WORDSW⊙

C000263331

WILLIAM WORDSWORTH was born in the Lake District in April 1770, and died there eighty years later on 23 April 1850. He had three brothers and a sister, Dorothy, to whom throughout his life he was especially close. When she was six and he was nearly eight, their mother died. Dorothy was sent away to be brought up by relatives and a year later William was sent to Hawkshead Grammar School, scene of the great childhood episodes of *The Prelude*. Wordsworth was cared for in lodgings and led a life of exceptional freedom, roving over the fells that surrounded the village. The death of his father, agent to the immensely powerful land-owner Sir James Lowther, broke in on this happiness when he was thirteen, but did not halt the education through nature that complemented his Hawkshead studies and became the theme of his poetry. As an undergraduate at Cambridge Wordsworth travelled (experiencing the French Revolution at first hand) and wrote poetry. His twenties were spent as a wanderer, in France, Switzerland, Wales, London, the Lakes, Dorset and Germany. In France he fathered a child whom he did not meet until she was nine because of the War. In 1794 he was reunited with Dorothy, and met Coleridge, with whom he published *Lyrical Ballads* in 1798, and to whom he addressed *The Prelude*, his epic study of human consciousness. In the last days of the century Wordsworth and Dorothy found a settled home at Dove Cottage, Grasmere. Here Wordsworth wrote much of his best-loved poetry, and Dorothy her famous *Journals*. In 1802 Wordsworth married Dorothy's closest friend, Mary Hutchinson. Gradually he established himself as the great poet of his age, a turning-point coming with the collected edition of 1815. From 1813 Wordsworth and his family lived at Rydal Mount in the neighbouring valley to Grasmere. In 1843 he became Poet Laureate.

Best known for her prize-winning and bestselling books *The Brontës* (1994) and *Wordsworth: A Life* (2000), Juliet Barker has been widely acclaimed for setting new standards of literary biography. She is also author of *The Brontës: A Life in Letters*, *The Brontës: Selected Poems* and *Charlotte Brontë: Juvenilia 1829–35*, as well as two books on medieval tournaments, *The Tournament in England c. 1100–1400* and *Tournaments:*

Jousts, Chivalry and Pageants in the Middle Ages. Born in Yorkshire, she was educated at Bradford Girls' Grammar School and St Anne's College, Oxford, where she obtained a doctorate in medieval history. From 1983 to 1989 she was the curator and librarian of the Brontë Parsonage Museum. She has, for many years, been a frequent contributor to national and international television and radio as a historian and literary biographer and has lectured as far afield as the United States and New Zealand. In 1999 she was one of the youngest ever recipients of an Honorary Doctorate of Letters, awarded by the University of Bradford in recognition of her outstanding contribution to literary biography, and in 2001 she was elected a Fellow of the Royal Society of Literature. She is married, with two children, and lives in the South Pennines.

JULIET BARKER

Wordsworth:
A Life in Letters

PENGUIN BOOKS

PENGUIN BOOKS

Published by the Penguin Group
Penguin Books Ltd, 80 Strand, London WC2R 0RL, England
Penguin Group (USA) Inc., 375 Hudson Street, New York, New York 10014, USA
Penguin Group (Canada), 90 Eglinton Avenue East, Suite 700, Toronto, Ontario, Canada M4P 2Y3
(a division of Pearson Penguin Canada Inc.)
Penguin Ireland, 25 St Stephen's Green, Dublin 2, Ireland (a division of Penguin Books Ltd)
Penguin Group (Australia), 250 Camberwell Road, Camberwell,
Victoria 3124, Australia (a division of Pearson Australia Group Pty Ltd)
Penguin Books India Pvt Ltd, 11 Community Centre,
Panchsheel Park, New Delhi – 110 017, India
Penguin Group (NZ), 67 Apollo Drive, Mairangi Bay, Auckland 1310, New Zealand
(a division of Pearson New Zealand Ltd)
Penguin Books (South Africa) (Pty) Ltd, 24 Sturdee Avenue, Rosebank, Johannesburg 2196, South Africa

Penguin Books Ltd, Registered Offices: 80 Strand, London WC2R 0RL, England

www.penguin.com

First published by Viking 2002
Published in Penguin Books 2007
1

Introduction, editorial matter and transcripts copyright © Juliet Barker, 2002
All rights reserved

The moral right of the editor has been asserted

Printed in England by Clays Ltd, St Ives plc

ISBN: 978-0-141-44213-6

For James, Edward and Sophie
the three stars in my firmament

Contents

List of Illustrations

Illustration Acknowledgements

The author and publishers are grateful to the following for permission to reproduce illustrations: 1, 2, courtesy The Francis Frith Collection, Salisbury, Wiltshire SP3 5QP, www.francisfrith.co.uk; 3, 6, 17, 27–31, The Wordsworth Trust, Grasmere; 4, 7, 8, 21, 23, Mary Evans Picture Library; 5, 20, 22, National Portrait Gallery, London; 9, John Garbutt; 10, John Marsh; 11, 12, 26, The Armitt Trust, Ambleside; 13, Mallett Gallery, London, UK/Bridgeman Art Library; 14, The National Gallery, London; 16, 25, Abbott Hall Art Gallery, Kendal, Cumbria, UK/ Bridgeman Art Library; 18, The Ashmolean, Oxford; 19, Boston Museum of Fine Arts, USA; 24 from *The Lake District, Life and Traditions* by William Rollinson (J. M. Dent & Son Ltd, 1974).

Introduction and Acknowledgments

The least objection to publishing private Letters or parts of them is that they are a burthen to the Press, and their perusal a waste of time.
William Wordsworth to Basil Montagu, [?September 1844]

Wordsworth said that for his own part, such was his horror of having his letters *preserved*, that, in order to guard against it he always took pains to make them as bad & dull as possible. –
The Journal of Thomas Moore, 10 August 1837[1]

William Wordsworth is not, on the face of it, a promising subject for a 'life in letters' biography. The very idea of publishing private letters was anathema to him. 'You concur with me, I dare say, in condemning the raking together every thing that may have dropped from a distinguished Author's pen', he wrote to a friend in December 1835.

Of this abuse we have had many instances lately; & it may be observed, by the bye, that these voluminous Ed[itio]ns are also an imposition upon the public . . . Not only has the public to pay for all that an Author may himself have written, but for the revival of no small portion of the forgotten trash that may have been written about him.[2]

Not for the first or last time in his life, William was out of step with contemporary taste and opinion. There was an insatiable appetite for this type of publication, as was demonstrated by the unseemly and opportunistic rush into print by friends and acquaintances after the deaths of Samuel Taylor Coleridge and Charles Lamb in 1834. Knowing both men better than any of their would-be biographers, it was not surprising that William objected so strongly to the intimate details of their lives being laid bare for the prurient reader. 'The Editor is a man without judgement, & therefore appears to be without feeling:' he stormed after glancing through the two volumes of Thomas Allsop's *Letters, Conversations and Recollections of S. T. Coleridge.*

> His rule is to publish <u>all the truth</u> that he can scrape together about his departed Friend; not perceiving the difference between the real truth and what <u>appears to him</u> to be true. The maxim de mortuis nil nisi <u>verum</u> was never meant to imply that <u>all</u> truth is to be told, only nothing but what <u>is</u> true. This distinction also has escaped his sagacity, and ever will escape those of far superior talents to Mr A[llsop] who care not what offence or pain they give to living persons provided they have come to a conclusion, however inconsiderately, that they are doing justice to the dead.[3]

William's sensitivity on this subject was all the more raw because he knew that he could not escape the dissecting table himself. His own private letter to Charles James Fox (no. 89 below), written in 1801 to accompany a gift of *Lyrical Ballads*, was published in 1838 in a collection of the correspondence of a former Speaker of the House of Commons, earning the editor an unexpectedly mild rebuke: 'publishing the Letters of a living Person without his consent previously obtained furnishes a precedent the effect of which, as far as it acts, cannot but be to check the free communication of thought between Man and Man.'[4] The following year Thomas de Quincey went a stage further: also acting without William's consent or knowledge, he wrote a series of articles for *Tait's Magazine* in which he included not only lengthy quotations from *The Prelude*, the poem William was preserving for posthumous publication, but also intimate personal details about all the Wordsworth family. Such was the hunger for this type of material that throughout this decade and the next, William was repeatedly asked to provide an autobiography for publication in periodicals and foreign editions of his own works. His answer was always robust: 'that my course of life had been altogether private, & that nothing could be more bare of entertainment or interest than a biographical notice of me must prove, if true.'[5]

As William was well aware, such flat denials of the intrinsic interest of his own life, however often or loud they were repeated, could not be enough to deflect public curiosity. He therefore took every opportunity to impress his views upon his friends, telling Basil Montagu, for instance, that 'it seems to me that in this gossiping age it is not desireable, to leave to others the discretion of making any kind of public use of documents if evidently private. – '[6] To Edward Moxon, his own publisher (who was also responsible for some of the biographies which had so offended William), he was equally forthright.

> For my own part, I do most earnestly wish that not a single letter I ever wrote should survive me: & I shall endeavour to make it known to all my correspondents, whether accidental or regular, that such is my wish: & farther that I sh[oul]d deem a breach of the laws of social intercourse, as I wish them to be maintained, between me & my friends & acquaintances, if either they do not destroy my letters, or send them to myself or representatives.[7]

In the event that such moral pressure failed to produce the desired effect, William had yet another card up his sleeve. As he told his fellow poet, Thomas Moore, 'such was his horror of having his letters *preserved*, that, in order to guard against it he always took pains to make them as bad & dull as possible.'[8]

Fortunately for the biographer (and reader), most of William's friends ignored his request to destroy his letters, thus giving us not only just the insight into his private life that he most objected to and feared, but also the opportunity to judge their merit for ourselves. It cannot be argued that he was always the most sparkling of letter writers; he acknowledged himself that his prose style had suffered from an early schooling in Johnsonian rhetoric and his habit of dictating his letters exacerbated his tendency to long-windedness. Some of them are undoubtedly both 'bad & dull'. On the other hand, whenever he felt passionately about a subject or wrote in the mood to please or entertain, his letters are a genuine pleasure to read, and he always retained the poet's ability to turn a casual but memorable phrase. A few days of unseasonal summer weather in the early spring of 1830, for instance, are described as appearing 'with the suddenness of a Pantomime trick'(no. 342), and when he apologized to Lord Lonsdale for his failure to send some verses, he commented that 'the promises of Poets are like the Perjuries of Lovers, things at which Jove laughs' (no. 283).

Independent of their inherent literary merit, William's letters are crucially important for the insights they give into his poetry. They reveal his own creative processes in producing the poems and what he intended their effect to be on readers. His inability to write to order, even when he wished to do so, is repeatedly illustrated, as is his ability both to throw off a poem over breakfast and to hold an idea in his head for thirty years before being able to commit it to verse (nos. 95, 510). His fanatical insistence on the importance of a particular choice of words, such as describing the Leech-gatherer in *Resolution and Independence* who 'was' by a lonely pond, 'not stood, not sat, but "*was*"' (no. 96), reveals how carefully he crafted even deceptively simple poems and explains his frustration at ill-informed criticism from those who did not read them as carefully and attentively as he wrote them (no. 137).

Whilst these 'sweating pages' in defence of his poetry, as Charles Lamb so appositely called them, now seem slightly risible, it is only because we have forgotten that the provocation was so great. Those unfamiliar with William's life will be surprised to learn that he wrote and published without profit for more than thirty years and that, for at least half that time, he was subjected to what one can only describe as a sustained campaign of vitriolic abuse by literary critics. To set William's reaction in context, therefore, a representative selection of contemporary reviews has been included in this selection of letters, charting his long, slow, elevation from despised buffoon to sage and seer.

The desire to place both the poet and man in context is also responsible for the decision to widen the selection to include letters and journal entries from other members of the extended Wordsworth family, their circle of intimate friends and, occasionally, passing strangers. The descriptive skills and sensitivity of William's sister, Dorothy, are well known, but they were shared to a lesser degree by his wife, Mary, his sister-in-law Sara Hutchinson, his daughter, Dora, and his son-in-law, Edward Quillinan. Sara, Dora and 'Q', as Quillinan was familiarly known, were also blessed with an irreverent wit and an ironic sense of humour which did not spare even the Bard himself. Quillinan's accounts of his first meeting with a decidedly grumpy William at Rydal Mount (no. 270), or later accompanying him to a Brixton school where a brawny, cross-eyed schoolmaster drew out a touching appreciation of *Composed Upon Westminster Bridge* from an unlikely group of schoolboys (no. 358), or, later still, climbing Helvellyn with the poet, who was engrossed in composing a poem, his daughter, who was trying to keep her seat on a recalcitrant pony, and a posse of tourists who, having recognized the great man, dogged their footsteps (no. 461), are little comic masterpieces – but they also serve to illustrate the day-to-day difficulties William had to face in coming to terms with unexpected fame and almost unprecedented levels of public adulation.

Few men protested so much against the threat to their privacy posed by biography but few could benefit as much as William Wordsworth from the publication of his letters. The private man, in the bosom of his family, was the antithesis of his cold, remote, arrogant and ruthlessly egocentric public image – an undeserved image which has been given a renewed lease of life in recent years by unsympathetic and biased portrayals of his relationship with Coleridge. Here is the real William: a man who inspired tremendous loyalty and love in those who knew him best and was so devoted to and dependent on his own family that the death of his daughter Dora destroyed him emotionally and physically; one who could exchange passionate love-letters like a teenager with his own wife after almost ten years of marriage and the birth of five children (nos. 157–8, 170–71); who, at sixty, was still 'the crack skater on Rydal Lake' (no. 341); and who, in his seventies, was trailed on his walks by the village children, the youngest clinging to his cloak or trousers, as he patiently cut ash switches from the hedgerows for them (no. 514). Here is a man who, contrary to one of the most frequently levelled charges against him, was not so entirely obsessed with his own poetry that he was unable to see the merit in others: he wrote encouragingly and with great kindness to many a hopeful young poet (for example, nos. 207, 281) but also, as he grew older, expressed dissatisfaction with his own poems and admitted that he felt that he had lived and written to little purpose (nos. 160, 293). The private man who emerges from the letters is more complex, more human and fallible, and ultimately altogether more likeable than either his detractors or his apologists would have us believe.

The object of this book is to allow the poet to speak for himself and to tell his own story in his own words, assisted by those who knew him most intimately. Extracts from only a few hundred of the many thousand relevant letters and diaries are quoted here, but they give an indication of the remarkable extent of William Wordsworth's vast circle of correspondents, which ranged from family and friends to complete strangers. For the assistance of the reader, a very brief description of each correspondent will be found in either the accompanying text or the introductory sentence to the letter. Anyone seeking more detailed biographical information or analysis of the letter itself should refer to my biography, *Wordsworth: A Life* (Viking, 2000). Explanatory text has been kept to a minimum, and has only been used where essential for chronological purposes or to point out where sometimes heated opinions expressed in the letters were contradicted by maturer thought and action. An important case in point is William's frequently cited refusal to give his daughter an allowance when she married against his wishes. His harsh comment 'That she may be somewhat straitened, acting as She has chosen to do with my strongest disapprobation I deem fit and right.'(no. 498) might fit the popular image of him as a typically cold and obdurate Victorian father, but it is untrue. William relented to the extent that he devoted a considerable portion of his own income (£80 a year) to providing his daughter, her husband and two stepdaughters with a suitable house and servants at Rydal.

The standard text of the Wordsworth letters is the eight-volume *The Letters of William and Dorothy Wordsworth* edited by Ernest de Selincourt and revised by Chester L. Shaver, Mary Moorman and Alan Hill (Oxford, Clarendon Press, 1967–93). In preparing this edition, however, the letters have, wherever possible, been newly transcribed from the manuscripts. This has revealed a considerable number of misreadings and even some mislocations: the latter have been indicated in the notes and correct locations substituted wherever possible. The text is as accurately and exactly transcribed from the manuscripts as it is possible to do; this is easier where the letters were dictated to one of his female amanuenses, but William's own appalling handwriting is sometimes impenetrable. Questionable readings and editorial insertions have been placed in square brackets and the former marked with a question mark; the erratic spellings and capitalizations of the originals have been retained but, to avoid confusion, abbreviated words and names have been printed in full, again with the editorial expansion placed in square brackets.

Attention has not been drawn to misreadings, however, which range from minor emendations in punctuation and capitalization to the first-time inclusion of omissions and completely new readings. Some examples of these prove instructive; though apparently minor in themselves, they do change the meaning of a sentence, sometimes significantly. The book that William sought from his friend Mathews was Bell's 'fugitive poetry', not 'forgotten poetry' (no. 38); his ears were (not surprisingly) 'stone-deaf' to the idle buzz of criticism, not 'stone-dead' (no. 134); his loathing at the thought of publication was 'almost insurmountable' not 'almost insupportable' (no. 139). Sara Hutchinson described Rydal as being beautiful 'beyond all conception' not 'beyond all description'(no. 181), which is quite a different thing. William did not trust favourable criticism from friends because it was liable to a suspicion of personal 'partiality', not 'particularity' (no. 192). He thought Keats' sonnet, 'Great Spirits now on earth are sojourning', was both 'vigorously conceived and exprest', not simply the more lukewarm 'vigorously conceived and well expressed', and, in the same letter, he did not consign Thelwall's poetry writing to the past by saying that he 'wrote' blank verse well, but referred to him as a poet who 'writes' well (no. 207). In Dorothy's letter of 23 July [1820] about the Continental Tour, she apparently states 'all, except my Brother, write a journal – Oh! Mine is nothing but notes . . .', but the manuscript shows that a whole phrase has dropped out: the last few words actually read 'Oh! no Mrs Monkhouse does <u>not</u> – Mine is nothing but notes . . .' (no. 244). William's letter to Sir George Beaumont is actually dated the 6th, not the 10th of January 1821, and in it, like a true north-country man, he describes the lofty 'fells', not 'hills', near the junction of the rivers Eden and Emont (no. 252). In 1826 William rebutted the suggestion that 'my tone of mind at present is somewhat melancholy', adding ' – it is not by any means peculiarly so', not 'particularly so' (no. 305). The females of the family, according to Dorothy, wanted him to publish a small volume of 'the numerous poems now in store' so that they could have 'a Run', not 'a Boom', before he reprinted his five-volume edition of collected poems (no. 343). Complaining that it was out of his power to spend a day quietly in London, William actually wrote 'People put so many questions to me, and think it so necessary to endeavour to put me upon *talking*, and to talk to me', which makes far more sense than 'People put so many questions to me, and think it so necessary to endeavour to put me upon *something*, and to talk to me' [my italics] (no. 411). On his tour of Italy in 1837, the 67-year-old poet felt that he was too old for such excessive exertions and that his bodily strength was not just 'diminished' but, rather pathetically, 'much diminished' (no. 422). The fan letters that William regularly received in the last decade of his life were written, he said, in a language of 'veneration', not merely 'admiration', and he was particularly pleased by 'the frequent mention of the consolation which my Poems have afforded the Writer under affliction, & the calmness and elevation of mind which they have produced in him': note that this is 'elevation *of mind*' [my italics] not just 'elevation' (no. 449). In a particularly moving letter of condolence to the poet, William Lisle Bowles, William mentions first reading Bowles' sonnets with his brother John in a recess 'upon London Bridge', not 'from London Bridge'; at the end of the letter, quoting his own 'But not without hope we sorrow and we mourn', he declares, 'So I wrote when I lost that dear brother. So have I felt ever since, and so I am sure, *my dear Friend*, you do now – ', not ' . . . so I am sure, *in my heart*, you do now.' [my italics] (no. 495). Perhaps saddest of all is the heart-wrenching letter William wrote to Isabella Fenwick in

December 1847 – the first he had written in the five months since Dora's death. The two misreadings in this letter are particularly poignant. William did not write baldly 'The thing I have to say . . .' but the infinitely more touching 'The *best* thing I have to say is that the Mother of our departed Child preserves her health, and stirs about the House upon every occasion, as heretofore' [my italics]. And William did not suffer most 'in head and mind' before he left his bed in the morning, but 'in heart and mind' (no. 539), a much more appropriate and moving description for a man whose life and work had indeed been a synthesis of heart and mind.

In preparing this edition I have had to rely on the assistance of many dedicated people who have gone out of their way to locate documents for me, often in very difficult circumstances. Librarians and archivists are the unsung heroes and heroines of the literary world, without whom no biographer, editor or researcher could operate. With remarkably few exceptions, my requests for information have been treated with exemplary efficiency and courtesy, even when a search has failed to locate a missing manuscript. Whilst it may seem invidious to name particular individuals, I owe an especial debt to the following, all of whom have acted above and beyond the call of duty: Jeff Cowton, Registrar of The Wordsworth Trust at Dove Cottage, Grasmere; Gayle Barkley of The Huntington Library; Dr Iain Brown of The National Library of Scotland; Robert E. Parks of The Pierpont Morgan Library; AnnaLee Pauls of Princeton University Library; and Andrew Russell of the National Art Library at the Victoria and Albert Museum. I am also indebted to Dr Marcus Ackroyd, who undertook the correction of transcriptions of manuscripts at The British Library, Dr Williams's Library, University College, London and the Victoria and Albert Museum on my behalf with his usual cheerfulness and thoroughness: any mistakes in these transcripts are entirely attributable to him. For the rest I must (reluctantly) take personal responsibility.

I am grateful to the following for permission to quote from manuscripts in their collections: Archives and Special Collections, Amherst College Library, USA; The Henry W. and Albert A. Berg Collection of English and American Literature, Room 320, The New York Public Library, USA; The Bodleian Library, Oxford; The Paul C. Richards Collection, Special Collections, Boston University, Massachusetts, USA; Special Collections, University of Bristol; The British Library, London; Department of Manuscripts and Archives, Cornell University, Ithaca, New York, USA; The Cumbria Record Office, The Castle, Carlisle; Special Collections, Edinburgh University Library; The Houghton Library,

Harvard University, Cambridge, Massachusetts, USA; The Historical Society of Pennsylvania, Philadelphia, USA; The Huntington Library, San Marino, California, USA; The Lilly Library, Indiana University, Bloomington, Indiana, USA; Special Collections, University of Iowa Libraries, Iowa City, Iowa, USA; The Librarian and Director, The John Rylands University Library of Manchester; Manuscripts Division, The National Library of Scotland, Edinburgh; The Pierpont Morgan Library, New York, USA; The Carl H. Pforzheimer Collection of Shelley and his Circle, The New York Public Library, USA; Department of Rare Books and Special Collections, Princeton University Library, Princeton, New Jersey, USA; The Sharpe Collection, University College, London; Miriam Lutcher Stark Collection, Harry Ransom Humanities Research Center, University of Texas at Austin, USA; Department of Special Collections, University of California, Davis, California, USA; The Rector, Visitors and Special Collections Department, University of Virginia Library, Charlottesville, Virginia, USA; The Victoria and Albert Museum, London; Dr Williams's Library, London; Her Majesty Queen Elizabeth II and The Royal Archives, Windsor Castle, Berkshire; The Wordsworth Trust and the Trustees of Dove Cottage, Grasmere; The Beinecke Rare Book and Manuscript Library, Yale University, New Haven, Connecticut, USA.

I would also like to thank the following for taking the trouble to respond to my requests for information: The Board of the Trustees of the Chevening Estate, Kent; The Centre for Kentish Studies, Maidstone, Kent; The Library, Clifton College, Bristol; Department of Manuscripts and Printed Books, Fitzwilliam Museum, Cambridge; The New York Genealogical and Bibliographical Society, USA; The Historical Manuscripts Commission, London; Ms C. M. Williams.

My agent, Andrew Lownie, and my editor, Eleo Gordon, together with the talented and friendly team at Penguin are also due their mead of praise. Last, but by no means least, I would like to thank the direct descendants of William and Mary Wordsworth, and the curators of Rydal Mount, Peter and Marian Elkington, all of whom have treated me with unfailing kindness and generosity. I am especially grateful to Susan Andrew and her son, Christopher, who, in true romantic literary tradition made the exciting discovery of an unpublished letter by Dora Wordsworth in an old trunk in the family attic. The letter (no. 522) is a particularly poignant one: it is amongst the last Dora ever wrote and mentions that her husband had vetoed her attendance at her brother's wedding in

Brighton for fear that she might catch cold. Instead, she went to Carlisle to prepare the newly-weds' cottage in readiness for their home-coming – and there caught the cold which her family believed caused her death from tuberculosis a few months later. Susan and Christopher not only told me about this remarkable discovery but also offered the letter to me so that it could appear in print for the first time in this book. I am indebted to them.

Chapter One

1770–92

1. William Wordsworth, autobiographical memoranda, dictated at Rydal Mount, November 1847

I was born at Cockermouth, in Cumberland, on April 7th, 1770, the second son of John Wordsworth, attorney-at-law, as lawyers of this class were then called, and law-agent to Sir James Lowther, afterwards Earl of Lonsdale. My mother was Anne, only daughter of William Cookson, mercer [cloth merchant], of Penrith, and of Dorothy, born Crackanthorp, of the ancient family of that name, who from the times of Edward the Third had lived in Newbiggen Hall, Westmoreland. My grandfather was the first of the name of Wordsworth who came into Westmoreland, where he purchased the small estate of Sockbridge. He was descended from a family who had been settled at Peniston in Yorkshire, near the sources of the Don, probably before the Norman Conquest. Their names appear on different occasions in all the transactions, personal and public, connected with that parish . . .

The time of my infancy and early boyhood was passed partly at Cockermouth, and partly with my mother's parents at Penrith, where my mother, in the year 1778, died of a decline, brought on by a cold, the consequence of being put, at a friend's house in London, in what used to be called "a best bedroom." My father never recovered his usual cheerfulness of mind after this loss, and died when I was in my fourteenth year, a schoolboy, just returned from Hawkshead, whither I had been sent with my elder brother Richard, in my ninth year.

I remember my mother only in some few situations, one of which was her pinning a nosegay to my breast when I was going to say the catechism in the church, as was customary before Easter. I remember also telling her on one week day that I had been at church, for our school stood in the churchyard, and we had frequent opportunities of seeing what was going on there. The occasion was, a woman doing penance in the church in a white sheet. My mother commended my having been present, expressing a hope that I should remember the circumstance for the rest of my life. "But," said I, "Mama, they did not give me a penny, as I had been told they would." "Oh," said she, recanting her praises, "if that was your motive, you were very properly disappointed."

My last impression was having a glimpse of her on passing the door of her bedroom during her last illness, when she was reclining in her easy chair. An intimate friend of hers, Miss Hamilton by name, who was used to visit her at Cockermouth, told me that she once said to her, that the only one of her five children about whose future life she was anxious, was William; and he, she said, would be remarkable either for good or for evil. The cause of this was, that I was of a stiff, moody, and violent temper; so much so that I remember going once into the attics of my grandfather's house at Penrith, upon some indignity having been put upon me, with an intention of destroying myself with one of the foils which I knew was kept there. I took the foil in hand, but my heart failed. Upon another occasion, while I was at my grandfather's house at Penrith, along with my eldest brother, Richard, we were whipping tops together in the large drawing-room, on which the carpet was only laid down upon particular occasions. The walls were hung round with family pictures, and I said to my brother, "Dare you strike your whip through that old lady's petticoat?" He replied, "No, I won't." "Then," said I, "here goes;" and I struck my lash through her hooped petticoat, for which no doubt, though I have forgotten it, I was properly punished. But possibly, from some want of judgment in punishments inflicted, I had become perverse and obstinate in defying chastisement, and rather proud of it than otherwise.

Looking back on his youthful self after the passage of almost seventy years, William Wordsworth recognized that a dominant emotion in his early life had been a burning sense of injustice and, consequently, a desire to rebel. This was not surprising. The death of his mother when he was eight had been unfortunate, but the death of his father before William reached his fourteenth birthday was a disaster which shaped his life for years to come. John Wordsworth's employer, Sir James Lowther, not only owned the family house at Cockermouth but also refused to honour his debt of £4,700 (the equivalent of £250,000 today) to his estate. The five young Wordsworths, Richard, William, Dorothy, John and Christopher, the eldest of whom was fifteen, the youngest just nine, were left homeless and impoverished; until they came of age and unless – or until – the Lowther debt was paid, they were dependent on the charity of their relatives. It was a state of affairs which would last almost exactly twenty years, depriving the young Wordsworths of both the financial security they had a right to expect and the opportunities dependent on it. Lack of money would be a constant source of frustration throughout William's life.

Richard and William, who had entered Hawkshead Grammar School in the spring of 1779, were joined there in due course by their younger brothers. During term time they boarded together in the village with a kindly local couple, Ann and Hugh Tyson, who created a second and much-loved home for them. William did not find his schoolwork difficult or onerous and his leisure hours, as he would later describe them in his autobiographical poem, *The Prelude*, were idyllic. They were spent companionably with the other boys in boisterous sports such as riding, sailing, fishing, hunting and ice-skating, or exploring the length and breadth of the Lake District. Christmas holidays were also spent happily with the large family of one of their guardian uncles, Richard Wordsworth, at Whitehaven. It was only during the longer summer vacations that the brothers had to endure the joyless and disapproving atmosphere of their grandparents' home at Penrith. Dorothy, who was only six when her mother died in 1778, had then left Cockermouth to live with her beloved 'Aunt' Threlkeld (actually an older cousin) and a bevy of orphaned cousins in the West Riding town of Halifax, more than ninety miles away. Shortly after her sixteenth birthday, however, she was summoned to Penrith to take up residence with her uncongenial Cookson grandparents and uncles, Christopher (Kit) and William. The only consolation for this second removal from a home she had loved was the prospect of meeting her brothers again for the first time in more than nine years.

2. Dorothy Wordsworth to a Halifax schoolfriend, Jane Pollard; Sunday evening, [Penrith, late July 1787]

. . . I might perhaps have employed an hour or two in writing to you but I have so few, so very few to pass with my Brothers that I could not leave them. You know not how happy I am in their company, I do not now want a friend who will share with me my distresses. I do not now pass half my time alone. I can bear the ill nature of all my relations, for the affection of my brothers consoles me in all my Griefs, but how soon alas! shall I be deprived of this consolation! & how soon shall I again become melancholy, even more melancholy than before. They are just the boys I could wish them, they are so affectionate & so kind to me as makes me love them more & more every day. W[illia]m & Christopher are very clever b[oys] at least so they appear in the partial eyes of a Sist[er], no doubt I am partial & see virtues in them that by [every]body else will pass unnoticed. John, (who is to be the Sailor,) has a most excellent heart, he is not so bright as either W[illia]m or Christopher but he has very good common sense & is very well calculated for the profession he has chosen. Richard (the oldest) I have seen, he is equally affectionate & good, but is far from being as clever as William, but I have no doubts of his succeeding in his business for he is very diligent & far from being dull, he only spent a night with us. Many a time have W[illia]m, J[ohn], C[hristopher], & myself shed tears together, tears of the bitterest sorrow, we all of us, each day, feel more sensibly the loss we sustained when we were deprived of our parents, & each day do we receive fresh insults, you will wonder of what sort; believe me of the most mortifying kind; the insults of servants, but I will give you the particulars of our distresses as far as my paper will allow, but I cannot tell you half what I wish & I fear that when I have finished you will feel yourself almost as much in the dark as ever. I was for a whole week kept in expectation of my Brothers, who staid at school all that time after the vacation begun owing to the ill-nature of my Uncle [Kit] who would not send horses for them because when they wrote they did not happen to mention them, & only said when they should break up which was always before sufficient. This was the beginning of my mortifications for I felt that if they had had another home to go to they would have been behaved to in a very different manner, & received with more chearful countenances, indeed nobody but myself expressed one wish to see them, at last however they were sent for, but not till my Brother W[illia]m had hired a horse for himself & came over, because he thought some one must be ill; the servants are every one of them so insolent to us as makes the kitchen as well as the parlour quite insupportable. James has even gone so far as to tell us that we had nobody to depend upon but my Grandf[athe]r for that our fortunes were but very small, & my B[rothe]rs can not even get a pair of shoes cleaned without James's telling them they require as much waiting upon as any Gentlemen, nor can I get a thing done for myself without absolutely entreating it as a [fav]our. James happens to be a particular favorite [with] my Uncle Kit, who has taken a dislike to my B[rothe]r W[illia]m & never takes any notice of any of us, so that he thinks [whi]le my Uncle behaves in this way to us he may do any thing, we are found fault with every hour of the day both by the servants & my Grandf[athe]r & Grandm[othe]r, the former of whom never speaks to us but when he scolds which is not seldom. I daresay our fortunes have been weighed thousands of times at the tea table in the kitchen & I have no doubt but they always conclude their conversations with 'they have nothing to be proud of'. Our fortunes will I fear be very small as Lord Lonsdale will most likely only pay a very small part of his debt which is 4700 pound. My uncle Kit, (who is our Guardian) having said many disrespectful things of him and having always espoused the Cause of the Duke of Norfolk [Lonsdale's political opponent], has insensed him so much that I fear we shall feel through life the effects of his imprudence. we shall however have sufficient to educate my Brothers. John poor fellow! says that he shall have occasion for very little, two hundred pounds will be enough to fit him out, & he should wish W[illia]m to have the rest for his education, as he has a wish to be a Lawyer if his health will permit, & it will be very expensive. we shall have I believe about six hundred pounds a piece if Lord L – does not pay, it is but very little, but it will be quite enough for my Brother's education & after they are once put forward in the world there is little doubt of their succeeding, & for me, while they live I shall never want a friend. – Oh Jane! when they have left me I shall be quite unhappy, I shall long more ardently than ever for you my dearest, dearest Friend. we have been told thousands of times that we were liars but we treat such behaviour with the contempt it deserves[. We] always finish our conversations which generally take a melancholy turn with wishing we had a father & a home.

3. William Wordsworth, autobiographical memoranda, dictated at Rydal Mount, November 1847

Of my earliest days at school I have little to say, but that they were very happy ones, chiefly because I was left at liberty, then and in the vacations, to read whatever books I liked. For example, I read all Fielding's works, Don Quixote, Gil Blas, and any part of Swift that I liked; Gulliver's Travels, and the Tale of the Tub, being both much to my taste. I was very much indebted to one of the ushers of Hawkshead School, by name Shaw, who taught me more of Latin in a fortnight than I had learnt during two preceding years at the school of Cockermouth. Unfortunately for me this excellent master left our school, and went to Stafford, where he taught for many years. It may be perhaps as well to mention, that the first verses which I wrote were a task imposed by my master; the subject, "The Summer Vacation;" and of my own accord I added others upon "Return to School." There was nothing remarkable in either poem; but I was called upon, among other scholars, to write verses [*Lines Written as a School Exercise at Hawkshead, Anno Aetatis 14*] upon the completion of the

second centenary from the foundation of the school in 1585, by Arch-
bishop Sandys. These verses were much admired, far more than they
deserved, for they were but a tame imitation of Pope's versification, and
a little in his style. This exercise, however, put it into my head to compose
verses from the impulse of my own mind, and I wrote, while yet a
schoolboy, a long poem running upon my own adventures, and the
scenery of the country in which I was brought up. The only part of that
poem which has been preserved is the conclusion of it ['Dear native
regions, I foretell'], which stands at the beginning of my collected Poems.

*4. John Spedding to his schoolfriend, William Wordsworth; [Mirehouse,
Keswick], 8 March 1838*

A letter from you carries back my thoughts to ancient days to the
early youth of 60 years – among w[hi]ch while I remember all with
thankfulness & most with pleasure – I cannot but dwell with particular
interest on those five – during w[hi]ch I sat with you on the same hard
bench at Hawkshead. The y[ea]r before last I visited that Seat of Learning
. . . Near half a century had been added to the 200 years w[hi]ch in our
time had elapsed

> 'Since Science first with all her heavenly train
> Beneath that roof began her heavenly reign – '[1]

& in this ½ Century – during w[hi]ch I had not [seen] the place a mighty
revolution seemed to have taken place in the Grammar   Science & her
train had surely been both effectually deposed for no vestige there remained
either of one or of the other. The School & the Yard & the Church all
seemed little & disappointing to my mind = The grass formerly worn
down by the rambling of 100 feet was growing in unrestrained profusion
– not a mark of a [hoop?] nor a [quoit?] nor a hep [marble] nor a ball to
be seen = even the very pissing corner seemed to have been disused for
50 years = within all was equally silent dull & desolate – The Study where
poor Barns used to have his ears so well boxed & whence Penny & I have
so often been driven headlong with blows & obloquy – seemed so quiet
that a mouse, c[oul]d she have found food, might have lived there
undisturbed = & it was only in the writing School that I at length found
not Varty laying his heavy ebony ruler over the heads of 50 boys – but
one dirty lad teaching six dirtier boys their multiplication task . . .

*5. Recollections of William Wordsworth, 1784–9, for the tercentary of
Hawkshead Grammar School by the son of Thomas Bowman, headmaster,
1786–1829*

My father used to say that he believed that he did more for William
Wordsworth by lending him books than by his teaching, though Wordsworth, mind you, did well enough under him at both Classics and
Mathematics, so I understood. But it was books he wanted, all sorts of
books; Tours and Travels, which my father was partial to, and Histories
and Biographies, which were also favourites with him; and Poetry – that
goes without saying. My father used to get the latest books from Kendal
every month, and I remember him telling how he lent Wordsworth
Cowper's 'Task' when it first came out, and Burns' 'Poems' . . .

Mr Wordsworth wrote to me after my father died, and in thanking him
I mentioned this. He wrote again – and I have his letter yet – saying
that my father also introduced him to Langhorne's poems and Beattie's
'Minstrel' & Percy's 'Reliques', and that it was in books or periodic works
my father lent him that he first became acquainted with the poetry of
Crabbe & Charlotte Smith & the two Wartons . . .

A story he used to tell about W[illia]m Wordsworth is that he left him
in his study once for what he thought would only be a minute or two,
telling him to be looking for another book in place of the one he had
brought back. As it happened he was kept half an hour or more by one
of the school tenants. When he got back, there was W[ordsworth] poring
over a book, so absorbed in it he did not notice my father's return. And
'what do you think it was' my father would say, or 'you'll never guess what
it was'. It was Newton's 'Optics', And that was the book Wordsworth
was for borrowing next. He was one of the very few boys, who used to
read the old books in the School Library, George Sandys' 'Travels in the
East' and his Ovid's 'Metamorphosis', Fox's [*sic*] 'Book of Martyrs' &
Evelyn's 'Forest Trees'. There were others, but these I remember . . . My
father continued to lend Wordsworth books when he was at Hawkshead
on holiday from Cambridge . . .

At the age of seventeen, William won a sizar's place at St John's College. This
was a form of scholarship intended for bright but impecunious students, entitling
them to pay reduced fees and receive free dinners, in the expectation that they
would win high honours for their college in university examinations. William
won further scholarships and exhibitions on his arrival at Cambridge and it was

generally expected that, after graduation, he would be ordained and succeed his uncle, Dr William Cookson, as a fellow. Constant family pressure was applied to this end but William's rebellious streak soon began to reassert itself.

6. William Wordsworth, autobiographical memoranda, dictated at Rydal Mount, November 1847

In the month of October, 1787, I was sent to St. John's College, Cambridge, of which my uncle, Dr [William] Cookson, had been a fellow. The master, Dr Chevallier, died very soon after; and, according to the custom of that time, his body, after being placed in the coffin, was removed to the hall of the college, and the pall, spread over the coffin, was stuck over by copies of verses, English or Latin, the composition of the students of St. John's. My uncle seemed mortified when upon inquiry he learnt that none of these verses were from my pen, "because," said he, "it would have been a fair opportunity for distinguishing yourself." I did not, however, regret that I had been silent on this occasion, as I felt no interest in the deceased person, with whom I had had no intercourse, and whom I had never seen but during his walks in the college grounds.

When at school, I, with the other boys of the same standing, was put upon reading the first six books of Euclid, with the exception of the fifth; and also in algebra I learnt simple and quadratic equations; and this was for me unlucky, because I had a full twelve-month's start of the freshmen of my year, and accordingly got into rather an idle way; reading nothing but classic authors according to my fancy, and Italian poetry. My Italian master was named Isola, and had been well acquainted with Gray the poet. As I took to these studies with much interest, he was proud of the progress I made. Under his correction I translated the Vision of Mirza, and two or three other papers of the Spectator, into Italian.

7. John Robinson, MP, to his second cousin, William Wordsworth; Sion Hill, London, 6 April 1788

Believe me that I shall be truly glad to see you here, at all times, but my earnest recommendation to you is to stick close to College for the first two or three years; a little excursion now and then may be allowed, and in some of those I hope we may see you here. It will give me great pleasure to hear you go out high in your year, and I cannot by words alone express to you the satisfaction I shall feel in hearing you go out Senior

Wrangler, strive for that, and establish a reputation at College which will go with you, and serve you thro' Life. To find this will give me much heartfelt Joy, for I most truly wish you well . . .

8. Christopher Cookson to his nephew, Richard Wordsworth; Penrith, 22 October 1789

Your Bro[the]r W[illia]m called here on Friday last in his road to Cambridge he looks very well. I should have been happy if he had favour'd me with more of his Company, but I'm afraid I'm out of his good graces –

9. Christopher Cookson to his nephew, Richard Wordsworth; Penrith, 18 December 1789

Im sorry to say that I think your Bro[the]r W[illia]m very extravagant he has had very near £300 since he went to Cambridge w[hi]ch I think is a very shameful sum for him to spend, considering his expectations – . . . Your Grandmother Desires her Love in the warmest manner both to you and John . . .

10. Dorothy Wordsworth to Jane Pollard; Forncett, 30 April 1790

My Brothers I hope are all well – I long to have an opportunity of introducing you to my Dear W[illia]m. I am very anxious about him just now, as he will shortly have to provide for himself: next year he takes his degree; when he will go into orders I do not know, nor how he will employ himself, he must, when he is three and twenty either go into orders or take pupils; he will be twenty in April –

In the summer of 1790 William committed his greatest act of rebellion yet. Instead of spending the vacation studying for his degree examinations at the end of the following term, he decided to abandon any hope of getting a fellowship and take a walking tour of Europe. His principle objective was to visit Switzerland to see for himself the 'sublime and beautiful' landscapes which were the inspiration of the Romantic movement. To get there, however, he would have to travel through France, which was still in a state of considerable political upheaval after the revolution of the year before. Anticipating the likely reaction of his relations, he kept his plans secret. Even Dorothy, who was now living with her uncle, Dr

William Cookson, his wife, and a fast-growing brood of children, at Forncett, near Norwich, did not find out until he wrote to her from the other side of the English Channel.

11. William Wordsworth, autobiographical memoranda, dictated at Rydal Mount, November 1847

In the month of August [sic; but see no. 12], 1790, I set off for the Continent, in companionship with Robert Jones, a Welshman, a fellow-collegian. We went staff in hand, without knapsacks, and carrying each his needments tied up in a pocket handkerchief, with about twenty pounds apiece in our pockets. We crossed from Dover and landed at Calais on the eve of the day when the king was to swear fidelity to the new constitution: an event which was solemnised with due pomp at Calais. On the afternoon of that day we started, and slept at Ardres. For what seemed best to me worth recording in this tour, see the Poem of my own Life [*The Prelude*, Book VI].

12. William Wordsworth to his sister, Dorothy; Kesswil, Switzerland, 6 [and 16] September [1790]

Septr. 6th Keswill (a small village
on the lake of Constance[)]

My dear Sister

My last letter was addressed to you from St Valier and the Grande Chartreuse. I have since that period gone over a very considerable tract of country and I will give you a sketch of my route, as far as relates to mentioning the places where I have been, after I have assured you that I am in excellent Health and Spirits, and have had no reason to complain of the contrary during our whole tour. My Spirits have been kept in a perpetual hurry of delight by the almost uninterrupted succession of sublime and beautiful objects which have passed before my eyes during the course of the last month, and you will be surprized when I assure you that our united expenses since we quitted Calais which was on the Evening of the 14th of July have not amounted to more than twelve pounds. Never was there a more excellent school for frugality than that in which we are receiving instructions at present. I am half afraid of getting a slight touch of avarice from it. It is the end of travelling by communicating Ideas to enlarge the mind; God forbid that I should stamp upon mine the strongest proof of a contracted Spirit . . .

I am a perfect Enthusiast in my admiration of Nature in all her various forms; & I have looked upon and as it were conversed with the objects which this country [Switzerland] has presented to my view so long, and with such encreasing pleasure, that the idea of parting from them oppresses me with a sadness similar to what I have always felt in quitting a beloved friend. There is no reason to be surprized at the strong attachment which the Swiss have always shewn to their native country, much of it must undoubtedly have been owing to those charms which have already produced so powerful an effect upon me, and to which the rudest minds cannot possibly be indifferent. Ten thousand times in the course of this tour have I regretted the inability of my memory to retain a more strong impression of the beautiful forms before me, and again and again in quitting a fortunate station have I returned to it with the most eager avidity, with the hope of bearing away a more lively picture. At this moment when many of these landscapes are floating before my mind, I feel a high [enjoyment] in reflecting that perhaps scarce a day of my life will pass, [in] which I shall not derive some happiness from these images – –

With regard to the manners of the inhabitants of this singular country, the impression which we have had often occasion to receive has been unfavourable. But it must be remembered that we have had little to do but with inn keepers and those corrupted by perpetual intercourse with strangers. Had we been able to speak the language, which is German, and had time to insinuate ourselves into their cottages, we should probably have had as much occasion to admire the simplicity of their lives as the beauties of their country. My partiality to Swisserland excited by its natural charms induces me to hope that the manners of it's Inhabitants are amiable, but at the same time I cannot help frequently contrasting them with those of the French, and as far as I have had opportunity to observe they lose very much by the comparison. We not only found the French a much less imposing people, but that politeness diffused thro the lowest ranks had an air so engaging, that you could scarce attribute it to any other cause than real benevolence. During the time which was near a month which we were in France, we had not once cause to complain of the smallest deficiency in civility in any person, much less of any positive rudeness. We had also perpetual occasion to observe that chearfulness & sprightliness for which the French have always been remarkable. But I must remind you that we crossed it at the time when the whole nation was mad with joy, in consequence of the revolution. It was a most interesting period to be in France, and we had many delightful scenes where the interest of the picture was owing solely to this cause . . .

But it is time to talk a little about England – when you write to my Brothers I must beg of you to give my love, and tell them I am sorry it has not been in my power to write to them. Kit [Christopher] will be surprized he has not heard from me, as we were almost upon terms of regular correspondence – I had not heard from Richard for some time before I set out; I did not call on him when I was in London, not so much because we were determined to hurry thro, but because he as many of our friends at Cambridge did, would look upon our scheme as mad & impracticable .. I expect great pleasure on my return to Cambridge, in exulting over those of my friends who threathned [*sic*] us with such an accumulation of difficulties as must undoubtedly render it impossible for us to perform the tour. Every thing however has succeeded with us far beyond my most sanguine expectations. We have it is true met with little disasters occasionally, but far from depressing us they rather gave us additional resolution & Spirits. We have both enjoyed most excellent health, and we have been this some time so inured to walking, that we are become almost insensible of fatigue. We have several times performed a journey of thirteen leagues [about forty miles] over the most mountainous parts of Swisserland, without any more weariness, than if we had been walking an hour in the groves of Cambridge. Our appearance is singular, and we have often observed that in passing thro' a village, we have excited a general smile. Our coats which we had made light on purpose for our journey are of the same piece; and our manner of bearing our bundles, which is upon our heads, with each an oak stick in our hands, contributes not a little to that gene[ral] curiosity which we seem to excite. But I find I hav[e] again relapsed into Egotism, and must here entreat y[ou not only] to pardon this fault, but also to make allowance for [the] illegible hand and desultory stile of this Letter. It has been written as you will see by it's different shades at many sittings and is in fact the produce of most of the leisure which I have had since it was begun – and is now

<u>finally drawing to a conclusion</u> at Berne on <u>the 16th of</u> Sept[em]b[e]r.
I flatter myself still with the hopes of seeing you for a forthnight [*sic*]
or three weeks, if it be agreeable to My Uncle, as there will be no
necessity for me to be in Cambridge before the 10th of Nov[em]b[e]r
but I shall be better able to judge whether I am likely to enjoy this
pleasure in about three weeks. I shall probably write to you again
before I quit France, if not most certainly, immediately on my landing
in England. You will remember me affectionately to my Uncle &
Aunt – as he was acquainted with my having given up all thoughts
of a fellowship, he may perhaps not be so much displeased at this
journey. I should be sorry if I have offended him by it – – –

*13. William Wordsworth, autobiographical memoranda, dictated at Rydal
Mount, November 1847*

After taking my degree in January, 1791, I went to London, stayed there
some time, and then visited my friend Jones, who resided in the Vale of
Clwydd, North Wales. Along with him I made a pedestrian tour through
North Wales . . .

*14. William Wordsworth to his friend, George Huntly Gordon; Rydal
Mount, 14 May 1829*

I was introduced to Mr. Thomas by my old friend & fellow Pedestrian
among the Alps, Robert Jones, fellow of St. John's Cambridge   one day
we sate down une partie quarrèe at the Squire's Table himself at the head
the Parson of the Parish a bulky broad-faced man between <u>50</u> & <u>60</u> at the
foot & Jones & I opposite each other – I must observe that "the Man of
God" had not unprofessionally been employed most part of the morning
in bottling the Squires "Cwrrw" anglisè strong Ale, this had redden'd his
visage (we will suppose by the fumes) but I sat at table not apprehending
mischief, the conversation proceeded with the cheerfulness good appetite, & good cheer, naturally inspire – the Topic – the powers of the Welsh
Language. "They are marvellous," said the revd Taffy "Your English is
not to be compared especially in conciseness, we can often express in one
word what you can scarcely do in a long sentence – ["] "That," said I, "is
indeed wonderful be so kind as to favor me with an instance?" "That I
will" he answered – "You know perhaps the word Tad?" "Yes." "What
does it mean?" "Father" I replied – "Well," stammer'd the Priest in

triumph, "Tad & Father there you have it" – on hearing this odd illustration of his confused notions I could not help smiling on my friend opposite whereupon, the incensed Welshman rose from his Chair & brandished over me a huge sharp pointed carving knife I held up my arm in a defensive attitude; judge of the consternation of the Squire, the dismay of my friend, & my own astonishment not unmixed with fear whilst he stood threat[e]ning me in this manner & heaping on my poor English head every reproachful epithet which his scanty knowledge of our language could supply to lungs almost stifled with rage – "You vile Saxon!" I recollect was one of his terms "To come here & insult me an ancient Briton on my own territory" At last his wrath subsided "et me servavit Apollo" [and Apollo (God of Poetry) saved me].

15. *Dorothy Wordsworth to Jane Pollard; Forncett, Sunday morning 26 June [1791]*

I often hear from my brother William who is now in Wales where I think he seems so happy that it is probable he will remain there all the summer or a great part of it: Who would not be happy enjoying the company of three young ladies in the Vale of Clewyd & without a rival? His friend, Jones is a charming young man, & has five sisters, three of whom are at home at present, then there are mountains, rivers, woods & rocks, whose charms without any other inducement would be sufficient to tempt William to continue amongst them as long as possible. So that most likely he will have the pleasure of seeing you when he visits Halifax, which I hope he will do in his road to the North; he thinks with great pleasure of paying that place a visit where I have so many friends. I confess you are right in supposing me partial to William. I hope when you see him you will think my regard not misplaced; probably when I next see Kitt [Christopher] I shall love him as well, the difference between our ages at the time I was with him was much more perceptible than it will be at our next meeting; his disposition is of the same cast as William's, and his inclinations have taken the same turn, but he is much more likely to make his fortune; he is not so warm as William but has a most affectionate heart, his abilities though not so great perhaps as his brothers may be of more use to him as he has not fixed his mind upon any particular species of reading, or conceived an aversion to any. He is not fond of Mathematics but has resolution sufficient to study them because it will be impossible for him to obtain a fellowship without a knowledge of them. William you may have heard lost the chance, indeed the certainty of a fellowship by not combating his inclinations, he gave way to his natural dislike of studies so dry as many parts of the mathematics, consequently could not succeed at Cambridge. He reads Italian, Spanish, French, Greek & Latin, & English but never opens a mathematical book. We promise ourselves much pleasure from reading Italian together at some time, he wishes that I was acquainted with the Italian poets, but how much have I to learn which plain English will teach me. William has a great attachment to poetry; indeed so has Kitt, but William particularly, which is not the most likely thing to produce his advancement in the world; his pleasures are chiefly of the imagination, he is never so happy as when in a beautiful country. Do not think from what I have said that he reads not [at] all, for he does read a great deal & not only poetry & those languages he is acquainted with but history &c &c –

16. William Wordsworth to his university friend, William Mathews; Plas-yn-Llan, Denbighshire, 3 August [1791]

You desire me to communicate to you copiously my observations on modern Literature, and transmit to you a cup replete with the waters of that fountain. You might as well have solicited me to send you an account of the tribes inhabiting the central regions of the African Continent. God knows my incursions into the fields of modern literature, excepting in our own language three volumes of Tristram Shandy, and two or three papers of the Spectator, half subdued – are absolutely nothing. Were I furnished with a Dictionary & a Grammar, and other requisites, I might perhaps make an attack upon Italy, an attack valiant, tho' probably my expedition, like a redoubted one of Caligula's of old, tho' of another kind, might terminate in gathering shells out of Petrarch, or sea weed from Marino. The truth of the matter is that when in Town I did <u>little</u>, and since I came here I have done nothing. a miserable account! However I have not in addition to all this to complain of bad spirits. That would be the devil indeed. I rather think that my gaiety encreases with my ignorance, as a spendthrift grows more extravagant, the nearer he approximates to a final dissipation of his property. I was obliged to leave all my books but one or two behind me. I regret much not having brought my Spanish Grammar along with me. By peeping into it occasionally I might perhaps have contrived to keep the little Spanish or some part of it, that I was master of.

William could not remain idle in Wales for long. By the autumn he was back in London, evading family pressure to return to university to study oriental languages and enlisting the support of his brother Richard, now a highly respectable and hard-working London lawyer, to persuade his guardian uncles to allow him to spend abroad the intervening years until he was old enough to be ordained a clergyman.

17. Richard Wordsworth to his uncle, Richard Wordsworth of Whitehaven; Gray's Inn, London, 7 November 1791

I found my Bro[the]r W[illia]m in London: he is advised to pass the Time previous to the Time of his Taking Orders in some retired Place in France w[hi]ch will be less expensive and more improving than in England it is his wish to set off immediately and he wo[ul]d be much obliged if You co[ul]d advance for him £40 w[hi]ch will support him till next Summer –.

18. William Wordsworth to William Mathews; Brighton, 23 November [1791]

Brighton Novbr. 23d [1791]

Dear Mathews,

I have been prevented from replying to your Letter, by an uncertainty respecting the manner in which I should dispose of myself for the winter, & which I have expected to be terminated every day this month past. I am now on my way to Orleans, where I purpose to pass the Winter, & am detained here by adverse winds . . .

I expect I assure you considerable pleasure from my sojourn on the other side of the water, and some little improvement, which God knows I stand in sufficient need of.

I am doomed to be an idler thro' my whole life. I have read nothing of this age, nor indeed did I ever. Yet with all this I am tolerable happy; do you think this ought to be a matter of congratulation to me, or no? For my own part I think certainly not. My Uncle the clergyman [Dr Cookson] proposed to me a short time ago to begin a course of Oriental Literature, thinking that that was the best field for a person to distinguish himself in as a man of Letters. To oblige him I consented to pursue the plan upon my return from the continent. But what must I do amongst that immense wilderness, who have no resolution, and who have not prepared myself for the enterprise by any sort of discipline amongst the Western languages?

who know little of Latin, & scarce anything of Greek. A pretty
confession for a young gentleman whose whole life ought to have
been devoted to study.

19. Dorothy Wordsworth to Jane Pollard; Forncett, 7 December [1791]

. . . William is, I hope, by this time arrived at Orleans, where he means
to pass the Winter for the Purpose of learning the French Language which
will qualify him for the office of travelling Companion to some young
Gentleman if he can get recommended, it will at any rate be very useful
to him, and as he can live at as little Expense in France as in England (or
nearly so), the Scheme is not an inelligible one. He is at the same Time
engaged in the Study of the Spanish Language and if he settles in England
at his return, (I mean if he has not the opportunity of becom[ing] travelling
Tutor) he [w]ill begin t[he] Study of the oriental Languages.

*20. William Wordsworth to his brother, Richard Wordsworth; chez M. Gillet
du Vivier, Rue Royale, Orléans, 19 December [1791]*

Dear Brother,

I have not been able to write to you as soon as I wished in
consequence of the time that my journey took me, and of a wish to
defer my Letter till I could give you some account of my arrangements. I was detained at Brighthelmstone [Brighton] from Tuesday till
Saturday Evening which time must have past in a manner extremely
disagreeable if I had not bethought me of introducing myself to Mrs
Charlotte Smith[2], she received me in the politest manner, and shewed
me every possible civility . . . On Sunday Morning I got to Dieppe,
and the same night to Rouen, where I was detained two days for the
diligence, and on the Wednesday night I reached Paris, where I
remained till the Monday following, and on the Tuesday arrived
here [Orléans], just a fortnight [*sic*] after quitting London.

I will now give you a criterion by which you may judge of my
expenses here. I had in Paris six hundred and forty three livres for
20£. – I give for my Lodging, which is a very handsome appartment
on the first floor, 30 Livres p[e]r month if I stay only three months
27 if I stay six and 24 and ten sous viz halfpence if I stay 8 months. My
board which is in the same house with two or three officers of the
Cavalry & a young gentleman of Paris, costs me fifty Livres p[e]r

month breakfast excluded. There are other little expenses which it would be not easy to sum up. But this as you will perceive is the bulk. And I think extremely reasonable considering the comfortable manner in which I live. Mrs Smith who was so good as to give me Letters [of introduction] for Paris furnished me with one for Miss Williams[3] an English Lady whom [*sic*] resided here lately, but was gone before I arrived. This circumstance was a considerable disappointment to me however I have in some respects remedied it by introducing myself to a Mr Foxlow an Englishman who has set up a Cotton manufactory here. I called upon him yesterday & he received me very politely, he & Mrs Foxlow are going into the country for a few days but when they return I shall I flatter myself by their means be introduced to the best society this place affords.

I have as yet no acquaintance but in the house, the young Parisian & the rest of the tables and one Family which I find very agreeable & with which I became acquainted by the circumstance of going to look at their Lodgings, which I should have liked extremely to have taken but I found them too dear for me. I have p[assed some] of my evenings there. – – –

. . . We are all perfectly quiet here [and] likely to continue so; I find [almost] all the people of any opulen[ce are] aristocrates and all the oth[ers] democrates. I had imagined [that] there were some people of wealth & circumstance favorers of the revolution, but here there is not one to be found.

I have every prospect of liking this place extremely well, the country tho' flat is pleasant and abounds in agreeable walks, particularly by the side of the Loire which is a very magnificent river. I am not yet able to speak french with decent accuracy but must of course improve very rapidly. I do not intend to take a master. I think I can do nearly as well without one, and it would be a very considerable augmentation of my expences . . .

I have said nothing of Paris & its splendors it is too copious a theme, besides I shall return that way & examine it much more minutely. I was at the national assembly, introduced by a member of whose acquaintance I shall profit on my return to Paris. Adieu, Adieu –

France had been William's destination of choice for pragmatic and sentimental reasons: he needed to improve his facility in the language and he had liked the people he had met on his Continental walking tour in 1790. He had not then been interested in politics so the French Revolution of 1789 had meant little to him. This would change dramatically during the year he spent in Orléans and Blois. The Revolution was now entering its second, more extreme, phase, which would lead to popular massacres, large-scale public executions and foreign invasions. William could not avoid being politicized: sympathizing with the suffering of the poor and repelled by the excesses of the *ancien régime*, he became an ardent radical and republican.

21. *Dorothy Wordsworth to Jane Pollard; Forncett, [8] May 1792*

William is still in France, & I begin to wish he was in England; he assures me however that he is perfectly safe, but as we hear daily accounts of Insurrections & Broils I cannot be quite easy; though I think he is wise enough to get out of the way of Danger.

22. *William Wordsworth to William Mathews; Blois, 19 May [1792]*

Since my arrival [in Blois] day after day and week after week has stole insensibly over my head with inconceivable rapidity . . .

You will naturally expect that writing from a country agitated by the storms of a revolution, my Letter should not be confined merely to us and our friends. But the truth is that in London you have perhaps a better opportunity of being informed of the general concerns of france, than in a petty provincial town in the heart of the kingdom itself. The annals of the department are all with which I have a better opportunity of being acquainted than you, provided you feel sufficient interest in informing yourself . . . The approaching summer will undoubtedly decide the fate of france. It is almost evident that the patriot army, however numerous, will be unable [to] withstand the superior discipline of their enemies. But suppose that the German army is at the gates of Paris, what will be the consequence[?] It will be impossible to make any material alteration in the constitution, impossible to reinstate the clergy in its antient guilty splendor, impossible to give an existence to the noblesse similar to that it before enjoyed, impossible to add much to the authority of the King: Yet there are in France some [? millions] – I speak without exaggeration – who expect that this will take place. I shall expect your Letter with impatience, tho', I little deserve, from my general remissness this attention on your part. I shall return to England in the autumn or the beginning of Winter.

23. *Dorothy Wordsworth to an unidentified correspondent; Forncett, 22 December 1792*

... William is in London; he writes to me regularly, and is a most affectionate brother.

William claimed in *The Prelude* that 'Nothing less than absolute want/Of funds for my support' compelled his return to England; if this was true, he was fortunate, for he narrowly escaped arrest and imprisonment which was the fate of most other Englishmen – even supporters of the Revolution – who remained in France at that time. In January 1793, King Louis XVI was executed and France declared war on England, effectively putting an end to all communication between the two countries. For William this was a disaster: his political sympathies were entirely with France and against his own country. Worse still, while in Orléans, he had met and fallen in love with Marie-Anne (Annette) Vallon, the 25-year-old daughter of a surgeon from Blois. He had left her on the understanding that he would return as soon as he could but the outbreak of war made that impossible. He would not see her again for almost ten years. Worst of all, however, he had to leave France shortly before Annette gave birth to their daughter, Caroline, who would therefore grow up a stranger. Whether William intended to return and marry Annette or not, he maintained as frequent a correspondence with her as the censors of their warring countries would allow (all of which has been destroyed, with the exception of three letters from Annette) and sent her money whenever possible. Before he left Orléans he also made arrangements for himself to be legally represented at the child's christening and for his name to appear in the church registers as the father.

24. *Register of Baptisms, Sainte Croixe, Orléans, 15 December 1792*

On the fifteenth day of December of the year 1792, the first year of the Republic, by me, the undersigned, was baptised a girl, born on this day in this parish of Williams Wordwodsth, Englishman, and of Marie-Anne Vallon, her father and mother; named Anne-Caroline by Paul Vallon and Marie-Victoire-Adelaïde Peigné, wife of André-Augustin Dufour. Williams Wordsodsth, absent, was represented in the capacity of father of the child by the aforesaid citizen, André-Augustin Dufour, court clerk of the tribunal of the district of Orléans, by virtue of a power ad hoc presented to us and signed 'Williams Wordworsth'; which signature citizens André-Augustin Dufour, Paul Vallon and Marie-Victoire-Adelaïde Peigné, aforesaid, have certified to us as authentic by their signatures below and on their responsibility.

M. V. A. Peigné. Vallon. Dufour

Perrin, Vicaire épiscopal.

The year William had spent living in France was arguably the most important of his life. His separation from his lover and child was an unending source of grief and guilt which the passage of the years softened but could not completely eradicate. His experience of the French Revolution coloured his political views permanently, his initial enthusiasm turning to fear and revulsion as he watched the rise of Napoleon Bonaparte and saw how easily democratic power could be usurped by a clever tyrant. Again and again he would revert in his letters to the painful political lessons he had learnt at this time. And because his poetry was imbued with his political beliefs, it too could trace its roots back to 1792.

Chapter Two

1793–8

On 29 January 1793 William published not one, but two, thin volumes of poetry. *An Evening Walk* was a revision of a poem he had written as a schoolboy at Hawkshead; *Descriptive Sketches* was a poetic account of his Continental walking tour of 1790. His reasons for publishing were twofold: to earn money and 'as I had done nothing by which to distinguish myself at the university, I thought these little things might shew that I could do something.' He was to be disappointed in both hopes.

25. *Dorothy Wordsworth to Jane Pollard; Forncett, 16 February [1793]*

By this Time, you have doubtless seen my Brother Williams Poems, & they have already suffered the Lash of your Criticisms. I should be very glad if you would give me your opinion of them with the same Frankness with which I am going to give you Mine. The Scenes which he describes have been viewed with a Poet's eye and are pourtrayed with a Poet's pencil; & the Poems contain many Passages exquisitely beautiful, but they also contain many Faults, the chief of which are Obscurity, & a too frequent use of some particular expressions & uncommon words for instance <u>moveless</u>, which he applies in a sense if not new, at least different from its ordinary one; by moveless when applied to the Swan he means that sort of motion which is smooth without agitation; it is a very beautiful epithet but ought to have been cautiously used, he ought at any rate only to have hazarded it once, instead of which it occurs three or four times. The word <u>viewless</u> also, is introduced far too often, this, though not so uncommon a word as the former ought not to have been made use of ᴏre than once or twice – I regret exceedingly that he did not submit ᴏrks to the Inspection of some Friend before their Publication, & ins with me in this Regret. Their Faults are such as a young Poet ly to fall into & least likely to discover, & what the Suggestions ld easily have made him see & at once correct –

26. Dorothy Wordsworth to Jane Pollard; Forncett, 16 June [1793]

I often hear from my dear Brother William & I am very anxious about him just now as he has not yet got any settled Employment. He is looking out and wishing for the Opportunity of engaging himself as Tutor to some young Gentleman, an Office for which even Friends less partial than I am, allow him to be particularly well qualified. You can have no Idea how much I wish to introduce him to you, I am sure you would be pleased with him, he is certainly very agreeable in his manners & he is so amiable, so good, so fond of his Sister! Oh Jane the last Time we were together he won my Affect[ion] to a Degree which I cannot describe; his Attentions to me were su[ch] as the most insensible of mortals must have been touched with – there was no Pleasure that he would not have given up with joy for half an Hour's Conversation with me; It was in Winter (at Christmas) [1790] that he was last at Forncett, & every Day as soon as we rose from Dinner we used to pace the Gravel Walk in the Garden <u>till</u> <u>six o'clock</u> when we received a Summons (which was always unwelcome) to Tea. Nothing but Rain or Snow prevented our taking this walk. Often have I gone out when the keenest North Wind has been whistling amongst the Trees over our Heads. I have paced that walk in the garden which will always be dear to me from the Remembrance of those long, long conversations I have had upon it supported by my Brother's arm. Ah! Jane! I never thought of the cold when he was with me. I am as heretical as yourself in my Opinions concerning Love & Friendship; I am very sure that Love will never bind me closer to any human Being than Friendship binds me to you my earliest female Friend, and to William my earliest & my dearest Male Friend.

Much as Dorothy longed for a reunion with her brother, her Cookson uncles refused to permit it. They disapproved of his politics, his affair with Annette and his illegitimate daughter. When he now announced that he had no intention of being ordained as a clergyman, even Dr Cookson washed his hands of his recalcitrant nephew. William and Dorothy were reduced to plotting a secret 'accidental' meeting at Halifax, which led to an idyllic few weeks spent together as guests of William Calvert at Windy Brow, his house overlooking Keswick in the Lake District.

27. Dorothy Wordsworth to Jane Pollard; [Forncett, 10 and 12 July 1793]

<u>none of this is to be read aloud so be upon your guard</u>

I cannot . . . resist my desire of making <u>you</u> acquainted with the scheme which we have in agitation of bringing about a meeting at Halifax. Ever since he saw Mr & Mrs Rawson [the former 'Aunt' Threlkeld] in London he has wished for an opportunity of accepting their very pressing invitation to their house but he has not been in the North since that time. He is now going upon a tour to the West of England along with a gentleman [William Calvert] who was formerly a school-fellow, a man of fortune, & who is to bear all the expenses of the journey and only requests the favour of William's company as he is averse to the idea of going alone. As William has not the prospect of any immediate employment I think he cannot pursue a better scheme, as his expences will be reduced to the articles of cloaths and washing, and he is perfectly at liberty to quit his companion as soon as any thing more advantageous shall offer.

. . . my brother's tour will not be completed till October at which time they will perhaps make a stand in <u>North</u> Wales from whence he can very conveniently take a trip to Halifax. It is more than two years and a half since we last saw each other & so ardent is our desire for a meeting that we are determined upon procuring to ourselves this happiness if it were even to be purchased at the price of a journey cross the Kingdom; but from North Wales into Yorkshire the distance is nothing . . .

28. Dorothy Wordsworth to Jane Pollard; Forncett, 30 August [1793]

His Tour was put a Stop to by an accident which might have had fatal consequences. Calvert's horse was not much accustomed to draw in a Whiskey (the carriage in which they travelled) and he began to caper one day in a most terrible manner, dragged them & their vehicle into a Ditch and broke it to shivers. Happily neither Mr C[alvert] nor William were the worse but they were sufficiently cautious not to venture again in the same way; Mr C[alvert] mounted his Horse and rode into the North and William's firm Friends a pair of stout Legs supported him from Salisbury through South into North Wales, where he is now quietly sitting down in the Vale of Clwydd, where he will wait my arrival at Halifax & join me there, I mean if he does not enter into some Engagement which may interfere with our schemes. He is staying with his Friend Jones the

companion of his continental Tour, and passes his Time as happily as he
could desire; exactly according to his Taste, except alas! (Ah here I sigh),
that he is separated from those he loves. He says that 'their House is quite
a cottage just such an one as would suit us' & oh! how sweetly situated in
the most delicious of all Vales, the Vale of Clwyd! You can have no Idea
of my Impatience to see this dear Brother. It is nearly three years since we
parted. It will be exactly three years when we meet again.

29. William Wordsworth to William Mathews; Mr Rawson's, Mill-house, near Halifax, 17 February [1794]

You have learned from Myers [William's cousin and fellow student at
Cambridge] that, since I had the pleasure of seeing you, I have been
do[ing] nothing and still continue to be doing nothing. What is to become
of me I know not: I cannot bow down my mind to take orders, and as
for the law I have neither strength of mind purse or constitution, to engage
in that pursuit. – It gives me great pleasure to hear you speak in such
affectionate terms of our former conversations, such language adds to the
desire which the recollection of those enjoyments inspires me with of
repeating them. I am happy to hear that you are master of Spanish and
Portuguese. Of Spanish I have read none these three years and little Italian,
but of French I esteem myself a tolerable master. My Italian studies I am
going to resume immediately, as it is my intention to instruct my sister in
that language . . .

  I [do not] know when I am likely to see you, as I am uncertain when
I shall be in London, nor do I think it worth while to take my master's
degree next summer. as an honour you know it is nothing, and in a
pecuniary light it would be of no use to me, on the contrary, it would
cost me a good deal of money.

30. Dorothy Wordsworth to an unidentified correspondent; Windy Brow, April 1794

After having enjoyed the company of my brother William at Halifax, we
set forward by coach towards Whitehaven, and thence to Kendal. I walked,
with my brother at my side, from Kendal to Grasmere, eighteen miles,
and afterwards from Grasmere to Keswick, fifteen miles, through the most
delightful country that was ever seen. We are now at a farm-house, about
half a mile from Keswick. When I came, I intended to stay only a few

days; but the country is so delightful, and, above all, I have so full an enjoyment of my brother's company, that I have determined to stay a few weeks longer. After I leave Windybrow I shall proceed to Whitehaven.

31. Dorothy Wordsworth to Jane Pollard; Windy Brow, near Keswick [21 April 1794]

You would hear from my aunt of my wonderful prowess in the walking way, and of my safe arrival at Grasmere. Since I wrote to her I walked from Grasmere to Keswick, 13 miles, and at Keswick I still remain. I have been so much delighted with the people of this house, with its situation, with the cheapness of living, and above all with the opportunity which I have of enjoying my brother's company that, though at my arrival I only talked of staying a few days, I have already been here above a fortnight & I intend staying still a few weeks longer – perhaps three or four. You cannot conceive any thing more delightful than the situation of this house. It stands upon the top of a very steep bank, which rises in a direction nearly perpendicular from a dashing stream below. From the window of the room where I write I have a prospect of the road winding along the opposite banks of this river, of a part of the lake of Keswick, and of the town, and towering above the town a woody steep of a very considerable height whose summit is a long range of silver rocks. This is the view from the house, but a hundred yards above, it is impossible to describe its grandeur. There is a natural terrace along the side of the mountain which shelters Windy Brow, whence we command a view of the whole vale of Keswick (the vale of Elysium, as Mr Grey[1] calls it). This vale is terminated at one end by a huge pile of grand mountains in whose lap the lovely lake of Derwent[water] is placed, at the other end by the lake of Bassenthwaite, on one side Skiddaw towers sublime and on the other a range of mountains not of equal size but of much grandeur, & the middle part of the vale is of beautiful cultivated grounds interspersed with cottages and watered by a winding stream which runs between the lakes of Derwent and Bassenthwaite. I have never been more delighted with the manners of any people than of the family under whose roof I am at present. They are the most honest cleanly sensible people I ever saw in their rank of life – & I think I may safely affirm <u>happier</u> than any body I know. They are contented with a supply of the bare necessaries of life, are active and industrious & declare with simple frankness unmixed with ostentation that they prefer their cottage at Windy Brow to any of the showy edifices in the neighbourhood, & that they believe there is not to be found in the whole vale a happier family than they are. They are fond of reading, & reason not indifferently upon what they read. We have a neat parlour to ourselves which Mr Calvert has fitted up for his own use and the lodging-rooms are very comfortable. Till my brother gets some employment he will lodge here. Mr Calvert is not now at windy brow as you will suppose. We please ourselves in calculating, from our present expences for how very small a sum we could live. We find our own food, our breakfast and supper are of milk & our dinner chiefly of potatoes & we drink no tea. We have received great civilities from many very pleasant families particularly from a Mrs Spedding of Armathwaite . . . William is very intimate with her oldest son [John, his schoolfellow at Hawkshead] and has always received great kindness from the family.

William was now twenty-four and his lack of employment was becoming a major cause for concern: somehow or other he had to earn his living. Having prudently shelved publication of a republican tract he had just written in defence of the execution of the King of France, he was now exploring the possibility of setting up a radical political journal, to be called *The Philanthropist*, with his university friend, William Mathews. In the fevered political climate of the day this was exactly the sort of anti-government activity which might result in prosecution, imprisonment or even transportation, as Richard Wordsworth warned him. His advice fell on deaf ears.

32. Richard Wordsworth to his brother, William; Staple Inn, London, 23 May 1794

tell me . . . how you mean to dispose of yourself this summer. I hope you will be cautious in writing or expressing your political Opinions by the suspension of the Habeas Corpus acts the Ministers have great powers – I have forwarded the Italian Gram[mar] Tasso & Ari[o]sto for you at Keswick.

33. William Wordsworth to William Mathews; Whitehaven, 23 May [1794]

I assure you it would give me great pleasure to cultivate your friendship in person, but I really cannot on any account venture to London unless upon the certainty of a regular income.

Living in London must always be expensive however frugal you may

be. as to the article of eating that is not much; but dress, and lodging, are
extremely expensive. – But I must do something to maintain myself even
in this country. You mention the possibility of setting on foot a monthly
miscellany from which some emolument might be drawn. I wish I assure
you most heartily to be engaged in something of that kind, and if you
could depend on the talents, and above all the industry of the young man
you speak of, I think we three would be quite sufficient with our best
exertions to keep alive such a publication. But as you say how to set it
afloat!

I am so poor that I could not advance any thing, and I am afraid you
are equally unable to contribute in that way! Perhaps however this might
be got over if we could be sure of the patronage of the public. I do not
see that my being in the country would have any tendency to diminish
the number or deduct from the value of my communications. It would
only prevent me from officiating as an editor, and, as you are I suppose both
resident in town that circumstance would not be of much consequence. I
wish much to hear further from you on this head, as I think if we could
once raise a work of this kind into any reputation it would really be of
consequence to us both. But much is to be attended to before we enter
the field. What class of readers ought we to aim at procuring; in what do
we, each of us, suppose ourselves the most able either to entertain or
instruct[?]

Of each others political sentiments we ought not to be ignorant; and
here at the very threshold I solemnly affirm that in no writings of mine
will I ever admit of any sentiment which can have the least tendency to
induce my readers to suppose that the doctrines which are now enforced
by banishment, imprisonment, &c, &c, are other than pregnant with
every species of misery. You know perhaps already that I am of that odious
class of men called democrats, & of that class I shall for ever continue. In
a work like that of which we are speaking, it will be impossible (and
indeed it would render our publication worthless were we to attempt it,)
not to inculcate principles of government and forms of social order of
one kind or another. I have therefore thought it proper to say this much
in order that if your sentiments or those of our coadjutor are dissimilar,
we may drop the scheme at once. Besides essays on morals and politics I
think I could communicate critical remarks upon poetry, &c, &c, upon
the arts of painting, gardening, and other subjects of amusement. But I
should principally wish our attention to be fixed upon life and manners, &
to make our publication a vehicle of sound and exalted morality. all the

periodical miscellanies that I am acquainted with except one or two of
the reviews, appear to be written to maintain the existence of prejudice
and to disseminate error. To such purposes I have already said I will not
prostitute my pen . . .

I am at present nearly quite at leisure, so that with industry I think I
can perform my share. I say nearly at leisure for I am not quite so as I am
correcting and considerably adding to those poems [*An Evening Walk* and
Descriptive Sketches] which I published in your absence. It was with great
reluctance I huddled up those two little works and sent them into the
world in so imperfect a state. But as I had done nothing by which to
distinguish myself at the university, I thought these little things might
shew that I could do something. They have been treated with unmerited
contempt by some of the periodical publications, and others have spoken
in higher terms of them than they deserve. I have another poem [the
'Salisbury Plain' poem][2] written last summer ready for the press though
I certainly should not publish it unless I hoped to derive from it some
pecuniary recompence – as I am speaking on this subject pray let me
request you to have the goodness to call on Johnson my publisher, and
ask him if he ever sells any of those poems and what number he thinks
are yet on his hands. You will be doing me a great favor.

34. *William Wordsworth to William Mathews; Whitehaven, [8] June [1794]*

I read the explicit avowal of your political sentiments with great pleasure;
any comments which I have to make upon it will be expressed in the best
manner by a similar declaration of my own opinions. I disapprove of
monarchical & aristocratical governments, however modified. Hereditary
distinctions and privileged orders of every species I think must necessarily
counteract the progress of human improvement: hence it follows that I
am not amongst the admirers of the British constitution . . . [but] . . . The
destruction of those institutions which I condemn appears to me to be
hastening on too rapidly. I recoil from the bare idea of a revolution;
yet, if our conduct with reference both to foreign and domestic policy
continues such as it has been for the last two years how is that dreadful
event to be averted? aware of the difficulty of this it seems to me that a
writer who has the welfare of mankind at heart should call forth his best
exertions to convince the people that they can only be preserved from a
convulsion by oeconomy in the administration of the public purse &
a gradual and constant reform of those abuses which, if left to themselves,

may grow to such a height as to render, even a revolution desirable . . . I deplore the miserable situation of the French; & think we can only be guarded from the same scourge by the undaunted efforts of good men in propagating with unremitting activity those doctrines which long and resolute[3] meditation has taught them are essential to the welfare of mankind. Freedom of inquiry is all that I wish for; let nothing be deemed too sacred for investigation; rather than restrain the liberty of the press I would suffer the most atrocious doctrines to be recommended: let the field be open & unencumbered, & truth must be victorious. On this subject I think I have said enough, if it be not necessary to add that, when I observe the people should be enlightened upon the subject of politics, I severely condemn all inflammatory addresses to the passions of men, even when it is intended to direct those passions to a good purpose. I know that the multitude walk in darkness. I would put into each man's hand a lantern to guide him & not have him to set out upon his journey depending for illumination on abortive flashes of lightning, or the coruscations of transitory meteors.

. . . as to coming to town this step I must at present decline. I have a friend in the country who has offered me a share of his income. It would be using him very ill to run the risque of destroying my usefulness by precipitating myself into distress & poverty at the time when he is so ready to support me in a situation wherein I feel I can be of some little service to my fellow men . . . I have not been much used to composition of any kind particularly in prose, my style therefore may frequently want fluency & sometimes perhaps perspicuity but these defects will wear off; an ardent wish to promote the welfare of mankind will preserve me from sinking under them.

The friend who had offered William a share of his income was Raisley Calvert, the younger brother of the Wordsworths' host at Windy Brow. Recognizing that William had the ability to make his mark in the world, if only he were freed from the necessity of having to earn his living, Calvert had made the practical offer of financial support. His generosity acquired an altogether more poignant aspect when, within weeks, it became clear that he was terminally ill. During the long, trying months William spent devotedly nursing his dying friend, the plans for establishing *The Philanthropist* fell through and he was forced to contemplate finding employment of a different kind.

35. William Wordsworth to William Mathews; Keswick, 7 November 1794

My friend, of whom I have spoken to you, has every symptom of a confirmed consumption of the lungs, & I cannot think of quitting him in his present debilitated state. If he should not recover, indeed whatever turn his complaint takes, I am so emboldened by your encouragement that I am determined to throw myself into that mighty gulph which has swallowed up so many, of talents and attainments infinitely superior to my own. One thing however I can boast and on that one thing I rely, extreme frugality. This must be my main support, my chief vectigal . . . You say a newspaper would be glad of me; do you think you could ensure me employment in that way on terms similar to your own? I mean also in an opposition paper, for really I cannot in conscience and in principle, abet in the smallest degree the measures pursued by the present ministry. They are already so deeply advanced in iniquity that like Macbeth they cannot retreat. When I express myself in this manner I am far from reprobating those whose sentiments on this point differ from my own; I know that many good men were persuaded of the expediency of the present war, and I know also that many persons may think it their duty to support the acting ministry from an idea of thereby supporting the government, even when they disapprove of most of the present measures.

. . . I begin to wish much to be in town; cataracts and mountains, are good occasional society, but they will not do for constant companions; besides I have not even much of their conversation, and still less of that of my books as I am so much with my sick friend, and he cannot bear the fatigue of being read to. Nothing indeed but a sense of duty could detain me here under the present circumstances. This is a country for poetry it is true; but the muse is not to be won but by the sacrifice of time, and time I have not to spare.

36. William Wordsworth to William Mathews; [Penrith, c.24 December 1794 and 7 January 1795]

I sincerely thank you for the exertions you are ready to make in my behalf. I certainly mean to visit London as soon as the case of my friend is determined; and request you would have the goodness to look out for me some employment in your way. I must premise however that I have neither strength of memory, quickness of penmanship, nor rapidity of composition to enable me to report any part of the parliamentary debates.

I am not conscious of any want of ability for translating from the French
or Italian Gazettes and with two or three weeks reading I think I could
engage for the Spanish . . .

There is still a further circumstance which disqualifies me for the office
of parliamentary reporter, viz. my being subject to nervous headaches,
which invariably attack me when exposed to a heated atmosphere or to
loud noises and that with such an excess of pain as to deprive me of all
recollection . . .

I should be happy to hear that you could give me grounds to suppose
you could find employment for me in any other part of a newspaper for
which you think me qualified.

Raisley Calvert died at Penrith in January 1795, leaving William a bequest of
£900 which was to be invested 'to secure me from want if not to render me
independent . . . and to enable me to pursue my literary views or any other views
with greater success or with a consciousness that if these should fail me I would
have something at last to turn to.' Having attended his friend to the grave, William
left for London, where newspaper employment continued to elude him. Mixing
in a highly intellectual circle of Cambridge graduates, who were radicals and
followers of the philosopher William Godwin, William befriended a struggling
lawyer, Basil Montagu, and his motherless son, who was almost two years old. In
doing so, he inadvertently stumbled on a solution to his and Dorothy's problems.

37. *Dorothy Wordsworth to Mrs Jane Marshall [née Pollard]; Mill House, [Halifax], 2 September [1795]*

I am going now to tell you what is for your own eyes & ears alone. I need
say no more than this I am sure, to insure your most careful secrecy. Know
then that I am going to live in Dorsetshire. Let me, however, methodically
state the whole plan, & then my dearest Jane I doubt not you will rejoice
in the prospect which at last opens before me of having, at least for a time
a comfortable home, in a house of my own, you know the pleasure which
I have always attached to the idea of home, a blessing which I so early lost
(though made up to me as well as the most affectionate care of relations
not positively congenial in pursuits & pleasures could do, & with separate
and distinct views). I think I told you that Mr Montague had a little boy,
who as you will perceive could not be very well taken care of either in
his father's chambers or under the uncertain management of various
friends of Mr M[ontagu] with whom he has frequently stayed. He was

lamenting this circumstance, & proposed to William to allow him 50£ a year for his board provided I should approve of the plan, at the same time W[illia]m had the offer of a ready furnished house rent free with a garden, orchard & every other convenience. A natural daughter of Mr Tom Myers (a cousin of mine whom I daresay you have heard me mention) is coming over to England by the first ships which are expected in about a month, to be educated, she is I believe about 3 or 4 years old, & T[om] Myers's Brother who has the charge of her has requested that I will take her under my care. With these two children & the produce of Raisley Calvert's legacy we shall have an income of at least 170 or 180£ per annum. W[illia]m finds that he can get 9 per cent for the money upon the best security. He means to sink half of it upon my life, which will make me always comfortable and independent, without taking into consideration the addition to it which I have every reason to expect from the liberality of Richard. The house belongs to a Mr Pinney a very rich Merchant of Bristol. He had given it up to his son to dispose of it as he pleased he has hitherto kept a man and maidservant in it, & has now with his father's approbation[4] offered it to my brother; he is to come occasionally for a few weeks to stay with us, paying for his board. It is a very good house, & in a pleasant situation, & there is nothing wanted for us to purchase, except linen of which we are to have the use till we have provided ourselves with it. William is staying at Bristol, at present, with Mr Pinney, & is very much delighted with the whole family, particularly Mr Pinney the father . . .

It will be a very great charge for me I am sensible, but it is of a nature well suited to my inclinations. You know I am active, not averse to household employments, & fond of children. I have laid my plans as distinctly as I can but many things must depend upon unforeseen circumstances, I am, however, determined to adhere with the strictest attention to certain rules. In the first place economy & an attention to the overlooking every thing my self will be absolutely necessary for this purpose, not much time is necessary if it is done with regularity. I shall also have a good deal of work, (needlework) to do – & I am determined to take the whole care of the children such as washing, dressing them &c upon myself. I forgot in enumerating the comforts of Racedown (so the place is called) to tell you that we may have land to keep a cow & that there is a cow there of which we may have the use. I think it is probable that there may be a cottager near us to whose charge we may commit it, for a share of the milk or some trifling recompense. I mean to keep one maidservant, she must be a strong girl and cook plain victuals tolerably well as we shall occasionally have both Mr Montague & Mr Pinney to stay with us. I have now told you all the <u>certain</u> income we shall have, added to which W[illia]m has great hopes of having a son of Mr Pinney for a pupil a boy about thirteen years of age, if he should be entrusted with him, then his income would be large, as he would have a very handsome salary. A Friend of Williams had the care of one of his brothers in his own house & had two hundred a year with him. I have great satisfaction in thinking that William will have such opportunities of studying as I hope will be not only advantageous to his mind but his purse, living in the unsettled way in which he has hitherto lived in London is altogether unfavourable to mental exertion. By the bye I must not forget to tell you that he has had the offer of ten guineas for a work [a political satire, *Imitation of Juvenal, Satire VIII*, which was never published in William's lifetime] which has not taken him up much time, & half the profits of a second edition if it should be called for. It is but a little sum but it is one step & promises that something may be done . . .

I am expecting a letter from my uncle William [Cookson] every day with his opinion of the scheme. I think he cannot disapprove of it. There are so many arguments in its favour. One of the first & greatest is that it may put William into a way of getting a more permanent establishment, and on my account that it will greatly contribute to my happiness & place me is such a situation that I shall be <u>doing something</u>, it is a painful idea that one's existence is of very little use which <u>I</u> really have always been obliged to feel; above all it is painful when one is living upon the bounty of one's friends, a resource of which misfortune may deprive one & then how irksome & difficult is it to find out other means of support, the mind is then unfitted, perhaps for any new exertions, & continues always in a state of dependence, perhaps attended with poverty.

38. William Wordsworth to William Mathews; Racedown Lodge [Dorset], Saturday, 24 October [1795]

I stayed at Bristol at least five weeks with a family whom I found amiable in all its branches; the weather was delightful, and my time slipped insensibly away . . . Coleridge was at Bristol part of the time I was there. I saw but little of him. I wished indeed to have seen more – his talents appear to me very great. I met with Southey also, his manners pleased me exceedingly and I have every reason to think very highly of his powers of mind. He is about publishing an epic poem on the subject of the maid of orleans. From the specimens I have seen I am inclined to think it will have many beauties. I recollect your mentioning you had met Southey and thought him a coxcomb. This surprizes me much, as I never saw a young man who seemed to me to have less of that character. We are now at Racedown and both as happy as people can be who live in perfect solitude. We do not see a soul. Now and then we meet a miserable peasant in the road or an accidental traveller. The country people here are wretchedly poor; ignorant and overwhelmed with every vice that usually attends ignorance in that class, viz – lying and picking and stealing &c &c. Yesterday I walked over to Lyme [Regis] not without a hope of meeting Leader,[5] but I was disappointed. I therefore returned home to dinner. Nota bene. Lyme is at least eight miles and a half from Racedown. My walk over the hills was charming. I could hear the murmuring of the sea for three miles; of course I often stopped "listening with pleasing dread to the deep roar of the wide weltering waves". This is from the minstrel [i.e. Beattie's *The Minstrel*] and has reminded me of a request I have to make to you which is that you would accept of my edition of Cato's Letters, and in return make me a present of that vol[ume] of Bells fugitive poetry which contains The minstrel and Sir martyn. I know you are possessed of it; so was I once but one of my brothers lent it to a person who valued it so highly as to deny himself the pleasure of returning it.

39. William Wordsworth to a university friend, Francis Wrangham; Racedown, 20 November [1795]

I have said no thing of Racedown; it is an excellent house and the country far from unpleasant but as to society we must manufacture it ourselves. Will you come and help us? we expect Montagu at Christmas and should be very glad if you could make it convenient to come along with him, if not, at all events we shall hope to see you in the course of next summer. Have you any interest with the booksellers? I have a poem [the 'Salisbury Plain' poem] which I should wish to dispose of provided I could get any thing for it. – I recollect reading the first draught of it to you in London. But since I came to Racedown I have made alterations and additions so material as that it may be looked on almost as another work. Its object is partly to expose the vices of the penal law and the calamities of war as they affect individuals – Adieu

40. Dorothy Wordsworth to Mrs Jane Marshall; Racedown, 30 November [1795]

We are now surrounded by winter prospects without doors, & within have only winter occupations, books, solitude and the fire-side, yet I may safely say we are never dull. Basil is a charming boy, he affords us perpetual entertainment, do not suppose from this that we make him our perpetual play-thing, far otherwise, I think that is one of the modes of treatment most likely to ruin a child's temper & character. But I do not think there is any Pleasure more delightful than that of marking the development of a child's faculties, & observing his little occupations. We found every thing at Racedown much more complete with respect to household conveniences than I could have expected. You may judge of this when I tell you we have not had to lay out ten shillings for the use of the house. We were a whole month without servant, but now we have got one of the nicest girls I ever saw; she suits us exactly, & I have all my domestic concerns so arranged that every thing goes on with the utmost regularity. We wash once a month. I hire a woman, to whom I give ninepence for one day, to wash, on the next we have got the clothes dried & on the third have finished ironing. It is the only time in which I have any thing to do in the house, but then I am very active & very busy as you will suppose. I have been making Basil coloured frocks, shirts, slips, &c, & have had a good deal of employment in repairing his clothes & putting my brothers into order. We walk about two hours every morning – we have many very pleasant walks about us & what is a great advantage, the roads are of a sandy kind & are almost always dry. We can see the sea 150 or 200 yards from the door, & at a little distance have a very extensive view terminated by the sea seen through different openings of the unequal hills. We have not the warmth and luxuriance of Devonshire though there is no want either of wood or cultivation, but the trees appear to suffer from the sea blasts. We have hills, which seen from a distance almost take the character of mountains, some cultivated nearly to their summits, others in their wild state covered with furze & broom. These delight me the most as they remind me of our native wilds. Our common parlour is the prettiest little room that can be; with very neat furniture, a large book [case?] on each side [of] the fire, a marble chimney piece, bath stove, & an oil cloth for the floor. The other parlour is rather larger, has a good carpet, side boards in the recesses on each side [of] the fire, & has upon the whole a smart appearance, but we do not like it half so well as our little breakfast room . . .

The greatest inconvenience we suffer here is in being so far from the post office; with respect to household conveniences we do very well, as the butcher coming from Cruikhern brings us every thing we want. With respect to letters we are however, more independent than most people as William is so good a walker, & I too have walked over twice to Crewkhern (the distance is 7 miles) to make purchases, & what is more we turned out of our way three miles, in one of our walks thither to see a house of Lord Powlett's & a very fine view. We were amply repaid for our trouble. If you want to find our situation out, look in your maps for Crewkhern, Chard, Axminster, Bridport & Lime; we are nearly equi-distant from all those places. A little brook which runs at the distance of one field from us divides us from Devonshire. This country abounds in apples; in some of our walks we go through orchards without any other enclosure or security than as a common field. When I spoke of the sea I forgot to tell you that my brother saw the West India fleet sailing in all its glory before the storm had made such dreadful ravages.[6] The peasants are miserably poor; their cottages are <u>shapeless</u> structures (I may almost say) of wood & clay – indeed they are not at all beyond what might be expected in savage life.

41. *Azariah Pinney to James Tobin; Bristol, 12 April 1796*

After I left London ... I remained three Weeks with Wordsworth at Race-down, who desired me to say, how happy it will make him to see you there – but not to expect any thing more than democratic fair [*sic*] – His Salisbury Plain is so much altered that I think it may in truth be called a new Poem – I brought it with me to Bristol – It is now at Coleridge's, by whom it has been attentively read and pronounced a very fine Poem – I doubt not but you will see it in Print within the duration of a few Weeks – While we were with him he relaxed the rigour of his philosophic Nerves so much as to go a Coursing several times, and I assure you did not eat the unfortunate Hares with less relish because he heard them heave their death groans, and saw their Eyes directed towards Heaven with that glare of vacant sadness which belongs to the expiring creature – for his usual Appetite shewed itself at the dining Table – Miss Wordsworth has undoubted claim to good humour, but does not possess, in my opinion, that je ne sais quoi, so necessary to sweeten the sour draught of human misfortune and smooth the [?rough] road of this Life's Passage –

42. William Wordsworth to William Mathews; Racedown, 21 March [1796]

You were right about Southey, he is certainly a coxcomb, and has proved it completely by the preface to his Joan of Arc, an epic poem which he has just published. This preface is indeed a very conceited performance and the poem though in some passages of first-rate excellence is on the whole of very inferior execution. Our present life is utterly barren of such events as merit even the short-lived chronicle of an accidental letter. We plant cabbages, and if retirement in its full perfection, be as powerful in working transformations as one of Ovid's Gods, you may perhaps suspect that into cabbages we shall be transformed. Indeed I learn that such has been the prophecy of one of our London friends. In spite of all this I was tolerably industrious in reading, if reading can ever deserve the name of industry, till our good friends the Pinneys came amongst us; and I have since returned to my books. as to writing it is out of the question. Not however entirely to forget the world, I season my recollection of some of its objects with a little ill-nature, I attempt to write satires! and in all satires whatever the authors may say there will be found a spice of malignity.

The frustration of being cut off from the stimulus of intellectual conversation and exiled from the centre of political events eventually drove William to London in the summer of 1796. He returned enthused with the idea for a new project, a philosophical drama, *The Borderers*, which would occupy him for months to come. No other pupils materialized but the monotony of life at Racedown was relieved by visitors. Mary Hutchinson, a childhood friend of the Wordsworths from Penrith, came in November and stayed until June 1797. It was an important visit for though neither William nor Mary declared their feelings at the time, they later recognized that it was during this period that their love for each other was rekindled. Basil Montagu also paid his first (short) visit to his son in the spring of 1796. Most dramatically of all, Samuel Taylor Coleridge literally leapt into the Wordsworths' lives as Mary left, vaulting over the gate in the field in his haste to visit them. William had met Coleridge several times before and had corresponded with him, but it was only on this occasion – and significantly in Dorothy's presence – that the two sparks ignited into a single flame that was to become a dazzling literary friendship and partnership.

43. Dorothy Wordsworth to unidentified correspondent; [Racedown], 24 October 1796

[William is] now ardent in the composition of a tragedy . . .

44. William Wordsworth to Francis Wrangham; [Racedown, c.25 February 1797]

As to your promoting my interest in the way of pupils upon a review of my own attainments I think there is so little that I am able to teach that this scheme may be suffered to fly quietly away to the paradise of fools . . .

I have lately been living upon air & the essence of carrots cabbages turnips & other esculent vegetables, not excluding parsely [*sic*] the produce of my garden –

45. Dorothy Wordsworth to Mrs Jane Marshall; Racedown, 19 March [1797]

Mr M[ontagu] came upon us unexpectedly before we were risen on Wednesday morning. W[illia]m has accompanied him to Bristol where they will spend about a fortnight & then William will return to Racedown. I am excessively pleased with Mr M[ontagu] – He is one of the pleasantest men I ever saw, & so amiable, & so good that every body who knows him must love him. You perhaps have heard that my friend Mary Hutchinson is staying with me; she is one of the best girls in the world & we are as happy as human beings can be; that is when William is at home, for you cannot imagine how dull we feel & what a vacuum his loss has occasioned, but this is the first day; tomorrow we shall be better. We feel the change more severely as we have lost both Montague & him at once. M[ontagu] is so chearful & made us so merry that we hardly know how to bear the change. Indeed William is as chearful as any body can be   perhaps you may not think it but he is the life of the whole house.

46. Dorothy Wordsworth to Mary Hutchinson; Racedown, [June 1797]

. . . You had a great loss in not seeing Coleridge. He is a wonderful man. His conversation teems with soul, mind, and spirit. Then he is so benevolent, so good tempered and cheerful, and, like William, interests himself so much about every little trifle. At first I thought him very plain, that is, for about three minutes: he is pale, thin, has a wide mouth, thick lips, and not very good teeth, longish, loose-growing, half-curling, rough, black hair[.] But, if you hear him speak for five minutes you think no more of them. His eye is large and full, and not very dark, but grey, such an eye as would receive from a heavy soul the dullest expression; but it speaks every emotion of his animated mind: it has more of 'the poet's eye in a fine frenzy rolling'[7] than I ever witnessed. He has fine dark eyebrows, and an overhanging forehead.

The first thing that was read after he came was William's new poem, 'Ruined Cottage,' with which he was much delighted; and after tea he repeated to us two acts and a half of his tragedy, 'Osorio.' The next morning, William read his tragedy, 'The Borderers.'

47. *Samuel Taylor Coleridge to his publisher, Joseph Cottle; [Racedown] Thursday [8 June 1797]*

Wordsworth admires my Tragedy – which gives me great hopes. Wordsworth has written a Tragedy himself. I speak with heart-felt sincerity & (I think) unblinded judgement, when I tell you, that I feel myself a *little man by his* side; & yet do not think myself the less man, than I formerly thought myself. – His Drama is absolutely wonderful. You know, I do not commonly speak in such abrupt & unmingled phrases – & therefore will the more readily believe me. – There are in the piece those *profound* touches of the human heart, which I find three or four times in 'The Robbers' of Schiller, & often in Shakespere – but in Wordsworth there are no *inequalities*. T[om] Poole's opinion of Wordsworth is – that he is the greatest Man, he ever knew – I coincide.

Such was the chemistry between William, Dorothy and Coleridge that none of them could face a parting, so Coleridge carried his new friends back with him to his home at Nether Stowey, a small village in Somerset. Within a matter of weeks the Wordsworths had given up Racedown and moved to Alfoxton, a gracious house in the Quantock Hills, a mere four miles from Coleridge.

48. *Dorothy Wordsworth to Mary Hutchinson; Alfoxton, 14 August 1797*

Here we are, in a large mansion, in a large park, with seventy head of deer around us. But I must begin with the day of leaving Racedown to pay Coleridge a visit. You know how much we were delighted with the neighbourhood of Stowey. The evening that I wrote to you, William and

I had rambled as far as this house, and pryed into the recesses of our little brook, but without any more fixed thoughts upon it than some dreams of happiness in a little cottage, and passing wishes that such a place might be found out. We spent a fortnight at Coleridge's: in the course of that time we heard that this house was to let, applied for it, and took it. Our principal inducement was Coleridge's society. It was a month yesterday since we came to Alfoxden.

The house is a large mansion, with furniture enough for a dozen families like ours. There is a very excellent garden, well stocked with vegetables and fruit. The garden is at the end of the house, and our favourite parlour, as at Racedown, looks that way. In front is a little court, with grass plot, gravel walk, and shrubs; the moss roses were in full beauty a month ago. The front of the house is to the south, but it is screened from the sun by a high hill which rises immediately from it. This hill is beautiful, scattered irregularly and abundantly with trees, and topped with fern, which spreads a considerable way down it. The deer dwell here, and sheep, so that we have a living prospect. From the end of the house we have a view of the sea, over a woody meadow-country; and exactly opposite the window where I now sit is an immense wood, whose round top from this point has exactly the appearance of a mighty dome. In some parts of this wood there is an under grove of hollies which are now very beautiful. In a glen at the bottom of the wood is the waterfall of which I spoke, a quarter of a mile from the house. We are three miles from Stowey, and not two miles from the sea. Wherever we turn we have woods, smooth downs, and valleys with small brooks running down them, through green meadows, hardly ever intersected with hedgerows, but scattered over with trees. The hills that cradle these valleys are either covered with fern and bilberries, or oak woods, which are cut for charcoal . . . Walks extend for miles over the hill-tops; the great beauty of which is their wild simplicity: they are perfectly smooth, without rocks.

The Tor of Glastonbury is before our eyes during more than half of our walk to Stowey; and in the park wherever we go, keeping about fifteen yards above the house, it makes a part of our prospect.

Alfoxton was far more accessible to visitors than Racedown and, with Coleridge frequently in residence, it drew many of his radical friends. One of the earliest and most controversial of these was John Thelwall, who had already been tried twice for his life, and acquitted, on charges of sedition and high treason. His presence attracted the attention of the government and an agent was despatched to investigate whether the new tenants of Alfoxton were French sympathizers or spies. Though the agent's report cleared the Wordsworths of suspicion, the rumours were sufficiently alarming to cause the owner to serve notice on them to quit. Coleridge's patron, Tom Poole, who had stood guarantor for the Wordsworths' lease, pleaded unsuccessfully for a change of heart.

49. John Thelwall, radical and poet, to his wife; Alfoxton, 18 July 1797

Everything but my Stella and my babes are now banished from my mind by the enchanting retreat (the Academus of Stowey) from which I write this, and by the delightful society of Coleridge and of Wordsworth, the present occupier of Allfox Den. We have been having a delightful ramble to-day among the plantations, and along a wild, romantic dell in these grounds, through which a foaming, rushing, murmuring torrent of water winds its long artless course. There have we . . . a literary and political triumvirate, passed sentence on the productions and characters of the age, burst forth in poetical flights of enthusiasm, and philosophised our minds into a state of tranquillity, which the leaders of nations might envy, and the residents of cities can never know.

50. Dr Daniel Lysons to the Duke of Portland at the Home Office; Bath, 11 August 1797

On the 8th. inst. I took the liberty to acquaint your Grace with a very suspicious business concerning an emigrant family, who have contrived to get possession of a Mansion House at Alfoxton, late belonging to the Revd. Mr. St. Albyn, under Quantock Hills – I am since informed, that the master of the House has no wife with him, but only a woman who passes for his Sister – The man has Camp Stools, which he & his visitors carry with them when they go about the country upon their nocturnal or diurnal expeditions, & have also a Portfolio in which they enter their observations, which they have been heard to say were almost finished – They have been heard to say they should be rewarded for them, & were very attentive to the River near them . . . These people may *possibly* be under Agents to some principal at Bristol –

*51. James Walsh, government agent, to the Duke of Portland; [Nether Stowey]
16 August 1797*

I last Night saw Thomas Jones who lives at Alfoxton House. He exactly
confirms Mogg of Hungerford, with this addition that the Sunday after
Wordsworth came, he Jones was desired to wait at Table, that there were
14 persons at Dinner. Poole & Coldridge were there, and there was a little
Stout Man with dark cropt Hair and wore a White Hat and Glasses
[Thelwall] who after Dinner got up and talked so loud and was in such a
Passion that Jones was frightened and did not like to go near them since.
That Wordsworth has lately been to his former House and brought back
with him a Woman Servant, that Jones has seen this Woman who is very
Chatty, and that she told him that Her Master was a Phylosopher.

52. Tom Poole to Mrs St Albyn; Nether Stowey, 16 September 1797

As for Mr. Wordsworth, I believe him to be in every respect a gentleman.
I have not known him personally long, but I had heard of his family
before I knew him. Dr. Fisher, our late Vicar, and one of the Canons of
Windsor, had often mentioned to me as his particular and respected
friend, Mr. Cookson, Mr. Wordsworth's uncle, and also one of the Canons
of Windsor. This circumstance was sufficient to convince me of the
respectability of Mr. Wordsworth's family. You may, upon my honour,
rest assured that no tenant could have been found for Allfoxen whom, if
you knew him, you would prefer to Mr. Wordsworth. His family is small,
consisting of his sister, who has principally lived with her uncle, Mr.
Cookson, a child of five years old, the son of a friend of his, and one
excellent female servant. Such a family can neither wear nor tear the
house or furniture, and I will venture to say they were never both in better
order. How different would be the case with a large family – full of careless
servants, a run of idle company, hunting, breaking down fences, etc.

But I am informed you have heard that Mr. Wordsworth does keep
company, and on this head I fear the most infamous falsehoods have
reached your ears. Mr. Wordsworth is a man fond of retirement – fond of
reading and writing – and has never had above two gentlemen at a time
with him. By accident Mr. Thelwall, as he was travelling through the
neighbourhood, called at Stowey. The person he called on at Stowey
[Coleridge] took him to Allfoxen. No person at Stowey nor Mr. Wordsworth knew of his coming. Mr. Wordsworth had never spoken to him

before, nor, indeed, had any one of Stowey. Surely the common duties of hospitality were not to be refused to any man; and who would not be interested in seeing such a man as Thelwall, however they may disapprove of his sentiments or conduct?

God knows we are all liable to err, and should bear with patience the difference in one another's opinions. Be assured, and I speak it from my own knowledge, that Mr. Wordsworth, of all men alive, is the last who will give any one cause to complain of his opinions, his conduct, or his disturbing the peace of any one. Let me beg you, madam, to hearken to no calumnies, no party spirit, nor to join with any in disturbing one who only wishes to live in tranquillity.

53. Dorothy Wordsworth to Mary Hutchinson; Alfoxton, 20 November 1797

We have been on another tour: we set out last Monday evening at half-past four. The evening was dark and cloudy; we went eight miles, William and Coleridge employing themselves in laying the plan of a ballad [*The Ancient Mariner*], to be published with some pieces of William's . . .

William's play is finished, and sent to the managers of the Covent Garden Theatre. We have not the faintest expectation that it will be accepted.

54. Dorothy Wordsworth to her brother Christopher; Mr Nicholson's, Cateaton Street, London, 8 December [1797]

My dear Kitt –
  You will be not a little surprized to hear that I am in London. William has been induced to come up to alter his play for the stage at the suggestion of one of the principal Actors of Covent Garden to whom he transmitted it. We have been in town more than a week, he has finished it, and it is presented to the Manager and we wait his decision which is expected in the course of a few days . . . If the play is accepted we shall probably stay a fortnight or three weeks longer, if not we shall probably return home in about ten days.

55. Elizabeth Threlkeld, a second cousin of the Wordsworths' mother, to her cousin, Samuel Ferguson; 14 February 1798

Dorothy and William Wordsworth have been in London, and at Mr Nicholsons the motive of their Journey was to offer a Tragedy for the inspection of the Manager at Covent Garden theatre which they were induced to believe he would accept and that it would have a prodigious run. They had planned many schemes to follow if it succeeded, one of which was a pedestrian tour through Wales and by Yorkshire into Cumberland. This would *by many* be thought rather a *wildish* scheme, but by them it was thought very practicable and would certainly have been put in execution, had not the play been unfortunately rejected. I received a very entertaining letter from Dorothy on the occasion, she says they are not disappointed with its rejection, but I cannot give implicit credit to her assertion. William is not determined whether he shall publish it or no, he expects a reform to take place in the Stage, and then it may be brought forward to great advantage. These are visionary plans the distant prospect of which may be very pleasant, but which on a nearer view, almost always disappoint one. However they are happy in having very fertile imaginings which are a continual source of entertainment to them, and serve to enliven many of their solitary hours. I believe Williams Play has very great merit; the language is beautiful, and it is uncommonly interesting Miss Nicholson tells me; but the metaphysical obscurity of one character, was the great reason of its rejection. I wish we could send you a copy of it, for I dare say you will be as anxious as we are, to read the performance of our relation, and that of so excentric a young man.

56. William Wordsworth to his friend, James Tobin; Alfoxton, 6 March [1798]

There is little need to advise me against publishing; it is a thing which I dread as much as death itself. This may serve as an example of the figure – by rhetoricians called hyperbole, but privacy & quiet are my delight . . . We leave Allfoxden at Midsummer, the house is lett to Crewkshank of Stowey so our departure is decided, what may be our destination I cannot say. If we can raize the money we shall make a tour on foot. Probably through Wales, & northwards.. At present we are utterly unable to say where we shall be. We have no particular reason to be attached to the neighbourhood of Stowey but the society of Coleridge, & the friendship of Poole. News we have none, our occupations continue the same, only I rise early in the mornings.

I have written 1300 lines of a Poem ['The Recluse'][8] in which I can contrive to convey most of the knowledge of which I am possessed. My object is to give pictures of nature, Man, & Society. Indeed I know not any thing which will not come within the scope of my plan. If ever I attempt another drama; it shall be written either purposely for the closet or purposely for the Stage, there is no middle way. But the work of composition is carved out for me, for at least a year and a half to come.

Coleridge's enthusiasm and support had not only confirmed William in his desire to be a poet but had also inspired him to embark on 'The Recluse', which they both considered would be his most important work. Vague in concept and definition, it would haunt William for the rest of his poetic career and, to his lasting regret, it would never be completed. Preoccupation with this major project did not preclude writing smaller poems, however, and in the spring of 1798 William was enjoying a period of remarkable creativity, working at such a pace that by mid July he had almost enough to fill two small volumes. Despite his personal disinclination to publish, he was determined that these poems would finance a scheme, inspired by Coleridge, on which he had set his heart.

57. *William Wordsworth to his publisher, Joseph Cottle of Bristol; Alfoxton, 12 April 1798*

. . . You will be pleased to hear that I have gone on very rapidly adding to my stock of poetry. Do come and let me read it to you, under the old trees in the park. We have a little more than two months to stay in this place. Within these four days the season has advanced with greater rapidity than I ever remember, and the country becomes almost every hour more lovely. God bless you,   Your affectionate friend,

                                                        W. Wordsworth

58. *Dorothy Wordsworth to her brother Richard; Alfoxton, 30 April [1798]*

We are to quit Allfoxden at Midsummer. Our present plan is to go into Germany for a couple of years. William thinks it will be a great advantage to him to be acquainted with the German language; besides that translation is the most profitable of all works. He is about to publish some poems.

He is to have twenty guineas for one volume, & he expects more than twice as much for another which is nearly ready for publishing. As we shall most probably go by London we shall see you before we go. Our journey as far as Hamburgh will cost us between twenty & five & twenty guineas; we have reason to think we can live cheaper in Germany than in England. Our design is to board in a family.

59. *William Wordsworth to his friend, James Losh; Alfoxton, 11 March [1798]*

We are obliged to quit this place at Midsummer. I have already spoken to you of its enchanting beauty. Do contrive to come and see us before we go away. Coleridge is now writing by me at the same table. I need not say how ardently he joins with me in this wish & how deeply interested he is in [every]thing relating to you. We have a delightful scheme in agitation which is rendered still more delightful by a probability which I cannot exclude from my mind that you may be induced to join in the party. We have come to a resolution, Coleridge, Mrs. Coleridge, my Sister & myself of going into Germany, where we purpose to pass the two ensuing years, in order to acquire the German language, & to furnish ourselves with a tolerable stock of information in natural science. Our plan is to settle if possible in a village near a university, in a pleasant, &, if we can a mountainous country, it will be desirable that this place should be as near as may be to Hamburg on account of the expense of travelling. What do you say to this?

60. *Dorothy Wordsworth to Mrs William Rawson; Alfoxton, 13 June [and Bristol, 3 July] 1798*

We are advised to go into Saxony. Some parts of that country are extremely beautiful and boarding is very cheap. It is our intention (William's and mine) to board in some respectable family for the benefit, or rather the obligation of talking German constantly. The Coleridges, if they can, will take a ready-furnished house as they have two children and must of course keep a servant.

Such are our plans for one year, at least; what we shall do afterwards it is impossible at present to say. If the state of Europe will permit we shall endeavour to get into Switzerland; at any rate we shall travel as far as the tether of a slender income will permit. We hope to make some addition to our resources by translating from the German, the most profitable species of literary labour, and of which I can do almost as much as my Brother . . .

When I am just upon the point of concluding my letter I recollect that you may perhaps think that we are going upon an expensive scheme into Germany and that our income will not suffice to maintain us. I must put you to the expense of a double letter to explain this to you. Notwithstanding Mr Montagu, (from having changed the course of his application to the law) has not been able to fulfil his engagement respecting Basil, we have lived upon our income and are not a farthing poorer than when we began house-keeping. We can live for less money in Germany while we are stationary than we can in England, so that you see our regular income (independent of what we may gain by translation) will be sufficient to support us when we are there, and we shall receive, before our departure much more than sufficient to defray the expenses of our journey, from a bookseller to whom William has sold some poems that are now printing, for which he is to have a certain present price and is to be paid afterwards in proportion to their sale. Our expenses last year 23£ for rent, our journey to London, clothes, servant's wages &c included, only amounted to 110£.

Chapter Three

1798–1802

Lyrical Ballads, a collection of nineteen poems by William and four by Coleridge, was printed in Bristol by Cottle and published anonymously in London by J. & A. Arch on 4 October 1798. The volume opened with Coleridge's *Rime of the Ancyent Marinere* and closed with William's *Tintern Abbey*, a last minute addition which had been written while the poems were actually being printed. Anticipating the criticism that his radical use of ordinary language and humbly-born characters would offend contemporary poetic taste, William also added a justificatory preface, which failed to convince at least one reviewer, Coleridge's friend, Robert Southey.

61. William Wordsworth, notes on his own poems, dictated to Isabella Fenwick, 1843

Tintern Abbey. July 1798. No poem of mine was composed under circumstances more pleasant for me to remember than this: I began it upon leaving Tintern, after crossing the Wye, and concluded it just as I was entering Bristol in the evening, after a ramble of 4 or 5 days, with my sister. Not a line of it was altered, and not any part of it written down till I reached Bristol.

62. William Wordsworth, advertisement to Lyrical Ballads *(1798), c. 30 April – 13 September 1798*

The majority of the following poems are to be considered as experiments. They were written chiefly with a view to ascertain how far the language of conversation in the middle and lower classes of society is adapted to the purposes of poetic pleasure. Readers accustomed to the gaudiness and inane phraseology of many modern writers, if they persist in reading this book to its conclusion, will perhaps frequently have to struggle with feelings of strangeness and aukwardness: they will look round for poetry, and will be induced to enquire by what species of courtesy these attempts can be permitted to assume that title. It is desirable that such readers, for their own sakes, should not suffer the solitary word Poetry, a word of very disputed meaning, to stand in the way of their gratification; but that, while they are perusing this book, they should ask themselves if it contains a natural delineation of human passions, human characters, and human incidents; and if the answer be favorable to the author's wishes, that they should consent to be pleased in spite of that most dreadful enemy to our pleasures, our own pre-established codes of decision.

63. *Robert Southey, review of* Lyrical Ballads *(1798), the* Critical Review, *October 1798*

Admirable as this poem ['The Female Vagrant'] is, the author seems to discover still superior powers in the Lines written near Tintern Abbey. On reading this production, it is impossible not to lament that he should ever have condescended to write such pieces as the Last of the Flock, the Convict, and most of the ballads. In the whole range of English poetry, we scarcely recollect any thing superior to a part of the following passage . . . [quotes lines 65–111].

The 'experiment,' we think, has failed, not because the language of conversation is little adapted to 'the purposes of poetic pleasure,' but because it has been tried upon uninteresting subjects. Yet every piece discovers genius; and, ill as the author has frequently employed his talents, they certainly rank him with the best of living poets.

The Wordsworths and Coleridge were unaware of the critical reception of *Lyrical Ballads*, having arrived in Germany even before the volume was published. Within days of their arrival, however, they unexpectedly went their separate ways: Coleridge (who had left his family at home) and his wealthy friend, John Chester, taking expensive lodgings in the fashionable town of Ratzeburg and the Wordsworths travelling south to Goslar, in Lower Saxony, in search of 'obscurer & cheaper Lodgings without boarding'. Immured for months on end in a snow-bound provincial town without books or company, William took refuge in his poetry, producing some twenty short poems, including the *Lucy* and *Matthew* poems, and the first version of what was to become his great autobiographical poem, *The Prelude*.

64. *William Wordsworth to Henry Gardiner; Hamburg, 3 October 1798*

We arrived at Hamburgh a fortnight ago, after a very pleasant voyage, of three days and three nights. We are now on the point of setting off to Brunswick whence we shall proceed into upper Saxony. The place of our destination is yet undetermined, but we intend to fix on some pleasant village or small town . . .

We can scarcely say how we like Germany. Hamburgh is, I hope, a miserable specimen of what we are to find –

Every thing is very dear & the inn-keepers, shop-keepers &c are all in league to impose upon strangers. We intend to apply with the utmost assiduity to learning the language when we are settled.

65. *Samuel Taylor Coleridge to Tom Poole; Ratzeburg, 20 November 1798*

I have heard from Wordsworth – He is at Goslar – where he arrived six weeks ago & his violent hatred of letter-writing had caused his ominous silence – for which he accuses himself in severe terms. – Goslar is an old decaying city at the Foot of the Hartz Mountain[s] – provisions very cheap, & lodgings very cheap; but no Society – and therefore as he did not come into Germany to learn the Language by a Dictionary, he must remove: which he means to do at the end of the Month. His address is – la Grand Rue de Goslar en Basse Saxe. – Dorothy says – 'William works hard, but not very much at the German.' – This is strange – I work at nothing else, from morning to night –

66. *William Wordsworth to Samuel Taylor Coleridge; [Goslar, 14 or 21 December 1798]*

Dorothy has written the other side of this sheet while I have been out – She has transcribed a few descriptions [from *The Prelude*] – You will read them at your leisure. She will copy out two or three little Rhyme poems which I hope will amuse you. As I have had no books I have been obliged to write in self-defence – I should have written five times as much as I have done but that I am prevented by an uneasiness at my stomach and side with a dull pain about my heart – I have used the word pain, but uneasiness & heat are words which more accurately express my feeling. At all events it renders writing unpleasant. Reading is now become a kind of luxury to me. When I do not read I am absolutely consumed by thinking & feeling & bodily exertions of voice or of limbs, the consequences of those feelings.

67. Dorothy Wordsworth to her brother Christopher; Goslar, 3 February 1799

For more than two months past we have intended quitting Goslar in the course of each week – but we have been so frightened by the cold season the dreadful roads, & the uncovered carts; that we needed no other motives (adding these considerations to our natural aversion to moving from a place where we live in comfort & quietness) to induce us to linger here. We have had a succession of excessively severe weather, once or twice interrupted with a cold thaw; & the cold of Christmas day has not been equalled even in this climate during the last century. It was so excessive that when we left the room where we sit we were obliged to wrap ourselves up in great coats &c – in order not to suffer much pain from the transition, though we only went into the next room or down stairs for a few minutes. No wonder then that we were afraid of travelling all night in an open cart!

. . . Coleridge is in a very different world from what we stir in, he is all in high life, among Barons counts & countesses. He could not be better placed than he is at Ratzeberg for attaining the object of his journey; but his expences are much more than ours conjointly. I think however he has done perfectly right in consenting to pay so much, as he will not stay longer in Germany than till March or April. It would have been impossible for us to have lived as he does; we should have been [ruined]. We shall certainly return to England before the end of summer, but very probably in the Spring. As soon as we are perfectly satisfied with our knowledge of the language we shall think about returning unless we should meet with so pleasant a residence in Saxony as should induce us to stay there longer than seems at present likely.

68. William Wordsworth to Samuel Taylor Coleridge; Nordhausen, 27 February [1799]

We must pursue a different plan. We are every hour more convinced that we are not rich enough to be introduced into high or even literary german society. We should be perfectly contented if we could find a house where there were several young people some of whom might perhaps be always at leisure to converse with us. We do not wish to read much but should both be highly delighted to be chattering & chatter'd to, through the whole day. As this blessing seems to be destined for some more favoured sojourners, we must content ourselves with pshaw for the ears – eyes for ever! We are resolved if the weather be tolerable to saunter about for a fortnight or three weeks at the end of which time you may be prepared to see us in Gottingen. I will not say to tarry long there for I do not think it would suit our plan; but to have the pleasure of seeing and conversing with you. There we can arrange every thing respecting our return.

My progress in German considered with reference to literary emolument is not even as dust in the balance. If I had had opportunities of conversing I should not have cared much if I had not read a line. My hope was that I should be able to learn German as I learn'd French, in this I have been woefully deceived. I acquired more french in two months, than I should acquire German in five years living as we have lived. In short sorry am I to say it I do not consider myself as knowing <u>any</u> thing of the German language. Consider this not as spoken in modesty either false or true but in simple verity.

69. Samuel Taylor Coleridge to Tom Poole; [Germany], 6 May 1799

– Wordsworth & his Sister passed thro' here, as I have informed you – I walked on with them 5 english miles, & spent a day with them. They were melancholy & hypp'd – W[ordsworth] was affected to tears at the thought of not being near me, wished me, of course, to live in the North of England near the Sir Frederic Vane's great Library – I told him, that independent of the expence of removing, & the impropriety of taking Mrs Coleridge to a place where she would have no acquaintance, two insurmountable objections, the Library was no inducement – for I wanted old books chiefly, such as could be procured any where better than in a Gentleman's new fashionable Collection . . . W[ordsworth] was affected to tears, very much affected; but he deemed the vicinity of a Library absolutely *necessary* to his health, nay to his existence. It is painful to me too to think of not living near him; for he is a *good* and *kind* man, & the only one whom in *all* things I feel my Superior – & you will believe me, when I say, that I have few feelings more pleasurable than to find myself in intellectual Faculties an Inferior. But my Resolve is fixed, *not to leave you till you leave me!* I still think that Wordsworth will be disappointed in his expectations of relief from reading, without Society – & I think it highly probable, that where I live, there he will live, unless he should find in the North any person or persons, who can feel & understand him, can reciprocate & react on him. – My many weaknesses are of some advantage to me; they unite me more with the great mass of my fellow-beings – but dear Wordsworth appears to me to have hurtfully segregated & isolated his Being Doubtless, his delights are more deep and sublime; but he has likewise more hours, that prey on his flesh & blood.

Coleridge clearly did not believe that William would find anyone in the North of England who could 'feel & understand him ... reciprocate & react on him', but he had not then met the Hutchinson family. The Hutchinsons and Wordsworths had been friends since their childhood together in Penrith, sharing both the same background and remarkably similar family circumstances. Though farmers by profession, the Hutchinsons were also highly literate and articulate, boasting not one but three poet brothers, Jack, Henry (a sailor like John Wordsworth) and George. Of the four sisters who were most intimate with the Wordsworths, Margaret (who died young), Mary, Sara and Joanna, it was Mary who assumed the most importance. Dorothy's closest Penrith friend, she had enjoyed a youthful romance with William which had been rekindled during her residence at Racedown. Significantly, the first thing the Wordsworths did when they returned from Germany was to pay her a visit at her brother Tom's farm – a visit that would last until the end of the year.

70. Jack Hutchinson to his cousin, John Monkhouse; Penrith, Saturday night, [19 May 1799]

The great Poet Mr Wordsworth and his Sister are now at Sockburn – I have not seen them yet but mean to visit them soon after my return. –

71. William Wordsworth to his publisher Joseph Cottle; Sockburn, [c. 20 May 1799]

> My address at Mr Hutchinson's,
> Sockburn near Northallerton,
> Yorkshire,

My dear Cottle,

   ... We are now in the County of Durham, just upon the borders of Yorkshire. We have spent our time pleasantly enough in Germany,

but we are right glad to find ourselves in England for we have learnt
to know its value.

We left Coleridge well at Gottingen a month ago.

72. Dorothy Wordsworth to Tom Poole; [Sockburn], 4 July [1799]

We are yet quite undetermined where we shall reside – we have no house
in view at present. It is William's wish to be near a good library, and if
possible in a pleasant country. If you hear of any place in your neighbourhood that will be likely to suit us we shall be much obliged to you if you
will take the trouble of writing to us.

The Wordsworths' dilemma was eventually solved almost by chance. In November
Coleridge came to visit them and accompanied William on a walking tour of
the Lakes. At Temple Sowerby they were unexpectedly joined by William's
brother, John, now an officer in the East India Company, who had just attended
their uncle Christopher Cookson's funeral. The brothers had not met for four
years, so the walking tour became a rediscovery not only of their native Lakes
but also of each other. All three men were profoundly affected by what became
a meeting of minds and all three decided that they would, eventually, make their
homes in the Lakes. William was the first to do so, encouraged by John and
Coleridge to rent a cottage they had seen in the Vale of Grasmere. On 20
December 1799 William and Dorothy took up residence at Town End, Grasmere
in what is now known as Dove Cottage; appropriately, their first visitors were
John Wordsworth and Mary Hutchinson.

73. Samuel Taylor Coleridge and William Wordsworth to Dorothy Wordsworth;
[Keswick, 8 or 10 November 1799]

[Coleridge writes] At Temple Sowerby we met your B[rothe]r John who
accompanied us to Hawes Water, Windermere, Ambleside & the divine
Sisters, Rydal & Grasmere – here we stayed two days, & left on Tuesday.
We accompanied John over the fork of Helvellyn on a day when light &
darkness coexisted in contiguous masses, & the earth & sky were but *one*!
Nature lived for us in all her grandest accidents – we quitted him by a
wild Tarn just as we caught a view of the gloomy Ulswater. Your B[rothe]r
John is one of you; a man who hath solitary usings of his own Intellect,
deep in feeling, with a subtle Tact, a swift instinct of Truth & Beauty. He
interests me much.

[William writes] C[oleridge] was much struck with Grasmere & its neighbourhood & I have much to say to you, you will think my plan a mad one, but I have thought of building a house there by the Lake side. John would give me £40 to buy the ground, & for £250 I am sure I could build one as good as we can wish. I speak with tolerable certainty on this head as a Devonshire Gentleman has built a Cottage there which cost a £130 which would exactly suit us every way, but the size of the bed rooms; we shall talk of this . . .

We shall go to Buttermere the day after tomorrow but I think it will be full ten days before we shall see you. There is a small house at Grasmere empty which perhaps we may take, & purchase furniture but of this we will speak; but I shall write again when I know more on this subject.

74. *William Wordsworth to Samuel Taylor Coleridge; Grasmere, Christmas Eve [1799]*

My dearest Coleridge

We arrived here last Friday, and have now been four days in our new abode without writing to you, a long time! but we have been in such confusion as not to have had a moment's leisure . . .

I arrived at Sockburn the day after you quitted it, I scarcely knew whether to be sorry or no that you were no longer there, as it would have been a great pain to me to have parted from you. I was sadly disappointed in not finding Dorothy; Mary was a solitary housekeeper and overjoyed to see me. D[orothy] is now sitting by me racked with the tooth-ache. This is a grievous misfortune as she has so much work for her needle among the bedcurtains &c that she is absolutely buried in it: We have both caught troublesome colds in our new & almost empty house, but we hope to make it a comfortable dwelling. Our two first days were days of fear as one of the rooms up stairs smoked like a furnace, we have since learned that it is uninhabitable as a sitting room on this account; the other room however & which is fortunately the one we intended for our *living* room promises uncommonly well; that is, the chimney draws perfectly, and does not even smoke at the first lighting of the fire. In particular winds most likely we shall have <u>puffs</u> of <u>inconvenience</u>, but this I believe will be found a curable evil . . . D[orothy] is much pleased with the house and <u>appurtenances</u> the orchard especially; in imagination she has already built a seat with a summer shed on the highest platform in this our little domestic slip of mountain. The spot commands a view over the roof of our house, of the lake, the church, helm cragg, & two thirds of the vale. We mean also to enclose the two or three yards of ground between us & the road, this for the sake of a few flowers, and because it will make it more our own. Besides, am I fanciful when I would extend the obligation of gratitude to insensate things? may not a man have a salutary pleasure in doing something gratuitously for the sake of his house, as for an individual to which he owes so much. The manner of the neighbouring cottagers have far exceeded our expectations; they seem little adulterated; indeed as far as we have seen not at all. The people we have uniformly found kind-hearted frank & manly, prompt to serve without servility. This is but an experience of four days, but we have had dealings with persons of various occupations, & have had no reason whatever to complain. We do not think it will be necessary for us to keep a servant. We have agreed to give a woman who lives in one of the adjoining cottages two shillings a week for attending two or three hours a day to light the fires wash dishes &c &c In addition to this she is to have her victuals every Saturday when she will be employed in scouring, & to have her victuals likewise on other days if we should have visitors & she is wanted more than usual. We could have had this attendance for eighteen pence a week but we added the sixpence for the sake of the poor woman, who is made happy by it – – The weather since our arrival has been a keen frost, one morning two thirds of the lake were covered with ice which continued all the day but to our great surprize the next morning, though there was no intermission of the frost had entirely disappeared. The ice had been so thin that the wind had broken it up, & most likely driven it to the outlet of the lake. Rydale is covered with ice, clear as polished steel, I have procured a pair of skates and tomorrow mean to give my body to the wind – not however without reasonable caution. – We are looking for John every day; it will [be] a pity, if he should come, that D[orothy] is so much engaged, she has scarcely been out since our arrival; one evening I tempted her forth; the planet Jupiter was on the top of the hugest of the Rydale mountains, but I had reason to repent of having seduced her from her work as she returned with a raging tooth-ache.

*75. Dorothy Wordsworth to her friend Lady Margaret Beaumont; Grasmere,
Friday evening, 29 November [1805]*

. . . [My brother John] paced over this floor in pride before we had been
six weeks in the house, exulting within his noble heart that his Father's
Children had once again a home together. We did not know on what day
he would come, though we were expecting him every hour, therefore he
had no reason to fear that he should surprize us suddenly; yet twice did
he approach the door & lay his hand upon the latch, & stop, & turn away
without the courage to enter (we had not met for several years) he then
went to the Inn and sent us word that he was come. This will give you a
notion of the depth of his affections, and the delicacy of his feelings –
While he stayed with us he busied himself continually with little schemes
for our comfort – At this moment, when I cast my eyes about I scarcely
see any thing that does not remind me of some circumstance of this kind.

*76. William Wordsworth to his friend and patron, Sir George Beaumont;
Grasmere, postmarked 1 March [1805]*

. . . after a separation of 14 years (I may call it a separation for we only saw
him four or five times & by glimpses) he came to visit his Sister & me in
this Cottage & passed eight blessed months with us. He was then waiting
for the command of the Ship to which he was appointed when he quitted
us. As you will have seen, we had little to live upon & he as little (Lord
Lonsdale being then alive). But he encouraged me to persist, & to keep
my eye steady on its object. He would work for me, (that was his language),
for me, & his Sister; & I was to endeavour to do something for the world.
A thousand times has he said could I but see you with a green field of
your own, & a Cow, & two or three other little comforts, I should be
happy! He went to sea as Commander with this hope . . .

*77. Dorothy Wordsworth to Mrs Jane Marshall; [Grasmere], [15 & 17] March
[1805]*

. . . how happily we lived together those eight months that he was under
our Roof – he loved solitude & he rejoiced in society – he would wander
alone among these hills with his fishing-rod, or led on merely by the
pleasure of walking, for many hours – Or he would walk with William
or me, or both of us, & was continually pointing out with a gladness

which is seldom seen but in very young people some-thing which perhaps would have escaped our observation, for he had so fine an eye that no distinction was unnoticed by him, & so tender a feeling that he never noticed any thing in vain. Many a time has he called me out in an evening to look at the Moon or Stars, or a cloudy sky, or this vale in the quiet moonlight – but the stars & moon were his chief delight, – he made of them his companions when he was at Sea, & was never tired of those thoughts which the silence of the night fed in him – then he was so happy by the fire-side, any little business of the house interested him, he loved our cottage, he helped us to furnish it, & to make the gardens – trees are growing now which he planted –

78. Joanna Hutchinson to her cousin, John Monkhouse; [Penrith], Saturday night, [c.12–18 April 1800]

My Sister Mary was very much delighted indeed with Grasmere, and the Wordsworth way of living, She says she ne[ver sa]w so compleat a Cottage in her life – and ev[ery thing] so very comfortable as they have –

79. Charles Lamb to Thomas Manning; 9 August 1800

Coleridge is settled with his Wife (with a child in her Guts) and the young philosopher [his son Hartley] at Keswick with the Wordsworths. They have contriv'd to spawn a new volume of Lyrical Ballads, which is to see the Light in about a month, & causes no little excitement in the Literary World.

The new edition of *Lyrical Ballads*, which William had been considering for some time, was given added impetus by Coleridge's presence. It was he who persuaded William to add a pugnacious and controversial preface explaining the literary principles which underpinned it and to send complimentary copies to 'persons of eminence'. What he could not do was offer any contribution of his own. His most important poem, *Christabel*, remained unfinished and had to be left out, so that the entire second volume consisted solely of William's new poems. The new, two volume edition would no longer be anonymous: for the first time William's name appeared (alone) on the title page.

80. William Wordsworth to his publisher, Joseph Cottle; Sockburn, 24 June [1799]

You tell me the poems have not sold ill. If it is possible, I should wish to know <u>what number</u> have been sold. From what I can gather it seems that The ancyent Mariner has upon the whole been an injury to the volume, I mean that the old words and the strangeness of it have deterred readers from going on. If the volume should come to a second Edition I would put in its place some little things which would be more likely to suit the common taste.

81. William Wordsworth to Joseph Cottle; Sockburn, 27 July [1799]

P.S. – My aversion from publication increases every day, so much so, that no motives whatever, nothing but pecuniary necessity, will, I think, ever prevail upon me to commit myself to the press again . . .

82. Joseph Cottle, Reminiscences of Samuel Taylor Coleridge and Robert Southey, *[November 1799]*

On my reaching London [after his visit to the Wordsworths at Sockburn], having an account to settle with Messrs. Longman and Rees, the booksellers of Paternoster Row, I sold them all my copyrights, which were valued as one lot, by a third party. On my next seeing Mr. Longman, he told me, that in estimating the value of the copyrights, Fox's "Achmed," and Wordsworth's "Lyrical Ballads," were "reckoned *as nothing.*" "That being the case," I replied, "as both these authors are my personal friends, I should be obliged, if you would return me again these two copyrights, that I may have the pleasure of presenting them to the respective writers." Mr. Longman answered, with his accustomed liberality, "You are welcome to them." On my reaching Bristol, I gave Mr. Fox his receipt for twenty guineas; and on Mr. Coleridge's return from the north, I gave him Mr. Wordsworth's receipt for his thirty guineas; so that whatever advantage has arisen, subsequently, from the sale of this volume of the "Lyrical Ballads," I am happy to say, has pertained exclusively to Mr. W[ordsworth].

83. *William Wordsworth to his brother, Richard; Grasmere, 8 [June] 1800*

The first edition of the Lyrical Ballads is sold off and another is called for
by the Booksellers, for the right of printing 2 editions of 750 each of this
vol[ume] of poems and of printing two editions one of 1000 and another
of 750 of another vol[ume] of the same size I am offered by Longman
80£. I think I shall accept this offer as if the books sell quickly I shall soon
have the right of going to market with them again when their merit will
be known, and if they do not sell tolerably, Longman will have given
enough for them.

84. *Dorothy Wordsworth, journal, [Grasmere, 31 July 1800]*

Thursday All the morning I was busy copying poems – gathered peas, &
in the afternoon Coleridge came very hot, he brought the 2nd volume
of the Anthology – –

   The men went to bathe, & we afterwards sailed down to Loughrigg
read poems on the water & let the boat take its own course – we walked
a long time upon Loughrigg & returned in the grey twilight – The moon
just setting as we reached home

85. *William Wordsworth to Messrs Longman & Rees; Grasmere, near*
Ambleside, Westmoreland, 18 December 1800

I have this day sent off the last Sheet of the second Volume of the Lyrical
Ballads. I am exceedingly sorry that bad health should have prevented
me from fulfilling my engagements sooner. A Poem of Mr Coleridge's
[*Christabel*] was to have concluded the Volumes; but upon mature deliberation, I found that the Style of this Poem was so discordant from my own
that it could not be printed along with my Poems with any propriety. I
had other Poems by me of my own which would have been sufficient for
our purpose but some of them being connected with political subjects I
judged that they would be injurious to the sale of the Work. I therefore,
since my last letter, wrote the last Poem of the 2nd Volume [*Michael*]. I
am sure when you see the work you will approve of this delay, as there
can be no doubt that the Poem alluded to will be highly serviceable to
the Sale ... The Preface which I have prefixed to the first volume is
long, & I hope will be of use.

86. William Wordsworth to John Abraham Heraud; Trinity Lodge, Cambridge, 23 November [1830]

The preface which I wrote long ago to my own Poems I was put upon by the urgent entreaties of a friend, and heartily regret I ever had any thing to do with it; though I do not believe the principles then advanced erroneous.

87. William Wordsworth, Preface to the second edition of Lyrical Ballads *(1800)*

The principal object . . . which I proposed to myself in these Poems was to make the incidents of common life interesting by tracing in them, truly though not ostentatiously, the primary laws of our nature: chiefly as far as regards the manner in which we associate ideas in a state of excitement. Low and rustic life was generally chosen because in that situation the essential passions of the heart find a better soil in which they can attain their maturity, are less under restraint, and speak a plainer and more emphatic language; because in that situation our elementary feelings exist in a state of greater simplicity and consequently may be more accurately contemplated and more forcibly communicated; because the manners of rural life germinate from those elementary feelings; and from the necessary character of rural occupations are more easily comprehended; and are more durable; and lastly, because in that situation the passions of men are incorporated with the beautiful and permanent forms of nature. The language too of these men is adopted (purified indeed from what appear to be its real defects, from all lasting and rational causes of dislike or disgust) because such men hourly communicate with the best objects from which the best part of language is originally derived; and because, from their rank in society and the sameness and narrow circle of their intercourse, being less under the action of social vanity they convey their feelings and notions in simple and unelaborated expressions. Accordingly such a language arising out of repeated experience and regular feelings is a more permanent and a far more philosophical language than that which is frequently substituted for it by Poets, who think that they are conferring honour upon themselves and their art in proportion as they separate themselves from the sympathies of men, and indulge in arbitrary and capricious habits of expression in order to furnish food for fickle tastes and fickle appetites of their own creation . . .

From such verses the Poems in these volumes will be found distinguished at least by one mark of difference, that each of them has a worthy *purpose*. Not that I mean to say, that I always began to write with a distinct purpose formally conceived; but I believe that my habits of meditation have so formed my feelings, as that my descriptions of such objects as strongly excite those feelings, will be found to carry along with them a *purpose*. If in this opinion I am mistaken I can have little right to the name of a Poet. For all good poetry is the spontaneous overflow of powerful feelings; but though this be true, Poems to which any value can be attached, were never produced on any variety of subjects but by a man who being possessed of more than usual organic sensibility had also thought long and deeply. For our continued influxes of feeling are modified and directed by our thoughts, which are indeed the representatives of all our past feelings . . .

I have said that Poetry is the spontaneous overflow of powerful feelings: it takes its origin from emotion recollected in tranquillity: the emotion is contemplated till by a series of reaction the tranquillity gradually disappears, and an emotion, similar to that which was before the subject of contemplation, is gradually produced, and does itself actually exist in the mind. In this mood successful composition generally begins, and in a mood similar to this it is carried on . . .

88. William Wordsworth to Messrs Longman & Rees; Grasmere, near Ambleside, Westmoreland, 18 December 1800

I have forgotten a part of my Letter which I think of great importance. The Lyrical Ballads are written upon a theory professedly new, and on principles which many persons will be unwilling to admit. I think therefore there would be a propriety in your sending a few copies to the amount of half a dozen or so to persons of eminence either in Letters or in the state. If you approve of this I will write Letters to accompany each of these copies. I cannot but think that if the choice of the persons were judiciously made, that this step would very much quicken the sale of the work. Pray let me know if you approve of this and also have the goodness to point out to me the persons whom you think the most fit to have the copies presented to them.

89. William Wordsworth to Charles James Fox, Whig statesman and opposition leader; Grasmere, 14 January 1801

Sir,

It is not without much difficulty, that I have summoned the courage to request your acceptance of these Volumes. Should I express my real feelings, I am sure that I should seem to make a parade of diffidence and humility . . .

Being utterly unknown to you as I am, I am well aware, that if I am justified in writing to you at all, it is necessary, my letter should be short; but I have feelings within me which I hope will so far shew themselves in this letter, as to excuse the trespass which I am afraid I shall make . . . were I assured that I myself had a just claim to the title of a Poet, all the dignity being attached to the word which belongs to it, I do not think that I should have ventured for that reason to offer these volumes to you: at present it is solely on account of two poems in the second volume, the one entitled "the Brothers", and the other "Michael", that I have been emboldened to take this liberty.

It appears to me that the most calamitous effect, which has followed the measures which have lately been pursued in this country, is a rapid decay of the domestic affections among the lower orders of society. This effect the present Rulers of this country are not conscious of, or they disregard it. For many years past, the tendency of society amongst almost all the nations of Europe has been to produce it. But recently by the spreading of manufactures through every part of the country, by the heavy taxes upon postage, by workhouses, Houses of Industry, and the invention of Soup-shops &c &c superadded to the encreasing disproportion between the price of labour and that of the necessaries of life, the bonds of domestic feeling among the poor, as far as the influence of these things has extended, have been weakened, & in innumerable instances entirely destroyed . . . parents are separated from their children, & children from their parents; the wife no longer prepares with her own hands a meal for her husband, the produce of his labour; there is little doing in his house in which his affections can be interested, and but little left in it which he can love. I have two neighbours, a man and his wife, both upwards of eighty years of age; they live alone; the husband has been confined to his bed many months and has never had, nor till within these few weeks has ever needed, any body to attend to him but his wife. She has recently been seized with a lameness which has often prevented her from being able to carry him his food to his bed; the neighbours fetch water for her from the well, and do other kind offices for them both, but her infirmities encrease. She told my Servant two days ago that she was afraid they must both be boarded out among some other Poor of the parish (they have long been supported by the parish) but she said, it was hard, having kept house together so long, to come to this, and she was sure that "it would burst her heart". I mention this fact to shew how deeply the spirit of independence is, even yet, rooted in some parts of the country. These people could not express themselves in this way without an almost sublime conviction of the blessings of independent domestic life. If it is true, as I believe, that this spirit is rapidly disappearing, no greater curse can befal a land.

I earnestly entreat your pardon for having detained you so long. In the two Poems, "the Brothers" and "Michael" I have attempted to draw a picture of the domestic affections as I know they exist amongst a class of men who are now almost confined to the North of England. They are small independent <u>proprietors</u> of land here called Statesmen, men of respectable education who daily labour on their own little properties. The domestic affections will always be strong amongst men who live in a country not crowded with population, if these men are placed above poverty. But if they are proprietors of small estates which have descended to them from their ancestors, the power which these affections will acquire amongst such men is inconceivable by those who have only had an opportunity of observing hired labourers, farmers, and the manufacturing Poor. Their little tract of land serves as a kind of permanent rallying point for their domestic feelings, as a tablet upon which they are written which makes them objects of memory in a thousand instances when they would otherwise be forgotten. It is a fountain fitted to the nature of social man from which supplies of affection, as pure as his heart was intended for, are daily drawn. This class of men is rapidly disappearing ... The two poems which I have mentioned were written with a view to shew that men who do not wear fine cloaths can feel deeply ... The poems are faithful copies from nature; & I hope, whatever effect they may have upon you, you will at least be able to perceive that they may excite profitable sympathies in many kind and good hearts, and may in some small degree enlarge our feelings of reverence for our species, and our knowledge of human nature, by shewing that our best qualities are possessed by men whom we are too apt to consider, not with reference to the points in which they resemble us, but to those in which they manifestly differ from us. I thought, at a time when these feelings are sapped in so many ways that the two poems might co-operate, however feebly, with the illustrious efforts which you have made to stem this and other evils with which the country is labouring, and it is on this account alone that I have taken the liberty of thus addressing you.

90. *Catherine Clarkson, wife of the anti-slavery campaigner, Thomas Clarkson, to the Reverend R. E. Garnham; Eusemere, Ullswater, 12 February 1801*

I think I told you in my last that I expected Wordsworth & his Sister to visit us. well – they have been here & staid more than three weeks & have left us with a very favourable opinion of them – You must buy W – two volumes of Lyrical Ballads & tell me what you think of them. We have not got them yet. I am fully convinced that Wordsworths Genius is equal to the Production of something very great, & I have no doubt but he will produce "something that Posterity will not willingly let die", if he lives ten or twenty years longer. – I was very much affected by "the Brothers" when I saw it in manuscript – pray tell me how it affects you, & any body else whom you may happen to converse with who has read it – I want to ascertain how much of the feeling w[hic]h it excited in me, was occasion'd by the Knowledge I have of the country & the manners of the Inhabitants – The Brothers, Lucy Gray, poor Susan, Timothy & the Poem where Bewick is praised are all that I have seen of the second Volume – Lucy Gray is I think inimitable.

91. *John Wordsworth to his sister, Dorothy; Staple Inn, 21 February [1801]*

I am out of all patience with the impudence of Longman for only offering 80£ for the L[yrical] B[allads]   it is little better than swindling – I am a great man with Mr Arch [bookseller and publisher of the first edition] tho' he does not know my name – I talk knowin[g]ly of Col[e]rid[g]e Southey. Wordsworth – Lamb &c –

Arch has had a great Sale of the 2d Vol tho I was surprised to find he had sold but few very few of the 2d edition[1] – he said his customers complain'd of being cheated out of a preface –

92. William Wordsworth to his brother, Richard; [Grasmere, c.23 June 1801]

A Few days ago I had a Letter from Mr Fox in which he says that he read the poems with greatest pleasure especially those in rime, he is not partial to blank verse. He mentioned Goody Blake &c the Mad Mother, The Idiot Boy, & We are seven, as having given him particular pleasure. I have had high encomiums on the poems from the most respectable quarters, indeed the highest authorities both in literature, good sense, and people of consequence in the state;. – – There is no doubt but that if my health should enable me to go on in writing I shall be able to command my price with the Booksellers. Longman has written to inform me that the last edition is sold to within 130 copies, & that I must prepare another. As soon as this next shall be disposed of, the copyright will revert to me, & I shall take care to know precisely, upon what terms a Bookseller can afford to take it, and he shall not have a farthing under. These two last editions, I have sold for 1 third less than they were worth.

William's optimism was not to be justified but, for the moment, his idyllic life in Grasmere and his deepening love for Mary led to a period of extraordinary poetic creativity, into which Dorothy's journal for the period provides an insight.

93. Dorothy Wordsworth, journal, [Grasmere], 31 January 1802

31st, Sunday. William had slept very ill – he was tired & had a bad headache – We walked round the two lakes – Grasmere was very soft & Rydale was extremely beautiful from the pasture side – Nab Scar was just topped by a cloud which cutting it off as high as it could be cut off made the mountain look uncommonly lofty   We sate down a long time in different places – I always love to walk that way because it is the way I first came to Rydale & Grasmere & because our dear Coleridge did also – When I came with W[illia]m 6½ years ago it was just at sunset there was a rich yellow light on the waters & the Islands were reflected there   Today it was grave & soft but not perfectly calm – William says it was much such a day as when Coleridge came with him – The sun shone out before we

reached Grasmere we sate by the roadside at the foot of the Lake close to
Mary's dear name which she had cut herself upon the stone – William
cut[2] at it with his knife to make it plainer.

94. Dorothy Wordsworth, journal, [Grasmere], 7 February 1802

Mr Simpson called before William had done shaving – William had had
a bad night & was working at his Poem – We sate by the fire & did not
walk, but read the Pedlar[3] thinking it done but lo, though W[illia]m could
find fault with no one part of it – it was uninteresting & must be altered
– Poor William!

95. Dorothy Wordsworth, journal, [Grasmere], 14 March 1802

Sunday morning – William had slept badly = he got up at 9 o clock but
before he rose he had finished the Beggar Boys = & while we were at
Breakfast that is (for I had Breakfasted) he, with his Basin of Broth before
him untouched & a little plate of Bread and butter he wrote the Poem to
a Butterfly! – He ate not a morsel, nor put on his Stockings but sate with
his Shirt neck unbuttoned, & his waistcoat open while he did it – The
thought first came upon him as we were talking about the pleasure we
both always feel at the sight of a Butterfly. I told him that I used to chase
them a little but that I was afraid of brushing the dust off their wings – &
did not catch them – He told me how they used to kill all the white ones
when he went to School because they were frenchmen. Mr Simpson
came in just as he was finishing the Poem – After he was gone I wrote it
down & the other poems & I read them all over to him – We then called
at Mr Olliffs – Mr O[lliff] walked with us to within sight of Rydale – the
sun shone very pleasantly, yet it was extremely cold – we dined and then
W[illia]m went to bed – I lay upon the fur gown before the fire but I
could not sleep – I lay there a long time – it is now half past 5 I am going
to write letters – I began to write to Mrs Rawson – William rose without
having slept we sate comfortably by the fire – till he began to try to alter
the Butterfly and tired himself he went to bed tired.

96. William Wordsworth to Sara Hutchinson; [Grasmere], 14 June [1802]

I am exceedingly sorry that the latter part of the Leech-gatherer has
displeased you, the more so because I cannot take to myself (that being

the case) much pleasure or satisfaction in having pleased you in the former part. I will explain to you in prose my feeling in writing that Poem, and then you will be better able to judge whether the fault be mine or yours or partly both. I describe myself as having been exalted to the highest pitch of delight by the joyousness and beauty of Nature and then as depressed, even in the midst of those beautiful objects, to the lowest dejection and despair. A young Poet in the midst of the happiness of Nature is described as overwhelmed by the thought of the miserable reverses which have befallen the happiest of all men, viz Poets – I think of this till I am so deeply impressed by it, that I consider the manner in which I was rescued from my dejection and despair almost as an interposition of Providence. 'Now whether it was by peculiar grace A leading from above'. A person reading this Poem with feelings like mine will have been awed and controuled, expecting almost something spiritual or supernatural – What is brought forward? 'A lonely place, a Pond' 'by which an old man *was*, far from all house or home' – not stood, not sat, but '*was*' – the figure presented in the most naked simplicity possible. This feeling of spirituality or supernaturalness is again referred to as being strong in my mind in this passage – '*How came he here* thought I or what can he be doing?' I then describe him, whether ill or well is not for me to judge with perfect confidence, but this I can *confidently* affirm, that, though I believe God has given me a strong imagination, I cannot conceive a figure more impressive than that of an old Man like this, the survivor of a Wife and ten children, travelling alone among the mountains and all lonely places, carrying with him his own fortitude, and the necessities which an unjust state of society has entailed upon him. You say and Mary (that is you can say no more than that) the Poem is *very well* after the introduction of the old man; this is not true, if it is not more than very well it is very bad, there is no intermediate state. You speak of his speech as tedious: everything is tedious when one does not read with the feelings of the Author – '*The Thorn*' is tedious to hundreds; and so is the *Idiot Boy* to hundreds. It is in the character of the old man to tell his story in a manner which an *impatient* reader must necessarily feel as tedious. But Good God! Such a figure, in such a place, a pious self-respecting, miserably infirm, and [?] Old Man telling such a tale!

My dear Sara, it is not a matter of indifference whether you are pleased with this figure and his employment; it may be comparatively so, whether you are pleased or not with *this* Poem; but it is of the utmost importance that you should have had pleasure from contemplating the fortitude, independence, persevering spirit, and the general moral dignity of this old man's character. Your feelings upon the Mother, and the Boys with the Butterfly, were not indifferent: it was an affair of whole continents of moral sympathy. I will talk more with you on this when we meet – at present, farewell and Heaven for ever bless you!

W.W.

Chapter Four

1802–8

On 24 May 1802 Lord Lonsdale died. He had successfully resisted all legal attempts to force him to pay his debt to John Wordsworth's estate and had never paid a penny of what he owed. Having left no legitimate children, his vast estates and huge wealth were inherited by the son of his third cousin, Sir William Lowther, who let it be known that he would settle all just claims. The Wordsworths leapt into action.

97. Dr William Cookson to his nephew, Richard Wordsworth; Forncett, 22 June 1802

Now that Lord Lonsdale is called to give an Account where his Knavery & his money will nothing avail him, may it not be expedient to try what can be done with his Successor? If your Claim is not to be maintained upon legal Grounds (either from it's lying too long dormant or from the great Expence of prosecuting it) it may be proper to try what an Appeal to Lord Lowther's Honour & Conscientiousness may produce. He has hitherto born an excellent character and surely if the Case were properly represented to him, it might do some Good –

98. William Wordsworth to his brother, Richard; Eusemere, Thursday, 24 June [1802]

From the facts which are at present before me I conclude that the account should be sent in as soon as possible. –

If we have a legal right to the principle we have likewise to <u>the interest</u>.

Do you then mean to demand payment of principle & <u>interest</u>?

If you do, have you sufficiently considered the immense sum which will be required to discharge these & all Lord Lonsdale's other old debts principal & <u>interest</u>?

Have you sufficiently reflected on the probability of Lord Lowther's laying it down as a general rule that he will not pay such old debts principal & <u>interest</u>, without being compelled thereto by <u>Law</u>?

Should Lord Lowther reject the payment of this debt of ours & others of the like kind from their enormous amount, with what greater success could you carry on a suit against him, with his immense fortune, than against his predecessor?

You will reply to this perhaps that Lord Lowther is a man of a fair character, & would have a suit conducted in a fair way. – But will his agents Attornies & people about him be men of honour & principle? Will not they measure his hear[t] & wishes by their own? and will not they deem every measure justifiable which may be likely to give them success?

What success was a poor man ever known to have against a very rich one in a Law suit – especially of a complex kind?

Despite William's scepticism, Richard persisted in lodging a claim for £10,388 6s 8d, 'the sum of £4660. 4s. 10 ³/₄d, which still remains due to my father's Estate, besides Interest and Costs', but settled, the following year, for £8,500 (the equivalent of £306,000 today). Twenty years after their father's death, the Wordsworths finally received their inheritance. The money came very opportunely for William, who was about to marry Mary Hutchinson. Before he did so, however, he and Dorothy travelled to France during the brief Peace of Amiens to meet Annette and Caroline (now aged nine). Though Dorothy kept a journal, it is singularly unenlightening about this first meeting of father and daughter, though she waxed lyrical about the distant views of England from Calais beach. William and Annette must have come to some sort of understanding for, after a bare month together in Calais, he returned to England with Dorothy. On 4 October 1802 he married Mary in a quiet early-morning ceremony in the village church of Brompton-by-Sawdon, which lay just across the fields from Tom Hutchinson's farm at Gallow Hill in the East Riding of Yorkshire. Dorothy looked forward to her brother's marriage with mixed feelings.

99. Dorothy Wordsworth, journal, [Calais], 1–29 August 1802

We arrived at Calais at 4 o'clock on Sunday morning the 31st of July [actually 1 August]. We stayed in the vessel till ¹/₂ past 7. Then W[illia]m went for Letters, at about ¹/₂ past 8 or 9. We found out Annette and C[aroline] chez Madame Avril dans la Rue de la Tete d'or. We lodged opposite two Ladies in tolerably decent-sized rooms but badly furnished, &

with large store of bad smells & dirt in the yard, & all about. The weather was very hot. We walked by the sea-shore almost every Evening with Annette & Caroline or W[illia]m & I alone. I had a bad cold & could not bathe at first but William did. It was a pretty sight to see as we walked upon the Sands when the tide was low, perhaps a hundred people bathing about ¹/₄ of a mile distant from us, and we had delightful walks after the heat of the day was passed away – seeing far off in the west the Coast of England like a cloud crested with Dover Castle, which was but like the summit of the cloud – the Evening star & the glory of the sky . . .

On Sunday the 29th of August we left Calais at 12 o'clock in the morning & landed at Dover at 1 on Monday the 30th. I was sick all the way.

100. Dorothy Wordsworth to Mrs Jane Marshall; Gallow Hill, 29 September 1802

. . . I have long loved Mary Hutchinson as a Sister, & she is equally attached to me this being so, you will guess that I look forward with perfect happiness to this Connection between us, but, happy as I am, I half dread that concentration of all tender feelings, past, present, & future which will come upon me on the wedding morning. There never lived on earth a better woman than Mary H[utchinson] & I have not a doubt but that she is in every respect formed to make an excellent wife to my Brother, & I seem to myself to have scarcely any thing left to wish for but that the wedding was over, & we had reached our home once again.

101. Dorothy Wordsworth, journal, [Gallow Hill], 4 October 1802

– on Monday, 4th October 1802 – my Brother William was married to Mary Hutchinson   I slept a good deal of the night and rose fresh & well in the morning. At a little after 8 o'clock I saw them go down the avenue towards the Church. William had parted from me up stairs. – I gave him the wedding ring – with how deep a blessing! I took it from my forefinger where I had worn it the whole of the night before – he slipped it again on to my finger and blessed me fervently.[1] When they were absent my dear little Sara [Hutchinson] prepared the breakfast. I kept myself as quiet as I could, but when I saw the two men running up the walk, coming to tell us it was over, I could stand it no longer & threw myself on the bed where I lay in stillness, neither hearing or seeing any thing till Sara came up stairs to me & said "they are coming – " This forced me from the bed where I lay & I moved I knew not how straight forward, faster than my strength could carry me till I met my beloved William & fell upon his bosom. He & John Hutchinson led me to the house & there I stayed to welcome my dear Mary.

102. Mary Wordsworth, memoranda for her son, Willy, November 1851

I do not know if I ever told you in what spirit some of my Relatives looked upon my marriage with your distinguished & honoured Father, so upon the back of your letter, not to waste good paper, for your amusement, & to divert my own loneliness I will record what has just passed thro' my mind.

My Father's Bachelor Brother Henry, – upon whom we were, as Orphans, in some measure dependent, & with whom I had lived when I went to School, at Stockton, – had no high opinion of Young Men without some Profession, or Calling;

Hence, knowing that he had designated your Father, as "a Vagabond", when our minds were made up to marry, I knew it would be useless, or worse than useless to ask his <u>consent</u>, but as in duty bound, I wrote to inform him of the intention, & craved his good wishes, or perhaps his Blessing, but I do not remember the words. However I received no answer; and we never met for several years. Visiting Stockton, afterwards, he was glad to see us both, in his way, & was then no doubt proud of his Nephew – – I know he had read <u>some</u> of his Poems, the "Happy Warrior", being his favourite; After his death my Brother found that the Old Gentleman had carefully preserved my letter in his private Desk, & by his will it appeared that all was right.

Not so with my other wealthy Friends, Cousins of my Father, the Son & three daughters of Dr Scurfield, my Grandmother's Brother. These cousins were a quaint Party, but I was a favorite both with the Bachelor Brother, & the three Maiden Sisters . . . Before my Marriage, we were in correspondence, when I lived with your Uncle Tho[ma]s, & they used to send me little presents now & then.

I <u>also</u> respectfully informed them of the <u>coming</u> Event. Their reply was, "they hoped I had my Uncle's consent". Not being able to respond to this <u>hope</u> favourably, I heard <u>no more of them</u>.

And your dear Father used to joke with me on the non-arrival of the <u>expected silver Coffee Pot</u> (which as that was the <u>marriage present</u> they sent to my Cousins Hutchinson) I naturally thought would have been presented to me; at the same time I used to express a wish that something might come, to remember them by, more suited to our then Establishment. The <u>disappointment</u>, however brought its reward, by the many jocund sallies of wit your dear Father used to launch upon my <u>blasted expectations</u>; & we have done very well without a <u>Silver Coffee Pot</u> to this day.

Whether it was in consequence of our friends' thinking us an improvident Pair, I do not know – but it is a fact that we did not receive a single <u>Wedding Present</u>.

Dorothy, the devoted sister, was soon to become Dorothy, the devoted aunt. When William and Mary's first child, John, made his appearance on 19 June 1803, she was in such ecstasies that even the prospect of going on her first tour of Scotland with William and Coleridge paled into insignificance by comparison. The tour was not a great success in terms of personal relationships – Coleridge, whose opium addiction made him depressed and ill, decided to quit them after only a fortnight – but it provided William with material for many new poems, including *Yarrow Unvisited*, *To a Highland Girl* and *The Solitary Reaper*.

103. *Dorothy Wordsworth to Catherine Clarkson; [Grasmere], 26 June 1803*

I have only one moment to say that Mary & the Child are quite well – She has never ailed any thing since his Birth . . .

Oh my dear Friend how happy we are in this blessed Infant! He sleeps sweetly all night through loves the open air – he has been out two hours today at one time, & by Snatches at different times all the day through He is a noble looking Child, has a very fine head, & a beautiful nose & thrives rarely – He takes no food but his mother's milk. Our Nurse left us last Tuesday[2] morning. – We have had no want of her, Mother & Child have gone on so nicely. I have been their sole attendant.

104. *Dorothy Wordsworth to Catherine Clarkson; Grasmere, 15 [actually 17] July [1803]*

We expect to set off on our Scotch tour in about ten days – William and C[oleridge] talk of it with thorough enjoyment, & I have no doubt I shall be as happy as they when I am fairly off; but I do not love to think of leaving home, and parting with the dear Babe who will be no more the same Babe when we return – besides, Sara does not come. This is a sad

mortification to us particularly as she had given us the strongest reason to
expect her, however we still hope for Joanna who can be very easily spared
from Gallow hill. Our dear Mary does not look forward to being left
alone with one gloomy thought – indeed how should she with so sweet
a Babe at her Breast? But both for her sake & Sara's we earnestly wished
that they might have been together.

105. *Samuel Taylor Coleridge to Robert Southey; [Keswick], 14 August 1803*

I never yet commenced a Journey with such inauspicious Heaviness of
Heart before. We – Wordsworth, Dorothy, and myself – leave Keswick
tomorrow morning. We have bought a stout Horse – aged but stout &
spirited – & an open vehicle, called a Jaunting Car – there is room in it
for 3 on each side, on hanging seats – a Dicky Box for the Driver & a
space or hollow in the middle, for luggage – or two or three Bairns. – It
is like half a long Coach, only those in the one seat sit with their *back* to
those in the other instead of face to face. – Your feet are not above a foot
– scarcely so much – from the ground so that you may get off & on while
the Horse is moving without the least Danger there are all sorts of
Conveniences in it.

106. *Samuel Taylor Coleridge to his wife; postmarked Fort William, [2] September [1803]*

It rained all the way – all the long long day – we slept in a hay loft, that
is, Wordsworth, I, and a young man who came in at the Trossachs &
joined us – Dorothy had a bed in the Hovel which was varnished *so rich*
with peat smoke, an apartment of highly polished [oak] would have been
poor to it: it would have wanted the *metallic* Lustre of the smoke-varnished
Rafters. – This was [the pleasantest] Evening, I had spent, since my Tour:
for [Wordsworth's] Hypochondriacal Feelings kept him silent, & [self]-
centred – . The next day it still was rain & rain the ferry boat was out for
the Preaching – & we stayed all day in the Ferry [house] to dry, wet
to the skin O such a wretched Hovel! – but two highland Lasses who kept
house in the absence of the Ferry man & his Wife, were very kind – &
one of them was beautiful as a Vision & put both me & Dorothy in mind
of the Highland Girl in William's Peter Bell. – We returned to E. Tarbet,
I with the rheumatism in my head and now William proposed to me to
leave them, & make my way on foot, to Loch Ketterin, the Trossachs,

1. Main Street, Cockermouth, photographed in 1906. The Wordsworth family home, where William, Dorothy and their brothers were born, stands on Main Street and overlooks the River Derwent at the back.

2. Flag Street, Hawkshead (1892), a typical street in the picturesque village where the Wordsworth boys attended the Grammar School.

3. William Wordsworth, aged thirty-six, a pencil portrait drawn in 1806 by Henry Edridge, ARA (1769–1821).

4. A view of the old town of Blois, *c.* 1820, engraved by R. Brandard, after a drawing by J. M. W. Turner. William lived in Blois for several months in 1792.

5. Robert Southey (1774–1843), a portrait dating from 1804 by Henry Edridge.

6. Samuel Taylor Coleridge (1772–1834), painted in 1804 by George Dance (1741–1825), the artist and architect of Sir George Beaumont's Coleorton Hall.

7. Old Westminster Bridge, London, 1827, engraved by M. J. Starling, after a drawing by Thomas H. Shepherd. William's famous poem *Composed Upon Westminster Bridge* was inspired by the view from this bridge, which he crossed, on the roof of a coach, on his way to France in July 1802.

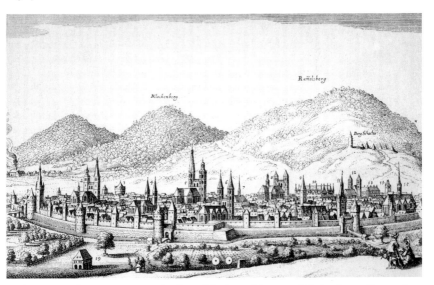

8. A seventeenth-century panoramic view of the imperial town of Goslar, Lower Saxony. It was whilst living in lodgings here with Dorothy during the winter of 1798–9 that William composed the *Lucy* and *Matthew* poems and the first version of *The Prelude*.

9. The tiny cottage at Town End, Grasmere, to which William and Dorothy moved in December 1799. They lived there for almost eight years, sharing it with Mary Hutchinson, whom William married in October 1802, three of their children, and visiting friends and relatives.

10. Rydal Mount, from 1813 the Wordsworths' much-loved family home which overlooked the Vale of Rydal and the lakes of Windermere, Rydal Water and Grasmere. It was here that they entertained writers, statesmen, churchmen and even royalty from around the world.

11. A view across Grasmere Lake towards the village of Grasmere, the 'inverted arch' of Dunmail Raise and the 'old woman' on top of Helm Crag. Three Wordsworth homes can be seen: Allan Bank on the lower slopes of Silver How fell on the left, the Parsonage, next to the Church in the centre of the village, and the cottage at Town End on the right.

12. The Vale of Rydal, an early photograph taken from Loughrigg Fell. Rydal Hall, the seat of the le Fleming family, is the large mansion in parkland on the right. The le Flemings built Rydal Church in 1823–4 and owned Rydal Mount, the house half-hidden in vegetation above and to the left of it which the Wordsworths rented from them for almost half a century. The field between Rydal Mount and the church is 'Dora's Field', which William purchased in 1825 as a potential site for a new house when Lady le Fleming threatened to end his lease of Rydal Mount.

13. Lowther Castle, the Lakeland home of the Earls of Lonsdale, from the north-east, 1814, by John Buckler.

14. Sir George Beaumont (1753–1827): artist, collector and generous supporter of the arts, he was one of William's earliest patrons and a life-long friend. An undated portrait by John Hoppner (1758–1810).

15. 'William the Good', Earl of Lonsdale (1757–1844), who repaid the twenty-year-old debt to the Wordsworth family owed by his predecessor and continued to be a generous patron to the poet and his children for the rest of his long life.

16. 'A picnic by the lake', 1825. A pen-and-ink work by the Wordsworths' friend, John Harden (1772–1847) of Brathay Hall, Ambleside.

17. A drawing of Rydal Mount by Dora Wordsworth, 1832.

18. Plaster bust of William Wordsworth, made in 1820 as a model for a marble version commissioned by Sir George Beaumont from Sir Francis Leggatt Chantrey, RA (1781–1842). Casts of the bust were made for sale and were widely available.

whence it is only 20 miles to Stirling, where the Coach runs thro' for Edingburgh – He & Dorothy resolved to fight it out – I eagerly caught at the Proposal: for the *sitting* in an open Carriage in the Rain is Death to me, and somehow or other I had not been quite comfortable. So on Monday I accompanied them to Arrochar . . . & there I parted with them, having previously sent on all *my* Things to Edinburgh by a Glasgow Carrier who happened to be at E. Tarbet. The worst thing was the money – they took 29 Guineas, and I six – all our remaining Cash!

107. Dorothy Wordsworth to Catherine Clarkson; Grasmere, 9 October [1803]

It is a fortnight this day since we returned home after our absence from Mary & the Babe of six weeks – a long long absence it seemed to be, though we were very happy during our tour, particularly the last month, for at first we were but half weaned from home & had not learnt the way of enjoying ourselves – We seemed to consider the whole Tour as a business to be by us performed for some good end or other, but when we had fairly got forward the rambling disposition came upon us & we were sorry to turn back again or rather we wished to go forward. We had a joyful meeting. Mary, though thin was quite well, & John had thrived & grown to our very hearts contentment . . .

Perhaps Mary may have told you that it was my intention to write while we were on the Tour. So indeed it was & I was even bold enough to hope that I should send you long & entertaining accounts of what we saw & what we did, that might enliven you in your absence from your dear home. I blame myself very much that I never once should have written one word to you . . .

Long letters it was out of my power to write unless I had had a thousand times more activity & strength than I am mistress of, for I was always tired when I reached the Inn at night & glad to put my Body in the state to receive all possible enjoyment of the few comforts a Scotch Inn affords. I was glad to lay my legs up & loll in indolence before the fire.

108. Dorothy Wordsworth to Catherine Clarkson; [Grasmere], 13 November [1803]

William has not yet done any thing of importance at his great work ['The Recluse'] – he is very well & looks better than for some time past. His Tour did him good. By the Bye I am writing not a journal, for we took no notes, but <u>recollections</u> of our Tour in the form of a journal, you will be amused with it for our sakes, but I think journals of Tours except as far as one is interested in the travellers are very uninteresting things. Wretched, wretched writing! I can hardly read it myself.

109. Dorothy Wordsworth to Catherine Clarkson; [Grasmere], 21 November [1803]

William has written two little poems on subjects suggested by our Tour in Scotland – that is all that he has actually done lately, but he is very well & I hope will soon be more seriously employed. It would do you [good] to see him with John upon his knee, he is a very nice nurse & a very happy Father.

Though everyone hoped and expected that William would now at last embark upon 'The Recluse', the poet himself found it impossible to know where to begin. Instead, he reverted to what he called his autobiographical poem (*The Prelude*), in the hope that this would lead him into his greater, philosophical work.

110. William Wordsworth to Francis Wrangham; Grasmere, [c.24 January – 7 February 1804]

You do not know what a task it is to me, to write a Letter; I absolutely loath the sight of a Pen when I am to use it. I have not written Three Letters except upon indispensable business during the last three Years. – I should not mention a circumstance so discreditable to me, were it not to justify myself from any apprehension on your part that I may have slighted You. It is not in my Nature to neglect old Friends, I live too much in the past for any thing of that kind to attach to me ...

    You enquire how I am & what doing. As to the first I am tolerably well, and for the second, I have great things in meditation but as yet have only been doing little ones. At present I am engaged in a Poem on my own earlier life which will take five parts or books to complete, three of which are nearly finished. – My other meditated works are a Philosophical Poem and a narrative one – These two will employ me some I ought to say several years, & I do not mean to appear before the world again as an Author till one of them at least be finished.

111. Dorothy Wordsworth to Catherine Clarkson; [Grasmere], 13 February [1804]

We are all well. William, which is the best news I can tell you, is chearfully engaged in composition, & goes on with great rapidity. He is writing the Poem on his own early life which is to be an appendix to the Recluse. He walks out every morning, generally alone, and brings us in a large treat almost every time he goes. The weather with all its pleasant mildness, has been very wet in general, he takes out the umbrella & I daresay, stands stock-still under it during many a rainy half-hour, in the middle of road or field.

112. William Wordsworth to Samuel Taylor Coleridge; [Grasmere], 6 March [1804] .

I finished 5 or 6 days ago another Book of my Poem amounting to 650 Lines. And now I am positively arrived at the subject I spoke of in my last. When this next book is done which I shall begin in two or three days time, I shall consider the work as finish'd. Farewell.

I am very anxious to have your notes for the Recluse. I cannot say how much importance I attach to this, if it should please God that I survive you, I should reproach myself for ever, in writing the work if I had neglected to procure this help. –

113. William Wordsworth to his young admirer, the writer, Thomas de Quincey, who was then at Oxford University; Grasmere, 6 March [1804]

I am now writing a Poem on my own earlier life; and have just finished that part in which I speak of my residence at the University: it would give me great pleasure to read this work to you at this time. As I am sure, from the interest you have taken in the L[yrical] B[allads] that it would please you, and might also be of service to you. This Poem will not be published these many years, and never during my lifetime, till I have finished a larger and more important work to which it is tributary. Of this larger work I have written one Book and several scattered fragments: it is a moral and Philosophical Poem; the subject whatever I find most interesting, in Nature Man Society, most adapted to Poetic illustration. To this work I mean to devote the Prime of my life and the chief force of my mind. I have also arranged the plan of a narrative Poem. And if I live to finish these three principal works I shall be content. That on my own life, the least important of the three, is better [than] half complete: viz 4 Books amounting to about 2500 lines. They are all to be in blank verse. I have taken this liberty of saying this much of my own concerns to you, not doubting that it would interest you. You have as yet have [*sic*] had little knowledge of me but as a Poet; but I hope, if we live, we shall be still more nearly united.

114. Dorothy Wordsworth to Catherine Clarkson; [Grasmere], 24 [actually 25] March 1804

We have been engaged, Mary and I, in making a complete copy of William's Poems for poor Coleridge to be his companions in Italy, & it was really towards the conclusion, a work of great anxiety for we were afraid they would not reach London or Portsmouth in time for him, and his desire to have them almost made him miserable, while there was any doubt about it. The last pacquet we sent off would arrive in London, as we now learn, three days before his departure, a great comfort to us! Thinking of his banishment, his loneliness, the long distance he will be from all the human beings that he loves, it is one of my greatest consolations that he has those poems with him. There are about eight thousand lines. a great addition to the poem on my Brother's life he has made since C[oleridge] left us, 1500 Lines, & since we parted from you a still greater; he has also written a few small poems. I hope my dear Friend a happy time for you and all of us will come when we shall read these Poems to you – I am sure your heart will swell with exultation and joy – I ought to tell you that besides copying the verses for Coleridge we have recopied them entirely for ourselves as we went along, for the manuscripts which we took them from were in such wretched condition and so tedious to copy from, besides requiring Williams almost constant superintendance that we considered it as almost necessary to save them alive that we should recopy them, for I think William would never have had the resolution to set us to work again. Judge then how fully we have been employed, what with nursing, & the ordinary business of the house which is really not a little.

115. Dorothy Wordsworth to Lady Margaret Beaumont; Grasmere, 24 August 1804

It will give you pleasure to hear that my Sister was safely delivered of a fine Girl seven days ago, namely on Thursday the 16th, and that both Mother & Child are going on perfectly well. As I told you was before determined, the old fashioned name of Dorothy is given to her – She is to be christened in about a month, when we shall be most happy to call upon you for the performance of your promise in her behalf, regretting only that you will not be in the North at that time; I hope however, that before the end of next summer your God-daughter may be put into your arms and receive a blessing from your own mouth. She is a nice Baby, healthy enough – stout enough – pretty enough; but in nothing <u>extraordinary</u>, as John certainly was at his Birth & continued to be during the first months of his Babyhood – he was remarkably large & there was a certain dignity & manliness about him which I have never seen in any other Child.

116. Dorothy Wordsworth to Lady Margaret Beaumont; Grasmere, 7 October 1804

His [Coleridge's] returning to <u>live</u> in the North of England is quite out of the question therefore we intend to keep ourselves unfettered here, ready to move to any place where he may chuse to settle with his family. We find ourselves sadly crowded in this small Cottage since the Birth of the little Girl & we are looking about for another house but we should only take it from year to year, that we may have nothing to bind us down. We cannot, however, hear of a house, & though we are very industrious inquirers yet I think we are half glad of it; for though when we have any single person staying with us we are forced to wish ourselves in another place, when we are alone we gather ourselves together, & looking round our lowly sitting-room we feel as if we could never find another home – –

In the spring of 1805 the Wordsworths were struck by a tragedy which would profoundly affect William both as a man and as a poet. On 5 February his brother, John, who was setting out on the final voyage to India and China which would make his fortune and allow him to retire, was wrecked in storms off the Isle of Portland. The ship, more than 300 men and John himself were all lost. The news took six days to reach Grasmere.

117. Richard Wordsworth to his brother, William; Staple Inn, 7 February [1805]

My dear Brother,

It is with the most painful concern that I inform you of the loss of the Ship Abergavenny, off Weymouth last night.

I am acquainted with but few of the particulars of this Melancholy Event. I am told that a great number of Persons have perished, & that our Brother John is amongst that number. Mr Joseph Wordsworth [their second cousin] is amongst those who have been saved. The Ship struck against a Rock, & went to the Bottom.

You will impart this to Dorothy in the best manner you can, & remember me most affect[ionatel]y to her & your wife, believe me Yours most sincerely

                                    R[ichar]d Wordsworth

118. William Wordsworth to Sir George Beaumont; Grasmere, 11 February 1805

The public papers will already have broken the shock which the sight of this Letter will give you; you will have learned by them the loss of the Earl of Abergavenny East Indiaman, & along with her & a great proportion of the crew, that of her Captain Our Brother: and a most beloved Brother he was. This calamitous news we received at 2 o clock to day; & I write to you from a house of mourning. My poor Sister, & Wife who loved him almost as we did (for he was one of the most amiable of men) are in miserable affliction, which I do all in my power to alleviate; but heaven knows I want consolation myself. – I can say nothing higher of my ever dear Brother than that he was worthy of his Sister who is now weeping beside me, & of the friendship of Coleridge; meek, affectionate, silently enthusiastic, loving all quiet things, & a Poet in every thing but words . . .

I shall do all in my power to sustain my Sister under her sorrow, which is & long will be bitter & poignant. – We did not love him as a Brother merely, but as a man of original mind, & an honour to all about him. O dear Friend forgive me for talking thus.

119. William Wordsworth to his friend, the anti-slavery campaigner, Thomas Clarkson; Grasmere, 16 February [1805]

I will not speak of John. You & your Wife knew much of what he was; but I could tell you tales of his goodness to his Sister & me which would melt you to the soul. – We shall endeavour to be resigned: this is all I can say; but grief will have its course. Our loss is one which never can be made up; had it come earlier in life or later it would have been easier to bear; we are young enough to have had hope of pleasure & happiness in each others company for many years, & too old to outgrow the sorrow. Besides such a man as our Brother, considering his education &c &c, is not to be looked for; & we were not Brother & sister with him in blood only but had the same pleasures the same loves in almost everything. – But I must not talk any more about him, you will have sorrow enough of your own, without any need of my lamentations.

120. William Wordsworth to James Losh; Grasmere, 16 March 1805

For myself I feel that there is something cut out of my life which cannot be restored, I never thought of him but with hope & delight, we looked forward to the time not distant as we thought when he would settle near us when the task of his life would be over & he would have nothing to do but reap his reward. By that time I hoped also that the chief part of my labours would be executed & that I should be able to shew him that he had not placed a false confidence in me. I never wrote a line without a thought of its giving him pleasure, my writings printed & manuscript were his delight & one of the chief solaces of his long voyages. But let me stop – I will not be cast down were it only for his sake I will not be dejected. I have much yet to do & pray God to give me strength & power – his part of the agreement between[3] us is brought to an end, mine continues & I hope when I shall be able to think of him with a calmer mind that the remembrance of him dead will even animate me more than the joy which I had in him living –

121. William Wordsworth to Sir George Beaumont; Grasmere, 1 May 1805

My dear Sir George,
    I have wished to write to you every day this long time, but I have also had another wish which has interfered to prevent me – I mean

the wish to resume my poetical labours. Time was stealing away fast from me and nothing done and my mind still seeming unfit to do any thing. At first I had a strong impulse to write a poem that should record my Brother's virtues & be worthy of his memory. I began to give vent to my feelings, with this view, but I was overpowered by my subject & could not proceed: I composed much, but it is all lost except a few lines, as it came from me in such a torrent that I was unable to remember it; I could not hold the pen myself, and the subject was such, that I could not employ Mrs Wordsworth or my Sister as my amanuensis. This work must therefore rest awhile till I am something calmer, I shall however never be at peace till, as far as in me lies, I have done justice to my departed Brother's memory. His heroic death (the particulars of which I have now accurately collected from several of the survivors) exacts this from me, & still more, his singularly interesting character & virtuous & innocent life. –

Unable to proceed with this work I turned my thoughts again to the Poem on my own life, and you will be glad to hear that I have added 300 lines to it in the course of last week. Two Books more will conclude it. It will be not much less than 9,000 lines, not hundred but thousand, lines, long; an alarming length! and a thing unprecedented in Literary history that a man should talk so much about himself. It is not self-conceit, as you will know well, that has induced [me] to do this, but real humility; I began the work because I was unprepared to treat any more arduous subject & diffident of my own powers. Here at least I hoped that to a certain degree I should be sure of succeeding, as I had nothing to do but describe what I had felt and thought, therefore could not easily be bewildered. This might certainly have been done in narrower compass by a man of more address, but I have done my best. If when the work shall be finished it appears to the judicious to have redundancies they shall be lopped off if possible. But this is very difficult to do when a man has written with thought, & this defect whenever I have suspected it or found it to exist in any writings of mine, I have always found incurable. The fault lies too deep, and is in the first conception.

122. William Wordsworth to Sir George Beaumont; Grasmere, 3 June 1805

I have the pleasure to say that I finished my Poem about a fortnight ago, I had looked forward to the day as a most happy one; and I was indeed grateful to God for giving me life to complete the work such as it is; but it was not a happy day for me I was dejected on many accounts; when I looked back upon the performance it seemed to have a dead weight about it, the reality so far short of the expectation; it was the first long labour that I had finished, and the doubt whether I should ever live to write the Recluse and the sense which I had of this Poem being so far below what I seem'd capable of executing, depressed me much; above all, many heavy thoughts of my poor departed Brother hung upon me; the joy which I should have had in shewing him the Manuscript and a thousand other vain fancies & dreams. I have spoken of this because it was a state of feeling new to me, the occasion being new. – This work may be considered as a sort of portico to the Recluse, part of the same building, which I hope to be able erelong to begin with, in earnest; and if I am permitted to bring it to a conclusion, and to write, further, a narrative Poem of the Epic kind, I shall consider the <u>task</u> of my life as over. – I ought to add that I have the satisfaction of finding the present Poem not quite of so alarming a length as I apprehended.

123. Dorothy Wordsworth to Lady Margaret Beaumont; Grasmere, 11 June 1805

My Brother is at Patterdale, he took his fishing-rod over the mountains, there being a Pass from Grasmere thither. My Sister & I accompanied him to the top of it, & parted from him near a Tarn under a part of Helvellyn – he had gone up on Saturday with a neighbour of ours to fish there, but he quitted his companion, & poured out his heart in some beautiful verses to the memory of our lost Brother [*Elegiac Verses to the Memory of my Brother, John Wordsworth*], who used to go sometimes alone to that same Tarn; for the pleasure of angling in part, but still more, for his love of solitude & of the mountains. Near that very Tarn William & I bade him farewell the last time he was at Grasmere, when he went from us to take the command of the Ship. We were in view of the head of Ulswater, & stood till we could see him no longer, watching him as he <u>hurried</u> down the stony mountain – Oh! my dear Friend – You will not wonder that we love that place. I have been twice to it since his death – the first time was agony, but it is now a different feeling – poor William was overcome on Saturday – & with floods of tears wrote those verses – he parted from us yesterday (Monday) very chearfully – & indeed his spirits are far better than I could have thought possible at this time – he will return to us we hope in three days – he went for the sake of relaxation, having finished his long Poem, & intending to pause a short time before he begins the other. You will judge that a happy change has been wrought in his mind when he chuses John's employments, & one of John's haunts, (for he delighted in the neighbourhood of Patterdale) for such a purpose.

124. Dorothy Wordsworth to Lady Margaret Beaumont; Grasmere, 4 November [1805]

You asked me about my Brother's small poems – It is true that he has sometimes talked of publishing a few of the longest of them; but he has now entirely given up the idea – he has a great dislike to all the business of publishing – but that is not his reason – he thinks that having been so long silent to the world he ought to come forward again with a work of greater labour; & has many other lesser objections.

125. Dorothy Wordsworth to Lady Margaret Beaumont; Grasmere, Christmas Day 1805

I have transcribed two thirds of the Poem addressed to Coleridge [*The Prelude*], and am far more than pleased with it as I go along – I often think of the time when William shall have the pleasure of reading it to you and Sir George. He is very anxious to get forward with The Recluse, and is reading for the nourishment of his mind, preparatory to beginning; but I do not think he will be able to do much more till we have heard of Coleridge.

126. William Wordsworth to Sir George Beaumont; Grasmere, 1 August 1806

Within this last month I have returned to the Recluse and have written 700 additional lines; would Coleridge return so that I might have some conversation with him upon the subject I should go on swimmingly. – We have been very little interrupted with Tourist-Company this summer, and, of course, being for the most part well have enjoyed ourselves much. I am now writing in the Moss hut which is my Study, with a heavy thunder shower pouring down before me. It is a place of retirement for the eye, (though the Public Road glimmers through the apple Trees a few Yards below), and well suited to my occupations.

William had taken refuge in the moss hut at the top of the garden because the little cottage at Town End was bursting at the seams after the birth of a third child, Thomas, on 15 June 1806. The Wordsworths were also in daily expectation of the return of Coleridge from Malta and, aware that he intended to separate from his wife, had offered him and his sons a home with them. A temporary solution, at least for the winter months, was found in Sir George Beaumont's offer of a farmhouse, rent-free, on his Leicestershire estate. It was there that William began to put together his next publication, *Poems, in Two Volumes*.

127. William Wordsworth to his friend, the poet and novelist, Walter Scott, Coleorton, near Ashby-de-la-Zouche, 10 November 1806

Here I am with my whole family, a flight of 160 miles south! The smallness of my House at Grasmere rendered it impossible to winter in it; and I have availed myself of a kind offer of my Friend Sir G[eorge] Beaumont and taken possession of a House of his for six months; about the end of which time we shall return to Grasmere; I hope to have a sight of the last primroses. You see therefore that I cannot profit by your friendly invitation to take up my abode with you for any part of the ensuing winter; which, most likely I should have been tempted to do if we had remained at G[rasmere].

. . . I am going to Press with a Volume which Longman will find easy to convey to you; it will consist entirely of small pieces & I publish with great reluctance, but the day when my long work will be finished seems farther & farther off; & therefore I have resolved to send this Vol[ume] into the world. It would look like affectation if I were to say how indifferent I am to its present reception; but I have a true pleasure [in] saying to you that I put some value upon it; and hope that it will one day or other be thought well of by the Public.

128. Dorothy Wordsworth to Lady Margaret Beaumont; Coleorton, 15 November [1806]

We like this place more & more every day; for every day we find fresh comfort in having a roomy house – The sitting-room, where by the fire-side we have seen some glorious sunsets, we far more than like, – we already <u>love</u> it. These sunsets are a gift of our new residence, for shut up as we are among the mountains in our small deep valley; we have but a glimpse of the glory of the evening through one gap called the Rays gap, the inverted arch which you pass through in going to Keswick . . .

My Brother works very hard at his poems preparing them for the press – Miss [Sara] Hutchinson is the transcriber – She also orders dinner & attends to the kitchen; so that the labour being so divided we have all plenty of leisure.

129. *William Wordsworth to Walter Scott; Coleorton, 20 January [1807]*

The printing of my work which is now to be extended to two small Vols of 150 pages or so each has met with unexpected delays, & as the sheets are sent down to me for correction, & three are only yet gone through it will be full three months before it is out; for we do not get on faster than at the rate of a Sheet a week – A Copy will be sent to you in the parcel that goes to Edingborough. –

130. *Dorothy Wordsworth to Catherine Clarkson; Coleorton, 17 [actually 16] February [1807]*

Coleridge has determined to make his home with us; but <u>where</u>? There is no house vacant in the North, and we <u>cannot</u> spend another winter in the cottage, nor even a <u>summer</u> with Coleridge & his two Boys, therefore how can we go again into the North this summer? Besides there would be something very unpleasant (not to say <u>indelicate</u>, for that in a case of <u>necessity</u> might be got over) in going so near to Mrs. Coleridge immediately after their separation . . .

Poems, in Two Volumes was published by Longman on 28 April 1807. It included most of the shorter poems William had written since taking up residence in the Lakes, including the memorials of his brother, *Daffodils, Composed upon Westminster Bridge* and his great *Ode: Intimations of Immortality*. The critics, taking their cue from Francis Jeffrey of the *Edinburgh Review,* who had long attacked what he called 'the Lake School of Poetry', were venomous, prompting a lengthy defence and somewhat unconvincing declaration of indifference from the poet himself.

131. Lord Byron, review of Poems, in Two Volumes, *Monthly Literary Recreations, July 1807.*

The pieces least worthy of the author are those entitled 'Moods of my own Mind,' we certainly wish these 'Moods' had been less frequent, or not permitted to occupy a place near works, which only make their deformity more obvious; when Mr W[ordsworth] ceases to please, it is by 'abandoning' his mind to the most commonplace ideas, at the same time clothing them in language not simple, but puerile . . .

132. Francis Jeffrey, review of Poems, in Two Volumes, *Edinburgh Review, October 1807*

[*The Redbreast and the Butterfly*]: The three last lines seem to be downright raving.
[*The Small Celandine*]: a piece of namby-pamby . . .
[*Yarrow Unvisited*]: a very tedious, affected performance . . .
[*To the Cuckoo*]: the author, striving after force and originality, produces nothing but absurdity.
[*Ode: Intimations of Immortality*]: This is, beyond all doubt, the most illegible and unintelligible part of the publication.
[*Alice Fell*]: If the printing of such trash as this be not felt as an insult on the public taste, we are afraid it cannot be insulted.

133. Anonymous review of Poems, in Two Volumes, *the* Critical Review, *August, 1807*

. . . when the man to whom, in early youth, Nature 'was all in all: who cannot paint what then he was . . .'; when that man is found in his riper years, drivelling to the redbreast . . . and to a common pilewort [celandine] . . ., how can we sufficiently lament the infatuation of self-conceit and our own disappointed hopes?

Is it possible for Mr. Wordsworth not to feel that while he is pouring out his nauseous and nauseating sensibilities to weeds and insects, he debases himself to a level with his idiot boy . . .?

134. William Wordsworth to Lady Margaret Beaumont; Coleorton, Tuesday 21 May 1807

It is impossible that any expectations can be lower than mine concerning the immediate effect of this little work upon what is called the Public. I do not here take into consideration the envy and malevolence, and all the bad passions which always stand in the way of a work of any merit from a living Poet; but merely think of the pure, absolute, honest ignorance, in which all Wordlings of every rank and situation must be enveloped with respect to the thoughts, feelings and images on which the life of my Poems depends. The things which I have taken whether from within or without what have they to do with routs, dinners, morning calls, hurry from door to door, from street to street, on foot or in Carriage, with Mr Pitt or Mr Fox . . . It is an awful truth that there neither is, nor can be, any genuine enjoyment of Poetry among nineteen out of twenty of those persons who live or wish to live in the broad light of the world, among those who either are, or are striving to make them selves, people of consideration in society. This is a truth and an awful one because to be incapable of a feeling of Poetry in my sense of the word is to be without love of human nature & reverence for God –

Upon this I shall insist elsewhere; at present let me confine myself to my object which is to make you my dear Friend as easy-hearted as myself with respect to these Poems. Trouble not yourself upon their present reception; of what moment is that compared with what I trust is their destiny, to console the afflicted, to add sunshine to daylight by making the happy happier, to teach the young & the gracious of every age, to see to think and feel, and therefore to become more actively & securely virtuous; this is their office which I trust they will faithfully perform long after we, (that is, all that is mortal of us) are mouldered in our graves. I am well aware how far it would seem to many I overrate my own exertions when I speak in this way in direct connection with the Volumes I have just made public . . . never forget what I believe was observed to you by Coleridge that every great and original writer in proportion as he is great or original, must himself create the taste by which he is to be relished, he must teach the art by which he is to be seen: this in a certain degree, even to all persons, however wise and pure may be their lives, and however unvitiated their taste: but for those who dip into books in order to give an opinion of them, or talk about them to take up an opinion, for this multitude of unhappy & misguided & misguiding Beings, an´ entire regeneration must be produced; and if this be possible it must be a work of time. To conclude; my ears are stone-deaf to this idle buzz, and my flesh as insensible as iron to these petty stings; & after what I have said, I am sure yours will be the same.

William had long considered that writing a narrative poem was one of the three main tasks of his life as a poet and, in the winter of 1807–8, he composed a long ballad, *The White Doe of Rylstone*. The popular success enjoyed by Walter Scott's *The Lay of the Last Minstrel* (1805) encouraged him to hope that he could demand a high price for the manuscript but, when he went to London in the spring to sell it, he changed his mind. Much to the dismay of his family, who had only managed to spend the winter in Grasmere because they had taken over a neighbouring cottage, and were relying on a successful publication to finance a move to a larger house, he decided not to publish.

135. *William Wordsworth to Walter Scott; Grasmere, 18 January 1808*

– I must say a word of my own employments; after I left you I had a thoroughly idle summer; & part of the Autumn was as idle – but latterly I have been busy, though with many interruptions; & have written a narrative Poem of about 1700 lines; I finished it two days ago – –

136. *Dorothy Wordsworth to Catherine Clarkson; Grasmere, 5 February 1808*

William has finished his poem of the White Doe of Rylston or The Fate of the Nortons and it will probably be sent to the press in less than a month. The length of the poem is nearly 1700 lines and I think it very beautiful. It is to be published in Quarto. He means to demand 100 guineas for 1,000 copies. Before he publishes it he intends to send the Manuscript to Coleridge.

137. *William Wordsworth to Sir George Beaumont; [Grasmere], [c.20 February 1808]*

Thanks for dear Lady B[eaumont]'s transcript from your Friends Letter. – it is written with candour, but I must say a word or two not in praise of it. "Instances of what I mean says your Friend are to be found in a poem on a Daisy (by the bye it is on the Daisy a mighty difference!)., and on Daffodils reflected in the Water." is this accurately transcribed by Lady

Beaumont? if it be, what shall we think of criticism or judgement founded upon and exemplified by a Poem which must have been so inattentively perused? My Language is precise, and therefore it would be false modesty to charge my self with blame.   – "Beneath the trees

> Ten thousand dancing in the <u>breeze</u>.
> The <u>waves beside</u> them danced, but they
> Outdid the <u>Sparkling waves</u> in glee.["]

Can explanation be more distinct? And let me ask your Friend how it is possible for flowers to be <u>reflected</u> in water where there are <u>waves</u>. they may indeed in still water – but the very object of my Poem is the trouble or agitation both of the flowers & the water. I must needs respect the understanding of every one honoured by your friendship; but sincerity compels me to say that my Poems must be more nearly looked at before they can give rise to any remarks of much value, even from the strongest minds – With respect to this individual Poem Lady B[eaumont] will recollect how Mrs Fermor [her sister] expressed herself upon it. – A Letter also was sent to me addressed to a Friend of mine and by him communicated to me in which this identical Poem was singled out for fervent approbation. What then shall we say? Why let the Poet first consult his own heart as I have done and leave the rest to posterity; to, I hope, an improving posterity. – The fact is, the English <u>Public</u> are at this moment in the same state of mind with respect to my Poems, if small things may be compared with great, as the French are in respect to Shakespear[e]; and not the French alone but almost the whole Continent. – In short, in your Friends Letter, I am condemned for the very thing for which I ought to have been praised; viz: that I have not written down to the level of superficial observers and unthinking minds. – – Every great Poet is a Teacher; I wish either to be considered as a Teacher, or as nothing –

138. Dorothy Wordsworth to Lady Margaret Beaumont; [Grasmere], [c.20 February 1808]

It has been a long & most severe winter, particularly unfortunate for us, as it has added to the inconveniences of our two small houses; and has also often confined my Brother to the Sitting-room; when in a milder season he would have composed his verses in the open air: indeed I cannot but admire the fortitude, and wonder at the success with which he has laboured, in that one room, common to all the Family, to all visitors, & where the children frequently play beside him.

*139. William Wordsworth to his sister, Dorothy; [London], Saturday morning
[25 March 1808]*

I have not yet seen Longman about the Poem as he expects a sight of the
Manuscript, and I do not chuse to send it to be thumbed by his Criticasters
– I do not think it likely I shall publish it [at] all – indeed I am so thoroughly
disgusted with the wretched & stupid Public, that though my wish to
<u>write</u> for the sake of the People is not abated yet my loathing at the
thought of publication is almost insurmountable. – Therefore trouble
yourselves no more about it. –

140. Dorothy Wordsworth to her brother, William; [Grasmere], 31 March [1808]

We are exceedingly concerned to hear that you, William! have given up
all thoughts of publishing your Poem. As to the Outcry against you, I
would defy it – what matter, if you get your 100 guineas into your pocket?
Besides it is like as if they had run you down, when it is known you have
a poem ready for publishing, and keep it back. It is our belief, and that of
all who have heard it read, that the *Tale* would bear it up – and without
money what CAN we do? New House! new furniture! such a large
family! two servants & little Sally![4] we *cannot* go on so another half-year:
and as Sally will not be fit for another place, we must take her back again
into the old one, and dismiss one of the Servants, and work the flesh *off
our poor bones*. Do, dearest William! do pluck up your Courage – overcome
your disgust to publishing – It is but a *little trouble*, and all will be over, and
we shall be wealthy, and at our ease for one year, at least.

141. William Wordsworth to Sir George Beaumont; Grasmere, 8 April [1808]

You will deem it strange, but really some of the imagery of London, has
since my return hither been more present to my mind, than that of this
noble Vale. I will tell you how this happens to be. – I left Coleridge at 7
o clock on Sunday morning, and walked towards the City in a very
thoughtful & melancholy state of mind; I had passed through Temple Bar
and by St Dunstan's, noticing nothing, and entirely occupied with my
own thoughts, when looking up, I saw before me the avenue of Fleet
street, silent, empty, and pure white with a sprinkling of new-fallen snow,
not a cart or Carriage to obstruct the view, no noise, only a few soundless &
dusky foot passengers, here & there; you remember the elegant line of

the curve of Ludgate Hill in which this avenue would terminate, and beyond and towering above it was the huge and majestic form of St Pauls, solemnized by a thin veil of falling snow – I cannot say how much I was affected at this unthought of sight, in such a place, and what a blessing I felt there is in habits of exalted Imagination. My sorrow was controuled, and my uneasiness of mind not quieted and relieved altogether, seemed at once to receive the gift of an anchor of security.[5]

Chapter Five

1808–13

In the spring of 1808 the Wordsworths moved from the cottage at Town End to Allan Bank, a grand, new (and, as they were soon to discover, badly-built) house on a spur of land overlooking Grasmere Lake. At last they had plenty of room to accommodate their growing family (a fourth child, Catharine, was born on 6 September 1808) and assorted guests who took up semi-permanent residence. Amongst the latter were Coleridge and a young Thomas de Quincey, who encouraged William in his decision to write a series of articles, which became a pamphlet, denouncing the Convention of Cintra, a British agreement which procured the withdrawal of French troops from Portugal but allowed them to keep all their spoils of war. Coleridge himself was preoccupied with a political project of his own, setting up a monthly periodical, *The Friend*, which required all the support the Wordsworths could give. Tensions between them were reaching crisis point, however, as Coleridge's anti-social habits – the result of consumption of opium on a heroic scale – made life impossible for a family with young children and on a very restricted income.

142. Dorothy Wordsworth to Catherine Clarkson; [Allan Bank] Grasmere, 5 April [actually June] [1808]

We are now, however, tolerably settled; though there is much to do for Henry [Hutchinson, Mary's sailor brother] & me, who are the only able-bodied people in the house except the servant and <u>William</u>, who you know is not expected to do anything. Henry is the most useful creature in the world, &, being very poor, we are determined to make the Carpets & do everything ourselves, for he is as good as a tailor, & at the same time a very pleasant companion, & fellow-labourer. Judge how busy I must have been for this fortnight past – papers, linen, books, everything to look over in the old house and put by in the new – besides curtains to make &c. &c. &c. – In another fortnight all will be over we hope; for Henry and I work body & soul, & with less we should never be done – Sara sews a little, but we suffer nothing that can fatigue her[1] and Dearest Mary sprained her right arm three weeks ago and cannot yet use it even to write a letter.

143. Sara Hutchinson to her cousin, Mary Monkhouse; [Grasmere, October 1808]

... you can have no conception of the uncomfortableness, not to say <u>misery</u>, of this House in these storms – not a chimney will draw the smoke! and one day we could not have a fire except in the Study; & then you could not <u>see</u> each other. – In the rest of the rooms the fire was actually blown out of the Grates – We have at last got the chimney Doctor who has begun his operations in the kitchen; but he works slowly, and I fear it will be an age before they are all cured. It has been a most ungenial Autumn – we have not been able to stir out; indeed it seems to be almost winter already, the Waterfalls are in all their glory if one could but travel abroad to see them –

144. Dorothy Wordsworth to Jane Marshall; [Grasmere], 4 December 1808

– – – There was one stormy day in which we could have no fire but in my Brother's Study – & that chimney smoked so much that we were obliged to go to bed with the Baby in the middle of the day to keep it warm, & I, with a candle in my hand, stumbled over a chair, unable to see it. – – – We cooked in the study, & even heated water there to wash dishes, for the Boiler, in the Back-kitchen could not be heated, much less the kitchen fire endured; & in fact partly on account of smoke in windy weather, & partly because of the Workmen we have been for more than a week together at different times without a kitchen fire. The Servants, you may be sure, have been miserable, & <u>we</u> have had far too much labour, & too little quiet; but, thank God! my health has stood it very well, & my Sister has not looked so healthy for these two years or been so strong.

145. William Wordsworth to Daniel Stuart, editor and proprietor of the Morning
Post; *[Grasmere], postmarked 9 February 1809*

I am greatly pleased that you think so favourably of my labours, both
because I value your judgement and because my heart is deeply interested
in this affair. Never did any public event cause in my mind so much
sorrow as the Convention of Cintra, both on account of the Spaniards
and the Portuguese, and on our own – – Every good and intelligent man
of my Friends or Acquaintances has been in his degree agitated and
afflicted by it – I do not feel so much inclined to express my thanks for
the trouble which you have taken with this Pamphlet, as my pleasure to
find that you attach so lively a feeling to it on account of the cause which
it is intended to support.

*146. William Wordsworth to Daniel Stuart; [Grasmere], postmarked 31 March
1809*

I confess I have no hopes of the thing making any impression: the style
of thinking and feeling is so little in the Spirit of the age. This Country is
in fact fallen as low in point of moral philosophy (and of course political)
as it is possible for any country to fall. We should have far better <u>books</u>
circulated among us, if we were as thoroughly enslaved as the Romans
under their Emperors . . .

Two things are absolutely wanted in this Country – a thorough reform
in Parliament – and a new course of education, which must be preceded
by some genuine philosophical writings from some quarter or other, to
teach the principles upon which that education should be grounded. We
have in our language better books than exist in any other, and in our land
better institutions, but the one nobody reads, and the others are fallen
into disorder and decay. What can be expected from a Parliament consisting
of such pitiful drivellers as the Members of our two Houses are with
scarcely an exception? and as to the Heads of the Army, there's Fergusson
who has behaved like a man of sense and honour; but heaven preserve us
from the rest!

147. William Wordsworth to Francis Wrangham; [Grasmere], franked 3 April 1809

What I have written has been done according to the best light of my Conscience, it is indeed very imperfect, and will I fear be little read, but if it is read cannot I hope fail of doing some good – though I am aware it will create me a world of enemies; and call forth the old yell of Jacobinism . . . Verses have been out of my Head for some time . . .

148. Dorothy Wordsworth to Thomas de Quincey; Grasmere, Monday, 1 May [1809]

My Brother has begun to correct and add to the poem of the White Doe, & has been tolerably successful – He intends to finish it before he begins with any other work, & has made up his mind, if he can satisfy himself in the alterations he intends to make, to publish it next winter, & to follow the publication on by that of Peter Bell & [Benjamin] the Waggoner. He has also made a resolution to write upon publick affairs in the Courier or some other newspaper for the sake of getting money – not wholly however on that account for unless he were animated by the importance of his subject & the hope of being of use he could do nothing in that way – Coleridge, however, writes to desire that he will not withdraw himself from poetry, for he is assured that there will be no need of it as he (Coleridge) can get money enough – I have, indeed, better hopes of him at present than I have had for this long time, laying together his own account of himself, & the account which Mrs C[oleridge] gives us of him. He intends to go to Penrith on Wednesday to superintend the Press, therefore you may expect a visit from the Friend on Monday morning (I believe that is the Day on which it will arrive in London) As to my Brother's writing for a newspaper I do not much like the thought of it but, unless the pamphlet [*The Convention of Cintra*] (the most improbable thing in the world) should make his poems sought after I know not how we can go on without his employing some portion of his time in that way – but the misfortune is, that he cannot lay down one work & begin with another – It was never intended that he should make a trade out of his faculties. His thoughts have been much employed lately in the arrangement of his published poems, as he intends to blend the 4 volumes together whenever they are re-printed – or should I say if ever? for we hear no more from Longman, & I believe that the two last volumes scarcely sell at all.

149. William Wordsworth to Samuel Taylor Coleridge; [Grasmere, 5 May 1809]

I am very sorry to hear of your being taken ill again, were it only on account of the effect these seizures may have upon the work in which you are engaged. They prove that it is <u>absolutely necessary</u> that you should always be <u>before hand</u> with your work. On the general question of your health, one thing is obvious, that health of mind, that is, resolution, self-denial, and well-regulated conditions of feeling, are what you must depend upon – and that Doctors can do you little or no good, and that Doctors stuff has been one of your greatest curses, – and of course, of ours through you. – I should not speak now upon this subject were it not on account of what you say about Mr. Harrison – You must know better than Mr. Harrison, Mr. King, or any Surgeon what is to do you good; what you are to do, and what to leave undone. Do not look out of yourself for that stay which can only be found within.

150. William Wordsworth to Tom Poole; [Grasmere, May 1809]

I have yet another and far more important reason for writing to you; connected as no doubt you will guess, with Coleridge. I am sorry to say that nothing appears to me more desirable than that his periodical essay should never commence. It is in fact <u>impossible</u> utterly impossible – that he should carry it on; and, therefore, better never begin it – far better, and if begun, the sooner it stop, also the better – the less will be the loss, and not greater the disgrace. You will consider me as speaking to you now in the most sacred confidence, and as under a strong sense of duty; from a wish to save you from anxiety and disappointment; and from a further and still stronger wish that, as one of Coleridge's nearest and dearest Friends, you should take into most serious consideration his condition, above all with reference to his children. I give it to you as my deliberate opinion, formed upon proofs which have been strengthening for years, that he neither will nor can execute any thing of important benefit either to himself his family or mankind. Neither his talents nor his genius mighty as they are nor his vast information will avail him anything; they are all frustrated by a derangement in his intellectual & moral constitution – In fact he has no voluntary power of mind whatsoever, nor is he capable of acting under any <u>constraint</u> of duty or moral obligation. Do not suppose that I mean to say from this that The Friend may not appear – it may – but it cannot go on for any length of time. I am <u>sure</u> it cannot.

151. William Wordsworth to Daniel Stuart; [Grasmere], postmarked 17 June 1809

Coleridge arrived here yesterday morning, after an absence of nearly four months. As I thought it my duty some time since, upon substantial grounds, to express my apprehension, that from the irresolution of the author "The Friend" might not prosper, which opinion I expressed in order to break the force of your disappointment should my forebodings prove true; I now think it right to say that such appear to be the present dispositions, resolutions, and employments of Coleridge that I am encouraged to entertain more favourable hopes of his exerting himself steadily than I ever have had at any other period of this business.

152. Dorothy Wordsworth to Catherine Clarkson; Grasmere, 18 November [1809]

Sara has been kept almost constantly busy in transcribing: for William, and for 'The Friend'; therefore she has desired me to write to you. For William she has been transcribing the introduction to a collection of prints to be published by Mr. Wilkinson of Thetford (of which I believe you know the history as your husband's name is down among those of the subscribers). I hope you will be interested with W[illia]m's part of the work (he has only finished the general introduction, being unable to do the rest till he has seen the prints). It is the only regular and I may say scientific account of the present & past state & appearance of the country that has yet appeared. I think, if he were to write a Guide to the Lakes & prefix this preface, it would sell better, & bring him more money than any of his higher labours. He has some thoughts of doing this; but do not mention it, as Mr. W[ilkinson]'s work should have its just fair run.

153. William Wordsworth to John Miller; Grasmere, 4 January [1810]

Shall I be believed when I say that in ninety nine cases out of a hundred praise and censure are things to me of equal indifference and that I attach no interest to my poems in their connection with the world further than as I think they are fitted to communicate knowledge, to awaken kindly or noble dispositions, or to strengthen the intellectual powers; in a word to promote just thinking and salutary feelings. With this habit of mind how can I be in the slightest degree affected by what this Scribbler, whether simple dunce or compound of dunce & malignant, says or thinks of them; or this or that goodnatured man who knows no more of Poetry than our Parish Clerk of Hebrew. If my Poems are inspired by Genius and Nature they will live, if not, they will be forgotten & the sooner the better; this being so, and their Author habitually feeling that it must be so, what matters it who is pleased or displeased . . . Let it not however be concluded that I have not received pleasure from praise in some instances when, as upon the present occasion it has been accompanied with evidence that what I write is really understood in the Spirit in which it was written.

154. Dorothy Wordsworth to Lady Margaret Beaumont; [Grasmere], 28 February [1810]

How have you liked the Epitaphs from Chiabrera [in *The Friend*]? The Essay [on Epitaphs] of this week, No 25, is by my Brother. He did not intend it to be published now; but Coleridge was in such bad spirits that when the time came he was utterly unprovided . . . so my Brother's Essay being ready was sent off . . . My Brother's Essay (as indeed most of the Essays) is sadly misprinted . . . My Brother has written two more Essays on the Same subject which will appear when there is need. He is deeply engaged in composition – Before he turns to any other labour I hope he will have finished 3 books of the Recluse – He seldom writes less than 50 Lines every day. After this Task is finished he hopes to complete ["]the White Doe" & proud should we all be if it could be honoured by a Frontispiece from the Pencil of Sir George Beaumont – [2]

155. Dorothy Wordsworth to Catherine Clarkson; [Grasmere], 12 April [1810]

As to Coleridge, if I thought I should distress you, I would say nothing about him; but I hope that you are sufficiently prepared for the worst. We have no hope of him – none that he will ever do anything more than he has already done. If he were not under our Roof, he would be just as much the slave of stimulants as ever; & his whole time and thoughts, (except when he is reading and he reads a great deal), are employed in deceiving himself, and seeking to deceive others. He will tell me that he has been writing, that he <u>has</u> written half a Friend; when I <u>know</u> that he has not written a single line. This Habit pervades all his words & actions, and you feel perpetually new hollowness and emptiness. I am loth to say this, & burn this letter, I entreat you. I am loth to say it, but it is the truth. He lies in bed, always till after 12 o'clock, sometimes much later; & never walks out – Even the finest spring day does not tempt him to seek the fresh air; & this beautiful valley seems a blank to him. He never leaves his own parlour except at dinner & tea, and sometimes supper, & then he always seems impatient to get back to his solitude – he goes the moment his food is swallowed. Sometimes he does not speak a word, & when he does talk it is always very much and upon subjects as far aloof from himself or his friends as possible. The Boys [his sons] come every week & he talks to them, especially to Hartley, but he never examines them in their books. He speaks of The Friend always as if it were going on, & would go on; therefore, of course, you will drop no hint of my opinion. I heartily wish I may be mistaken. – I hope in about 3 weeks to inform you of the Birth of our 5th little one. Mary is now better than she was before Catharine was taken ill [see below, no. 156], being free from the Heartburn. Her spirits are very good, being now full of hope. William goes on writing industriously . . .

With respect to Coleridge, do not think it is his love for Sara which has stopped him in his work – do not believe it: his love for her is no more than a fanciful dream – otherwise he would prove it by a desire to make her happy. No! He likes to have her about him as his own, as one devoted to him, but when she stood in the way of other gratifications it was all over. I speak this very unwillingly, & again I beg, burn this letter. I need not add, keep its contents to yourself alone.

156. Dorothy Wordsworth to Jane Marshall; Grasmere, 13 April [1810]

On Saturday Morn[in]g, poor little Catharine was seized with strong convulsions, & in spite of the warm bath, opening medicines, & lancing her gums, no effect was produced for 8 hours. Meanwhile her poor Mother was in agony of grief, & I feared more for her than the Child. She appeared to be perfectly restored, tho' very weak when the convulsions left her; but alas! the next day we discovered that she had lost the use of her right side. Thank God she has begun to use the leg again freely, but it is very weak; & she makes no use whatever of her arm; the Apothecary however, a very sensible & judicious man gives us the best hope of her perfect recovery, & her Mother has recovered her spirits. She has eaten heartily for three or four days & looks very well. The fits were brought on by having eaten a large quantity of raw carrot – but of this more when we meet.

Though nineteen-month-old Catharine gradually recovered most of the movement in her right side, she remained lame, had difficulty using her right hand and was extremely delicate for the rest of her life. Despite Mary's shock and distress, her last child, Willy, was safely delivered on 12 May 1810 and, after his christening a month later, William and Dorothy left Grasmere to visit the Beaumonts at Coleorton in Leicestershire; Dorothy then went to Bury St Edmunds to stay with the Clarksons, while William went to Hindwell, in Radnorshire, to visit Sara, who was recuperating at her brother, Tom's, new farm. For the first time in almost eight years of married life, William and Mary were able to write letters to each other which were not to be shared with Dorothy or Sara but were intended for their eyes only.

157. William Wordsworth to his wife, Mary; Hindwell, Monday 11 August [1810]

Every day every hour every moment makes me feel more deeply how blessed we are in each other, how purely how faithfully how ardently, and how tenderly we love each other; I put this last word last because, though I am persuaded that a deep affection is not uncommon in married life, yet I am confident that a lively, gushing, thought-employing, Spirit-stirring passion of love, is very rare even among good people. I will say more upon this when we meet, grounded upon recent observation of the condition of others. We have been parted my sweet Mary too long, but we have not been parted in vain, for wherever I go I am admonished how blessed, and almost peculiar a lot mine is. – . . .

O Mary I love you with a passion of love which grows till I tremble to think of its strength; your children and the care which they require must fortunately steal between you and the solitude and the longings of absence – When I am moving about in travelling I am less unhappy than when stationary, but then I am at every moment, I will not say reminded of you, for you never I think are out of my mind 3 minutes together however I am engaged, but I am every moment seized with a longing wish that you might see the objects which interest me as I pass along, and not having you at my side my pleasure is so imperfect that after a short look I had rather not see the objects at all . . .

158. Mary Wordsworth to her husband, William; [Grasmere], Wednesday morning, 14 [actually 15] August [1810]

Your beloved letter my William I never can be enough grateful to thee for – O William! I really am too happy to move about on this earth, it is well indeed that my employments keep me active about other things or I should not be able to contain my felicity – Good Heavens! that I should be adored in this manner by thee thou first & best of Men, is a lot so far beyond, not only all my hopes but all my desires & the blessing is so weighty it is so solemnly great that it would be even painful were I left to brood much upon the thought of it. I therefore feel a comfort in those salutary interruptions that will only admit of that delightful, happy chearing thought of thee which I can communicate to the Children & which they can in part enter into. – Our Conversations now are all of your return –

A second winter suffering from the smoking chimneys of Allan Bank convinced the Wordsworths that they would have to move again. Their lease was, in any case, coming to an end. By early June 1811 they were established in cheaper rented accommodation at the Parsonage in Grasmere, in the centre of the village and just across the road from the church. Though William was still writing poetry, he could not be prevailed upon to publish.

159. Dorothy Wordsworth to Catherine Clarkson; Grasmere, 30 December 1810

William the Father has written 15 fine political sonnets, which Mary & I would fain have him send to the Courier – both in order that they might be read, & that we might have a little profit from his industry: he is, however, so disgusted with Critics, Readers, newspaper-Readers – & the talking public, that we cannot prevail. The King of Sweden, Buonaparte, and the struggle of the Peninsula are the subjects of these sonnets.

160. William Wordsworth to the poet, John Edwards of Derby; Grasmere, 27 March [1811]

I cannot but be grateful to hear that my Poems are often looked at by you, as if they have any merit it is certainly of that kind which makes itself felt by little and little. I have been correcting some of them lately, and probably ere long may republish the whole arranged in a manner that will make more clear my intentions in writing them. But I am shocked to find how indifferent I am becoming concerning things upon which so much of my life has been employed. I am not quite 41 years of age, yet I seem to have lost all personal interest in everything which I have composed. When I read my poems, I often think that they are such as I should have admired and been delighted with if they had been produced by another, yet as I cannot ascertain how much of this approbation is owing to self-love, and how much to what my own powers and knowledge supply to complete what is imperfect in the poems themselves, upon the whole my own works at present interest me little, far too little, I am at that point where I seem to have small regard for them as my own, and yet cannot independently and purely admire them as I do what I deem good or excellent in those of another.

161. Dorothy Wordsworth to Catherine Clarkson; [Grasmere], 16 June 1811

Now I must tell you that we like our new house very much. There are only three important objections to it. First, that it fronts the East, & has no sitting-rooms looking westward, therefore we lose the sun very soon: secondly, that it is too public, but this evil will wear away every year, for we shall plant abundance of shrubs in the Autumn in addition to those already planted; & thirdly that the field in which the house stands is very wet, & cannot be drained. It is no playing-place for the children, & being at present not divided from the road to the house, it leads them into continual temptation to dirty & wet themselves; but, when all other things are done it is to be fenced off, & a plantation to be made all round the back part of the house.

162. Sara Hutchinson to her cousin, John Monkhouse; [Grasmere], 28 March [1812]

I have been transcribing the Peter Bell which is now completely finished and improved – and I intend to make another copy for myself when William has done with my Pen – A few weeks ago I transcribed the Preface to Wilkinson's Sketches for Luff with which I think I was almost more delighted than with anything else William ever wrote and intend to make another Copy as a present for you – but I shall not have time to do it before Mary [Monkhouse, John's sister] comes. William has been busy with the Recluse but the smoke put him off and he will not now begin again before his journey.

William's journey was to London, ostensibly for a social visit, but in reality to confront Coleridge. When he had left Allan Bank the previous autumn with the intention of taking up residence with Basil Montagu and his new wife, William had felt obliged to warn his old friend about Coleridge's drug-addiction and anti-social habits. Montagu repeated these criticisms to Coleridge, adding that William had 'authorized him' to do so. Coleridge, not unnaturally, took offence and, at every opportunity in London society, had accused the Wordsworths of betraying and neglecting him. Henry Crabb Robinson, a mutual friend, whose legal training as a barrister now proved invaluable, succeeded in brokering a peace between the two men and, with his help, William wrote a letter denying Coleridge's accusations but admitting he was to blame for speaking so frankly to such an indiscreet man as Montagu. Though the breach between the two men was thus healed, their old intimacy had gone for ever.

163. Dorothy Wordsworth to her brother and sister-in-law, William and Mary; [Grasmere], 3 May [1812]

These things are only worth noticing as additional proofs that he [Coleridge] cannot speak truth – The extract from his letter, written since his return to London, I shall transcribe . . . 'At <u>Keswick</u>, forsooth! he satisfied himself that no possibility remained of his being deluded.' – At <u>Keswick</u> where the weightiest of his charges was flatly contradicted! – at <u>Keswick</u> where nothing <u>was</u> done, nothing <u>could be</u> done to encrease the offence – whence the insult of total neglect was heaped upon us & received without murmuring [but no doubt he expected some submission on your part][3]. This only proves what we have long been sure of that he is glad of a pretext to break with us, & to furnish himself with a ready excuse for all his failures in duty to himself & others.

164. William Wordsworth to his wife, Mary; [London], Thursday afternoon, two o'clock, [7 May 1812]

I had also a long conversation with H[enry Crabb] Robinson, not a little interesting. He seemed to apprehend that there was in Coleridge's mind a lurking literary jealousy of me. I totally rejected that supposition, and told him that I believe in my soul that envy & jealousy of that kind were faults of which Coleridge was utterly free, and that if he had not chimed in with my praises it was because he was in ill-humour with me, and not because he was uneasy at any comparison between my intellectual Powers and his.

165. Samuel Taylor Coleridge to Daniel Stuart; 71 Berners Street, London, 8 May [1812]

Mr Wordsworth is in town: & at a time when I require the most perfect tranquillity of mind, I am plunged into the hot water of that bedeviled Cauldron, Explanation with alienated Friendship.

166. Henry Crabb Robinson, diary, 8 May 1812

I endeavoured to draw C[oleridge's] attention <u>from</u> words w[hic]h are so liable to misrepresentation – And w[hi]ch in repetition so entirely change their character, to the fact so positively denied by W[ordsworth] that he ever intended (least of all commissioned) M[ontagu] to repeat what W[ordsworth] stated to him – This in my mind is the only material fact. Every thing else admits of explanation. This does not.

167. Henry Crabb Robinson, diary, 11 May 1812

The conversation that accompanied the writing it [William's letter to Coleridge] was highly interesting & exhibited W[ordsworth] in a most honourable light. His integrity his purity, his delicacy are alike eminent – How preferable is the <u>coolness</u> of such a man to the heat of C[oleridge]. The opinion entertained by Wordsworth of Montagu and his wife greatly facilitated the writing a conciliatory letter. Wordsworth, I find, believed the latter [Coleridge] fully.[4]

168. Samuel Taylor Coleridge to Robert Southey; [London, 12 May 1812]

The affair between Wordsworth & me seems settled – much against my first expectation from the message, I received from him, & his refusal to open a Letter from me – I have not yet seen him, but an explanation has taken place – I sent by Robinson an attested avowed Statement of what Mr & Mrs Montagu told me – & Wordsworth has sent an unequivocal denial of the Whole *in spirit* & of the most offensive passages in letter as well as Spirit – & I then instantly informed him that were ten thousand Montagues to swear against it, I should take his word not ostensibly only but with inward Faith! –

169. Henry Crabb Robinson, diary, 19 May 1812

W[ordsworth] has seen C[oleridge] sev[era]l times & been much in his
Company but they have not yet touched upon the Subject of their
Correspondence – Thus, as I hoped, the Wound is healed, but as I
observed to Mrs C[larkson], probably the Scar remains in Coleridge's
bosom –

While William was in London, Mary was at Hindwell, with their son, Thomas,
who was recuperating from a serious illness. The four other children had been
left at Grasmere in the care of their aunts Dorothy and Sara. Once again, William
and Mary exchanged a series of love letters, but the mood was abruptly broken
by shocking news from Grasmere.

*170. William Wordsworth to his wife, Mary; [from the Beaumonts' house in
Grosvenor Square, London], Saturday night, 10 o'clock [9 May 1812]*

Thou sayst that thou art the blessedest of Women and surely I am the
most blessed of Men. The life which is led by the fashionable world in
this great city is miserable; there is neither dignity nor content nor love
nor quiet to be found in it. If it was not [for] the pleasure I find under
this roof, and that I am collecting something to think about; I should be
unable to resist my inclination to set off to morrow, to walk with thee by
the woody side of that quiet pool, near which thy days and nights are
passed. O. my Mary, what a heavenly thing is pure & ever growing Love;
such do I feel for thee, and D[orothy] and S[ara] and all our dear family
– . . .
    – My sweet Love how I long to see thee; think of me, wish for me,
pray for me, pronounce my name when tho[u] art alone, and upon thy
pillow; and dream of me happily & sweetly. – I am the blessedest of Men,
the happiest of husbands –

*171. Mary Wordsworth to her husband, William; [Hindwell], Saturday morning,
23 May [1812]*

I <u>do</u> long most intensely for the time when you are to join me here – I
never felt this more than when we were walking through those greenest
of all green fields this morning – the birds were singing, and the air was
so balmy, & I seemed to have so much leisure (a thing which I seldom

have at our own sweet home) to know how blessed above all blessed creatures I should be were you but here to wander with me, & enjoy the joys of this heavenly season – dearest William! the time will soon be here I trust, & long shall it be ere we part again – if this depends upon my choice – –

Yet I do not regret that this separation has been, for it is worth no small sacrifice to be thus assured, that instead of weakening, our union has strengthened – a hundred fold strengthened those yearnings towards each other which I used so strongly to feel at Gallow hill – & in which you sympathized with me at that time – that these feelings are mutual now, I have the fullest proof, from thy letters & from their power & the power of absence over my whole frame – Oh William I can not tell thee how I love thee, & thou must not desire it – but feel it, O feel it in the fullness of thy soul & believe that I am the happiest of Wives & of Mothers & of all Women the most blessed – . . .

[25 May] I have had no intelligence from Grasmere since the letter which you sent to me & I begin, not to be uneasy about them, but uneasy with myself that I do not hear again – it is a fortnight since that letter was written which seems a long time not to know what has passed at home – Those 2 littlest Darlings [Catharine and Willy] how my heart does beat when I think about them! Dear dear William – dost thou not love them & that Darling little Dorothy [Dora] at Appleby & dear John O how glad we shall be when we all get together again –

172. Dorothy Wordsworth to her brother, William; [Grasmere], 4 June [1812]

My dearest Brother –

Sara and John & William and I are all in perfect health – but poor Catharine died this morning at ¼ past 5 o'clock. She had been even better & more chearful than usual all yesterday – & we had fondly flattered ourselves for three or four days – in particularly noticing how much her lameness was abated, & how well she used her hand. Mr Scambler [the local physician] has promised us to write to you by this same post, with an account of her illness – I shall therefore say no more than that She began to be convulsed at a little before 10 last night; & died this morning at ¼ past 5 – – – Upon most mature deliberation we have concluded it best not to write to Mary – It would be impossible for her to be here at the Funeral; & we think that She will be better able to stand the shock when it is communicated by you,[5] – You will be by her side to impart all the consolation which can be given. May God bless & support you both – We are as well as we can be after so sudden a shock – & are greatly comforted in the Belief that all that <u>could</u> be done to save her <u>was</u> done – Yours evermore

D Wordsworth

June 4th Thursday afternoon

. . . We purpose burying the beloved Girl on Monday. This we do for the best – & we hope you will both be satisfied. If we had attempted to keep her till you & her Mother could come, you would not have been able to look upon her face, she would then be so changed – & it will be a calmer sorrow to visit her Grave. – –

173. William Wordsworth to Catherine Clarkson; Hindwell, Thursday, 18 June [1812]

. . . I found poor dear Mary in a most disconsolate State from which we have not yet been able to raise her. The suddenness of the shock & her not having been upon the spot have been great aggravations of her distress in losing this beloved child endeared to her by such long and tender anxieties of maternal care and love. – . . .

I had hopes to prevail upon Mary to take a little Excursion in this neighbourhood that might beguile her heaviness, but I now am inclined to give them up. She seems so afraid that some of her other Children may be taken from her before she reaches home, and has upon her mind so many tender offices of sorrow to perform for her departed Catharine, that I fear no benefit will be derived from any attempts to turn her attention to other objects.

174. William Wordsworth to his sister, Dorothy, and sister-in-law, Sara Hutchinson; [Hindwell], Friday evening [19 June 1812]

Yesterday we received your Letter – giving an account of the funeral of the Darling. I am pleased with the place you have [picked?] upon for her grave. We have broken ground in that Churchyard, through Gods blessing, as gently as well could have been. I hope that we shall all be sensible of this, and shew our dear remembrance & feeling of it by additional

tenderness & kindness to each other. Catharine is gone before to prepare
the way for us & make it somewhat less forbidding; sweet Innocent – I
have yet not felt my own sorrow, only I know well that it is to come. –
But as I said before, I do not mean to yield to the emotions of my heart
on this sad and unexpected privation. – I long to hear how little Dorothy
is & how she [is] looking – take care of the water, and of fire, and of all
dangers; especially for William.

Catharine was just three months short of her fourth birthday when she died. The
Wordsworths had not recovered from her loss when they were hit by a second
tragedy: six-year-old Thomas caught measles and died of pneumonia six months
after his sister.

*175. William Wordsworth to Robert Southey; [Grasmere], Wednesday evening
[2 December 1812]*

My dear Friend
   Symptoms of the measles appeared upon my Son Thomas last
Thursday; he was most favorable [*sic*] held till tuesday, between ten
and eleven at that hour was particularly lightsome and comfortable;
without any assignable cause a sudden change took place, an inflammation had commenced on the lungs which it was impossible to
check and the sweet Innocent yielded up his soul to God before six
in the evening. He did not appear to suffer much in body, but I fear
something in mind as he was of an age to have thought much upon
death a subject to which his mind was daily led by the grave of his
Sister. My Wife bears the loss of her Child with striking fortitude.
My Sister was not at home but is returned to day, I met her at
Threlkeld. Miss Hutchinson also supports her sorrow as ought to be
done. For myself dear Southey I dare not say in what state of mind I
am; I loved the Boy with the utmost love of which my soul is capable,
and he is taken from me – yet in the agony of my Spirit in surrendering
such a treasure I feel a thousand times richer than if I had never
possessed it. God comfort and save you & all our friends and us all
from a repetition of such trials – O Southey feel for me! If you are
not afraid of the complaint, I ought to have said if you have had it
come over to us! Best love from everybody – you will impart this
sad news to your Wife and Mrs Coleridge and Mrs Lovel & to Miss

Barker and Mrs Wilson.[6] Poor Woman! She was most good to him
– Heaven reward her.

> Heaven bless you
> Your Sincere Friend
> W. Wordsworth

Will Mrs Coleridge please to walk up to the Calverts and mention
these afflictive news with the particulars. I should have written but
my Sorrow overpowers me.

To add to the Wordsworths' distress, the three surviving children also caught
measles; the family moved to Ambleside to be nearer the doctor as their lives too
hung in the balance. The deaths of Catharine and Thomas had already convinced
William that he would have to make better financial provision for his depleted
family and he had been actively seeking a government office, to no avail. At the
height of this crisis, Lord Lonsdale offered a lifeline: he would give William an
annual pension until an appropriate office came available. Though William had
qualms about accepting, he was persuaded to do so, and the money enabled the
Wordsworths to move from the Parsonage, where the sight of the two children's
graves from almost every window was more than they could bear. In May 1813
they took a lease on Rydal Mount, a beautiful house a couple of miles away, in
an exquisite situation overlooking the wooded Vale and lake of Rydal. It was to
be their home for the remainder of their lives.

176. William Wordsworth to Lord Lonsdale; Ambleside, 17 December 1812

The suddenness of this blow [the death of Thomas] has overwhelmed me,
following so close upon another as sudden which deprived me of a
Daughter last midsummer. Of my three remaining Children the youngest
is now at the height of the fever attendant upon the measles, and the other
two are recovering one of whom has been severely held, so that you will
easily conceive, my Lord, that I can scarcely trust I am in a state of mind
that will allow me to decide upon the proposition laid before me in your
Lordship's Letter – Were I to trust to my present feelings I should indeed
have no difficulty, but oppressed with sorrow and distracted with anxiety
as I am, I fear that in a calmer state of mind I might hereafter disapprove
of a determination formed at once under such circumstances – I must
therefore beg leave to request that a few days may be allowed me to
consider the subject before I give a final answer to your Lordship's Letter.

177. William Wordsworth to Lord Lonsdale; Grasmere, 27 December 1812

After mature consideration, I have resolved to trust to the first feelings excited by that Letter; these were, rather to owe any addition to my income, required by my present occasions, to your Lordship's friendship than to the Government, or to any other quarter where it was not in my power to return what in the common sentiments of men would be deemed an equivalent. – Asking permission therefore to retract my former determination, which I am encouraged to do by the personal intercourse and marks of regard with which your Lordship has since distinguished me, and by the irresistible delicacy of your last Letter, I feel no scruple in saying that I shall with pride and pleasure accept annually the sum offered by your Lordship untill the Office becomes vacant, or any other change takes place in my circumstances which might render it unnecessary. – I cannot forbear to add, that I feel more satisfaction from this decision, because my opinions would not lead me to decline accepting a pension from Government, on the ground that Literary Men make some sacrifice of Independence by such acceptance, and are consequently degraded.

178. William Wordsworth to Lord Lonsdale; Grasmere, 8 January 1812

. . . you have been the means of relieving my mind, in an [*sic*] manner that, I am sure, will be gratifying to your Heart. – The House which I have for some time occupied is the Parsonage of Grasmere. It stands close by the Churchyard; and I have found it absolutely necessary that we should quit a Place; which, by recalling to our minds at every moment the losses we have sustained in the course of last year, would grievously retard our progress towards that tranquillity which it is our duty to aim at. By your Lordships goodness we shall be enabled to remove, without uneasiness from some additional Expense of Rent, to a most desirable Residence soon to be vacant at Rydale. I shall be further assisted in my present depression of mind (indeed I have already been so) by feeling myself at liberty to recur to that species of intellectual exertion which only I find sufficiently powerful to rouze me, and which for some time I could not have yielded to, on account of a task undertaken for profit. This I can now defer without imprudence till I can proceed with it more heartily than at present would be possible.

179. Dorothy Wordsworth to Jane Marshall; Rydal Mount, [13 May 1813]

When I tell you that we removed yesterday, you will not wonder that I write a short note. We are all well, though some of us, especially my Sister, jaded with our fatigues. The weather is delightful, & the place a paradise; but my inner thoughts <u>will</u> go back to Grasmere – I was the last person who left the House yesterday Evening – It seemed as quiet as the grave; & the very church-yard where our darlings lie, when I gave a last look upon it [seemed] to cheer my thoughts. There I could think of life & immortality – the house only reminded me of desolation, gloom – emptiness, & cheerless silence – but why do I now turn to these thoughts? the morning is bright & I am more chearful today.

180. Sara Hutchinson to her cousin, Tom Monkhouse; Rydal Mount, 23 June [1813]

We are all very well and comfortable in our new residence notwithstanding the noise which little Willy makes with his strong shoes upon the carpetless floors – and we have so much pleasure from the beauty which is around us without doors that we care little for the want of ornament within. I do wish you could have come to see us this summer – I fancy that much as I enjoy this place that I should love it far better if all my friends had seen and enjoyed it with me – It is the admiration of every body – the <u>crack</u> spot, and the envy, of the whole neighbourhood . . .

We have had abundance of other visitors; I think we have scarcely been one day unengaged for the last month – You who are fond of visiting and parties should always come into this neighbourhood in June, or July, or August – and then you would think that we live <u>in</u> the world; especially if you came at the Regatta season when there are the most genteel Balls.

181. Sara Hutchinson to her cousin and sister-in-law, Mary Hutchinson; [Rydal Mount, 1 August 1813]

We have two nice new boats upon Rydale at command & it is a sweet Lake to fish upon – there is plenty of Perch & Pike & we take our Tea [bathing?] & load with fuel at the Island & dr[ink] Tea on the opposite shore for the Islands are so full of wood that there is no safety in making a fire upon them – and from the opposite shore in an evening we have the most beautiful scene among the Lakes. I know not whether ever you were there at sun-set – It is beautiful beyond all conception.

Almost at the same time as the Wordsworths moved into Rydal Mount, the office came vacant which William had identified as likely to suit him. This was the post of Distributor of Stamps for Westmorland, Whitehaven and the Penrith area of Cumberland; the stamps were not postage stamps but government-issue stamped paper, on which legal documents were written and newspapers printed. There was no official salary but the Distributor and his sub-distributors each took a percentage from the sale, after which it was William's duty to make a quarterly return to the Treasury. The clerk, John Carter, whom he appointed to do the administrative work, became a loyal friend and trusted servant, who was as happy to help in the garden as in proof-reading later editions of William's poems. He remained in the Wordsworth family service until his death.

182. Sara Hutchinson to her cousin, Tom Monkhouse; [Rydal Mount, 16 May 1813]

William sets off tomorrow to Appleby to take upon him his new office – The income of it we expect will be about 500£ per an[num] – and the duty very easy. He will keep a Clerk therefore we hope it will not very much interfere with his other pursuits –

183. Sara Hutchinson to her cousin, John Monkhouse; [Rydal Mount], 27 August [1813]

We are all pretty well – Mary is at times in tolerable spirits i.e. when she is obliged to exert herself – but when she is alone she seems to have gained nothing towards subduing her affliction; and she is as thin and looks as miserably as ever. William is over head & ears in his verses so what with them, & company, & stamps, he is more busy than agreeable – but we all enjoy our house & the situation – and are as happy as it is permitted to most people to be.

184. Dorothy Wordsworth to Catherine Clarkson; [Rydal Mount, c.14 September 1813]

William is at Penrith on Stamp business. Till the end of this Month he will be entirely engaged with it. He has done nothing else for weeks & been from home 2 thirds of his time. Afterwards all will be easy, little for him to do. He has got a clerk who promises well. He is to work in the garden also.

185. William Wordsworth to Sara Hutchinson; [Rydal Mount], 4 October 1813

This is the anniversary of my Wedding Day, and every year whether fraught with joy or sorrow has brought with it additional cause why I should thank God for my connection with your family. Mary joins with me in blessing you as we have blessed each other.

186. Dorothy Wordsworth to Catherine Clarkson; [Rydal Mount, 4 October 1813]

I look forward to long evenings & winter's quiet; & I hope they will not be succeeded by such a bustling summer as the last, though of that we have had no reason to complain, for it has not been of a very fatiguing nature nor such as exclude the intervention of serious thought, and harshly banish reflections which will have their course at one time or another, & which must be indulged[7] or tranquillity can never come; & it has been much better for all of us, especially Mary than perfect stillness would have been. Yet in looking back upon it I feel that much of the knowledge which I had formerly gained from Books has slipped from me, & it is grievous to think that hardly one new idea has come in by that means. This in itself would be no great evil, but the sorrows of this life weaken the memory so much that I find reading of far less use than it used to be to me, & if it were not that my feelings were as much alive as ever there would be a growing tendency for the mind to barrenness. But how I have wandered from my point. We shall have more leisure in Winter, & we never can have such a summer, for consider the work of removal – and we have had so many visitors who had not been to see us for a long time before, and who came to see the new place as much as to see us. Our domestic occupations are now comparatively few. We have fitted up the house completely – Willy goes to school – & there is no likelihood of more children to nurse; and though, if we could nurse them with the same chearful confidence as before I should be glad that Mary were likely to have another Child, I do not now wish it. I should so dread the anxieties attending the common diseases of Infancy – but there is no prospect of it –

Chapter Six

1814–19

187. *William Wordsworth to Tom Poole; Rydal Mount, 28 April 1814*

My poetical Labours have often suffered long interruptions; but I have at last resolved to send to the Press a portion of a Poem which if I live to finish it, I hope future times will "not willingly let die". These you know are the words of my Great Predecessor [Milton], and the depth of my feelings upon some subjects seems to justify me in the act of applying them to myself, while speaking to a Friend, who I know has always been partial to me.

188. *Dorothy Wordsworth to Catherine Clarkson; Keswick, 24 April [1814]*

. . . now, above all other time I should have wished to be at home, for William is actually printing 9 books of his long poem – it has been copied in my absence, & great alterations have been made some of which indeed I had an opportunity of seeing during my week's visit. But the printing has since been going on briskly, & not one proof-sheet has yet met my eyes. We are all most thankful that William has brought his mind to consent to printing so much of this work; for the MSS. were in such a state that, if it had pleased Heaven to take him from this world, they would have been almost useless. I do not think the book will be <u>published</u> before next winter; but, at the same time, will come out a new edition of his poems in two Volumes Octavo, & shortly after – Peter Bell, The White Doe, & Benjamin the Waggoner. This is resolved upon, and I think you may depend upon not being disappointed.

If William was only concerned about the confused state of his manuscripts, he could have chosen simply to make clean, fair copies of his hitherto unpublished poems. His decision to publish, of all things, part of 'The Recluse', is an indication that, however much he protested to the contrary, he had taken the reviews of his work to heart and intended to answer all those critics who ridiculed him for wasting his talent on small poems on unworthy subjects. *The Excursion*, pointedly sub-titled, *Being a Portion of The Recluse, A Poem*, would prove that he was capable of writing a grand philosophical poem and that he was still engaged with the subject. *The Excursion* was published in August 1814 while William, with a show of apparent indifference as to its reception, was escorting Mary and Sara on a six-week tour of Scotland, in the hope of restoring his wife's spirits which were still deeply depressed after the loss of her two children. The publication of *The Excursion* marked a turning point in William's reputation: the initial reaction of the professional critics was hostile and contemptuous, but a significant number of readers now began to write privately to William expressing their gratitude and admiration.

189. Sara Hutchinson to her cousin and sister-in-law, Mary Hutchinson; Callander, Wednesday [3 August 1814]

. . . dearest Mary is much improved by her journey; she truly enjoys herself; & William is happy that the journey has accomplished this his chief aim –

190. William Wordsworth to his sister, Dorothy; Perth, Sunday morning, 11 o'clock, 19 or 20 [actually 21] August [1814]

– I forgot to say, that I stepped yesterday evening in to a Booksellers shop with a <u>sneaking</u> hope that I might hear something about the Excursion, but not a word; on the contrary, inquiry of the Bookseller what a poetical parcel which he was then opening consisted of, he said, that it was a new Poem, entitled Lara, a most exquisite thing, supposed to be written, by Lord Byron, and that all the world were running wild after it; this parcel they had down by the Coach – they had received one the day before which was carried off immediately. Now dont you think I am quite a hero not to be envious . . .[?]

191. Francis Jeffrey, Review of The Excursion, *the* Edinburgh Review, *November 1814*

This will never do. It bears no doubt the stamp of the author's heart and fancy; but unfortunately not half so visibly as that of his peculiar system . . . It is longer, weaker, and tamer, than any of Mr. Wordsworth's other productions; with less boldness of originality, and less even of that extreme simplicity and lowliness of tone which wavered so prettily, in the Lyrical Ballads, between silliness and pathos. We have imitations of Cowper, and even of Milton here, engrafted on the natural drawl of the Lakers – and all diluted into harmony by that profuse and irrepressible wordiness which deluges all the blank verse of this school of poetry, and lubricates and weakens the whole structure of their style . . .

What Mr. Wordsworth's ideas of length are, we have no means of accurately judging; but we cannot help suspecting that they are liberal, to a degree that will alarm the weakness of most modern readers. As far as we can gather from the preface, the entire poem – or one of them, for we really are not sure whether there is to be one or two – is of a biographical nature; and is to contain the history of the author's mind, and of the origin and progress of his poetical powers, up to the period when they were sufficiently matured to qualify him for the great work on which he has been so long employed. Now, the quarto before us contains an account of one of his youthful rambles in the vales of Cumberland, and occupies precisely the period of three days; so that, by the use of a very powerful *calculus*, some estimate may be formed of the probable extent of the entire biography.

192. William Wordsworth to Abigail Hodgson; Rydal Mount, 26 September 1814

I have ever been indifferent to the opinions of <u>professed</u> Critics concerning my writings; and as much as I have slighted these, even so much have I been accustomed to value the judgements of persons speaking or writing from their hearts and inner Spirit. From these sources have flowed the language which you have addressed to me; it could not therefore but be acceptable; and I sincerely thank you, for the assurances which (through means of your Letter) I have received from one who is a Stranger to me, that in my Poem of the 'Excursion', I have moved the affections and excited the Imagination to salutary purposes. Assurances of this kind given by Friends, however judicious, are liable to a suspicion of personal partiality, but when they proceed from Strangers an Author is convinced that it is the book and the book alone to which he is indebted for the tribute of gratitude and praise which he receives. Great, then, must be the pleasure, when, as in the present case, there is accompanying evidence that fervent admiration is the result of comprehensive thought, and feelings at once deep and delicately discriminative. –

I have only to add that if you should ever be led to revisit the scenes which have proved delightful to you, I hope you will not pass my door without favoring me with a call.

193. Mary Wordsworth to her sister-in-law, Dorothy; [Rydal Mount, 29 October 1814]

You will be surprised to hear that W[illiam] has completed a new poem of about 130 odd lines – the subject is from one of the greek Stories Laodamia – he has written it very quickly – I told you about it in my last but he made me put it out again for he said it would never be done – if it was promised. We shall order the Printer to send you a Copy of the proof when it is struck off – it is to be placed at the end of 'the Affections' – I doubt he has done this so readily that he will not be contented till he has made himself ill doing more for he is reading & hunting among his books – for no <u>good purpose</u>, but do not name this. –

194. William Wordsworth to Catherine Clarkson; [Rydal Mount], New Year's Eve [1814]

. . . I am encouraged by finding so much of your letter devoted to the Excursion. I am glad that it has interested you; I expected no less, and I wish from my Soul that it had been a thousand times more deserving of your regard. In respect to its final destiny I have neither care nor anxiety being assured that if it be of God – it must stand; and that if the spirit of truth, "The Vision and the Faculty divine" be not in it, and so do not pervade it, it must perish. So let the wisest & best of the present generation and of Posterity decide the question. Thoroughly indifferent as I am on this point, I will acknowledge that I have a wish for the <u>sale</u> of the present Edition, partly to repay the Expense of our Scotch Tour, and still more to place the book within reach of those who can neither purchase nor procure it in its present expensive shape.[1]

195. Dorothy Wordsworth to Catherine Clarkson; [Rydal Mount, 27 February 1815]

Last night's post brought two sheets of the White Doe. William will do all he can to hurry it through the press that it may come out in the busy time of London gaieties. I have no anxiety about the fate of either the

Excursion or the White Doe beyond the Sale of the first Edition – and
that I do earnestly wish for. There are few persons who can afford to buy
a two guinea Book, merely for admiration of the Book. The edition has
no chance of being sold except to the wealthy; & they buy books much
more for fashion's sake than any thing else – and alas! we are not yet in
the fashion.

In May 1815, William, Mary and Sara went to London for the publication of his
new collected edition, which was simply called *Poems*, and *The White Doe of
Rylstone, or the Fate of the Nortons*. Though the reviews were as disappointing as
ever, William for the first time encountered several young men who, through
The Excursion, had become devotees of his poetry and would do all in their power
to convert others. Amongst them was Benjamin Robert Haydon, an aspiring
painter and sculptor, who persuaded the poet to have a plaster cast taken of his
face. This was a lengthy and undignified process which entailed sitting completely
still, with a towel wrapped over the head and straws in the nostrils to enable him
to breathe through the plaster.

196. Benjamin Robert Haydon, diary, 13 June [1815]

June 13. I had a cast made yesterday of Wordsworth's face. He bore it like
a philosopher. [John] Scott[2] was to meet him at Breakfast. Just as he came
in the Plaister was covered over. Wordsworth was sitting in the other
room in my dressing gown, with his hands folded, sedate, steady, & solemn.
I stepped in to Scott, & told him as a curiosity to take a peep, that he
might say the first sight he ever had of so great a poet was such a singular
one as this.

I opened the door slowly, & there he sat innocent & unconscious of
our plot against his dignity, unable to see or to speak with all the mysterious
silence of a spirit.

When he was relieved he came into breakfast with his usual cheerfulness,
and delighted & awed us by his illustrations & bursts of inspiration. At
one time he shook us both in explaining the principles of his system, his
views of man, & his objects in writing.

197. Francis Jeffrey, review of The White Doe, *the* Edinburgh Review, *October 1815*

This, we think, has the merit of being the very worst poem we ever saw imprinted in a quarto volume; and though it was scarcely to be expected, we confess, that Mr. Wordsworth, with all his ambition, should so soon have attained to that distinction, the wonder may perhaps be diminished when we state, that it seems to us to consist of a happy union of all the faults, without any of the beauties, which belong to this school of poetry. It is just such a work, in short, as some wicked enemy of the school might be supposed to have devised, on purpose to make it ridiculous; and when we first took it up, we could not help suspecting that some ill-natured critic had actually taken this harsh method of instructing Mr. Wordsworth, by example, in the nature of those errors, against which our precepts had been so often directed in vain. We had not gone far, however, till we felt intimately that nothing in the nature of a joke could be so insupportably dull . . .

198. Anonymous review of Poems (1815), *the* Monthly Review, *November 1815*

We are so thoroughly overwhelmed by the high and mighty tone of this author's prose [in his preface], that we really must have immediate recourse to his verse, in order to get rid of the painful humiliation and sense of inferiority which he inflicts on his readers. There, (Dieu merci;) we are comforted by silliness instead of system; by want of harmony instead of abundance of pride; by downright vacancy instead of grandeur and presumption.

199. Dorothy Wordsworth to Catherine Clarkson; [Rydal Mount], 15 August [1815]

I once thought The White Doe might have helped off the other [*The Excursion*], but I now perceive it can hardly help itself. It is a pity it was published in so expensive a form because some are thereby deprived of the pleasure of reading it; but however cheap his poems might be I am sure it will be very long before they have an extensive sale – nay it will not be while he is alive to know it. God be thanked he has no <u>mortification</u> on this head & I may safely say that those who are most nearly connected with him have not an atom of that species of disappointment. We have too [?rooted?noticed] a confidence in the purity of his intentions, & the power with which they are executed. His writings will live – will comfort the afflicted & animate the happy to purer happiness when we and our little cares are all forgotten.

200. William Wordsworth to Benjamin Robert Haydon; Rydal Mount, 21 December 1815

I sit down to perform my promise of sending you the first little Poem I might compose on my arrival at home – I am grieved to think what a time has elapsed since I last paid my devoirs to the Muses, and not less so to know that now in the depth of Winter when I hoped to resume my Labours, I continue to be called from home by unavoidable engagements. To morrow I quit Rydale Mount and shall be absent a considerable time.

201. William Wordsworth to a young friend, the Scottish poet, Robert Pearce Gillies; Rydal Mount, postmarked 9 April 1816

In the Champion another weekly journal, have appeared not long since, five sonnets of mine, all of them much superior to the one you have sent me [William's own *September, 1815*, which had appeared in *The Examiner* in February]. They will form part of a Publication which I sent to the Press three weeks ago, which you have been given to understand was a *long* work; but it is in fact *very short*, not more than 700 verses, altogether. The principal poem is 300 lines long, a Thanksgiving Ode, and the others refer almost exclusively to recent public events. The whole may be regarded as a *Sequel* to the Sonnets dedicated to Liberty; and accordingly I have given directions for its being printed uniform with my Poems, to admit of being bound up along with them. – I have also sent to press a Letter in Prose, occasioned by an intended Republication of Dr Currie's Life of Burns. I ought to tell you that the Sonnet you have sent me is thus corrected.

> For me *who under kindlier laws belong*
> To *Nature's tuneful quire*, this rustling etc
> Mid frost and snow *the instinctive* joys of song
> And nobler cares etc.

When these little things will be permitted to see the light, I know not; as my Publisher has not even condescended to acknowledge the Receipt of the MSS, which were sent three weeks ago; from this you may judge of the value which the Goods of the author of the Excursion at present bear in the estimation of the Trader. N'importe, if we have done well we shall not miss our reward; farewell, yours faithfully

W. Wordsworth

William's slim volume of political poems inspired by the downfall of Napoleon and the ending of the war against France, *Thanksgiving Ode, January 18, 1816: With Other Short Pieces, Chiefly Referring to Recent Events*, and his prose essay, *A Letter to a Friend of Burns*, were published in May 1816. On the 19th of that month, William's oldest brother, Richard, died of liver disease, aged forty-seven, leaving a young widow, a one-year-old son and a hugely indebted estate. The enormous responsibility of sorting out Richard's affairs fell principally on William as his brother's executor and de facto head of the family.

202. Dorothy Wordsworth to Catherine Clarkson; [Rydal Mount], 26 May 1816

. . . the contemplation of the death of a <u>Brother</u> was solemn & distressing – & when all was over we felt it deeply, though we were very thankful when God had taken him from his sufferings – & heartily do we join in Christopher's prayer that God may give us grace to profit by the awful event. We have seen very little of Richard for many years therefore as a companion his loss will not be great; but when we did meet he was always amiable & affectionate; & there has been in all our connections with him a perfect harmony. It is a great comfort to us that he died in the house of his Brother [Christopher, now Rector of Lambeth] & that his body rests where Christopher may probably also spend his latter days. He was to be buried in the Church at Lambeth on Friday. He made his will about three weeks before his death, & has appointed William & Christopher joint guardians to his Son & executors with his Wife.

203. William Wordsworth to John Scott, editor of The Champion; *Rydal Mount, 11 June 1816*

I am only just returned after more than a week's absence upon painful and anxious business, which has devolved upon me as trustee under the will of my eldest brother, recently deceased. He has left an only child, a boy sixteen months old, and a widow not twenty-seven years, and though his property is considerable, yet the affairs are in an intricate and perplexed situation, so that much of my time and more of my thoughts will in future be taken up by them; and I need scarcely say to you that I am wholly inexperienced in things of this kind . . .

The queries you put to me upon the connection between genius and irregularity of conduct may probably induce me to take up the subject again, and yet it scarcely seems necessary. No man can claim indulgence for his transgressions on the score of his sensibilities, but at the expense of his credit for intellectual powers. All men of *first* rate genius have been as distinguished for dignity, beauty, and propriety of moral conduct. But we often find the faculties and qualities of the mind not well balanced; something of prime importance is left short, and hence confusion and disorder. On the one hand it is well that dunces should not arrogate to themselves a pharisaical superiority, because they avoid the vices and faults which they see men of talent fall into. They should not be permitted to believe that they have more understanding merely on that account, but should be taught that they are preserved probably by having less feeling, and being consequently less liable to temptation. On the other hand, the man of genius ought to know that the cause of his vices is, in fact, his deficiencies, and not, as he fondly imagines, his superfluities and superiorities. All men ought to be judged with charity and forbearance after death has put it out of their power to explain the motives of their actions, and especially men of acute sensibility and lively passions. This was the scope of my letter to Mr. Gray [*A Letter to a Friend of Burns*]. Burns has been cruelly used, both dead and alive . . . He asked for bread – no, he did not *ask* it, he endured the want of it with silent fortitude – and ye gave him a stone. It is worse than ridiculous to see the people of Dumfries coming forward with their pompous mausoleum, they who persecuted and reviled him with such low-minded malignity.

204. William Wordsworth to Henry Crabb Robinson; Rydal Mount, 2 August 1816

I am glad that you were pleased with my Odes &c [?] They were poured out with much feeling; but from mismanagement of myself the labour of making some verbal corrections cost me more health and strength than anything of that sort ever did before. I have written nothing since. –

and as to Publishing I shall give it up; as no-body will buy what I send forth, nor can I expect it seeing what stuff the public appetite is set upon.

205. *Sara Hutchinson to her cousin, John Monkhouse; [Rydal Mount], Tuesday evening [6 August 1816]*

. . . I guess that you have had pleasure in the Odes &c – as Mary, Tom, & all sensible people have had who have the necessary requisite, <u>feeling</u>, to enjoy them – but yet I dare say that few as were the copies printed they will not sell – & yet there is no doubt that William's reputation gains ground every day . . . William has been so much engaged with his Ex[ecuto]rship – his [Stamps?] & visitors that he has never composed a line since the Odes were written – and there is little prospect of leisure for him for some time to come – for he is not like Southey that he can write whatever may be the interruptions –

206. *Sara Hutchinson to her cousin, Tom Monkhouse; Rydal Mount, 21 February [1817]*

Since I last wrote there has been some Letters from London which appear to make William's presence there necessary – however we think they may do very well without him – Dr W[ordsworth, i.e., Christopher] must bestir himself – and I am sure he will do it far better for W[illiam] is so little fit for business that it worries him beyond all measure – These affairs of his Brother and some plaguy Stamp concerns have deranged him in a piteous manner – when he is thus employed – he is in a fever the whole time and unable to sleep – besides the expence of the journey is a serious affair – the times being so bad and he & D[orothy] having been so long kept out of a part of their income by Richard's embarrassments & demise. I should like very well to come with him – but I must be a little richer before I can venture upon another journey. Want of Cash also will prevent D[orothy] & I taking our long-talked-of trip to Paris – unless we can get a lottery prize or some such honey-fall.

207. William Wordsworth to Benjamin Robert Haydon; Rydal Mount, 20 January 1817

Your account of young Keats interests me not a little; and the Sonnet [Keats's 'Great Spirits now on earth are sojourning'] appears to be of good promise of course neither You nor I being both so highly complimented in the Composition can be deemed judges altogether impartial – but it is assuredly vigorously conceived and exprest; Leigh Hunts Compliment is well deserved – and the Sonnet is very agreeably concluded. – – Your account of [John] Scott causes me deep concern – I am sorry that he is about to publish upon so melancholy an occasion – His verses I fear will have too large an infusion of pain in them. to be either generally pleasing or serviceable whatever degree of genius they may exhibit. – Thelwall the Politician many years ago lost a Daughter about the age of Scott's child – I knew her She was a charming Creature – Thelwalls were the agonies of an unbeliever, and he expressed them vigorously in several Copies of harmonious blank verse, – a metre which he writes well for he has a good ear. These effusions of anguish were published, but though they have great merit, one cannot read them but with much more pain than pleasure. – You probably know how much I have suffered in this way myself; having lost within the short space of half a year two delightful Creatures a girl & a boy of the several ages of four[3] & six and a half. This was four years ago – but they are perpetually present to my eyes – I do not mourn for them; yet I am sometimes weak enough to wish that I had them again. They are laid side by side in Grasmere Churchyard – on the headstone of one is that beautiful text of Scripture "Suffer the little Children to come unto me and forbid them not for of such is the Kingdom of Heaven". And on that of the other are inscribed the following verses,

> Six months to six years added, he remained
> Upon this sinful earth, by sin unstained;
> O blessed Lord whose mercy then removed
> A Child whom every eye that look'd on loved,
> Support us – teach us calmly to resign
> What we possess'd – and now is wholly Thine!

These verses I have transcribed because they are embued with that sort of consolation which you say Scott is deprived of. – It is the only support to be depended upon, & happy are they to whom it is vouchsafed –

208. William Wordsworth to Daniel Stuart; Rydal Mount, 7 April 1817

The suspension of the Habeas Corpus Act[4] is a measure approved by all the well disposed, who are a large majority of the influential part of the Country. In fact also the spirit among the labouring classes (with the exception of the populace of Carlisle) is incomparably better than it was in 1794 & 5. The agricultural population of Cumberland and Westmoreland is at present sound; but I would not engage that it will continue so, in case rebellion should get the upper hand in other parts of the Island. a Revolution will, I think, be staved off for the present, nor do I even apprehend that the disposition to rebellion may not without difficulty be suppressed, notwithstanding the embarrassments and heavy distresses of the times. Nevertheless I am like you an alarmist, and for this reason, I see clearly that the principal ties which kept the different classes of society in a vital & harmonious dependence upon each other have, within these 30 years either been greatly impaired or wholly dissolved. Everything has been put up to market and sold for the highest price it would bring. Farmers used formerly to be attached to their Landlords, & labourers to their Farmers who employed them. all that kind of feeling has vanished – in like manner, the connexion between the trading & landed interests of country towns undergoes no modification whatsoever from personal feeling, whereas within my memory it was almost wholly governed by it. a country squire, or substantial yeoman, used formerly to resort to the same shops which his father had frequented before him, and nothing but a serious injury real or supposed would have appeared to him a justification for breaking up a connection which was attended with substantial amity, and interchanges of hospitality from generation to generation. all this moral cement is dissolved, habits and prejudices are broken & rooted up; nothing being substituted in their place but a quickened selfinterest – with more extensive views, – & wider dependencies, – but more lax in proportion as they are wider – The ministry will do well if they keep things quiet for the present, but if our present constitution in church & state is to last, it must rest as heretofore upon a moral basis. That they who govern the country must be something superior to mere financiers and political economists.

209. Dorothy Wordsworth to Catherine Clarkson; [Rydal Mount], 13 April [1817]

William has been sadly harassed by my poor brother Richard's affairs – delays of lawyers – difficulties in getting debts paid – threatenings of a Chancery Suit – perplexing letters – everything to disturb him, and all new – and what is worse one can see no end of it; but I think he begins to take things more quietly, &, for the first time during more than a year & a half he has taken to his old employments. To-day he has composed a Sonnet, & in our minds we sing 'Oh! be joyful!' It has indeed been most melancholy to see him bowed down by oppressive cares, which have fallen upon him through mismanagement, dilatoriness, or negligence. alas! that is the truth.

In the spring of 1817, Robert Southey was in Paris and, at the request of the Wordsworths, he went to visit Annette Vallon and her daughter, Caroline. William had not seen either of them since August 1802, when they had spent six weeks together at Calais during the brief Peace of Amiens. Since then they had continued to keep in touch by letter and William had supported them with an annual remittance of £35, but plans to attend Caroline's wedding to Jean Baptiste Baudouin in February 1816 had fallen through because of the unstable situation in France and the Wordsworths' financial difficulties. As Southey knew the whole story and had met Baudouin's brother, Eustace, when he was a French prisoner of war in England, he was commissioned to visit the family and William's first grandchild, Louise Marie Caroline Dorothée Baudouin.

210. Robert Southey to his wife, Edith; Paris, 16 May 1817

I got to M. Beaudouins brothers having seen half Paris on the way. I should tell you that Wordsworth in giving me his address had told me what I knew before, but he added that it would not be necessary nor pleasant to myself to appear to be acquainted with it. The daughter [Caroline] was the only person at home when I was admitted – she did not know my name, and spoke no English. I made myself understood with my French, explained that I [had] come to inquire to M. Eustace B[audouin] whom I had seen in Cumberland with Mr. W[ordsworth]. She immediately said M[r]. W[ordsworth] was her father, and we had a tete-a-tete of about an hour long, much like a scene in a sentimental comedy. She is a very interesting young woman, with much more of natural feeling than of French manners, and surprizingly like John Wordsworth [William's son], much more so than his own sister [Dora]. The little French Dorothy is very like her mother, a sweet infant, in perfect health and good humour. I waited some time in expectation that the husband would come in, and when I could afford to wait no longer, I promised to breakfast with them the next morning. She wept a good deal and was very much affected during our conversation . . .

[At nine o'clock next morning, Southey returned.] The mother [Annette] was there to meet me – not a word of English could any of the three speak, and I had to make my way in French which I did to admiration. M. Beaudouin is like his brother, but considerably taller, very fond of his child, a fair presumption that he is not less fond of his wife. She on her part (and her mother also) speaks of him as the best of husbands. We parted sworn friends, and I was stopt on the way down stairs to take leave of the baby, who had been pleased to smile very graciously upon us and take me into favour. They live in small lodgings pleasantly situated. I breakfasted in their fashion upon meat pie, gruyere cheese, and white wine, after which the mother made me drink coffee, would have made me drink tea also if I had not obstinately refused, and proposed *punch*. This was a curious visit. It lasted about two hours, after which I returned home and began this letter.

William's poetic reputation at home was now such that he was sought out by portrait painters. Mary's wealthy London cousin, Tom Monkhouse, commissioned a portrait from Richard Carruthers, a young northern painter, which would be widely reproduced. The following winter, while William was on a visit to London, his friend, Haydon, produced a striking chalk drawing which became known in family circles as 'the Brigand', and included William's head amongst other famous literati in the crowd paying homage in his vast picture, 'Christ's Entry into Jerusalem'.

211. Sara Hutchinson to her cousin, Tom Monkhouse; [Rydal Mount], 28 August [1817]

– William was engaged at home with Mr Carruthers, and as neither you or he could attend Joanna to the [Regatta] ball she did not go, though we learn from Tillbrooke & his friend that there was a great lack of Ladies – Before I have done with Balls let me tell you that there is to be one on the 9th of next month at Kendal at which Joanna intends to be, and

<u>William</u> also. It is on the Evening of the Book Club dinner at which all the Gentlemen of the county attend, & William always goes as a compliment to Lord L[onsdale] – and also for the benefit of the Landlord of the King's Arms – therefore Joanna intends to <u>go along</u> – & she hopes you will be here in time to meet them at Kendal & attend upon both these important occasions – it is reckoned the <u>genteelest</u> Ball at Kendal – no <u>Towns people</u> attend!!!!!!!

Mr Carruthers has nearly finished one picture of W[illia]m – but he is not satisfied himself neither are <u>we</u> though the picture will be thought like by all common observers – but he erred in chusing the attitude – one in which William is never seen – and the face is too fat & the expression unnatural – but this was not the Artist's fault for W[illia]m himself sate, as Joanna told him, in 'a <u>perpetual smirk</u>' – and would not put on one Schedoni glance[5] – however C[arruthers] we are almost certain will succeed in the next which he commences tomorrow –

212. Dorothy Wordsworth to Catherine Clarkson; Rydal Mount, 16 October 1817

William has sate for his picture, written a few small poems, entertained company, enjoyed the country, & paid some visits & so his summer has been passed; he intends to work hard at the Recluse in Winter –

213. Benjamin Robert Haydon, Autobiography, *[London, 28 December 1817]*

In December Wordsworth was in town, and as Keats wished to know him I made up a party to dinner of Charles Lamb, Wordsworth, Keats and [Tom] Monkhouse, his friend, and a very pleasant party we had . . .

On December 28th the immortal dinner came off in my painting-room, with [Christ's Entry into] Jerusalem towering up behind us as a background. Wordsworth was a fine cue, and we had a glorious set-to, – on Homer, Shakespeare, Milton and Virgil. Lamb got exceedingly merry and exquisitely witty; and his fun in the midst of Wordsworth's solemn intonations of oratory was like the sarcasm and wit of the fool in the intervals of Lear's passion. He made a speech and voted me absent, and made them drink my health. 'Now,' said Lamb, 'you old lake poet, you rascally poet, why do you call Voltaire dull?' We all defended Wordsworth, and affirmed there was a state of mind when Voltaire would be dull. 'Well,' said Lamb, 'here's Voltaire – the Messiah of the French nation, and a very proper one too.'

He then, in a strain of humour beyond description, abused me for putting Newton's head into my picture, – 'a fellow,' said he, 'who believed nothing unless it was as clear as the three sides of a triangle.' And then he and Keats agreed he had destroyed all the poetry of the rainbow by reducing it to the prismatic colours. It was impossible to resist him, and we all drank 'Newton's health, and confusion to mathematics'. It was delightful to see the good-humour of Wordsworth in giving in to all our frolics without affectation and laughing as heartily as the best of us. By this time other friends joined, amongst them poor Ritchie . . .

In the morning of this delightful day, a gentleman, a perfect stranger, had called on me. He said he knew my friends, had an enthusiasm for Wordsworth and begged I would procure him the happiness of an introduction. He told me he was a comptroller of stamps, and often had correspondence with the poet. I thought it a liberty; but still, as he seemed a gentleman, I told him he might come.

When we retired to tea we found the comptroller. In introducing him to Wordsworth I forgot to say who he was. After a little time the comptroller looked down, looked up and said to Wordsworth, 'Don't you think, sir, Milton was a great genius?' Keats looked at me, Wordsworth looked at the comptroller. Lamb who was dozing by the fire turned round and said, 'Pray, sir, did you say Milton was a great genius?' 'No, sir; I asked Mr Wordsworth if he were not.' 'Oh,' said Lamb, 'then you are a silly fellow.' 'Charles! my dear Charles!' said Wordsworth; but Lamb, perfectly innocent of the confusion he had created, was off again by the fire.

After an awful pause the comptroller said, 'Don't you think Newton a great genius?' I could not stand it any longer. Keats put his head into my books. Ritchie squeezed in a laugh. Wordsworth seemed asking himself, 'Who is this?' Lamb got up, and taking a candle, said, 'Sir, will you allow me to look at your phrenological development?'[6] He then turned his back on the poor man, and at every question of the comptroller he chaunted –

> Diddle diddle dumpling, my son John
> Went to bed with his breeches on.

The man in office, finding Wordsworth did not know who he was, said in a spasmodic and half-chuckling anticipation of assured victory, 'I have

had the honour of some correspondence with you, Mr Wordsworth.'
'With me, sir?' said Wordsworth, 'not that I remember.' 'Don't you, sir?
I am a comptroller of stamps.' There was a dead silence; – the comptroller
evidently thinking that was enough. While we were waiting for Wordsworth's reply, Lamb sung out

> Hey diddle diddle
> The cat and the fiddle.

'My dear Charles!' said Wordsworth, –

> Diddle diddle dumpling, my son John,

chaunted Lamb, and then rising, exclaimed, 'Do let me have another look
at that gentleman's organs.' Keats and I hurried Lamb into the painting-
room, shut the door and gave way to inextinguishable laughter. Monkhouse followed and tried to get Lamb away. We went back but the
comptroller was irreconcilable. We soothed and smiled and asked him to
supper. He stayed though his dignity was sorely affected. However, being
a good-natured man, we parted all in good-humour, and no ill effects
followed.

All the while, until Monkhouse succeeded, we could hear Lamb
struggling in the painting-room and calling at intervals, 'Who is that
fellow? Allow me to see his organs once more.'

It was indeed an immortal evening. Wordsworth's fine intonation as he
quoted Milton and Virgil, Keats' eager inspired look, Lamb's quaint
sparkle of lambent humour, so speeded the stream of conversation, that
in my life I never passed a more delightful time. All our fun was within
bounds. Not a word passed that an apostle might not have listened to. It
was a night worthy of the Elizabethan age, and my solemn Jerusalem
flashing up by the flame of the fire, with Christ hanging over us like a
vision, all made up a picture which will long glow upon –

> that inward eye
> Which is the bliss of solitude.[7]

*214. Sara Hutchinson to her niece, Dora; [from Tom Monkhouse's] Mortimer
Street, [London], 4 January 1818*

Mr Carruthers was here yesterday Evening. He brought your Fathers
Picture with him which is nearly finished & put into a frame – but it does

not strike the London People as being such a good likeness, because here your father is not in his thoughtful way and therefore the picture is not lively enough – indeed it does not seem half so like him as it did, even to me – beside your father looks so well & rosy, that the picture appears sickly. Mr C[arruthers] was so good as [to] try to make a pencil drawing of your Mother last night, but it is not like her – Mr Haydon intends to make a chalk drawing of your Father for your Mother –

The Wordsworths' visit to London was brought to a close by the news that there was about to be a general election. William was determined to repay the generosity of his patron, Lord Lonsdale, by doing all he could to further the Lowther cause and secure the election of his two sons as Members of Parliament. Though the fact that he held a government post legally prohibited him from overt intervention, 'William continues to imagine that he can be of use in Westmorland', as his wife wearily remarked. In fact, his local knowledge made him an invaluable adviser to the successful Lowther campaign, though he was forthright in expressing his opinions.

215. *William Wordsworth to Lord Lonsdale; Coleorton Hall, 21 January 1818*

I have . . . a firm conviction in my own mind, that if there did not exist in different parts of the Island that sort of political Power and Influence which your Lordship as a great Land holder possesses, the Government would be immediately subverted, and the whole Country thrown into confusion and misery. What else but the stability and weight of a large Estate with proportionate influence in the House of Commons can counterbalance the democratic activity of the wealthy commercial and manufacturing Districts? It appears to a superficial Observer, warm from contemplating the theory of the Constitution, that the political power of the great Land holders ought by every true lover of his Country to be strenuously resisted; but I would ask a well intentioned native of Westmorland or Cumberland who had fallen into this mistake, if he could point out any arrangement by which Jacobinism can be frustrated, except by the existence of large Estates continued from generation to generation in particular families, with parliamentary power in proportion. We have a striking proof of the efficacy of this state of things on the present occasion, where we see such a large body of all that is conspicuously respectable in Westmorland or connected with it rallying round your Lordship on the first alarm – –

216. William Wordsworth to Lord Lonsdale; Rydal Mount, 18 February [1818]

The more I see of this Contest the more I regret that circumstances should
have thrown the representation upon both your Sons. This is unpalatable
to many respectable people well-wishers to your Lordships Family; and
forces them to acknowledge a shew of reason in the opposite Party which
they would otherwise deny. 'Two Brothers, and these Sons of a Peer, for
one County!' is a frequent exclamation from quarters entitling it to regard.
Your Lordship is aware of the considerations which prompts [*sic*] me to
speak thus without reserve. I am fully persuaded that this unfortunate
circumstance is the only tenable ground of the enemy. – Notwithstanding
the clamor from some despicable quarters, your Lordship is loved honored
and respected throughout Westmorland, and your influence is looked up
to with satisfaction and pleasure by a vast majority of what is respectable
in all ranks of the County.

217. William Wordsworth to Lord Lonsdale; [Rydal Mount], 14 March 1818

If you continue to read the Kendal Chronicle you must be greatly
concerned to see that the Liberty of the Press should be so grossly abused.
– This Paper as now conducted reminds me almost at every sentence of
those which I used to read in France during the heat of the Revolution
– Notwithstanding the satisfactory result of the Canvass, there is a <u>ferment
of disaffection</u> in the County – excited by these Libellers and others who
talk as prompted by them; and I am convinced, at this moment there is
such hostility among the lower Ranks, including servants, day-labourers,
handicraftsmen, small shopkeepers, to whom must be added many who
from education and situation in life ought to know better, that if it went
by counting heads Mr B[rougham: the Whig candidate] would sweep all
before him, and be triumphant to a degree which I fear to contemplate.
– I will go farther and express my belief that if the Power of incitement
which these seditious doctrines have derived from the events now pending
in West[morla]nd were spread all over England the Government would
be in imminent danger. – Mr B[rougham] may at this moment be
regarded as the most prominent Demagogue in the Kingdom – His visit
to West[morla]nd is anxiously looked for by his adherents. I submit, but
with due deference, to your Lordship's consideration, whether <u>this</u> would

not be an eligible time to make known his former advances to turn the Lowther interest to his own profit – [8]

218. *Sara Hutchinson to Tom Monkhouse; [Playford Hall, Ipswich], Monday 13 April [1818]*

I have had several Letters from the north since I last wrote to you. Dorothys all full of election matters. I wish it were over for they are all possessed by it – and, as Mary says, it is pitiable that William should be thus diverted from his natural pursuits.

219. *Mary Wordsworth to her sister, Sara Hutchinson; [Rydal Mount, 1 December 1818]*

W[illiam] is at this moment sitting, as he has been all the morn[in]g, except while he dashed off a letter to Till[brook] with his feet on the Fender & his verses in his hand – nay now they have dropped upon his knee & he is asleep from sheer exhaustion – he has worked so long – he has written 21 Sonnets (including [2 o]ld ones) on the river Duddon – they all [to]gether comprise one Poem – he has also written 3 on the Yorkshire Caves by Westall[9] – you have heard of them I dare say – I will say no more of these till you see them – for they are too much to transcribe.

220. *Dr Christopher Wordsworth to his brother, William; Sundridge, Kent, 14 December 1818*

I looked to see something in your Letter about Poetry: and hoped for some tidings of my friend Benjamin the Waggoner – or Peter Bell – or something else as good. – In my retirement here, I read no poetry so much as yours: and none with so much delight, and gratitude to the author. I have daily had great enjoyment, in the wintery evenings, in the Excursion – and long so much to see it in octavo, that though I am not rich, and though my debts, though diminishing, are still large – (£600 to Mr Lloyd only), I will yet readily give £50 towards forwarding any edition of it in 8vo – or towards a little edition of the White Doe – or any editions of Benjamin the Waggoner – if you would like that better –

221. William Wordsworth to his brother, Christopher; [Rydal Mount], 1 January 1819

The Wordsworths are too poor to print at their own cost for the gratification of others – many thanks, however, for your good intentions and
wishes – ever most affectionately

Yours WW

222. Mary Wordsworth to her cousin, Tom Monkhouse; [Rydal Mount], 12 January [1819]

I am glad you have spent so pleasant a Xmas. We have had a noisy time
of it & a great deal of pleasure reflected upon us by the mirth of these 3 Girls
[the three poets' teenage daughters, Dora Wordsworth, Edith Southey and
Sara Coleridge], who are as happy as the day is long – We had a splendid
Ball last week & much I thought you would have enjoyed it had you been
here – The dining room was ridded of all superfluous furniture & dressed
out in Christmas's gayest garb – a festoon of glittering Holly with its red
berries &c &c was carried round the walls – the floor was chalked with
great taste, & all that youthful fancy could invent in a humble way to
make the thing splendid, was not wanting –

223. William Wordsworth to Lord Lonsdale; Rydal Mount, 13 January 1819

It was lately notified to me that my name has been inserted by the Lord
Chancellor in the Comm[issio]n of the Peace for West[morla]nd [i.e., as
a Justice of the Peace]: As an additional proof of Your Lordship's favorable
opinion, this official communication of an event which your last Letter
led me to expect could not but be gratifying to me – I wish I could add
that I feel myself properly qualified for the undertaking, and that I could
get rid of those apprehensions which they who know me better than I
know myself are perpetually pressing upon me, that my literary exertions
will suffer more than I am aware of from this engagement. They ground
their opinion upon an infirmity of which I am conscious; viz; that
whatever pursuit I direct my attention to, is apt to occupy my mind
too exclusively – – But why should I trouble Your Lordship with
these personal considerations? – I am anxious to discharge my obligations to society, and if it should continue to be thought proper for

me, in the failure of other eligible Persons, to attempt to be serviceable in this way, I must be upon my guard to suffer as little injury as possible.

224. William Wordsworth to Francis Wrangham; Rydal Mount, 19 February 1819

I find it difficult to speak publicly of good men while alive especially if they are persons who have power – the world ascribes the eulogy to interested motives or to an adulatory Spirit which I detest. But of Lord Lonsdale I will say to you that I do not think there exists in England a man of any rank more anxiously desirous to discharge his Duty in that station of life to which it has pleased God to call him: His thought and exertions are constantly directed to that object, & the more he is known the more is he beloved & respected and admired.

225. Dr Christopher Wordsworth to his brother, William; Hampstead, 17 April 1819

I long to hear of [your] getting on with the Recluse – and grieve therefore to think of your time being taken up in Executorship business, and in Justice Business (but this I hope is a premature report), and above all, I hope that (as you do not mention it) you have not persevered in the plan of instructing [your son] John yourself. Really your time is too valuable for such occupations –

226. George Ticknor, Professor of Belles Lettres, Harvard University, Life, Letters and Journals, [March 1818]

Wordsworth knew from Southey that I was coming, and therefore met me at the door and received me heartily. He is about fifty-three or four [he was actually almost forty-eight], with a tall, ample, well-proportioned frame, a grave and tranquil manner, a Roman cast of appearance, and Roman dignity and simplicity. He presented me to his wife, a good, very plain woman, who seems to regard him with reverence and affection, and to his sister, not much younger than himself, with a good deal of spirit and, I should think, more than common talent and knowledge. I was at home with them at once, and we went out like friends together to scramble up the mountains, and enjoy the prospects and scenery . . . We returned to dinner, which was very simple, for, though he has an office under the government and a patrimony besides, yet each is inconsiderable . . .

His conversation surprised me by being so different from all I had anticipated. It was exceedingly simple, strictly confined to subjects he understood familiarly, and more marked by plain good-sense than by anything else. When, however, he came upon poetry and reviews, he was the Khan of Tartary again, and talked as metaphysically and extravagantly as ever Coleridge wrote; but, excepting this, it was really a consolation to hear him. It was best of all, though, to see how he is loved and respected in his family and neighbourhood . . .

The peasantry treated him with marked respect, the children took off their hats to him, and a poor widow in the neighbourhood sent to him to come and talk to her son, who had been behaving ill . . .

In the evening he showed me his manuscripts, the longest a kind of poetical history of his life, which, in the course of about two octavo volumes of manuscript, he has brought to his twenty-eighth year, and of which the "Excursion" is a fragment. It is in blank-verse, and, as far as I read, what has been published is a fair specimen of what remains in manuscript. He read me "Peter Bell, the Potter," a long tale, with many beauties but much greater defects; and another similar story, "the Waggoner." . . . The whole amused me a good deal; it was a specimen of the lake life, doctrines, and manners, more perfect than I had found at Southey's, and, as such, was very curious. We sat up, therefore, late, and talked a great deal about the living poets. Of [Walter] Scott he spoke with much respect as a man, and of his works with judicious and sufficient praise. For [Thomas] Campbell he did not seem to have so much regard; and for Lord Byron none at all, since, though he admired his talent, he seemed to have a deep-rooted abhorrence of his character, and besides, I thought, felt a little bitterness against him for having taken something of his own *lakish* manner lately, and, what is worse, borrowed some of his thoughts. On the whole, however, he seemed fairly disposed to do justice to his contemporaries and rivals . . .

227. William Wordsworth to John Forbes Mitchell, treasurer of the fund for building a national monument to Robert Burns; Rydal Mount, 21 April 1819

. . . notwithstanding a cordial approbation of the <u>feeling</u> which has prompted the undertaking, and a genuine sympathy in admiration with the Gentlemen who have subscribed towards a Monument for Burns, I cannot unite my humble efforts with theirs in promoting <u>this</u> object. – Sincerely can I affirm that my respect for the motives which have swayed these Gentlemen has urged me to trouble you with a brief statement of the reasons of my dissent. In the first place, Eminent poets appear to me to be a Class of men who less than any other's stand in need of such marks of distinction, and hence I infer that this mode of acknowledging their merits is one for which they would not in general be themselves solicitous. Burns did indeed erect a monument to Ferguson, but I apprehend his gratitude took this course because he felt that Ferguson had been prematurely cut off, and that his fame bore no proportion to his deserts. In neither of these particulars can the fate of Burns justly be said to resemble that of his Predecessor, his years indeed were few, but numerous enough to allow him to spread his name far and wide, and to take permanent root in the affections of his Countrymen: in short, he has raised for himself a Monument so conspicuous, and of such imperishable materials; as to render a local fabric of Stone superfluous, and therefore comparatively insignificant.

Chapter Seven

1819–22

228. *Sara Hutchinson to her cousin, John Monkhouse; [Rydal Mount], 7 May [1819]*

You will have seen by the Newspapers that Peter Bell is published – as also a spurious Peter[1] who made his appearance a week before the true one – Some People attribute the latter to H. Smith (one of the Authors of the Rejected Addresses) but I believe it is Hazlitt (tho' W[illia]m says H[azlitt] could <u>not</u> write anything so foolish) because there are some expressions & rhymes, in the extracts which we have seen, that occur <u>only in Peter Bell</u> which Hazlitt saw many years ago – besides we find that Hazlitt's new Lectures have been printing at the same time & at the same office with William's Peter – The false one is very stupid, but I have no doubt that it has helped the sale of the true one – which has nearly all been sold in about a week, and a new Ed[ition] is called for – Some good-natured person – the Author no doubt – sent William a No[.] of the "Literary Gazette" in which is a most abominably abusive critique – it can only be written from personal <u>malice</u> – for the most beautiful passages are selected for ridicule – in many cases the very ones which are pointed out for admiration, in the complimentary Letters which W[illia]m has received – however, notwithstanding, it is exactly what I expected – and I wish you could see the article – for after all they confess indirectly that he influences all the poetry <u>in the Country</u> – This critique made us advise him to publish the Waggoner, just to give them another bone to pick, which he has consented to – and it will come out as soon as possible I hope with the second Ed[ition] of Peter.

229. *William Wordsworth to Lord Lonsdale; Rydal Mount, 22 May [1819]*

My bookseller will in a few days break in upon your Lordship with another little Piece in verse of mine [*The Waggoner*]. The subject is slight – but the Poem was written con amore, and in the opinion of my friends with

Spirit. – Peter Bell has furnished abundant employment to the Witlings and the small critics, who have been warring with me for more than 20 years, and seem more bitter than ever – Somebody, however, must have been pleased, for the Edition was sold in a few days.

230. *Anonymous review of* Peter Bell *in the* Monthly Review, *August 1819*

All past, present, and (probably) future performances, by the same author, must sink into nothing before *Peter Bell*. No lisping was ever more distinctly lisped than the versification of this poem ; and no folly was ever more foolishly boasted than that of the writer, whether in style or subject matter. The former is the style of Mr Newbery's best gilded little volumes for nurseries; the latter is subject for any of the Cheap Repository Tracts, intended for the reformation of the lowest orders . . . Can Englishmen write, and Englishmen read, such drivel, such daudling, impotent drivel, – as this . . . [?]

231. *Review of* Peter Bell *in the* Eclectic Review, *July 1819*

In spite of the imbecilities of style which run through the narrative, and in spite of our determination not to allow *Peter Bell*, the potter, to gain upon our feelings, the Poet got the better of us, and we closed the Tale resolved, even at the imminent risk of being set down for *Lakers* ourselves, to do its Author justice.

232. *Review of* The Waggoner *in the* Eclectic Review, *July 1819*

Mr. Wordsworth has one chance of being read by posterity. It rests upon his finding some judicious friend to do for him the kind office which Pope did for Parnell, and which has probably saved his fame. If Wordsworth's best pieces could be collected into one volume, some of his early lyrics, a few of his odes, his noble sonnets, all his landscape sketches, and the best parts of the *Excursion*, while his idiots and his waggoners were collected into a bonfire on the top of Skiddaw, then 'Sybilline leaves' would form a most precious addition to our literature, and his name and his poetry would live, when his system, and his absurdities, and his critics should be forgotten.

233. Review of The Waggoner *in the* Monthly Review, *September 1819*

For ourselves, we confess honestly that we consider 'the Waggoner' to be one of the best and most ingenious of *all* Mr. Wordsworth's poems. It manifests, occasionally, a classical style of language and versification which is wholly superior to his native manner; and, were it not for the internal evidence of several instances of extreme folly, we should really be disposed to suspect that some lighter and more joyous hand had here been at work.

234. William Wordsworth to Lord Lonsdale; Rydal Mount, 16 June 1819

– The Kendal Chronicle has been taking great pains in no less than four numbers to persuade my neighbours that I am a very bad Poet; from which I conclude that they do not much like me as a Politician –

235. Sara Hutchinson to her cousin, John Monkhouse; Rydal Mount, 25 July [1819]

– By the bye we females have a great curiosity to see the Reviews &c. of W[illia]ms Poems &c in Blackwood's Magazine; but [as] W[illia]m will not suffer it to come into the House with his knowledge <u>we must smuggle it</u> – So if <u>you take it in</u> bring those Nos. – but do not buy it I entreat you if you have it not already for it is not worth the money –

236. Mary Wordsworth to her cousin, Tom Monkhouse; [Rydal Mount, postmarked 8 November 1819]

We are looking forward to a very quiet winter – if William's eyes will allow it I trust that it may be a profitable one –

237. Sara Hutchinson to her cousin, John Monkhouse; [Rydal Mount, postmarked ?17 December 1819]

William intends to publish a batch of small poems immediately – & when a new Ed[ition] of the other poems is called for, which will be in a few months, these with the White Doe, Benjamin, Peter, & the Odes, will make a third volume – this ed[ition] will be a small octavo in a cheaper style – then <u>he says</u> he will never trouble himself with anything more but the Recluse –

William's good intentions with regard to 'The Recluse' were ephemeral. The death of George III on 29 January 1820 precipitated another general election and almost as soon as the campaigning was over, William, Mary and Dorothy set off on the tour of the Continent which they had all dreamed about for so many years. It would retrace much of the route of William's pedestrian tour of 1790, taking them through France, where they would visit Annette and Caroline, Switzerland and the Low Countries. Their companions would be Mary's cousin, Tom Monkhouse, his bride, Jane, whom he married two days before they set off, and her sister. William's friend, Henry Crabb Robinson, would join them in Switzerland. Before they could go, however, William was determined to see through the press his two latest works, *The River Duddon, A Series of Sonnets*, and the new collected edition of his poems in '4 nice pocket volumes'.

238. Sara Hutchinson to her cousin, Tom Monkhouse; [Rydal Mount], 10 April [1820]

Dorothy will inform you the moment of her arrival – Tell her that William expects She will lose no time in communicating with Longman – We have heard nothing from him since she went – & he is very anxious that the vol[ume] should be out & the reprint of the Poems commenced . . . William & I went to Kendal on Thursday Ev[enin]g & stayed till Saturday morning – and he is to be off again on Wednesday to meet Lord Lonsdale at Keswick & proceed with him to Whitehaven – This work will never have an end – Poetry & all good & great things will be lost in Electioneering –

239. William Wordsworth to Benjamin Robert Haydon; Rydal Mount, Friday [late April 1820]

. . . it is some time since I have been impelled to lay down a rule, not to lend to *a Friend* any money which I cannot afford *to lose*.

My income has at no period of my life exceeded my wants; within this last year it has been considerably reduced, while the education of my children is reaching its most expensive point. – It sounds paradoxical, but the fact is strictly true; that I have too great an admiration of your talents, and too much regard and respect for you to comply with your request: for I could not be easy were you to repay the money to your own inconvenience and I could not at the same time spare it without embarass-ment. I have for several years been obliged to defer my trip to the Continent because I could not afford it; and if it be executed next summer as I have promised, the engagement was incurred altogether in consequence of the offer of a friend [Sir George Beaumont] to supply the cash if needed. – It avails little to repeat how much this inability hurts me on the present occasion, – Had my literary labours brought me profit, it would have been otherwise – but I shall say no more. –

. . . I am sending to the press a collection of poems, that conclude the third and *last* Vol[ume] of my miscellaneous pieces. – In more than one passage their publication will evince my wish to uphold the cause of Christianity. – My industry has often been as much as my health could bear, since I saw you, but with a product by no means proportionate! – But with God's blessing I shall be remembered after my day. –

240. *Henry Crabb Robinson, diary, 21 June [1820]*

June 21st. – After taking tea at home I called at Monkhouse's, and spent an agreeable evening. Wordsworth was very pleasant. Indeed he is uniformly so now. And there is absolutely no pretence for what was always an exaggerated charge against him, that he could talk only of his own poetry, and loves only his own works. He is more indulgent than he used to be of the works of others, even contemporaries and rivals, and is more open to arguments in favour of changes in his own poems. Lamb was in excellent spirits. Talfourd came in late, and we stayed till past twelve. Lamb was at last rather overcome, though it produced nothing but humorous expressions of his desire to go on the Continent. I should delight to accompany him.

241. *Review of* The River Duddon *in the* Eclectic Review, *August 1820*

The River Duddon flows through a series of thirty-three sonnets which are for the most part of no ordinary beauty. Here and there, a little metaphysical mud, or a Lakish tincture, mingles with the stream, and it occasionally runs somewhat shallow: but the general character of the series is that of a very noble descriptive beauty.

242. *Review of* The River Duddon *in the* British Critic, *February 1821*

The volume before us . . . has less of Mr. Wordsworth's peculiarities than any preceding volume, and furnishes less food for the humerous critic; but it is more than commonly soft and sweet; a mild and moral pensiveness runs through the whole of it, and it gives us the idea of a mind not weakened indeed, but mellowed and sobred by time, and willing to concede something, in order that mankind, who cannot be benefited by poetry unless they be pleased by it, may be allured gradually in their original and naked simplicity.

243. *Mary and Dorothy Wordsworth to Sara Hutchinson and Dora Wordsworth; Dunkirk, 13 July 1820*

[Mary writes] We are now sailing in a Packet boat between Elmtrees – little Children playing, linen bleaching on the banks. I have been making a few memoranda sitting in our carriage. – D[orothy] has joined me & W[illiam] just gone to join the Company who now seem so merry that I believe I must quit you – he has been the very reverse sonneteering – but it is now written out, & as our affairs have suffered by his remissness I trust he will now cease . . . – we think of you perpetually & wish & wish for you – if ever we are rich enough depend upon it I shall come again with you & my children!

[Dorothy writes] Your Father has written a beautiful sonnet – so much the worse for us; for we rather mismanaged Bruges in consequence of that – but he has done & I hope finally – otherwise <u>he</u> will be no better for the journey. This morning he is well, & all alive & ready to plan for the best.

244. *Dorothy Wordsworth to Catherine Clarkson; Coblentz, 23 July [1820]*

Today I have been the strongest of the Females, yet I have resisted my inclination to take several tempting walks, in the environs of this singularly happily situated city. I certainly am not so strong as I was twenty years ago. This I am now obliged to confess & I must manage myself accordingly. Five years ago I used to say I felt no difference. – My Sister is an excellent Traveller – all alive & full of enjoyment – So indeed am I – and, with a little better arrangement, I expect that I shall not be obliged to give up any important gratification in the delightful countries whither we are bound. William's eyes are much better – & except during two days when nothing would serve him but he must write poetry he has been perfectly well . . .

Journals we shall have in number sufficient to fill a Lady's book shelf –

for all, except my Brother, write a journal – Oh! no Mrs Monkhouse does <u>not</u> – Mine is nothing but notes, unintelligible to any one but myself; I look forward, however, to many a pleasant hour's employment at Rydal Mount in filling up the chasms – But it is grievous to pass on through such a country as this, only glancing at the objects in the broad highway & leaving so many entirely unseen.

245. *Mary Wordsworth to her sister, Sara Hutchinson; Schaffhausen, 1 August [1820]*

. . . you will be sorry to find Mrs Monkhouse is of a very delicate constitution & unable at present to keep pace with us – In consequence of this, & of T[om] M[onkhouse] (whose spirits are bad in consequence) & she doing each other no good – D[orothy], who is the kindest creature in the world – being able to speak German – & the best of all persons in making her way amongst all sorts of strange people – has remained behind, to escort Mrs M[onkhouse] & Miss H[orrocks, her sister] – T[om] came forward with us – from Hornberg, a romantic town at the foot of the Black Forest . . . D[orothy] is an adept in making her way, for she never hesitates – going into the Kitchens talks to every body there. – & in the villages – on the roads, & makes friends & gains information & gabbers German every where. She astonishes us all. William's eyes are certainly much better – his attention being directed elsewhere – but I very much fear that were the same causes existing as irritated them before we left England, there would not be much change for the better yet – However I am willing to hope that our long absence will in the end prove serviceable – At present he is sadly annoyed with his Money – The Banker at Carlsruhe has given him some nasty small pieces that we find here will not pass – & they are gone in great perplexity to the Bank to see what can be done – You know what a stew he will be in.

246. *William Wordsworth to Lord Lonsdale; Lucerne, 19 August [1820]*

. . . Interlacken. Here our Alpine Tour might be said to commence; which has produced much pleasure, thus far; and nothing that deserves the name of difficulty; even for the Ladies. From the valley of Lauterbrunnen we crossed the Weigern Alp to Grindelwald, and thence over the grand Sheide to Meyringen. This journey led us over high ground, and for 15 leagues along the base of the loftiest Alps which reared their bare or snow-

clad ridges and Pikes, in a clear Atmosphere, with fleecy clouds now and
then settling upon & gathering round them. We heard and saw several
Avalanches. They are announced by a sound like thunder, but more
metallic and musical; this warning naturally makes one look about, and
we had the gratification of seeing [them] falling in the shape and appearance
of a torrent or cascade of foaming water, down the deep-worn crevices of
the steep or perpendicular granite mountains. No thing can be more
awful than the sound of these cataracts of ice & snow thus descending
unless it be the silence which succeeds. The elevations from which we
beheld these operations of nature, and saw such an immense range of
primitive mountains stretching to the East and West, were covered with
rich pasturage, and beautiful flowers, among which was abundance of the
Monkshood, a flower which I had never seen but in the trim borders of
our gardens, and which here grew not so much in patches as in little
woods or forests, towering above the other plants. At this Season the
Herdsmen are with their Cattle in still higher regions than these which
we have trod, the herbage where we travelled, being reserved 'till they
descend in the Autumn – We have visited the Abbey of Engleberg, not
many leagues from the borders of the Lake of Lucern. The tradition is
that the Site of this Abbey was pointed by Angels, singing from a lofty
mountain that rises from the plain of the valley, and which from having
been thus honored is called Engleberg, or the hill of the Angels. It is a
glorious position for such Beings; and I should have thought my self
repaid for the trouble of so long a journey by the impression made upon
my mind, when I first came in view of the vale in which this Convent is
placed, and of the mountains that enclose it. The light of the Sun had left
the valley, and the deep shadow spread over it heightened the splendor
of the Evening light spread upon the surrounding mountains, some of
which had their summits covered with pure snow, others were half-hidden
by vapours rolling round them, and the rock of Engleberg could not have
been seen under more fortunate circumstances, for masses of cloud
glowing with the reflexion of the rays of the setting sun were hovering
round it like choirs of spirits preparing to settle upon its venerable head.

247. Dorothy Wordsworth, journal, 14 and 17 September 1820

While standing on the brow of the precipice, above this shady deep recess,
the very image of pastoral life, stillness and seclusion, W[illia]m came up
to me; &, if my feelings had been moved before, how much more

interesting did the spot become when he told me it was the same dell, that "aboriginal vale", that "green recess" so often mentioned by him – the first of the kind that he had passed through in Switzerland, and "now," said he, "I find that my remembrance for thirty years has been scarcely less vivid than the reality now before my eyes!" . . .

We left the hut of Trientz musing on the strange connexions of events in human life; – how improbable, thirty years ago, that W[illiam] should ever return thither! – and <u>we</u> to be his companions! – And to pass a night within the hollow of that "aboriginal Vale" was a thing that the most romantic of our fancies could not have helped us even to dream of!

248. *Henry Crabb Robinson, diary, Milan, 1 September 1820*

We arrived just before dinner, and were placed at the upper end of a table reserved for the English, of whom there were five or six present, beside ourselves . . . A knot of young persons were listening to the animated conversation of a handsome young man, who was rattling away on the topics of the day with great vivacity. Praising highly the German poets Goethe, Schiller, &c., he said, "Compared with these, we have not a poet worth naming." I sat opposite him, and said, "Die gegenwartige Gesellschaft ausgenommen" (the present company excepted). Now, whether he heard or understood me I cannot possibly say. If so, the rapidity with which he recovered himself was admirable, for he instantly went on: "When I say no one, I always except Wordsworth, who is the greatest poet England has had for generations." The effect was ludicrous. Mrs. Wordsworth gave me a nudge, and said, "He knows that's William." And Wordsworth, being taken by surprise, said, "That's a most ridiculous remark for you to make. My name is Wordsworth." On this the stranger threw himself into an attitude of astonishment – well acted at all events – and apologized for the liberty he had taken. After dinner he came to us, and said he had been some weeks at Milan, and should be proud to be our cicerone. We thought the offer too advantageous to be rejected, and he went round with us to the sights of this famous city. But though I was for a short time taken in by him, I soon had my misgivings, and coming home the first evening, Wordsworth said, "This Mr. [Graham] is an amusing man, but there is something about him I don't like." And I discovered him to be a mere pretender in German literature – he knew merely the names of Goethe and Schiller. He made free with the names of our English literary notabilities, such as Shelley, Byron, Lamb, Leigh

Hunt; but I remarked that of those I knew he took care to say no more. One day he went to Mrs. Wordsworth with a long face, and said he had lost his purse. But she was not caught. Some one else must have paid the piper. At Paris we met the same gentleman again, and he begged me to lend him £15, as he had been robbed of all his money. I was enabled to tell him that I had that very morning borrowed £10. He was, however, more successful in an application to Monkhouse, who said, "I would rather lose the money than ever see that fellow again." It is needless to say he "lost his money and his friend," but did not, in the words of the song, "place great store on both." As usually happens in such cases, we learnt almost immediately after the money had been advanced, that Mr. [Graham] was a universal borrower . . . [who had] committed what was then a capital forgery, but made his escape . . . Some time afterwards we heard that this reckless adventurer had died on a bed of honour – that is, was killed in a duel.

249. *William Wordsworth to Lord Lonsdale; 45 Rue Charlot, Boulevards du Temple, [Paris], 7 October [1820]*

We have been in Paris, since Sunday last; and think of staying about a fortnight longer, as scarcely less will suffice for even a hasty view of the Town & neighbourhood. We took Fontainebleau in our way, and intend giving a day to Versailles . . . Nothing which I have seen in this City has interested me at all like the Jardin des Plantes, with the living animals and the Museum of natural History which it includes. Scarcely could I refrain from tears of admiration at the sight of this apparently boundless exhibition of the wonders of the creation. The Statues and pictures of the Louvre affect me feebly in comparison. – The exterior of Paris is much changed since I last visited it in 1792. I miss many antient Buildings, particularly the Temple; where the poor king and his family were so long confined. That memorable Spot where the Jacobin Club was held, has also disappeared. Nor are the additional buildings always improvements; the Pont des Arts, in particular, injures the view from the Pont Neuf greatly; but in these things public convenience is the main point.

250. Henry Crabb Robinson, journal, Paris, 3 October 1820

Having breakfasted alone I repaired to Rue Charlot & was introduced to Mrs Baudoin, a mild amiable woman in appearance. I liked every thing about her except that she called Wordsworth 'father' which I thought indelicate. The mother is said to be a clever woman and she seems so.[2]

251. Henry Crabb Robinson, diary, London, 20 November 1820

I was glad to accompany the Wordsworths to the British Museum. I had to wait for them in the anteroom, and we had at last but a hurried survey of the antiquities. I did not perceive that Wordsworth much enjoyed the Elgin Marbles; but he is a still man when he does enjoy himself, and by no means ready to talk of his pleasure, except to his sister. We could hardly see the statues. The Memnon, however, seemed to interest him very much. Took tea with the Lambs. I accompanied Mrs. and Miss Wordsworth home, and afterwards sat late with Wordsworth at Lamb's.

The Continental Tour had given William much food for thought and would, in time, inspire a whole collection of poems. In the meantime he found inspiration closer to home, though his efforts were hampered by a severe bout of the trachoma which now regularly afflicted his eyes.

252. William Wordsworth to Sir George Beaumont; [Rydal Mount], 6 January 1821[3]

Yesterday I performed a great feat – wrote no less than 7 Letters, reserving your's for to day; that I might have more leisure, and you consequently less trouble in reading. – I have been a good deal tossed about since our arrival here. Mrs W[ordsworth] & I were first called away by the sudden death of my near Kinsman, Mr [John] Myers. We went to College together; and were inseparables for many years. I saw him buried in Millom Church by the side of his Wife. The Churchyard is romantically situated; Duddon Sands on one side, and a rocky Hill scattered over with antient trees on the other. Close by are the remains of the old Castle of the Huddlestones, part of which are converted into farm Houses, and the whole embowered in tall trees, that tower up from the sides and bottom of the circular moat. The Churchyard is in like manner girt round with trees. The Church is of striking architecture and apparently of remote antiquity. – We entered with the funeral train, the day being too far advanced to allow the Clergyman to see to read the service, and no light had been provided; So we sate some time, in solemn silence. At last one candle was brought which served both for Minister and Clerk, casting a wan light on their faces. On my right hand were two stone figures in a recumbent Position (like those of the monument in Coleorton church) – Huddlestones of other years; and the voice of the Minister was accompanied and almost interrupted, by the slender sobbing of a young person, an Indian by half blood, and by the fathers side a niece of the deceased wife of the person whom we were interring. She hung over the coffin and continued this oriental lamentation till the service was over, every body else except one faithful Servant being apparently indifferent. Mrs W[ordsworth] I find has mentioned our return by Duddon-side and how much we were pleased with the winter appearance of my favourite River. – Since that expedition I have been called to Appleby, and detained there upon business. In returning I was obliged to make a circuit which showed me for the [first] time several miles of the Course of that beautiful stream the Eden, from the bridge near Temple Sowerby down to Kirkoswald. Part of this tract of Country I had indeed seen before but not from the same points of view. It is a charming region, particularly at the spot where the Eden & Emont join. The Rivers appeared exquisitely brilliant, gliding under Rocks & through green meadows, with woods, & sloping cultivated grounds, and pensive russet moors interspersed, and along the circuit of the Horizon lofty fells and mountains clothed rather than concealed in fleecy clouds & resplendent vapour.

253. William Wordsworth to his friend, the poet and philanthropist, John Kenyon; Rydal Mount, 5 February 1821

My dear Friend,

Many thanks for your valuable present of the [eye] Shades, which reached me two days ago by the hands of my Sister. I have tried them & they answer their purpose perfectly; Mrs W[ordsworth] says they have no fault but being over fine for the person they are intended for. I, on the other hand, am pleased to see Ornament engrafted upon infirmity, and promise that I will take care neither to sully nor spoil such elegant productions.

We have had a charming season since we reach[e]d West[morlan]d
winter disarmed of all his terrors; & proving that it is not necessary
always to run away from old England for the sake of fine weather –

*254. William Wordsworth to Henry Crabb Robinson; [Rydal Mount],
postmarked 13 March 1821*

Would that I could encourage the hope of passing a winter with you at
Rome, about the time you mention, which is just the period I should
myself select. – But the expense is greater than I dare think of facing,
though five years hence the education of my eldest Son will be nearly
finished; but in the mean time I cannot foresee how we shall be able to
lay by any thing either for travelling, or other purposes.

*255. Dorothy Wordsworth to Catherine Clarkson; [Rydal Mount], 27 March
[1821]*

William is quite well, and very busy, though he has not looked at the
Recluse or the poem on his own life; & this disturbs us. After fifty years
of age there is no time to spare, & unfinished works should not, if it be
possible, be left behind. This he feels, but the will never governs <u>his</u> labours.
How different from Southey, who can go as regularly as clockwork, from
history to poetry, from poetry to criticism, and so on to biography, or
anything else. If their minds could each spare a little to the other, how
much better for both! William is at present composing a series of Sonnets
on a subject which I am sure you would never divine, – the Church of
England, – but you will perceive that in the hands of a poet it is one that
will furnish ample store of poetic materials. In some of the sonnets he
has, I think, been most successful.

*256. Mary Wordsworth to her cousin, Tom Monkhouse, and his wife; Rydal
Mount, 9 April [1821]*

. . . Miss W[ordsworth] is not in her best way – her Swiss appetite is quite
gone – tracing her own steps <u>upon Paper</u>, the work she is at present
engaged in, has no effect in stimulating her appetite – at my daughter's
earnest request, <u>I</u> too am busy transcribing my notices – for she could not
read the original – but mine is a mere transcript – D[orothy]'s I hope, one
day or other will be a valuable production – but I have not seen it yet –

indeed a second copy must be made before her friends can read it. William's eyes I am most happy to tell you keep in their best state, but being very busy at present with composition, he sometimes aggravates their tendency to inflame – but they are notwithstanding much better.

257. Dorothy Wordsworth to Catherine Clarkson; [Rydal Mount, 31 May 1821]

I have not yet finished my journal, though at times I have worked very hard from ten o'clock in the morning till dinner time, at four; & when it is done, I fear it will prove very tedious reading even to <u>Friends</u>, who have not themselves visited the places where we were. Had not my Brother so very much wished me to do my best, I am sure I should never have had the resolution to go further than just re-copy what I did by snatches, & very irregularly, at the time; but to please him I have amplified & arranged; & a long affair will come out of it, which I cannot think any person can possibly have the patience to read through; but which, through sympathy & a desire to revive dormant recollections, may in patches be interesting to a few others. For my own sake, however, the time is not thrown away; & when we are dead and gone, any memorial of us will be satisfactory to the children, especially Dorothy [i.e. Dora]. Her mother's journal is already transcribed, & not being so lengthy as mine, it cannot but be interesting, & very amusing. She has read it to Mrs Gee & Miss Lockier & they were delighted. Her course was much wiser than mine. She wrote regularly & straightforward, & has done little more than re-copy, whereas all that I did would have been almost worthless, dealt with in that way. There is some excuse for me in my illness which threw me back. I have not read a single word of Mary's, being determined to finish my own first, & then make comparisons for correction, & insertion of what I may have omitted.

258. Dorothy Wordsworth to Catherine Clarkson; Rydal Mount, 25 August [1821]

The most important matter is the state of my dear Brother's eyes. During the winter he daily read several hours, & could use them freely without the slightest inconvenience, except by candle-light, & we flattered ourselves that the weakness was overcome; but in the spring he worked hard and incessantly and under great mental excitement, & the consequence was, that often, having the first threatenings of slight inflammation for a few days he was obliged to lay aside all employment, and if he had not been exceedingly careful in all respects he might probably have been as bad as ever again; but happily the inflammation never became violent, and it is now almost entirely gone; though still he cannot read more than a quarter of an hour without heat & prickings in the eye, & if he were to exercise his mind in composition all would be to be begun again. Undoubtedly the malady proceeds from the stomach. It is attended with heat & flushings in the face. I still hope as he is now going on perfectly well, that before winter he may be able to take to his studies. He has now two works unfinished (the Recluse & the [*Ecclesiastical*] Sonnets) & you may believe that it often disturbs him that he is forced to spend so much of his time in idleness. It is, however, a great consolation to us that he enjoys air, exercise, company & all the pleasures this delightful country spreads before us, & these are the best means of cure – & as I said I hope he will be cured before winter. The inflammation is solely in the eye-lids.

259. *Dorothy Wordsworth to Catherine Clarkson; Rydal Mount, 24 October [1821]*

Sara & I are alone. William & Mary left us this morning to spend a week at Keswick, & I am glad of this as he has had three weeks of labour in poetry, & I should fear that his eyes may suffer without a little pause. They are very much amended, & I do not think he has been at all the worse for his labour. He cannot bear the full light of a candle; nor can he read at all by candle-light.

260. *Sara Hutchinson to her cousin, Tom Monkhouse; [Rydal Mount] Friday night, 23 November [1821]*

I have been busy transcribing Poems for you the whole day – not that it was such a very long job, but William kept altering and improving as I went along to the no small <u>disfigurement</u> of my <u>m.s.</u>, and the delay of the Work – However, late as it is, I must write you a few hasty lines to thank you for your kind Letter – and to say that the Poems you asked for [*Ecclesiastical Sonnets*] being a long series of Sonnets (or rather intended to be for they are not completed) which are intended for publication soon, we thought those which I have sent would be more interesting to you as relating to your <u>Travels</u>; and also because you are not likely to see them in Print – having been written for the purpose of <u>ornamenting "the Journals"</u> – I have just finished a fair Copy of Mary's <u>Notes</u>, which I assure you make a very respectable figure in a Book, and is very <u>pretty</u> reading. She was so very shy of exposing it that I was resolved to have a copy of my own that I might lend to whom I liked – . . .

I must not forget to say that you are not to give any copy of the Poems to any one. If Mr Robinson should wish it you may let him read them but even he must have no copy. –

. . . He has been at work again, & before my M. S. leaves the House, I shall have to scratch & interline till you will not be able to blunder through – He says I am to tell you that it is all his fault & not my inaccurate transcription.

261. Sara Hutchinson to her cousin, Tom Monkhouse; [Rydal Mount, 26 November 1821]

. . . as I told you in my Letter we altered, improved, & added all the while the transcription was going forward – And now two new Poems are sent [whic]h have been written since the other went off – And though W[illia]m [says] he has finished probably there will be another <u>batch</u> f[or you] in a day or two. – You must put them into your Book as neatly as you can & press them to make them look <u>tidy</u>.

Tuesday. – As I augured here is another Poem for you besides alterations in the two former – . . .

Thursday Another & another, have been added – and now it will be impossible for you to put them in order so you must number them & <u>read</u> them in succession – There are more one [*sic*] the Stocks – but here are as many as the Frank will carry –

262. William Wordsworth to James Losh; Rydal Mount, 4 December 1821

There was another feeling which both urged & indisposed me to write to you, I mean the allusion which in so friendly a manner you make to a supposed change in my Political Opinions. To the Scribblers in Pamphlets & Periodical publications who have heaped so much obloquy upon myself & my friends Coleridge & Southey, I have not condescended to reply, nor ever shall; but to you my candid & enlightened Friend I will say a few words on this Subject, which if we have the good fortune to meet again, as I hope we may, will probably be further dwelt upon.

I should think that I had lived to little purpose if my notions on the Subject of Government had undergone no modification – my youth must in that case have been without enthusiasm & my manhood endued with small capability of profiting by reflexion. If I were addressing those who have dealt so liberally with the words Renegado, Apostate &c, I should retort the charge upon them & say, you have been deluded by Places & Persons, while I have stuck to Principles – I abandoned France & her Rulers when they abandoned the struggle for Liberty, gave themselves up to Tyranny & endeavoured to enslave the world – I disapproved of the war against France at its commencement, thinking, which was perhaps an error, that it might have been avoided – but after Buonaparte had violated the Independence of Switzerland my heart turned against him & against the Nation that could submit to be the Instrument of such an outrage. Here it was that I parted, in feeling, from the Whigs, & to a certain degree united with their Adversaries, who were free from the delusion (such I must ever regard it) of Mr Fox & his Party that a safe & honourable Peace was practicable with the French Nation, & that an ambitious Conqueror like B[uonaparte] could be softened down into a commercial Rival . . .

When I was young, giving myself credit for qualities which I did not possess, & measuring Mankind by that Standard, I thought it derogatory to human Nature to set up Property in preference to Person, as a title for Legislative power:[4] that notion has vanished. I now perceive many advantages in our present complex system of Representation which formerly eluded my observation, this has tempered my ardor for Reform – but if any plan could be contrived for throwing the Representation fairly into the hands of the Property of the Country, & not leaving it so much in the hands of the large Proprietors as it now is, it should have my best support – tho', even in that event, there would be a sacrifice of Personal rights, independent of property, that are now frequently exercised for the benefit of the community.

263. Dorothy Wordsworth to Catherine Clarkson; [Rydal Mount], 16 January [1822]

William has written some beautiful poems in remembrance of our late Tour. If you should go to London Mr Monkhouse will show them to you, he having a copy. I think of their kind he never wrote anything that was more delightful. He began (as in connection with my "Recollections of a Tour in Scotland") with saying "I will write some Poems for your journal", and I thankfully received two or three of them as a tribute to the journal, which I was making from notes, memoranda taken in our last summer's journey on the Continent; but his work has grown to such importance (and has continued growing) that I have long ceased to consider it in connection with my own lengthy narrative of events unimportant, & lengthy descriptions, which can only interest friends, or a few persons, who enjoy mountain scenery especially, may wish for minute details of what they cannot hope to view with their own eyes – or perhaps a few others who have themselves visited the countries which we visited. – The poems are as good as a descriptive tour – without describing. I was going to say more about them; but I will leave you to judge for yourself. The Ecclesiastical Sonnets, meanwhile, are at rest.

The fact that the poems inspired by the Continental Tour had now grown to such a substantial number persuaded William that he ought to publish them after all. In March 1822 *Memorials of a Tour on the Continent, 1820* and another slim volume, *Ecclesiastical Sketches*, containing the sonnets inspired by the Church of England, were both published by Longman. These were followed by *A Description of the Lakes in the North of England*, a substantial reworking of the prose work he had originally written in 1809 as an introduction to Thomas Wilkinson's engravings. This trio of publications would ensure that everything William had ever written which he wished to preserve for posterity, apart from 'The Recluse' and *The Prelude*, were now in print. It would be thirteen years before his name appeared again on the title page of a new publication.

264. Sara Hutchinson to her cousin, John Monkhouse; Rydal Mount, 22 February 1822

W[illia]m has just received the last proofs of his two little works which are in the Press – You will I am sure be delighted with them, especially with the 'Ecclesiastical [Ske]tches'. – But I dare say they will fall as flat upon the public as all his other works have done – And no wonder when such stuff as Lord Byron's is read with so much avidity – and when History is only interesting when dressed up in a barbarous Scotch Novel!

265. Dorothy Wordsworth to Henry Crabb Robinson; [Rydal Mount], 3 March 1822

With respect to the Tour poems, I am afraid you will think his notes not sufficiently copious – Prefaces he has none – except to the poem on Goddard's death.[5] Your suggestion of the Bridge at Lucern set his mind to work; and if a happy mood comes on he is determined, even yet, though the work is printed, to add a poem on that subject – You can have no idea with what earnest pleasure he seized the idea – yet before he began to write at all, when he was pondering over his recollections, & asking me for hints & thoughts, I mentioned that very subject & he then thought he could make nothing of it. – You certainly have the gift of setting him on fire –

266. William Wordsworth to his friend, Richard Sharpe; Rydal Mount, 16 April [1822]

The Ecc: Sketches labour under one obvious disadvantage, that they can only present themselves as a whole to the Re[ader w]ho is pretty well acquainted with the history of [this] Country; &, as separate pieces, several of t[hem] suffer as poetry, from the matter of fact – there being unavoidably in all history, except as it is a mere suggestion, something that enslaves the Fancy –

267. Francis Jeffrey, review of Memorials of a Tour on the Continent, 1820, *in the* Edinburgh Review, *November 1822*

. . . since he [Wordsworth] has . . . exchanged the company of leech-gatherers for that of tax-gatherers, he has fallen into a way of writing which is equally distasteful to his old friends and his old monitors – a sort of prosy, solemn, obscure, feeble kind of mouthing, – sadly garnished with shreds of phrases from Milton and the Bible – but without nature and without passion, – and with a plentiful lack of meaning, compensated only by a large allowance of affectation and egotism. This is the taste in which a volume of *Sonnets to the River Duddon* is composed and another which he calls *Ecclesiastical Sketches*, and these precious *Memorials of a Tour.*

The great characteristic of these works is a sort of emphatic inanity – a singular barrenness and feebleness of thought, disguised under a senten-tious and assuming manner and a style beyond example verbose and obscure. Most of the little pieces of which they are composed begin with the promise of some striking image or deep reflection; but end, almost invariably, in disappointment – having, most commonly, no perceptible meaning at all – or one incredibly puerile and poor – and exemplifying nothing but the very worthless art of saying ordinary things in an unintelligible way – and hiding no meaning in a kind of stern and pompous wordiness.

268. Review of Ecclesiastical Sketches *and* Memorials of a Tour on the Continent, 1820, *in* Blackwood's Magazine, *August 1822*

For our own parts, we believe that Wordsworth's genius has had a greater influence on the spirit of poetry in Britain, than was ever before exercised by any individual mind. He was the first man who impregnated all his descriptions of external nature with sentiment or passion . . . He was the first man that vindicated the native dignity of human nature, by shewing that all her elementary feelings were capable of poetry . . . He was the first man that stripped thought and passion of all vain or foolish disguises, and shewed them in their just proportions and unencumbered power. He was the first man who in poetry knew the real province of language, and suffered it not to veil the meanings of the spirit. In all these things, and in many more, Wordsworth is indisputably the most *Original Poet of the Age*; and it is impossible, in the very nature of things, that he ever can be eclipsed.

269. William Wordsworth to the poet and author, Walter Savage Landor; Rydal Mount, 20 April [1822]

. . . you commend the fine conclusion of Russel's sonnet upon Philoctetes & depreciate that form of composition. I do not wonder at this; I used to think it egregiously absurd, tho the greatest poets since the revival of literature has [*sic*] written in it. Many years ago my sister happened to read to me the sonnets of Milton, which I could at that time repeat – but somehow or other I was singularly struck with the style of harmony & the gravity & republican austerity of those compositions – In the course of the same afternoon I produced 3 sonnets & soon after, many others; & since that time & from want of resolution to take up anything of length, I have filled up many a moment in writing Sonnets, which, if I had never fallen into the practice, might easily have been better employed. The

Excursion is proud of your approbation. <u>The Recluse</u> has had a long sleep,
save in my thoughts. my MSS. are so ill-penned & blurred that they are
useless to all but myself – & at present I cannot face them. But if my
stomach can be preserved in tolerable order I hope you will hear of me
again, in the character chosen for the title of that Poem.

Chapter Eight

1822–7

270. Edward Quillinan, account of his first meeting with William Wordsworth, April 1821

Mr G[illies] of Edinburgh had given me a letter of introduction to Mr Wordsworth the Poet. It was unsealed, for my inspection; and I found it so flattering to me that I was unwilling to present it, though most anxious for the acquaintance of so admirable a Genius. – I rode over twice from Penrith & back again (50 miles, over Kirkstone, that is 25 & back) yet when I approached his dwelling, I lost heart; at last I went over a third time, & having made up my mind to quit the army, & settle in this delightful country, I screwed up my courage to the mark, and walked up the steep hill, & passed his gate, & rung his door-bell, resolved to introduce myself. – It so happened that Mr Marshall of Ullswater had heard me say at his house, that I had a letter for Mr W[ordsworth] & he had reported to him this fact. Several weeks elapsing without the delivery of the letter, Mr W[ordsworth], little aware of the cause of its detention, was prepared to be offended at my supposed neglect: I was ushered in to the library at Rydal. He rec[eive]d me very stiffly, but asked me for the letter. I told him, & it was true, that I had not brought it with me, but that it was an open letter of introduction, [but that it spoke of me in a manner so extravagantly laudatory that I had not the face to present it.][1] – He seemed quite angry: Hurled a chair about & made short & stiff remarks. I was getting indignant, and thought him most disagreeable. – Suddenly the door opened, and a young lady [Dora], rather tall of good features perhaps, not handsome but of most engaging innocence & ingenuousness of aspect, stood at the door, seemed impressed at seeing a stranger & half drew back. Then it was that I saw the Poet's countenance to advantage – All the father's heart was thrown into his eyes & voice as he encouraged her to come in. She did so; but only staid a few moments; It was a most timely interruption I have loved that sweet girl ever since. – Soon however the fine patriarchal expression vanished & the poet resumed his frigidity of tone & his twirl of the chair. I was about to retire much disappointed, when in came Miss Hutchinson, who saw at once that there was some awkwardness between us: she relieved me in a moment, with that fine tact & benign politeness thoroughly understood only by women. She civilly accosted me, rallied the Poet for twirling the chair, took it from him & appropriated it to her own use; made herself mistress of the cause of our restraint, laughed him into good humour, & sent him out to shew me the garden & the terrace. We rambled together for hours; talked of poetry, he taking the lion's share of the conversation, to which he was entitled, & in triumphe, I returned with him to dinner! – that day was the precursor to many & many a happy one under the same roof.

Quillinan, a poet in his own right, was soon on intimate terms with all the Wordsworth household. He brought his wife and daughter to live in one of the cottages at the foot of the hill and, when a second daughter, Rotha, was born in September 1821, William and Dora became her god-parents. The idyll was brought to an abrupt end only a few months later when Quillinan's wife died. The grieving widower, with his two daughters, was obliged to leave the Lakes but he kept in touch with the Wordsworths and urged William to write his wife's epitaph. Harassed by the continuing ill-health of his youngest son, Willy, who had been sent home from boarding school in such a state that his death was hourly expected, William could not apply himself to the task, until Mary tactfully proposed a solution.

271. *Dorothy Wordsworth to Edward Quillinan; Rydal Mount, 6 August 1822*

My Brother has not composed a single verse since you left us – At this you will not wonder – His feelings will I am sure lead him to pour out his first renewed song to the memory of her who is departed; but <u>when</u> that will be I cannot say – and will not.

272. *Mary Wordsworth to Edward Quillinan; Rydal Mount, 19 September [1822]*

With regard to the Monument, I quite agree with Sir E[gerton Brydges, Quillinan's father-in-law] & yourself; & wish it could be speedily executed – but knowing Mr W[ordsworth] as I do, if the inscription is to depend upon him (& I am sure his feelings would lead [him] to do something worthy of the subject at once could he but command his power) I must prepare you not to be disappointed if a long time elapses before he can satisfy himself – He is utterly unable to do any thing at a given time – & the stronger the desire is to accomplish his object, the more difficult does it become to him – An instance in point I can give – it took him years to produce those 6 simple lines upon the Stone at the head of the earthly remains of our own dear Boy who neighbours your own Treasure – Yet he could not give it up. Your letter will best <u>re</u>introduce the subject to his mind & I must leave it to work there.

273. Mary Wordsworth to Edward Quillinan; Rydal Mount, 19 October [1822]

The Stone, which is a very nice one, is laid down in the Church Yard – Respecting the Ins[cription] for the Monument, judging from many of your own elegant verses – & from my own knowledge of William's incapacity to bring his powers to act with his will, I think it would be best & most promptly done, were you yourself to attempt something & forward what you produce – then W[illiam] with your permission might improve upon or add to yours, or he would be stimulated to throw off something himself – I <u>know</u> the thing being done, would be a great relief to his mind – tho' we have not mentioned the subject to each other lately – I have not found a favourable season.

274. Dorothy Wordsworth to Edward Quillinan; [Rydal Mount], finished 19 November [1822]

– And now my dear Friend I must turn for a moment to the most interesting part of your very interesting letter – You desire to have no criticism – & I assure you I am not disposed to criticize. The verses are very affecting – & I think they will set my Brother's mind to flow in numbers, as they have already wrought on his feelings – He has mused upon your lines – but he must be left to himself – at present his nervous anxiety concerning William [his son] is not sufficiently settled down – He cannot go to any thing but vagrant reading by day light – He walks much it is true – yet seldom alone except to the Doctor's – .

275. Mary Wordsworth to Edward Quillinan, Rydal Mount; 21 December [1822]

. . . he has just satisfactorily finished a little Poem (which I wish you could hear read), & the presence of our late Absentees [Dorothy and Joanna Hutchinson, just returned from a tour of Scotland] I expect will divert him from going to any other employment for some time – as he stands in need of a little relaxation. The Poem in question is not to be spoken of <u>at</u> <u>present</u> – or I would transcribe it for you – the subject is the intended new church at Rydal – which her Ladyship [Lady le Fleming] makes such a secret of, that were it to be named, or if she had the least idea that <u>we</u> aided the business by any hints one way or other – perhaps the good work might not be done – However W[illiam] means, at a proper time, to honor her by presenting his Poem to her.

276. Dorothy Wordsworth to Henry Crabb Robinson; [Rydal Mount], 21 December 1822

– My Brother's mind, since our summer company left us has been so much taken up with anxiety that till within the last 3 weeks he has done nothing. Our first job was to prepare, with additions – a second Edition of his little Book on the Lakes. He is now giving his mind to Poetry again but I do not think he will ever, in his life-time – <u>publish</u> any more poems – for they hang on hand – never selling – the Sketches and the Memorials have not, I daresay <u>half</u> sold –

277. William Wordsworth to Lady le Fleming of Rydal Hall; [Rydal Mount, late January 1823]

Mr Wordsworth is far from desiring to entangle Lady le Fleming in a troublesome correspondence but he cannot refrain from expressing his sympathy with those feelings which have induced Lady le Fleming to decline meeting his wishes to honor the Verses by prefixing to them her name he will therefore not only abstain from introducing her Ladyship's name but will also alter the line in which Rydal is mentioned & take care that nothing shall be left in the poem which must obviously localize it – . . .

The purpose of the verses being to support however humbly & feebly the cause of religion & piety especially as connected with the ordinances

and institutions of the Church of England Mr W[ordsworth] is desirous
that they should be published at this time when the Church is assaulted
openly & unceasingly by enemies in all orders of society from the highest
to the lowest – In a few days Mr W[ordsworth] will enclose a revised
copy & if after what has been said & notwithstanding that this foundation
has already at great length been noticed in newspapers & will be so again
when it is consecrated Lady le Fleming should object to the verses being
published Mr W[ordsworth] will suppress them altogether out of respect
to the private feeling of <u>One</u> to whom this neighbourhood of Rydal is
upon this as it has been upon many other occasions so deeply indebted –

In the spring of 1823, William and Mary escorted their eldest son, John, to New
College, Oxford, where (unlike his father) he would enter university with the
privileged status of a gentleman-commoner. From Oxford his parents travelled
on to London, then visited the Quillinans at Lee Priory, in Kent, preparatory to
taking a short tour abroad.

278. *William Wordsworth to John Kenyon; Lee Priory, 16 May [1823]*

We came hither 5 weeks ago, meaning after a fortnight's stay, to cross the
Channel for a little Tour in Flanders & Holland – but we had calculated,
as the saying is, without our Host – the Spring was tardy & froward –
when a day or two of fine weather came, they were followed by blustering &
even tempestuous winds – these abated, & out came my own vernal
enemy the Inflammation in my eyes which dashed our resolutions – and
here I am still obliged to employ Mrs W[ordsworth] as my amanuensis.

This day however being considerably better we shall go to Dover with
a view to embark for Ostend tomorrow; unless detained by similar
obstacles. From Ostend we mean to go to Ghent, to Antwerp, Breda
Utrecht Amsterdam – to Rotterdam by Harlem the Hague & Leyden –
thence to Antwerp by another route & perhaps shall return by Mecklin
Brussels Lille & Ypres to Calais – or direct to Ostend as we came. We
hope to be landed in England within a month. We shall hurry thro'
London homewards – where we are naturally anxious already to be, having
left Rydal Mount so far back as February.

279. Mary Wordsworth, final entry in her 'Journal of a Tour of Holland' [11 June 1823]

– Adventures we have had few – William's eyes being so much disordered & so easily aggravated naturally made him shun society – & crippled us in many respects, but I trust we have stored up thoughts & Images that will not die.

It is worthy to record that our travelling expences, from our departure to our return to Lee Priory, inclusive of washing &c did not quite amount to 24 English pounds. A cheap Excursion!

280. Dorothy Wordsworth to Dora's friend, Elizabeth Crump; [Rydal Mount], Thursday afternoon [17 July 1823]

My Brother & Sister are delighted at finding themselves at home & seem to have nothing to complain of but the wet weather of our North of England. They declare that during their whole absence of 21 weeks they have not seen as much rain as has already fallen since their return.

281. William Wordsworth to an unidentified correspondent; Rydal Mount, 21 October 1823

You are yet very young, and I can therefore without any regret say that I know of no infallible test for ascertaining whether you are capable of becoming a poet or not: '*Try*, and *merit*', and in these two words lies the substance of what can with reason be said upon the Subject. – Nevertheless as my own experience may not be useless to you, I will add that at your age I had full as much of the poetic Spirit in me as I have ever had since – but with regard to Art and the power of expression I had made all advances, nor was it untill my 28th year, though I wrote much, that I could compose verses which were not in point of workmanship very deficient and faulty. –

> With many good wishes, I am dear Sir
> Sincerely yours
> Wm Wordsworth

282. William Wordsworth to Walter Savage Landor; Rydal Mount, 21 January 1824

. . . [you] remark in your last – 'that you are disgusted with all books that treat of religion.' I am afraid it is a bad sign in me, that I have little relish for any other – even in poetry it is the imaginative only, viz. that which is conversant [with], or turns upon infinity, that powerfully affects me, – perhaps I ought to explain – I mean to say, that unless in those passages where things are lost in each other, & limits vanish, & aspirations are raised, I read with something too much like indifference – but all great poets are in this view powerful Religionists, & therefore among many literary pleasures lost, I have not yet to lament over that of verse as departed. But politics, what do you say to Buonaparte on the one side, and the Holy Alliance on the other – to the prostrate Tories, & to the contumelious & vacillating Whigs, who dislike or despise the Church, and seem to care for the State only so far as they are striving, without hope, I honestly believe, to get the management of it? as to the low-bred & headstrong Radicals, they are not worth a thought. Now my politics used always to impel me more or less to look out for co-operation with a view to embody them in action – of this interest I feel myself utterly deprived, & the subject, as matter of reflection, languishes accordingly. Cool heads no doubt there are in the country – but moderation naturally keeps out of sight – & wanting associates I am less of an Englishman than I once was, or could wish to be.

283. William Wordsworth to Lord Lonsdale; Rydal Mount, 23 January 1824

I am quite ashamed of being so long in fulfilling my engagement. But the promises of Poets are like the Perjuries of Lovers, things at which Jove laughs. – At last, however, I have sent off the two first books of my Translations [of Virgil's *Aeneid*], to be forwarded by Mr Birkett. I hope they will be read by your Lordship with some pleasure, as they have cost me a good deal of pains. Translation is just as to labour what the person who makes the attempt is inclined to. If he wishes to preserve as much of the original as possible, and that with as little addition of his own as may be, there is no species of composition that costs more pains. A literal Translation of an antient Poet in verse, and particularly in rhyme, is impossible; something must be left out and something added; I have done my best to avoid the one & the other fault. I ought to say a prefatory word about the versification, which will not be found much to the taste of those whose ear is exclusively accommodated to the regularity of Popes Homer. I have run the Couplets freely into each other, much more even than Dryden has done. This variety seems to me to be called for, if any thing of the movement of the Virgilian versification be transferable to our rhyme[d] Poetry; and independent of this consideration, long Narratives in couplets with the sense closed at the end of each, are to me very wearisome –

284. *William Wordsworth to his friend, the poet, James Montgomery; Rydal Mount, 24 January 1824*

Dear Sir,

I am truly sorry that the benevolent society with which you are connected [The Society for Ameliorating the Condition of Infant Chimney-Sweepers] should have been at the trouble of addressing themselves to me, to write some thing in behalf of the poor Chimney-boy – I feel much for their unhappy situation, and should be glad to see the custom of employing such helpless creatures in this way abolished. – But at no period of my life have I been able to write verses that do not spring up from an inward impulse of some sort or other; so that they neither seem proposed or imposed. – Therefore I have no hope of meeting either the wishes of the Society or my own on this humane occasion. – If you are in communication with them may I beg you to mention my regret, accompanied with my earnest desires that their endeavour may prove successful.

> I am dear Sir
> with great respect
> very sincerely yours
> Wm Wordsworth

Rydal Mount
Jan[ua]ry 24th 1824

I should have written sooner, but it was possible that I might have fallen into a track that would have led to something.

The Wordsworths spent much of the spring and summer of 1824 away from home. William and Dorothy paid a round of visits to the Beaumonts at Coleorton, John at Oxford, the Quillinans at Lee Priory and their brother, Christopher, at

Cambridge, where he was now Master of Trinity College; they also spent several weeks in London, where they were joined by Dora, and stayed with Mary's cousin, Tom Monkhouse, who was already showing signs of the tuberculosis which would kill him the following year. In the autumn, William, Mary and Dora went on a tour of Wales with Robert Jones, William's old college friend and companion of his continental walking tour of 1790, which ended with a visit to Mary's brother and cousins at Hindwell and Stow on the Welsh Border. Unlike the previous year's tour of the Low Countries, this one was a resounding success, marred only by the knowledge that Tom, also a visitor at Hindwell, was dying.

285. Tom Monkhouse to his sister, Mary Hutchinson; [London], 26 March [1824]

I wish you could be with us (but where could we put you? Yet we <u>would</u> contrive it) when the Wordsworths are here – you would find more Entertainment in a Week – than a Month at another Time – They are such <u>seekers out</u>[2] of Pleasure – & you would see also so many interesting People – They are in the full Tide of Enjoyment from Morning to Night – it is quite delightful to see how compleatly happy Miss Wordsworth seems to be – she is an excellent Creature – & deserves to be happy – The Poet is in high <u>Feather</u> – never more agreable – & Dora is of so contented a Nature – that she is always happy among her friends – she has grown a fine Girl & is much admired by every Person –

286. William Wordsworth to his brother, Christopher; [Rydal Mount], 4 January 1825

Mary, Doro [i.e., Dora] and I reached home on the 13th Nov[embe]r after an absence of eleven weeks & ½, three of which were spent in a delightful ramble through North, and a part of South, Wales – five in a residence in Radnorshire & Herefordshire with Mr [Tom] Hutchinson and Mr [John] Monkhouse – and three at Sir George Beaumont's [Coleorton]. Our abode in South Wales, notwithstanding the pleasure we had in seeing such excellent Friends was made very melancholy by the state of Mr Thomas Monkhouse's health, who, you will be grieved to hear, is dying of a pulmonary Consumption – dying very, very slowly. He is now in Devonshire with his Wife and Child and Miss [Sara] Hutchinson. Their situation is sad, for he is not allowed by his Physicians to speak above a whisper, from which you may judge in what condition they suppose his lungs to be. I cannot help saying on this occasion that Mr M[onkhouse] has proved to us in all our various connexions a faithful & invaluable Friend, so that our loss will in every respect be severe.

Jones met us at Llanroost [Llanrwst], and was our companion during 13 days. We parted at the famous Devil's Bridge. If I find I have room I will send you a Sonnet, which I poured out in the chasm there, during a heavy storm, while Doro was at my side endeavouring to sketch the body of the place, leaving, poor Girl! the soul of it to her Father. Jones was the best of companions, being master of the language, very extensively known in the Country, a most affectionate Man, &, I verily believe, the best-tempered Creature imaginable; to me, who am apt to be irritable in travelling, an inestimable qualification. We did not ascend Snowden nor any high mountain but in other respects did justice to the country, by travelling very leisurely. It much exceeded in interest the expectations which the imperfect observations of one or two and twenty, & the faded recollections of two or three and thirty years allowed me to entertain. We were indeed all much delighted, and often wished for Dorothy and you.

287. Mary Wordsworth to Edward Quillinan; Stow, 27 September [1824]

You have heard of our North Wales tour – which ended as it commenced, most delightfully – the day passed at the Devil's bridge was a sublime finale to the whole – W[illiam] was well, & in excellent spirits all the 3 weeks we were afloat, & Doro enchanted with all we saw, – I could not therefore but be happy – & had we found dear Thos. Monkhouse in a state equal to the rest of our friends we should have had a thorough enjoyment of the whole expedition – but alas, he is far otherwise, as you must have learned from Sarah [Hutchinson] – & his present appearance is almost hopeless – Yet many symptoms are wanting to justify our giving up all hope – tho' the medical man he consults here, encourages very little, when speaking to his friends . . . we talk of remaining among our relatives until about the third week in Oct[obe]r – then return by way of Leicestershire to introduce Doro at Coleorton, by which means we shall anticipate our early-spring visit to the Beaumonts, & secure to ourselves the prospect of a long-continued, undisturbed settling at dear Rydal Mount when at length we reach home. It is high time, such a family of Ramblers as we have lately been, should become stationary.

288. Mary Wordsworth to Edward Quillinan; Stow, 27 September [1824]

W[illia]m has been murmuring verses during our wanderings; & is now so comfortable in health & his eyes so free from inflammation that I trust after we feel ourselves settled at Rydal, he will be able seriously to address himself to the Recluse – but I do not mention this hope, lest he should be scared by the prospect.

289. Sara Hutchinson to Edward Quillinan; 7 Strand, Torquay, 3 November [1824]

The Poet was quite well while with us [at Hindwell] – nobody ever saw him in better plight – & he was the life of our party – doing always his utmost to amuse & keep up our Spirits – which he always does God bless him! when there is a real necessity for his exertions – He had enjoyed his Tour in Wales very much & Do[ra] had been busy with her Pencil & is most surprizingly improved in Sketching –

290. Dorothy Wordsworth to Henry Crabb Robinson; Rydal Mount, 13 December [1824]

. . . Now for ourselves – We are all quite well – the Travellers were much improved both in looks & health by their journey, especially my Brother, whose eyes have been less troublesome than usual since his return – Notwithstanding bad weather we have had our daily walks. My Brother has not yet looked at the Recluse: he seems to feel the task so weighty that he shrinks from beginning with it . . . yet knows that he has now no time to loiter if another great work is to be accomplished by him – I say another – for I consider the Excursion as one work though the Title-page tells that it is but a <u>part</u> of one that has another Title. He has written some very pretty small poems. I will transcribe two of them, which have been composed by him with true feeling, & he has great satisfaction in having done them – especially that on Mary Monkhouse [Tom's infant daughter] for her dear Father's sake, who prizes it very much –

*291. William Wordsworth to his friend, the poet, Samuel Rogers; Rydal Mount,
23 March [1825]*

I shall not be in Town this year, nor can I foresee, since the loss of Mr
Monkhouse, when I shall revisit London; the Place does not suit me on
account of the irritability of my eyes – I must look for you & other friends
here. Pray come down this Summer – I could let you have a quiet room,
this House having lately been added to in a small way. Mr M[onkhouse]
is not only a loss to his Friends & Kindred but to Society at large – as in
all his dealings and transactions he was a Man of perfect integrity & the
most refined honour – he was not bright or entertaining but so gentle &
gracious, & so much interested in most of what ought to interest a pure
mind, that his company was highly prized by all who knew him intimately.

292. Dorothy Wordsworth to John Monkhouse; Rydal Mount, 3 April [1825]

William is well; but much thinner than he used to be, and this makes him
look old. He is thinking about a new Edition of his Poems (including the
Excursion) in six Volumes.

*293. William Wordsworth to his young admirer, the poet, Maria Jane Jewsbury;
Rydal Mount, 4 May 1825*

I am not altogether free from reflections natural to my time of life, such
as, that I have lived and laboured to little purpose, – assurances like yours
are correctives of this mistake, for how can it be other than one, when I
receive blossoms of such promise with declarations so fervent, yet evidently
sincere!

   . . . let me caution you, who are probably young, not to rest your hopes
or happiness upon Authorship. I am aware that nothing can be done in
literature without enthusiasm, and therefore it costs me more to write
in this strain – but of even successful Authors how few have become
happier Men – how few I am afraid have become better by their labours.
Why should this be? and yet I cannot but feel persuaded that it is so with
our sex, and your's is, I think, full as much exposed to evils that beset the
condition.

294. *Sir George Beaumont to William Wordsworth; 24 May 1825*

. . . I cannot but wish you & Mrs Wordsworth or your sister may go [to Italy] – I take it for granted both cannot leave home for such a time together the nature of your business considered & I have a great desire to assist on this occasion, if therefore another £100 added to Mrs Fermors [legacy] will be of any use I have it at your service, & I trust you will not be offended at this offer when you consider of what use you have been to my mind by your poetry & by your friendship & kindness on various occasions to my body – Your friendship has been one of the chief blessings of my life & I shall remain deeply in arrears –

295. *William Wordsworth to Sir George Beaumont; Rydal Mount, 28 May [1825]*

I wish we could transport her [Lady Beaumont] hither for a week at least under this quiet roof, in this bright and fragrant season of fresh leaves and blossoms. Never I think have we had so beautiful a spring; sunshine and showers coming just as if they had been called for by the spirits of Hope, Love, and beauty. This Spot is at present a Paradise, if you will admit the term when I acknowledge that yesterday afternoon the mountains were whitened with a fall of snow. – But this only served to give the landscape, with all its verdure blossoms and leafy trees, a striking Swiss air, which reminded us of Unterseken and Interlaken. –

   Most reluctantly do I give up the hope of our seeing Italy together; but I am prepared to submit to what you think best. My own going with any part of my family must be deferred till John is nearer the conclusion of his University studies: so that for this summer it must not be thought of. I am truly sensible of your kind offer of assistance, and cannot be affronted at such testimonies of your esteem. We sacrifice our time our ease, and often our health for the sake of our Friends (and what is Friendship unless we are prepared to do so?). I will not then pay <u>money</u> such a Compliment as to allow <u>it</u> to be too precious a thing to be added to the Catalogue; where Fortunes are unequal, and where the occasion is mutually deemed important. But at present this must sleep.

296. Dorothy Wordsworth to Henry Crabb Robinson; Rydal Mount, 2 July 1825

Though my Brother is preparing for the Press he has not yet even fixed upon a Publisher, so it will be some time before the poems are out. – He has had so little profit in his engagement with Longman, that he is inclined to try another, and he (Longman) after assuring him that it would not answer for the Concern to allow a larger share of profits – or, in other words, more than half (my B[rothe]r being secured from loss) assured him that they should not think themselves unhandsomely used if he applied elsewhere (as he had proposed to do). After all, I think, it will prove that he is not likely to <u>mend himself</u>;[3] and perhaps he may turn again to the Longmans, from whom if he parts, he parts on friendly terms. I wish he had made up his mind, and for my part, am sorry that he has ever entertained a thought of change; for <u>his</u> works are not likely to be much aided in the Sale by exertions even of the most active publishers.

297. William Wordsworth to Samuel Rogers; Rydal Mount, 23 March [1825]

My dear Friend,

I am much obliged by your kindness in taking so much trouble about my Poems, & more especially so by the tone in which you met Mr Murray,[4] when he was disposed to put on the airs of a Patron. I do not look for much advantage either to Mr M[urray] or to any other Bookseller with whom I may treat; and for still less to myself, but I assure you that I would a thousand times rather that not a verse of mine should ever enter the Press again, than allow any of them to say that I was to the amount of the strength of a hair dependant upon their countenance, consideration, Patronage, or by whatever term they may dignify their ostentation or selfish vanity. You recollect Dr Johnson's short method of settling precedence at Dilly's "No Sir, Authors above Booksellers."

I ought to apologize for being so late in my reply – & indeed I scarcely feel justified in troubling even so kind a friend about an affair in which I am myself so indifferent – as far as inclination goes. As long as any portion of the Public seems inclined to call for my Poems, it is my duty to gratify that inclination, & if there be the prospect of pecuniary gain, tho' small, it does not become me to despise it, otherwise I should not face the disagreeable sensations, &

injurious, & for the most part unprofitable labours in which the preparing for a new edition always entangles me: the older I grow, the more irksome does this task become – for many reasons which you as a pains-taking Author will easily divine, & with which you can readily sympathize . . .

As to your considerate proposal of making a Selection of the most admired, or the most popular, even were there not insuperable objections to it in my own feelings, I should be utterly at a loss how to proceed in that selection.

298. William Wordsworth to Alaric Watts, editor of the Leeds Intelligencer *newspaper and of the annual,* The Literary Souvenir; *Lowther Castle, Penrith, 13 August 1825*

I do not wish to dispose of the copyright of my works. The value of works of imagination it is impossible to predict; and it would be more mortifying to dispose of the copyright for less than might prove its value, than it would gratify me to sell it at a price beyond its worth. I would therefore wish to dispose of the right of printing an edition at a given sum.

299. Dorothy Wordsworth to William's university friend, Robert Jones; Rydal Mount, 7 October 1825

We really were not sorry that you did not arrive in the course of last summer; for you would have had no quiet enjoyment, & you are not made for bustling pleasures. We never in our lives had so many visitors. The newspapers (for I suppose newspapers are not excluded from the Valley of Meditation) will have announced to you the names of some of them – Mr. Canning, Sir Walter Scott &c. &c.; but if we had kept a private register of the names of others of less note you would really have been astonished with their numbers. Dora regrets that she did not do so.

300. William Wordsworth to Scottish poet and editor, Allan Cunningham; Rydal Mount, 23 November [1825]

Many thanks for your letter – the interest which yourself & family take in my writings & Person is grateful to my feelings – testimonies of this kind are among the very pleasantest results of a literary life. The ground upon which I am disposed to meet your anticipation of the spread of my

Poetry is, that I have endeavoured to dwell with truth upon those points of human nature in which all men resemble each other, rather than on those accidents of manners & character produced by times & circumstances; which are the favourite seasoning, & substance too often, of imaginative writings. If therefore I have been successful in the execution of my attempt, it seems not improbable, that as education is extended, writings that are independant of an over – not to say vicious – refinement will find a proportionate increase of readers, provided there be found in them a genuine inspiration.

. . . Do not say I ought to have been a Scotchman – tear me not from the Country of Chaucer, Spencer, Shakespear & Milton – yet I own that since the days of childhood, when I became familiar with the phrase "they are killing geese in Scotland & sending the feathers to England" which every one had ready when the snow began to fall, & I used to hear in the time of a high wind that

> "Arthur's Bower has broken his band
> And he comes roaring up the land
> King of Scotts with a' his Power
> Cannot turn Arthur's Bower,"

I have been indebted to the North for more than I shall ever be able to acknowledge. Thomson, Mickle, Armstrong, Leyden, Yourself, Irving a poet in <u>spirit</u> & I may add Sir Walter Scott were all Borderers – if they did not drink the water, they breathed at least the air of the two countries. The list of English Border Poets is not so distinguished – but Langhorn was a native of West[morlan]d & Brown, the Author of the Estimate of Manners & Principles, &c a Poet as his letter on the Vale of Keswick with the accompanying verses shews – was born in Cumberland. So also was Skelton a Demon in point of Genius; & Tickle in later times, whose style is superior in chastity to Pope's his contemporary. Addison & Hogarth were both within a step of Cum[berlan]d & West[morlan]d their several Fathers having been natives of those Counties; which are still crowded with their name & relatives. It is enough to me to be ranked in this catalogue & to know that I have touched the hearts of many by subjects suggested to me on Scottish Ground –

301. Sara Hutchinson to Edward Quillinan; Rydal Mount, 25 January [1826]

Mr W[ordsworth] has been, & kept every one else when they were not employed in nursing me, busy in preparing his Poems for republication – Hurst & Robinson were to have been the Publishers – but luckily the bargain was so made that until the delivery of the copy & the cash paid upon it, they had no claim upon it – else he would now have perhaps lost his Edition as they are become Bankrupt – . . .

William had had a fortunate escape, unlike his friend, Sir Walter Scott, who was personally bankrupted by the collapse of his publishing house, Constable. The same national financial crisis which precipitated these crashes also caused the failure of the Tees Bank, in which every member of the Hutchinson family lost money. At the same time as the Wordsworths faced financial ruin, they also had to contemplate losing their beloved home. Lady le Fleming decided to terminate their lease of Rydal Mount so that she could install her aunt in the house. Until she changed her mind, more than a year later, the Wordsworths were left in suspense.

302. Sara Hutchinson to Edward Quillinan; Rydal Mount, 25 January [1826]

I know not whether you were told that upon understanding that Mrs Huddlestone was positively to occupy Rydal Mount after May 1827 William bought the little field behind Tillbrooks Cottage, belonging to Backhouse, being resolved to build himself a House rather than quit Rydal – But we have still hopes that Mrs H[uddlestone] will not come hither; & that we may be permitted to stay to prevent the erection of another 'genteel Cottage' a thing very obnoxious to the dignity of the Lady of the Manor – but this is entre nous –

303. William Wordsworth to Robert Jones; Rydal Mount, 18 May [1826]

I have been very busy about the threatened contest for West[morlan]d – that is no excuse for not writing to you earlier; in fact I have no hope of visiting Wales this spring or summer; we have received notice to quit Rydal Mount & I am entangled in preparations for building a house in an adjoining field purchased at an extravagant fancy price. I enter upon this work with great reluctance & would feign hope that some turn of fortune may yet prevent it going forward . . . My Sister is still in

Herefordshire[5] wishing to avoid the bustle of our approaching election, when she went thither in Feb[ruar]y our plan was that I was to meet her in the Vale of Clwydd at the end of this month as you know – but this is impossible both on account of the possible building & the election.

304. Sara Hutchinson to Edward Quillinan; Rydal Mount, 22 May [1826]

We have little or no hope of spending another Summer at dear Rydal Mount. I know not whether I told you of Mr W[ordsworth]'s plan of building – the timber is bought – the plan & elevation all upon Paper &c – and he is eager to begin in good earnest – He – Dora – & Willy are the <u>Builders</u> – Miss W[ordsworth] & I anti Builders – Mary W[ordsworth] I think is neuter – only she will be satisfied when the determination is made which way ever it may be. – I cannot bear to think of leaving this place – and Mrs Huddlestone who is to succeed us as little relishes leaving her present situation – but My Lady has set her heart upon it – and I suppose, for the sake of her Son, Mrs H[uddlestone] will not refuse – tho' she is wise enough to know that even for his interest they had better have Kirkstone between them. It <u>vexes</u> me – so I will write no more about it –

305. William Wordsworth to John Kenyon; Rydal Mount, 25 July [1826]

You inquire after my Poetry – I have a poor account to give of my progress in Composition since I saw you – I cannot get over the idea which long ago haunted me, that I have written too much in common with almost every writer of our time – Of Publication I have only to say that I have been desirous to send forth a new Edition of all my Poetry that has seen the Light including the Excursion, and several small additional Pieces – One – a fragment of the Recluse viz an address to the Clouds upon which you may judge if any Spirit be left in me – but this scheme has been frustrated by the failures among the Booksellers – so that the Poems & Excursion, which have been long out of print are likely to remain so.

. . . A Thought has struck me, that as my Friend Mr Gee, tomorrow sets out for London from this place you may have a double Letter without the expense of Postage – I will therefore send you a Copy of Verses, part of which was written this very morning in the delightful wood that borders our Garden on the side towards Rydal Water – You may be inclined to think from these verses that my tone of mind at present is somewhat melancholy – it is not by any means peculiarly so except from the shade that has been cast over it recently by poor Southeys afflictions[6] – I laugh full as much as ever, and of course talk more nonsense; for, be assured that after a certain Period of life old sense slips faster away from one than new can be collected to supply the loss. This is true with all men, and especially true where the eyes fail for the purposes of reading and writing as mine have done. – But now for the Verses which are for yourself & Mrs Kenyon – and not for miscellaneous ears. Pray attend to this as they [are] not likely soon to be published –

306. William Wordsworth to an unidentified correspondent; [Rydal Mount, ?September 1826]

I have no news from this Quarter, but that our trees are of foliage this year unusually luxuriant; so much so, that many of the Dwellings of this neighbourhood seem packed in green leaves like precious Trinkets in cotton. Every thing about us looks bright, clear, soft, sheltered and peaceful: for the weather has been quite heavenly for many weeks . . .

307. Sara Hutchinson to her cousin, John Monkhouse; Rydal Mount, 19 September [1826]

We have been in such a bustle of <u>pleasure</u> it would have been could we have taken it by ease – but having so many friends to attend to unless it had been possible to make each limb do the duty of the whole body or the body could have been in two [or] three places at a time, instead of enjoying the pleasure we have had severe <u>labour</u> – Last week began with a large Party at home Sir George [Beaumont] & Mr [Samuel] Rogers & some smaller folk dined with us – & all the rest of our neighbours came in the Ev[enin]g when Dora's <u>Syren</u> Friend, Miss Ayling, charmed all hearts with Handel's music – Monday a wedding at the Crumps – some went to Breakfast – some to dinner – & all the neighbourhood joined the party in the Ev[enin]g – then came another Day at home with Sir G[eorge] &c – then W[illia]m M[ary] & D[ora] set off to Llagstone to a Christening – & I was left at home to entertain all comers, which were no few, & to escort Lady Farquhar & shew her the Lions, attend to Miss Cookson, & poor Miss Honeyman who always comes unluckily when we are in a scramble – which is very mortifying – as there is no one in the world we are more disposed to shew attention to, or who better deserves it – So went on last week – & yesterday, Monday, we had a huge

picnic party into Easedale – & came home to tea – W[illia]m was not
with us and poor Dora laid up with a cold – W[illia]m in the midst of all
this bustle busy among his verses – and only <u>agreeable by fits</u> – but he is
gone off this morning to Keswick to visit Southey – & at the end of the
week will join Dora at Halsteads [the Marshalls' home on Ullswater] if
her cold is well enough for her to leave home – Sir G[eorge] & R[ogers]
are at Keswick – we expect them back after their visit to Lowther is paid
– and we are <u>threatened</u> with a <u>visitation</u> from <u>Mrs Coleridge</u> – & have
had a Letter proposing a visit from W[illia]ms Welsh Friend Mr Jones –
so when our <u>Season</u> is to end I know not –

Among the many visitors of this summer was Frederic Mansel Reynolds, editor
of the popular Christmas annual, *The Keepsake*, who hoped to enlist William as
one of his contributors. He suggested that William might cure his trachoma by
rubbing his eyelids with 'blue stone', copper sulphate, a remedy which proved
surprisingly effective. Relieved of this painful complaint and reassured that his
family would now be able to stay in Rydal Mount, William decided to resolve
his remaining problem. Though his efforts to secure a new publisher had failed,
when he re-approached Longmans, they capitulated and agreed to pay him
improved terms for a new six-volume edition of his works.

*308. William Wordsworth to Frederic Mansel Reynolds; Halsteads, 24 October
[1826]*

It gives me great pleasure to say which I do with gratitude, that I have
derived, I am persuaded great benefit from your remedy. The Blue stone
was applied by Mrs W[ordsworth] to my eyes, five or six times; it distressed
them not a little for the time; but they have not been any thing like so
well for many years as since. It is but justice to ascribe this to the virtues
of the Stone; though it is proper to say that my having about the same
period entirely left off wine (fermented or spirituous liquors have never
made a part of my beverage) it is probable that this change may have
concurred in producing the beneficial effect. at all events I am thankful,
and shall always feel greatly indebted to your advice. If my Life were
thoroughly regulated as to diet, and exertion of body and mind, I have
reason to think that I should henceforth have comparatively little reason
to complain of my eyes. – If they become deranged again, depend upon
it I will persist in the use of the Blue Stone, and this will be the best way
of acknowledging my obligation to you.

309. Mary Wordsworth to John Kenyon; [Rydal Mount], 27 October [1826]

W[illiam] is paying his last summer visits for this season – our latest lingerers after pleasure have departed, Miss Wordsworth we expect at home (she having been an Absentee for 10 months) in the course of the next fortnight – so that after the rejoicings for her return are over we look forward to a quiet & industrious winter – without any harrassing fears that we are to be turned [out] of our favoured Residence – a fear that haunted us if I remember right, the last time I had the pleasure of writing to you.

310. Dorothy Wordsworth to Henry Crabb Robinson; Rydal Mount, 18 December [1826]

My Brother does really intend, by the same Lady who conveys this to London, to write respecting the publishing of his poems – to Longman. I heartily wish that an agreement, & speedy printing may follow. He has lately written some very good Sonnets. I wish I could add that the "Recluse" was brought from his hiding-place.

The eyes continue well, & as active and useful as any eyes in the house.

311. Dorothy Wordsworth to Henry Crabb Robinson; Rydal Mount, 6 January [1827]

I have the same good tidings for you of my Brother's eyes. We have now no dread of proof sheets; but are hoping for their arrival before the end of next week. Longman has agreed to his Terms, & the poems were to go to press immediately, and proceed with all possible speed.

312. William Wordsworth to Messrs Longman & Co.; Rydal Mount, 10 May [1827]

This day I have received six copies of the poems . . . I am pleased with the appearance of the books except an error in apportioning the matter in the third vol[ume] which is too large, the miscalculation was my own fault.

*313. William Wordsworth to George Husband Baird, convener of a committee
of the Church of Scotland appointed 'for enlarging the collection of Translations
and Paraphrases from sacred scripture, and . . . improving the Psalmody';
Rydal Mount, 15 June 1827*

The interest I take in all that concerns the welfare of the Church of
Scotland would have induced me to make an attempt at producing some
thing which might have suited the plan you have explained in a manner &
with a care that proves the importance you attach to it, if I could have
entertained the least hope of success. But I assure you Sir with frankness &
sincerity, that I am unequal to the task. My own devotional feelings have
never taken in verse a Shape that has connected them with scripture in a
degree that would encourage me to an effort of this kind – The Sacred
writings have a majesty, a beauty, a simplicity, an ardour, a sublimity, that
awes and overpowers the spirit of Poetry in uninspired men, at least this
is my feeling; and if it has deterred me in respect to compositions that
might have been entered upon without any view of their seeing the light,
how much more probable is it that I should be restrained, were I to make
the endeavour under a consciousness that I was writing with a national
purpose! Indeed, Sir, I dare not attempt it. –

Among the many pilgrims who made their way to Rydal Mount in the autumn
of 1827 was a young Irishman, William Rowan Hamilton, who instantly struck
up an intimate friendship with William, despite the thirty-five year difference in
their ages. Hamilton was a remarkable man, a competent poet as well as an
outstanding scientist; William would later say that he and Coleridge were 'the
two most wonderful men, taking all their endowments together', that he had
ever met.

*314. William Wordsworth to Robert Southey; [Rydal Mount, 15 September
1827]*

My dear S——

The Bearers are Gentlemen of whom I cannot say half so much
as they deserve. Mr Hamilton is Professor Astronomer in The University of Dublin, at 22 – years of – age –

Mr Nimmo is a civil engineer of distinction; Mr Otway is a
clergyman of the Irish Church – is acquainted with every corner of
Ireland –

You will find them all interesting – They did not ask for this
Introduction but I know they wished for it –

Ever yours W.W.

in extreme haste –

*315. William Rowan Hamilton to his sister, Eliza, Keswick; 16 September
1827*

I must shut up this letter and go present to Southey an introduction
which I have received from Wordsworth, with whom I spent the evening
– I might almost say the *night* – of yesterday, for he and I were taking a
midnight walk together for a long, long time, *without any companion* except
the stars and our own burning thoughts and words.

*316. William Wordsworth to William Rowan Hamilton; Rydal Mount, 24
September 1827*

. . . If I have the pleasure of see[ing] you [again] I will beg permission to
dissect these verses,[7] or any other you may be inclined to show me – but
I am certain that, without conference with me or any benefit drawn from
my practice in metrical composition your own high powers of mind will
lead you to the main conclusions – You will be brought to acknowlege
that the logical faculty has infinitely more to do with Poetry than the
Young & the inexperienced, whether writer or critic, ever dreams of.
Indeed, as the materials upon which that faculty is exercised in Poetry are
so subtle, so plastic, so complex, the application of it requires an adroitness
which can proceed from nothing but practice, a discernment which
emotion is so far from bestowing that at first it is ever in the way of it . . .

But again, my dear Sir, let me exhort you (and do you exhort your
Sister) to deal little with modern writers, but fix your attention almost
exclusively upon those who have stood the test of time. – <u>You</u> especially
have not leisure to allow of your being tempted to turn aside from the
right course by deceitful lights. My Household desire to be remembered
to you in no formal way – seldom have I parted, never I was going to say,
with one whom after so short an acquaintance I lost sight of with more
regret. I trust we shall meet again . . .

Chapter Nine

1828–31

317. *William Wordsworth to an unidentified correspondent; Rydal Mount, 30 January 1828*

Sir

Your Letter was not put into my hands till yesterday, on my return home after an absence of a few weeks. – A proposal, of the same kind has been repeatedly urged upon me by Mr Allan Cunningham, viz – that I would make a selection of my own Poetry to be circulated among the Scottish Peasantry, in a cheap Form; to which I have replied that I should be utterly at a loss what portions to select; and I may add that at present nothing of the sort could be done without permission of my Publishers, who have an interest in the Edition of my Works collected last year. – My present intention is to forward your Letter to Messrs Longman; if they object, there is of course an end to the matter – ; till this Edition shall be disposed of; if they do not; it will then be for me to consider, whether it is prudent to consent to the choice pieces or passages of my Poetry being presented to the public in this manner; in homelier language, to the plumbs being picked out of five expensive Volumes, the whole of which have probably not yet brought to their Author a return equal to what one of the slightest novels of the season may produce. – You will excuse this narrow, though not narrow-<u>minded</u> view of the case; for I take it without scruple, having never <u>composed</u> a line for the sake of pelf – though I have <u>sometimes</u> <u>published</u> from that immediate motive; and in so doing, as if the Muses resented even that indignity I have, through the intermeddling agency of the periodical critics, been disappointed.

The need to earn money was again at the forefront of William's mind in the winter of 1827–8 and it was for this reason alone that he finally succumbed to the temptation to write for the newly fashionable annuals, which he and Southey despised as 'picture books for grown-up children'. It was a sign of his growing fame that he was inundated with requests for contributions but, when Frederic Mansel Reynolds, editor of *The Keepsake*, offered him 100 guineas for a minimum of twelve pages of verse, William felt he could not refuse. He felt personally indebted to Reynolds, who had suggested the blue-stone cure for his trachoma, and he had to find the money to pay the debts of his eldest son, John, who had just left university and, thanks to the Beaumonts, had secured a curacy at Whitwick, near Coleorton, in Leicestershire.

318. Dorothy Wordsworth to the Reverend William Jackson, former curate of Grasmere; Rydal Mount, 12 February 1828

My Brother is writing verses – but has not yet turned to the Recluse – & we shall lose him again so soon that I fear this winter will produce nothing – and how years roll away! – – I am now 56 – & he two years older –

319. William Wordsworth to his wife and daughter, Mary and Dora, in Herefordshire; [Rydal Mount], Thursday [early March 1828]

John arrived [the] day before yesterday, looking well & apparently in good spirits – Bills to the amount of upwards of 60 pounds including the one paid by Mr Jackson have been sent for Battles [i.e., college bills] the Taylor's bill not included, 7 pounds for a new suit, one also left at Cambridge, so that with Whitwick furniture, & John's journey and settling etc the expenses on John's account will be very formidable.

This was my main inducement for closing with Mr. Reynolds's offer for the Keepsake. I have already written all that will be necessary to fulfill my engagement, but I wish to write a small narrative Poem by way of variety, in which case I should defer something of what is already written till another year if we agree. I have written one little piece 34 lines, on the Picture of a Beautiful Peasant Girl bearing a Sheaf of Corn. The Person I had in my mind lives near the Blue Bell Tillington – a sweet Creature, we saw her when going to Hereford – another Piece 82 lines same stanza as Ruth, is entitled The Wishing-gate at Grasmere. Both have I think merit . . .

Farewell, dearest Loves. I have shewn the above additions [to *The Triad*] to Nobody, even in this House; so I shall shut up my Letter that neither it nor they may be read. Love to all at both Houses. again farewell.

Your affectionate husband and father,

W.W.

William arranged to meet his wife and daughter, who had spent the winter at Brinsop Court with Tom Hutchinson's family, at his brother's in Cambridge in April. They all then went together to London where Mary quickly tired of the frenetic round of social activity and went to visit John at Whitwick, expecting that William and Dora would join her soon. Instead, however, father and daughter decided to take a seven-week-long trip down the River Rhine; even more surprisingly, they agreed to take Coleridge with them.

320. Dora to her cousin, Chris Wordsworth; from Quillinan's house, 12 Bryanston Street, Portman Square, London, postmarked 14 May 1828

Tonight we all go to Drury Lane; Mr. Reynolds, the Keepsake Friend, sent us four tickets, and we are to meet him there. This is a tidy man. I have been to the Diorama, but as yet nothing else in the sight-seeing way. Of friends, the most interesting, Sir Walter Scott, Rogers, Mr. Kenyon, and others too numerous to name. Mr. Quillinan has taken my mother to call upon Mrs. Hoare. Father at breakfast with Crabbe Robinson in the Temple, and I alone at home to receive all their visitors. Father dines with Mr. Joshua Watson on Friday. I wonder how dear uncle is. I want to see him, but shall be "fearfully shamed," for I have got such a hat! and had a Frenchman last night to dress my hair for the opera, who cut off all my dangling curls, and made my head precisely like the ladies you see in their windows. Breakfast, dinner, and evening engagements are over-whelming us; *truly*, I am sighing for Rydal rest.

321. Mary Wordsworth to Edward Quillinan; The Vicarage, Whitwick, Leicestershire, 26 July [1828]

I have not heard of their return tho' a week is passed since the time, fixed for their absence from home, expired – They would not be foolish enough to face the stormy weather we have had, & which seems to have been general – tho' Doro only speaks of showery weather. She says they 'get on famously, but that Mr C. sometimes detains them with his fiddle faddling, & that he likes prosing to the folks better than exerting himself to see the face of the Country & that Father with his few ¹/₂ doz[en] words of German makes himself much better understood than Mr C. with all his weight of German Literature'.

322. Thomas Colley Grattan, novelist and travel writer, on his first meeting with William Wordsworth, Brussels, 25 June 1828

Wordsworth . . . was a perfect antithesis to Coleridge – tall, wiry, harsh in features, coarse in figure, inelegant in looks. He was roughly dressed in a long brown *surtout*, striped duck trousers, fustian gaiters, and thick shoes. He more resembled a mountain farmer than a 'lake poet.' His whole air was unrefined and unprepossessing.

This was incontestably the first impression made on others as well as on me. But, on after observation, and a little reflection, I could not help considering that much that seemed unfavourable in Wordsworth might be really placed to his advantage. There was a total absence of affectation, or egotism; not the least effort at display, or assumption of superiority over any of those who were quite prepared to concede it to him. He seemed satisfied to let his friend and fellow-traveller take the lead, with a want of pretension rarely found in men of literary reputation far inferior to his; while there was something unobtrusively amiable in his bearing towards his daughter.

323. Dora Wordsworth to Edward Quillinan; Antwerp, 1 August 1828

This letter with the usual Wordsworthian coolness is to give notice that the two Poets and their amiable Daughter hope to Steam it from Ostend Monday evening & Tuesday the 6th & further hope to reach London the same day – . . . I shall be thankful to get home though not the least weary "we tramping" – I have made the best traveller of the trio – The heat – the first part of our journey overpower'd Mr Coleridge & when at Godesbergh for two days was very ill – but since he has been more than tolerable – & we get on delightfully – . . .

In spite of all our fears we have caught none of the illnesses prevalent among the "amphibious animals" – yesterday a day of pouring rain at Rotterdam gave Father time to <u>half</u> persuade himself into an Ague – but the symptoms have disappear'd – I am a saucy Child as you know full well – he had a little cold from damp feet – was a little doleful – & I was

wicked enough to say it was Ague – heavy showers every day since last
Monday week – & before we left Godesbergh – but nothing to keep us
Prisoners till yesterday –

324. William Wordsworth to William Jerdan, editor of the Literary Gazette,
*in answer to a request that he would write an account of his tour; Rydal Mount,
7 October 1828*

I really cannot change my opinion as to the little interest which would
attach to such observations as my ability or opportunities enabled me to
make during my ramble upon the Continent; or it would have given me
pleasure to meet your wishes. There is an obstacle in the way of my ever
producing any thing of this kind, viz – idleness, – and yet another which
is an affair of taste. – Periodical writing – in order to strike, must be
ambitious – and this style is, I think, in the record of Tours or Travels
intolerable – or at any rate the worst that can be chosen. My model would
be Gray's Letters & Journal if I could muster courage to set seriously about
any thing of the kind – but I suspect Gray himself would be found flat in
these days.

*325. Dora Wordsworth to Maria Jane Jewsbury; Rydal Mount, 1 December
1828*

I must tell you what a neighbour of ours said when he heard Daddy was
about to return after his long absence "Why than we shall hae him *booing*
agen int' that wood; he *boos* like a bull enough to *freighten* a body["] –
Poetical is it not[?]

*326. William Wordsworth to his brother, Christopher; Rydal Mount, Friday
[mid October 1828]*

On our return to the north we stopped a fortnight with John, with whom
his mother had resided during our absence of nearly 7 weeks; and found
John happy in the quiet and solitude of Whitwick, and in the discharge
of his professional duties. He wants nothing but more quietness and
regularly sustained energy. The latter I think he would possess did not his
Body hinder it; close application forces the blood into his head & eyes,
and otherwise disorders him. – I have been baffled in all my attempts to
find a situation for William, so that after having taken him off from his

Greek, & remitted his Latin reading in some degree, I am now obliged to
turn my thoughts again to College. With this view he must quit home
for a year's preparation. I have written to Mr Jackson to learn if he can
take him; if he cannot I must place him somewhere else; and should be
glad of a suggestion from you on the subject. His Brother would be quite
equal to instruct him, but that would never answer, as he would have no
authority over him.

*327. William Wordsworth to George Huntly Gordon; Rydal Mount, 10
November [1828]*

I have now to request your attention and <u>assistance</u> in a point of much
more importance; it is to trouble you to give me information respecting
your notions of the advantages and disadvantages of a situation in some
government office for a Young Man, with some talent, but which has not
been adequately cultivated, his studies having been interrupted by severe
illness. The individual is my Younger Son. The best way of explaining
myself will be to give briefly his history. He was 18 years of age last June.
Before the age of 10 he was sent to the Charterhouse where he was
obliged to quit after nearly three years trial; his health having been utterly
ruined by the confinement &c. In the Course of the summer after he
came down, for the last time, he was attacked with dropsy, first in the
abdomen & afterwards in the Chest; by care and medical skill, he was
restored, but he was not permitted to read except for the merest amusement
for more than two years – during which time, as it had been before, his
growth was utterly stopped – Afterwards I did not venture to send him to
a public School – for fear of a Relapse – but home is a bad place for
progress in study, though he had unusual advantages. The consequence
was, that a Mind not particularly disposed to Books by nature, was
rendered still less so – he dreaded the notion of College – and could think
of no thing but the Army, to which he is still strongly inclined, but which
we are decidedly averse to. The object which took me to Town last
Spring, was to procure him a situation either in a Counting House, or a
manufacturing concern – in this I failed – And though he is decidedly
averse to the scheme – I have been obliged to think of a situation for him
in some public office. I have no hope of succeeding immediately, though
my Friends of the Lowther family have the best disposition to serve me.
But my Son as I said before has a prejudice against such a situation,
grounded <u>mainly</u> I believe upon his humble sense of his own talents, by

the bye another disadvantage of his private education, and upon an apprehension that he cannot bear the Confinement. Now, dear Sir, be so good as to enlighten us upon these two points – how much confinement & what sort of labour are required in the offices with which you are acquainted . . .

I have yet another question to ask – as I have no means of procuring him such a situation at present, how could he pass the intermediate time with most advantage – at an english University, or abroad? where he might learn French & German . . .

– Pray excuse my vile penmanship – it is always bad – but today I have no command of my pen at all, for I am just come from 2 hours hard labour with the mattock and spade in my Garden, where we are making improvements, & a Labourer has disappointed me –

William's arrangement with *The Keepsake* had always seemed too good to be true: he now began to realize that Reynolds intended to obtain more poetry from him than had been agreed by the simple expedient of rejecting some of the poems and holding others back for later publication. To make matters worse, an enterprising Parisian publisher, Galignani, taking advantage of the absence of international copyright regulation, had just issued a cheap and unauthorized edition of William's poems, for which the poet would receive nothing at all.

328. William Wordsworth to Edward Quillinan; [Rydal Mount], postmarked 12 November 1828

Of the Keepsake I have neither seen nor heard any thing – Besides the Triad it contained two short pieces of mine, & 4 or 5 sonnets – [1]

I have not written a verse these 9 months past – my vein, I fear is run out. Gagliani [i.e Galignani] has printed my Poems in one Vol[ume] at Paris – so there is an end to the sale of the London Edition, his being to be had a[t] a third or a 4th of the price.

329. William Wordsworth to Frederic Mansel Reynolds; Rydal Mount, 19 December 1828

I hope you did not patronize Gagliani's piracy by yourself purchasing the work. My Friend Mr Robinson laudably declined doing so when at Paris – because he would not encourage so unfair a proceeding. – My last Edition is yet a few pounds in my debt – and I am certain that the sale will be much impeded by the Paris Edition at less than half the price of the London one. <u>Every</u> body goes to Paris now a days. – I see you are a conscientious Reckoner – I feared my Quota would prove short of my engagement – but not as you say "<u>very short</u> " of our stipulated Mark. The strict letter was 12 pages at the least and 15 at the most. Depend upon it one year with another you shall have no right to complain – And this year the account shall be set straight. I am rather rich having produced 730 verses during the last month – after a long fallow – . In the list are two stories – and three incidents – so that your wish may be gratified, by some one or more of these Pieces. But I will tell you frankly – I can write nothing better than a great part of the "<u>Triad</u> " – whether it be for your purpose or no – –

330. Dora Wordsworth to Edward Quillinan; Rydal Mount, 30 December 1828

He has just finished another Poem of 376 lines – Composed nearly a thousand lines in the last six or seven weeks – pretty well for a Man in his 59th year –

331. William Wordsworth to Frederic Mansel Reynolds; [Rydal Mount], postmarked 28 January 1829

I must now come to a principle – which I cannot allow to govern the agreement between us. In your former Letter – you observed that my Contributions only filled eleven pages and a half – upon which assurance I readily agreed to make up the deficiency – but I find that four Sonnets of mine have not been inserted – which would have occupied at least two pages, making altogether 13 – and a half pages – – Now I care nothing about my Contributions being inserted – I mean on the score of personal vanity – but I certainly don't expect that a claim for more should be grounded upon rejection, for you clearly see, if this principle be admitted – I might write on for ever, before my part of the Contract were fulfilled. You rely upon my fair dealing not to send you any thing I deem unworthy of myself – You have this confidence in me – and I shall take care not to abuse it – Pray send me back the rejected Sonnets at your leisure – if you recollect we took a good deal of pains together about one line in the Sonnet upon Roman antiquities – I corrected it – but I forget how – tell me when you wish for my Contribution.

332. William Wordsworth to George Huntly Gordon; Rydal Mount, 29 July
[1829]

I have not got my Mss back from the "Keepsake," whose managers have
between them used me shamefully – but my Complaint is principally of
the Editor for with the Proprietor I have had little direct connection – If
you think it worth while you shall at some future day, see such parts of
the correspondence as I have preserved. Mr Southey is pretty much in the
same predicament with them, though he has kept silence for the present
– He apprehends that they purpose to extend such of his last years
contributions as they did not publish, into this year, which they have no
right to do – – I am properly served for having had any connection with
such things – My only excuse is, that they offered me a very liberal sum, &
that I have laboured hard through a long life without more pecuniary
emolument, than a Lawyer gets for two special retainers, or a public
performer sometimes for two or three songs – farewell.

333. William Wordsworth to the Reverend Dionysius Lardner, editor of the
Cabinet Cyclopaedia of Eminent Literary and Scientific Men; *Rydal*
Mount, 22 January 1829[2]

The subject which I had thought of is much more limited than you
suppose – being nothing more than an Account of the Deceased Poetesses
of Great Britain – with an Estimate of their Works – but upon more
mature Reflection I cannot persuade myself that it is sufficiently interesting
for a separate subject, were I able to do it justice. The Dramatic & other
imaginative female Writers might be added – the interest would thereby
be encreased, but unity of subject would be sacrificed – –. It remains
therefore for me to regret that I should have held out the least hope that
I might undertake any thing of the Kind – for which I have no excuse
but what you I hope will be satisfied with, that I was taken by surprize.

   I still am of opinion that something is wanted upon the subject – neither
Dr Johnson, nor Dr Anderson, nor Chalmers, nor the Editor I believe of
any other Corpus of English Poetry takes the least notice of female Writers
– this, to say nothing harsher, is very ungallant.

334. William Wordsworth to Hugh James Rose, Christian Advocate of Cambridge University; [Rydal Mount, late January 1829]

Great principles, you hold, are sacrificed to shifts and expedients. I agree with you. What more sacred law of nature, for instance, than that the mother should educate her child? yet we felicitate ourselves upon the establishment of infant schools, which is in direct opposition to it.

. . . there are thousands of stirring people now in England, who are so far misled as to deem these schools *good in themselves*, and to wish that, even in the smallest villages, the children of the poor should have what *they* call 'a good education' in this way. Now, these people (and no error is at present more common) confound *education* with *tuition*.

Education, I need not remark to you, is everything that *draws out* the human being, of which *tuition*, the teaching of schools especially, however important, is comparatively an insignificant part. Yet the present bent of the public mind is to sacrifice the greater power to the less – all that life and nature teach, to the little that can be learned from books and a master . . .

In the present generation I cannot see anything of an harmonious co-operation between these schools and home influences. If the family be thoroughly bad, and the child cannot be removed altogether, how feeble the barrier, how futile the expedient! If the family be of middle character, the children will lose more by separation from domestic cares and reciprocal duties, than they can possibly gain from captivity with such formal instruction as may be administered . . .

We are as impatient under the evils of society as under our own, and more so; for in the latter case, necessity enforces submission. It is hard to look upon the condition in which so many of our fellow creatures are born, but they are not to be raised from it by partial and temporary expedients: it is not enough to rush headlong into any new scheme that may be proposed, be it Benefit Societies, Savings' Banks, Infant Schools, Mechanics' Institutes, or any other. Circumstances have forced this nation to do, by its manufacturers, an undue portion of the dirty and unwhole-some work of the globe. The revolutions among which we have lived have unsettled the value of all kinds of property, and of labour, the most precious of all, to that degree, that misery and privation are frightfully prevalent. We must bear the sight of this, and endure its pressure, till we have by reflection discovered the cause, and not till then can we hope

even to palliate the evil. It is a thousand to one but that the means resorted
to will aggravate it.

On 9 April 1829, Dorothy, who had spent the winter at Whitwick with her
nephew, John, was suddenly struck down with what may have been a form of
cholera. Reports that she was at death's door sent Mary hurrying to Whitwick
to nurse her back to health. It was the first serious illness of Dorothy's life but it
marked the beginning of a steady physical decline which, six years later, would
also lead to a complete mental breakdown.

335. Dorothy Wordsworth to Henry Crabb Robinson, Whitwick; 2 May 1829

It drew tears from my eyes to read of your affectionate anxiety concerning
me. In fact it is the first time in my life of fifty six years in which I have
had a serious illness, therefore I never before had an opportunity of
knowing how much some distant Friends care about me – Friends abroad
– Friends at home – all have been anxious – & more so, far more I am
sure, than I deserve; but I attribute much of this to my having been so
remarkably strong and healthy, it came like a shock to every one, to be
told of a dangerous illness having attacked me. – I am now, through God's
mercy, perfectly restored to health, & almost to strength; but quiet care –
for a time at least, I am assured is necessary; & indeed my own frame
admonishes me that it is. But for the sake of my kind friends I am bound
to take care, & I promise them all – including you who will be far away
from us, that I will be neither rash nor negligent – Indeed I never can
forget what I suffered myself nor the anxiety of those around me.

336. William Wordsworth to Henry Crabb Robinson; Rydal Mount, 26 April 1829

What a shock that was to our poor hearts. Were She to depart the Phasis
of my Moon would be robbed of light to a degree that I have not courage
to think of – during her illness we often thought of your high esteem of
her goodness, and of your kindness towards her upon all occasions – Our
last account was of the 19th & that morning she had been out in the
garden for ten minutes & we know that if she had not been going on well
since we should certainly have heard – We look for a letter in course
tomorrow – Mrs Wordsworth is still with her & I have entreated her to

stay ten days more – Dora is my house keeper, & did she not hold the Pen it would run wild in her Praises – Sara Coleridge, one of the loveliest and best of Creatures, is with me so that I am an enviable person notwithstanding our domestic impoverishment. Mrs Coleridge is here also – & if pity and compassion for others anxieties were a sweet sensation I might be envied on that account also for I have enough of it –

337. William Wordsworth to George Huntly Gordon; Rydal Mount, 16 June 1829

We have at last had a night of rain after a parching drought of many many weeks; the streams of the mountains are again foaming & vocal and the verdure already of the mountain turf reanimated . . .

You would have enjoyed a walk I had this morning with Miss Coleridge now our visitor. With a spade each a basket and an umbrella, for sunny showers were flying all about us – we went high up into a valley among the mountains behind this house to fetch the roots of a beautiful flower [bird's-eye primrose] which she had seen for the first time a few days ago – We have planted it in the garden with many fears however that the soil is not moist enough for it to thrive in.

338. Dorothy Wordsworth to her nephew, John Wordsworth of Cambridge; Rydal Mount, 18 November [1829]

You have heard of your aged Uncle's pedestrian feats . . . in Ireland [where William had just taken a five-week tour]; and now that he has been many weeks at home I am truly happy in being able to tell you that I never saw him more active or in better health. This morning – under a clear frosty sky with brilliant sunshine he is walking to Langdale to look after the Constellation Farm,[3] with Dora by his side, on her poney. He has paid all his visits (to Lowther – to Hallsteads Levens Park & Storrs Hall) and is vigorously disposed to commence his winter's labours – and, if the eyes keep tolerably well, I trust something important may be done. He does intend to fall to the 'Recluse' being seriously impressed with the faith that very soon it must be too late (His next Birth day will be his 60th) – but, in the mean time he has been busy with other less important matters – polishing the small poems he wrote last year – and actually he has written another Sonnet! This we were not glad of – fearing it might be but the beginning as heretofore, of a Batch: he has, however, promised that he will write no more – now I should have little faith in this promise, if it were not plain that his mind is set upon doing its best at the great Work.

339. Dora Wordsworth to Edward Quillinan; Rydal Mount, 21 November 1829

Upon one step Father is determined – that is, to have his Poems printed some way or other or in one little Vol[ume] so that the purchasers of the former Ed[ition] may procure them if they like. This he deems but common justice . . .

Father bids me tell you that he has removed the 1st Stanza of his 'Sound Poem' [*On the Power of Sound*] as I call it, with which you were pleased to a place where it tells more & has written another Stanza which is a better introduction – We all think there is a grandeur in this Poem but it ought to have been in the "Recluse" & Mother on that account but half enjoys it –

340. Dora Wordsworth to Edward Quillinan; [Rydal Mount], postmarked 19 December 1829

I am sorry to say Father has not yet heard from Longman – Aunt & I are exceedingly anxious something were done towards forwarding the printing of these small Poems, for till they are out of the way we feel convinced, his great work will never be touched, every day he finds something to alter or new stanzas to add – or a fresh Sonnet – or a fresh Poem growing out of one just finished – which he always promises shall be the last – Two or three stanzas are added to the Ode on Sound – "After thoughts" to The Rock & Primrose Poem & so on –

341. Dorothy Wordsworth to her friend Mary, sister of Charles Lamb; Rydal Mount, 9 January 1830

My Brother & Sister are both in excellent health. In him there is no failure except the tendency to inflammation in his eyes, which disables him from reading much or at all by candle-light – & the use of the pen is irksome to him: however he has a most competent and willing amanuensis in his Daughter, who takes all labour from Mother's & Aunt's aged hands – His muscular powers are in no degree diminished – indeed I think that he walks regularly more than ever, finding fresh air the best bracer of his weak eyes – he is still the crack skater on Rydal Lake – and as to climbing of mountains – the hardiest & the youngest are yet hardly a match for him. In composition I can perceive no failure & his imagination seems as vigorous as in youth – yet he shrinks from his great work and both during the last & present winter has been employed in writing small poems – Do not suppose, my dear Friends, that I write the above boastingly – Far from it It is in thankfulness for present blessings – yet always with a sense of the probability that all will have a sudden check – and if not so – the certainty that in the course of Man's life; but a few years of vigorous health and strength can be allotted to him. For this reason my Sister & I take every opportunity of pressing upon him the necessity of applying to his great work – & this he feels – resolves to do it – and again resolution fails – and now I almost fear habitually, that it will be ever so.

342. William Wordsworth to George Huntly Gordon; Rydal Mount, 6 April 1830

We have had here a few days of delicious summer weather – it appeared with the suddenness of a Pantomime trick – stayed longer than one had a right to expect – and was as rapidly succeeded by high wind, bitter cold, and Winter snow over hill and dale – . . .

You ask what are my employments – according to Dr Johnson they are such as entitle me to high commendation; for I am not only making two blades of grass grow where only one grew before, but a dozen. In plain language I am draining a bit of spungy ground. – But do not set me down for an Agricultural Patriot; my grasses are in my little Policy & grow more for beauty than profit. If the ground is to be depastured I must be Nebuchadnezzarized & e'en take to grazing myself, for I dare not trust to Cows nor Horses – they would trample & defile my Walks, nor to sheep – they would devour my Plantations, which are upon too small a scale to be worth being severally enclosed – In the field where this goes on I am making a green Terrace, that commands a beautiful view of our two Lakes Rydal & Windermere, & more than two miles of intervening vale with the Stream visible by glimpses flowing through it. I shall have great pleasure in shewing you this, among the other returns which I hope one day to make for your kindness.

Adieu Yours WW

*343. Dorothy Wordsworth to her nephew, Chris Wordsworth; [Rydal Mount],
13 April [1830]*

Your Uncle passed his 60th Birth-day on the 7th of this month – and
thankful am I to say that his activity & strength are hardly perceptibly
diminished during the last ten years (I date from 1820 recalling the
exertions he made on the Alps at that time) but he has of late complained
of head-aches after exertion, which used much to trouble him in his youth
but left him in middle life. I hope this return is only accidental. He has
lately laid aside poetical labours & has been much out of doors, presiding
over workmen who are making us a <u>third</u> Terrace in the field purchased
for the house – which – to my great satisfaction – was, you know, only
built in the air. This new Terrace is a beautiful thing – but I will not
describe it – you must all come & walk upon it – A new edition of the
Poems will soon be called for – We, females, wish him to publish
the numerous poems now in store immediately, in one small volume, –
that they may have a Run & this Edition get sold off before the 5 vol[ume]s
are again printed – when the new little volume might be incorporated
with them – which would be very fair, as the purchasers of the former
would have the opportunity of adding the new little volume. Now in his
heart, he approves of our plan; but his aversion to publication at all, is so
great that he <u>will not</u> resolve to do it – and would much rather smuggle
the new ones in among the rest – as he did before – & thus get nothing
for them. A much better plan than this would be to publish nothing new, &
let the whole remain for the benefit of his Family after death.

*344. William Wordsworth to his daughter, Dora; [Rydal Mount], Tuesday
morning [late April/early May 1830]*

I have given over writing Verses till my head becomes stronger or my
fancy livelier – you have there mightily the advantage of me, as a comparison between our Letters abundantly shows – farewell love & love and
love for ever –

W.W.

345. William Wordsworth to George Huntly Gordon; [Rydal Mount], 10 May [1830]

Now will you be so kind as to trouble yourself in your rambles to make enquiries occasionally among the Retail Booksellers whether they are of opinion that a cheap Edit[ion] of my Poems would answer for me; I mean make amends by encrease of Sale for diminution of price. If you could settle my mind on this subject I should be inclined to try the experiment, as the last Edition is I believe getting low.

346. William Wordsworth to his admirer, the surgeon, John Gardner; Whitehaven, 19 May 1830

May 19th 1830
Whitehaven
(I return home in a few days.)

My dear Sir,

I feel that I ought to thank you for your judicious Letter, and for the pains you have taken towards settling the question of the eligibility of low-priced Publications. Messrs Longman talk strangely when they say that my annual Account will shew what is advisable. How can that shew anything but what number of Purchases I have had? it cannot tell me how many I have missed by the heavy price. Again, Messrs L[ongman] affirm that my Buyers are of that class who do not regard prices – but that class, never perhaps very large, is every day going smaller with the reduced incomes of the time – and besides, in this opinion I believe these Gentlemen to be altogether mis-taken. My Poetry, less than any other of the day, is adapted to the taste of the Luxurious, and of those who value themselves upon the priviledge of wealth and station. And though it be true that several passages are too abstruse for the ordinary Reader, yet the main body of it is as well fitted (if my aim be not altogether missed) to the bulk of the people both in sentiment and language, as that of any of my contemporaries . . .

To the above considerations I would add the existence of the pirated editions, and above all an apprehension that there is a growing prejudice against high-priced books. Indeed I am inclined to think with my Friend Mr Southey that shortly few books will be published except low-priced ones, or those that are highly ornamented, for persons who delight in such luxuries. These considerations all seem in favor of the experiment which you recommend. Yet I am far from sure that it would answer. It is not to be questioned that the perpetually supplied stimulus of Novels stands much in the way of the purer interest which used to attach to Poetry. And although these poorer Narratives do but in very few instances retain more than the hold of part of a season upon public attention, yet a fresh crop springs up every hour. But to bring these tedious *pros* and *cons* to a close, I will say at once that if I could persuade myself that the Retail Bookseller you speak of is not mistaken in his notion that he could sell *ten* copies, (or less than half of that number,) when he now sells *one*, were the price something under a pound, I would venture upon such an edition. I ought to say to you, however, that I have changed my intention of making additions at present, and should confine myself to inter-mixing the few poems that were published in the Keep-sake of [the] year before last. I have already stated to you my notions as to the extreme injustice of the law of copy-right; if it has not been mis-represented to me, for I never saw the Act of Parliament. But I am told that, when an Author dies, such of his Works as have been twice fourteen years before the Public are public property, and that his heirs have no pecuniary interest in anything that he may leave behind, beyond the same period. My days are in course of nature drawing towards a close, and I think it would be best, in order to secure some especial value to any collection of my Works that might be printed after my decease, to reserve a certain number of new pieces to be inter-mixed with that collection. I am acquainted with a distinguished Author who means to hold back during his lifetime all the Corrections and additions in his several works for the express purpose of benefiting his heirs by the superiority which those improvements will give to the pieces which may have become the property of the public. I do sincerely hope and trust that the Law in this point will one day or other be brought nearer to justice and reason. Take only my own comparatively insignificant case. Many of my Poems have been upwards of 30 years subject to criticism, and are disputed about as keenly as ever, and appear to be read much more. In fact thirty years are no adequate test for works of Imagination, even from second or third-rate writers, much less from those of the first order, as we see in the instances of Shakespeare and Milton.

347. William Wordsworth to George Huntly Gordon; Rydal Mount, 30 May [1830]

As to the Portrait to be prefixed according to the suggestion of the Booksellers – the notion to me is intolerable. These Vanities should be avoided by living Authors – when a man is departed the world may do with him what it likes – but while he lives let him take some little care of himself –

348. Sara Hutchinson to Edward Quillinan; Rydal Mount, 31 July [1830]

We have, as usual, a throng of summer visitors & the house has been more like an Inn, for the last six weeks, than a private one – . . . For one <u>long</u> fortnight we had Mrs Hemans[4] & one of her boys – he was a sweet interesting creature – but she tho' a good-natured person is so spoilt by the adulation of 'the world' that her affectation is perfectly unendurable – Don't say this to Miss Jewsbury who idolizes her – Mr W[ordsworth] <u>pretends</u> to like her very much – but I believe it is only because we do not – for She is the very opposite, her good-nature excepted, of anything he ever admired before either in <u>theory or practice</u> – I wish you had been here – I am sure you would have been amused at least –

349. William Wordsworth to Samuel Rogers; Rydal Mount, Friday, postmarked 30 July 1830

How shall I dare to tell you that the Muses and I have parted company – at least I fear so, for I have not written a verse these twelve months past, except a few stanzas upon my return from Ireland, last autumn.

350. Hartley Coleridge, poet and son of Samuel Taylor Coleridge, to his brother, Derwent; finished 30 August 1830

Of Westmorland and the *old familiar faces*, what shall I say? All are not gone – but most are changed. The Rydal Mount family perhaps the least of any, tho' W. W. to me seems yearly less of the Poet, and more of the respectable, talented, hospitable Country gentleman. Unfortunately, his weakest points, his extreme irritability of self-approbation and parsimony of praise to contemporary authors are much *in statu quo*. This is a little ungrateful, for he always applauds my attempts; but what he would do, if they were favourites with the public, no matter . . .

John Wordsworth, a truly respectable Clergyman, and [since 1829] Rector of Moresby, a Parish on the coast of Cumberland – Patron Lord Lonsdale – is about to be married to Miss Curwen,[5] a very amiable young Lady, quite pretty enough, but whether rich enough I have my doubts, as old Capricorn [her grandfather] left his estates much encumbered – which I am sorry for, since Henry Curwen [her father] is a most excellent, right-hearted, and right-minded man, and John Wordsworth is so truly estimable, and so much what a Minister of the Gospel should be, and withal, so unlikely to fall foolishly in love, that I am sure the woman of his choice must be what a minister's wife should be. Dora, as sweet a creature as ever breath'd, suffers sadly from debility. I have my suspicions that she would be a healthier matron than she is a Virgin, but strong indeed must be the love that could induce her to leave her father, whom she almost adores, and who quite doats upon her. I am afraid there is little hope at present of another portion of the *Recluse*, but it must delight every lover of mankind to see how the influence of Wordsworth's poetry is diverging, spreading over society, benefitting the heart and soul of the Species, and indirectly operating upon thousands, who haply, never read, or will read, a single page of his fine Volumes.

Politics, rather than poetry, were foremost in William's mind in the stormy years leading up to the Reform Bill of 1832. He had opposed the Roman Catholic Emancipation Act of 1829, fearing it marked the death-knell of the Church of England and that Catholics appointed to state office would put their loyalty to the Pope above that to the Crown. He would also oppose, with equal vigour, the attempts to reform Parliament, not because he was intrinsically opposed to the idea of widening the franchise, but because he feared that too much change, too swiftly made, would destroy the delicate balance of the constitution and lead to the hijacking of an uneducated electorate by unprincipled demagogues and potential tyrants, just as it had done during the French Revolution. The revolutions in Europe in 1830 fed his fears and the hopes of British radicals in equal measure.

351. William Wordsworth to George Huntly Gordon; [Rydal Mount, mid August or later, 1830]

In France incompatible things are aimed at; a monarchy and democracy to be united without an intervening aristocracy to constitute a graduated scale of power & influence. I cannot conceive how an hereditary monarchy can exist, without an hereditary peerage, in a country so large as France, nor how either can maintain their ground if the Law of the Napoleonic Code compelling equal division of property by will, be not repealed. And I understand that a vast majority of the French are decidedly adverse to the repeal of that Law – which I cannot but think will erelong be found injurious both to France, & in its collateral effects to the rest of Europe. But why fatigue you with these dry speculations –

352. William Wordsworth to Edward Quillinan; [Rydal Mount], 10 September 1830

Dora has already by a short note thanked you for bearing us in mind while you were in Paris, & for your interesting Letter – My own notions of the late changes in France, you will be at no loss to form an opinion about – From what you have heard me say upon Politics and government, & reform, & revolution etc you will not doubt but that I must lament deeply that the Ex-King of France should have fallen into such a desperate course of conduct, and given his enemies so much the advantage over him. He has done much harm to the cause of rational monarchy all over the world by placing himself in the wrong, to a degree that one would have thought impossible. – As to the future, fair and smooth appearances are not to be trusted, though the French, having passed lately through so many commotions and disappointments, may be in some degree checked in this democratical career by their remembrance of those calamities – – –.

By the end of the year, William felt that it was an absolute necessity that he should be in London to be at the heart of the political agitation surrounding Parliamentary reform. He went via Cambridge where his daughter was to spend the winter with her uncle and cousins and he would meet many young acolytes, including the poet Alfred Tennyson, who was then an undergraduate at Trinity College. To get to Cambridge, the sixty-year-old poet rode Dora's pony all the way from Lancaster, an extraordinary feat which prompted a flood of poetry.

353. *William Wordsworth to his sister, Dorothy; Coleorton, Monday morning*
[8 November 1830]

Lancashire is but a dull county and in my long ride, I saw nothing that
pleased me so much as a sweet little Gainsborough cottage girl, with a
tiny wheelbarrow, which she was guiding along the Causeway, filled
with dung collected on the road; with a little basket enclosed in a red
handkerchief and slung upon one of the handles of the Barrow – in which
she had carried Dinner to her Father in the fields – I gave her a penny for
her industry, and she said, thank you Sir in the prettiest manner imaginable
– I regret I did not ask her whether she had learned to read –

354. *William Wordsworth to William Rowan Hamilton; Trinity Lodge,*
[Cambridge], 26 November 1830

It was my wish that Dora should have the benefit of her pony while at
Cambridge, and very valiantly and economically[6] I determined, unused
as I am to Horsemanship, to ride the creature myself. I sent James [Dixon,
the servant] with it to Lancaster – there mounted – stopped a day at
Manchester a week at Coleorton, and so reached the end of my journey
safe and sound, not however without encountering two days of tempestuous rain. Thirty seven miles did I ride in one day through the worse
[*sic*] of these Storms. And what was my resource? guess again – writing
verses – To the memory of my departed Friend Sir George Beaumont[7]
whose House I had left the day before. While buffetting the other Storm
I composed a Sonnet upon the splendid Domain of Chatsworth which I
had seen in the morning, as contrasted with the secluded habitations of
the narrow Fells in the Peak – and as I passed through the tame and
manufacture-disfigured Country of Lancashire I was reminded by
the faded leaves, of Spring – and threw off a few Stanzas of an Ode to
May.

355. *William Wordsworth to William Rowan Hamilton; from Christopher*
Wordsworth's country home, Buxted Rectory, Sussex, 24 January 1831

How came you not to say a word about the disturbances of your unhappy
country [Ireland]? O'Connell and his brother agitators I see are apprehended; I fear nothing will be made of it towards strengthening the
Government; and if the prosecution fails, it cannot but prove very mis-

chievous . . . Are you not on the brink of a civil war? Pray God it be not so! . . .

Parliament is soon to meet, and the Reform question cannot be deferred. The nearer we come to the discussion, the more am I afraid of the consequences.

356. William Wordsworth to his nephew, Chris Wordsworth; [Buxted], postmarked 18 February 1831

a Man must be blind as a mole who cannot see that the revolutionary movements of the present day are pointed for their ultimate aim against social inequality as based upon and upheld by accumulated Property – For many reasons I detest the ballot & not the least of these is a conviction that armed with this instrument the enemies of the present social system would be irresistible. Do not infer from this that I am reconciled either to those vast capitals & very great inequalities of <u>landed</u> property in particular which exist in these Islands but all this might be brought within reasonable bounds in due course of time without incurring the mischiefs which must inevitably arise out of the principles of [? another] system; mischiefs incalculably greater [? than those] which the liberals are set upon removing at [any] cost.

357. Charles Cavendish Fulke Greville, diarist and clerk to the Privy Council, Memoirs, 27 February 1831

I am just come from breakfasting with [Henry] Taylor to meet Wordsworth; the same party as when he had Southey – [John Stuart] Mill, Elliot, Charles Villiers. Wordsworth may be bordering on sixty; hard-featured, brown, wrinkled, with prominent teeth and a few scattered grey hairs, but nevertheless not a disagreeable countenance; and very chearful, merry, courteous, and talkative, much more so than I should have expected from the grave and didactic character of his writings. He held forth on poetry, painting, politics, and metaphysics, and with a great deal of eloquence; he is more conversable and with a greater flow of animal spirits than Southey. He mentioned that he never wrote down as he composed, composed walking, riding, or in bed, and wrote down after; that Southey always composes at his desk. He talked a great deal of Brougham, whose talents and moral virtues he greatly admires; that he was very generous and affectionate in his disposition, full of duty and attention to his mother, and had adopted and provided for a whole family of his brother's children, and treats his wife's children as if they were his own.

One very different meeting took place at the request of a schoolmaster, Joseph Hine, who, like so many others in his profession, had written urging William to publish a selection of his poems for school-children. For all Quillinan's teasing, Hine was clearly an inspired teacher and the occasion had its due effect on William.

358. Edward Quillinan to Dora Wordsworth; [12 Bryanston Street, London], postmarked 3 March 1831

While William Wordsworth Esq[ui]re Poet and Anti-Reformer is working away with a steel pen at, not in, my side, I may as well take another to give some account of her father to la mia dorabella. He is very busy indeed . . . His time is swallowed up in swallowing breakfasts, making morning visits, (where he gets cold collations) devouring dinners, and thundering denunciations against reform: and now and then "brooding over his own sweet voice" and Sir George Beaumont. – On Tuesday Captain Todd and I accompanied him to Brixton, not to the tread-mill, but to see a mad Schoolmaster named Hine or Hind. Now listen. This broad shouldered muscular Theban had one advantage over us besides his learning. His eyes are so arranged that you never know when he is looking at you; so that he may be staring hard at you all the time that he seems to look quite the other way. I shouldn't like to have such a cunning-eyed Schoolmaster. He received us all three with the most earnest cordiality, and gave us glasses of sherry and pound-cake. But to Mr Wordsworth he was crushingly affectionate. I wouldn't have had my hand in those brawny fingers so long and often for something. After wine and cake, we were ushered into the School-room. There were 54 boys at desks in rows of 8; as in the pit of a theatre. We were on the stage: viz. Poet, Pedagogue, Captain of Dragoons & I. – The boys rose and bowed; sate and gazed: one made a speech of welcome after formal introduction of Poet – Poet replied – pencils and slates were brought out at word of command; pedagogue gave out, line by line, the Sonnet supposed to be written on Westminster Bridge. All the Boys wrote it, one echoing the Master, as the clerk in certain cases, does the clergyman. When finished, several boys, in turn, read it aloud: very well too. They were then called upon to explain the meaning of "the river glideth at its own sweet will." One boy, the biggest, a red headed man-boy, with a ring on his right little finger, made a dissertation on the influence of the moon on the tides &c &c, and seemed rather inclined to be critical; another said there was no wind; another that there were no water breaks in the Thames to prevent its gliding as it pleased; another that the arches of the bridges had no locks to shut the water in or out: & so forth. One Boy said there were no boat[s] – that was the nearest. – Poet explained: was then called on by Pedagogue to read his sonnet himself: declined. Ped[agogue] entreated: Poet remonstrated: Ped[agogue] inexorable: Poet submitted. I never heard him read better. The Boys evidently felt it; a thunder of applause; Poet asked for a Half Holiday for them – granted – thunders on thunders Seriously speaking, – the whole scene was indescribably animated and interesting. – Got away from Ped[agogue] (who breakfasts here next Friday) and drove off. – Your Father has finished his own caligraphic duties; & insists on my finishing on pretence that he wants me to walk: the truth being that he is afraid I am making love to you all this time. – Love to your Mother. Ever Yrs. E.Q.

Chapter Ten

1831–6

William's meeting with Joseph Hine and the Brixton schoolboys marked a turning point in his poetic career: it resulted in the publication of *Selections from the Poems of William Wordsworth, Esq. Chiefly for the Use of Schools and Young Persons* (1831). The edition was prepared by Hine, though William checked the proofs, and published by another Wordsworthian devotee and poet, Edward Moxon. Selling at only 5s 6d, *Selections* was hugely successful in making William's poems available to a wider readership, convincing William that he should change his publisher from Longman to the more entrepreneurial Moxon. The two men had first met in 1826 when Moxon had made a pilgrimage to Rydal Mount. In the light of their subsequent relationship, William's advice then to the aspiring poet seems providential.

359. William Wordsworth to Edward Moxon; [Rydal Mount], postmarked 8 December 1826

– this little Vol[ume], with what I saw of yourself during a short interview, interests me in your welfare; and the more so as I always feel some apprehension for the destiny of those who in Youth addict themselves to the Composition of Verse. It is a very seducing employment; and though begun in disinterested love of the Muses is too apt to connect itself with self-love and the disquieting passions which follow in the train of that our natural infirmity. Fix your eye upon acquiring Independence by honorable business, and let the Muses come after rather than go before. –

360. William Wordsworth to Edward Moxon; [Rydal Mount, c.9 June 1831]

My dear Sir,

On the other side see a list of *errata*, some of which are so important and so mischievous to the sense that I beg they may be struck off instantly upon a slip of paper or separate leaf, and inserted in such

books as are not yet dispersed. For one of these *errata*, perhaps more,
I am answerable.

Tell Mr Hine, to whom I wish to write as soon as I can find time,
that I think the collection judiciously made. When you mentioned
'notes', I was afraid of them, and I regret much the one at the end
was not suppressed; nor is that about the editorial nut-cracks happily
executed. But Mr Hine is an original person, and therefore allowance
must be made for his oddities. He feels the poetry, and that is enough.
His preface does him great credit.

> ever and most truly yours,
> Wm Wordsworth

*361. William Wordsworth to William Rowan Hamilton and his sister, the poet
Eliza Hamilton; Rydal Mount, 13 June 1831*

I wish I could tell you that I had been busily employed in my own art;
but I have scarcely written a hundred verses during the last twelve months;
a sonnet, however, composed the day before yesterday, shall be transcribed
upon this sheet, by way of making *my* part of it better worth postage. It
was written at the request of the Painter Haydon, and to benefit him –
i.e., as he thought. But it is no more than my sincere opinion of his
excellent picture . . .

Have your sisters any interest with schoolmasters or *mistresses*? A selection from my poems has just been edited by a Dr. Hime [*sic*] for the benefit
chiefly of schools and young persons, and it is published by Moxon, of
Bond-street, an amiable young man of my acquaintance, whom I wish to
befriend, and of course I wish the book to be circulated, if it be found
to answer his purpose; 1500 copies have been struck off . . . The retail
price (bound) is only 5s. 6d., and the volume contains, I should suppose,
at least 1100 verses . . . and it would be found a good travelling companion
for those who like my poetry . . .

*362. Dorothy Wordsworth to the Reverend Francis Merewether, rector of
Coleorton; Rydal Mount, 6 June [1831]*

In spite of all that he [William] has suffered from the madness of the
Reformers – & of all that he dreads may happen to our long-favoured
Country & its glorious institutions, he is strong in health & even in spirits
chearful – He now no longer discusses, or attempts to <u>persuade</u>, He finds

it all in vain – & now he endeavours to wait in patience, trusting that by the wisdom & providence of God some changes (which he cannot foresee) may be wrought in the minds & actions of the infatuated multitudes – high & low – rich & poor.

The weather has been charming for many weeks – & is so still but the grass is beginning to pine for rain – So are all other fruits of the earth – This place (would that you & Mrs Merewether could see it) is enchanting – We have made great improvements, & the growth of the trees is astonishing – My Brother & his son William are fellow-labourers, & the Father almost as active as the Son – in lopping trees – making Seats – for sunshine or shade – a pool for the gold-fishes &c &c &c. These my Brother finds very worthy employments after the Turmoils of London in the late stormy times.

363. William Wordsworth to Benjamin Robert Haydon; [Rydal Mount], postmarked 8 July 1831

You ask my opinion about the Reform Bill. – I am averse (with that wisest of the Moderns Mr Burke) to all *hot* Reformations; i.e. to every sudden change in political institutions upon a large scale. They who are forced to part with power are of course irritated, and they upon whom a large measure of it is at once conferred have their heads turned and know not how to use it. To the *principle* of this particular measure, I object as *unjust*; and by its injustice opening a way for spoliation and subversion to any extent which the rash and iniquitous may be set upon . . . In short the whole of my proceedings would have been *tentative*, and in no case would I have violated a principle of justice. This is the sum of what I have to say.

364. William Wordsworth to John Kenyon; Rydal Mount, 9 September [1831]

The Summer that is over has been with us as well as with you a brilliant one, for sunshine & fair & calm weather – brilliant also for its unexampled gaiety in Regattas, Balls, Dejeuners, Pic-nics, by the Lake Side – on the Islands – & on the Mountain tops – Fire-works by night – Dancing on the greensward by day – in short a fever of pleasure from morn to dewy eve – from dewy eve till break of day. Our Youths & Maidens like Chaucer's Squire "hath slept no more than doth the Nightingale" & our Old Men have looked as bright as Tithonus when his withered cheek reflected the blushes of Aurora upon her first declaration of her passion for him.[1] In the room where I am now dictating, we had, three days ago a dance – forty beaus & belles, besides Matrons, ancient Spinsters & Greybeards – & tomorrow in this same room are we to muster for a Venison feast. Why are you not here, either to enjoy – or to philosophize upon this dissipation? – our Party tomorrow is not so large, but that we could find room for you & Mrs Kenyon. The disturbed state of the Continent is no doubt the reason why, in spite of the Reform bill, such multitudes of Pleasure Hunters have found their way this Summer to the Lakes.

In September 1831, William set off in the old jaunting car, driven by Dora, for a tour of Scotland. Their first objective, however, was to pay a farewell visit to William's old friend, Sir Walter Scott, at Abbotsford; Scott was seriously ill and about to go abroad in a vain attempt to recover his health. William, too, was suffering from a severe recurrence of his trachoma, which delayed his departure and accounted for his appearance, which caused some amusement.

365. *William Wordsworth to Sir Walter Scott; Carlisle, 16 September [1831]*

Carlisle, Friday Eve[ni]ng, Sept[ember] 16th [1831]

My dear Sir Walter,

"There's a man wi' a veil and a lass driving" exclaimed a little urchin as we entered "merrie Carlile" a couple of hours ago on our way to Abbotsford – From the words you will infer, & truly, that my eyes are in but a poor state – I was determined however to see you & yours & to give my daughter the same pleasure at all hazards; accordingly I left home last Tuesday but was detained two entire days at Halsteads on Ullswater by a serious increase of my complaint – this morning I felt so much better that we ventured to proceed, tomorrow we hope to sleep at Langholm on Sunday at Hawick & on Monday if the distance be not greater than we suppose under your roof

366. *William Wordsworth, notes dictated to Isabella Fenwick in January 1843*

Yarrow Revisited: . . . On Tuesday Morning Sir Walter Scott accompanied us & most of the party to Newark Castle on the Yarrow. When we alighted from the carriages he walked pretty stoutly & had great pleasure in revisiting these his favorite haunts – of that Excursion the Verses "Yarrow revisited" are a memorial . . . On our return in the afternoon we had to cross the Tweed directly opposite Abbotsford. The wheels of our carriage grated upon the pebbles in the bed of the stream that there flows somewhat rapidly – a rich but sad light of rather a purple than a golden hue was spread over the Eildon Hills at that moment & thinking it probable that it might be the last time Sir Walter would cross the stream I was not a little moved & expressed some of my feelings in the Sonnet beginning "A trouble[, not of clouds, or weeping rain]" . . .

367. *William Wordsworth to William Rowan Hamilton; Rydal Mount, 27 October [1831]*

You will naturally wish to hear something of Sir Walter Scott, & particularly of his health. I found him a good deal changed within the last three or four years, in consequence of some Shocks of the apoplectic kind; but his friends say that he is very much better, & the last accounts, up to the time of his going on board were still more favourable. He himself thinks his Age much against him, but he has only completed his 60th year – but a friend of mine was here the other day who has rallied, & is himself again, after a much severer [shock, and at an age several] years more advanced. So that I [trust the] world & his friends may be hopeful, with good reason, that the life & faculties of this Man, who has during the last six & twenty years diffused more innocent pleasure than ever fell to the lot of any human being to do in his own life-time may be spared.

368. *William Wordsworth to Basil Montagu; [Rydal Mount], postmarked 22 October 1831*

You say your disinclination to move encreases every year – it is not so with myself – travelling agrees with me wonderfully, I am as much Peter Bell as ever, & since my eyelids have been so liable to inflammation, after much reading especially, I find nothing so feeding to my mind as change of scene & rambling about; & my labours, such as they are, can be carried on better in the fields, & on the roads than any where else.

369. William Wordsworth to Lord Lonsdale's daughter, Lady Frederick Bentinck;
Rydal Mount, 9 November [1831]

I set off with a severe inflammation in one of my eyes, which was removed
by being so much in the open air; and for more than a month I scarcely
saw a newspaper, or heard of their contents. During this time we almost
forgot, my daughter and I, the deplorable state of the country. My spirits
rallied, and, with exercise – for I often walked scarcely less than twenty
miles a day – and the employment of composing verses, amid scenery the
most beautiful, and at a season when the foliage was most rich and varied,
the time flew away delightfully; and when we came back into the world
again, it seemed as if I had waked from a dream, that never was to return.
We travelled in an open carriage with one horse, driven by Dora; and
while we were in the Highlands I walked most of the way by the side of
the carriage, which left us leisure to observe the beautiful appearances.
The rainbows and coloured mists floating about the hills were more like
enchantment than anything I ever saw, even among the Alps. There was
in particular, the day we made the tour of Loch Lomond in the steamboat,
a fragment of a rainbow, so broad, so splendid, so glorious, with its
reflection in the calm water, it astonished every one on board, a party of
foreigners especially, who could not refrain from expressing their pleasure
in a more lively manner than we are accustomed to do.

370. Dora Wordsworth to Maria Jane Fletcher [nee Jewsbury]; Rydal Mount,
20 October 1831

Edinburgh is indeed a splendid city & the grandeur & beauty of the Scotch
Lakes far surpassed my expectation – & the best of all was I took dear
daddy away almost blind & brought him home with eyes as bright as any
of my little Turkies that you knew some 6 or 7 years back – & what was
more surprizing he was busy composing most of the time & he promises
that the Recluse shall be his winter's employment – but entre nous I think
his courage will fail him when winter really arrives –

371. William Wordsworth to William Rowan Hamilton; [Rydal Mount], 22 November 1831

You send me Showers of verses which I receive with much pleasure, as do we all; yet have we fears that this employment may seduce you from the Path of Science which you seem destined to tread with so much honour to yourself & profit to others. Again & again I must repeat, that the composition of verse is infinitely more of an art than Men are prepared to believe, & absolute success in it depends upon innumerable minutiae which it grieves me you should stoop to acquire a knowledge of. Milton talks of "pouring easy his unpremeditated verse" – it would be harsh, untrue & odious to say there is any thing like cant in this; but it is not true to the letter, & tends to mislead. I could point out to you 500 passages in Milton upon which labour has been bestowed, & twice 500 more to which additional labour would have been servicable: not that I regret the absence of such labour, because no Poem contains more proofs of skill acquired by practice. These observations are not called out by any defects or imperfections in your last pieces especially, they are equal to the former ones in effect; have many beauties, & are not inferior in execution – but again I do venture to submit to your consideration, whether the poetical parts of your Nature, would not find a field more favourable to their exercise in the regions of prose: not because those regions are humbler, but because they may be gracefully & profitably trod, with footsteps less careful & in measures less elaborate.

372. Dora Wordsworth to Maria Jane Fletcher; Rydal Mount, 3 December 1831

. . . – since I began this letter Father has taken up the Recluse with good earnest – Mother & he are both hard at work in this room – *but take no notice of this when you write to me or dont name it to any one* as perhaps he may not like my naming it – tho' he has never said so, I am sure you will rejoice with us in this work so I could not help telling you.

373. Dr Christopher Wordsworth to his son, Chris; postmarked 19 April 1832

They were very loath to part with him [Chris's brother John] from Rydal: for he has been of great value to all the family – more especially to your uncle – who having John to talk to in his walks, was very industrious through the whole winter at all other times of the day – and worked very hard – especially in the revising and finishing of his long autobiographic Poem.

374. William Wordsworth to the Reverend Joseph Kirkham Miller, in response to a request that he would write and publish on public affairs; Rydal Mount, 17 December 1831

My dear Sir,

You have imputed my silence, I trust, to some cause neither disagreeable to yourself nor unworthy to me. Your letter of the 26th of Nov[ember] had been misdirected to Penrith, where the postmaster detained it some time, expecting probably that I should come to that place, which I have often occasion to visit. When it reached me I was engaged in assisting my wife to make out some of my mangled and almost illegible MSS; which inevitably involved me in endeavours to correct and improve them. My eyes are subject to frequent inflammations, of which I had an attack (and am still suffering from it) while that was going on. You would nevertheless have heard from me almost as soon as I received your letter, could I have replied to it in terms in any degree accordant to my wishes. Your exhortations troubled me in a way you cannot be in the least aware of; for I have been repeatedly urged by some of my most valued friends, and at times by my own conscience, to undertake the task you have set before me. But I will deal frankly with you. A conviction of my incompetence to do justice to the momentous subject has kept me, and I fear will keep me, silent. My sixty-second year will soon be completed, and though I have been favoured thus far in health and strength beyond most men of my age, yet I feel its effects upon my spirits; they sink under a pressure of apprehension to which, at an earlier period of my life, they would probably have been superior. There is yet another obstacle: I am no ready master of prose writing, having been little practised in the art. This last consideration will not weigh with you; nor would it have done with myself a few years ago; but the bare mention of it will serve to show that years have deprived me of *courage*, in the sense the word bears when applied by Chaucer to the animation of birds in spring time. . . . Providence is now trying this empire through her political institutions. Sound minds find their expediency in principles; unsound, their principles in expediency. On the proportion of these minds to each other the issue depends. From calculations of partial expediency in opposition to general principles, whether those calculations be governed by fear or presumption, nothing but mischief is to be looked for; but, in the present stage of our affairs, the class that does the most harm consists of *well-intentioned* men, who, being ignorant of human nature, think that they may help the thorough-paced reformers and revolutionists to a *certain* point, then stop, and that the machine will stop with them. After all, the question is, fundamentally, one of piety and morals; of piety, as disposing men who are anxious for social improvement to wait patiently for God's good time; and of morals, as guarding them from doing evil that good may come, or thinking that any ends *can* be so good as to justify wrong means for attaining them.

William's sudden enthusiasm for 'The Recluse' ended almost as soon as it began, driven from his head by fears for his sister, who had suffered a serious relapse, and for the country, which, in June 1832, saw the passage of the Reform Bill which he had opposed so long.

375. *William Wordsworth to his brother, Christopher; Rydal Mount, 1 April [1832]*

Our dear sister makes no progress towards recovery of Strength – She is very feeble – never quits her room, and passes most of the day in or upon the bed. She does not suffer pain except now & then from wind and stitches – She is very chearful, and nothing troubles her but public affairs & the sense of requiring so much attention. Whatever may be the close of this illness, it will be a profound consolation to you my dear Brother, and to us all, that it is borne with perfect resignation; and that her thoughts are such as the good and pious would wish – She reads much – both religious and miscellaneous works. – . . .

I was so distressed with the aspect of public affairs, that were it not for our dear Sister's Illness, I should think of nothing else. – . . . I have witnessed one revolution in a foreign Country, and I have not courage to think of facing another in my own. Farewell. God bless you again.

*376. William Wordsworth to the Reverend Francis Merewether; Moresby, 18
June 1832*

The Reform bill being passed my <u>anxiety</u> for that cause is over but only
to be succeeded by dejection to despondency – the Parliament that has
past this bill was in profligacy & folly never surpassed since the parliament
that overthrew the monarchy in Charles the first's time; & it is to be
feared that it will give birth to a Monster still more odious than itself. Of
nine members to be returned by the county from which I write, seven
will to a certainty be, either down right Jacobin Republicans, or of a class,
in the present stage of our revolution, still more dangerous – rash or
complying Whig Innovators: of the other two members one will probably
be a Conservative & the ninth is in doubt, but I fear the good cause in
this instance also will not prevail.

*377. William Wordsworth to Henry Crabb Robinson; Rydal Mount, 21 July
[1832]*

You would observe that a cheap edition of my Poems is advertized in 4
Vol[ume]s. Help the sale, if you can till I get back my own money which
I shall have to advance to the amount of 4 or 500£. My terms of
Publication are 2 thirds of the risk & expence for what the Publisher calls
two thirds of the profit . . .

  Yesterday, notwithstanding the state of my Eyes, I was on the top of
Helvellyn with my friend Mr Julius Hare of Trinity Col[lege], Dr Arnold,
Master of Rugby as keen a reformer as your self, or any other Dissenting
Whig, & Mr [Thomas] Hamilton, Author of Cyril Thornton &c &c.
Also a Brother of Professor Buckland. We tempered our Bra[ndy] with
water from the highest, & we will therefore infer the pure[st], Spring in
England – & had as pleasant a day as any middle aged Gentlemen need
wish for – except for certain sad recollections that weighed upon my heart
– Once I was upon this summit with Sir H[umphry] Davy and Sir W[alter]
Scott – & many times have I trod it with my nearest & dearest relatives &
friends, several of whom are gone, & others going to their last abode –
But I have touched upon too melancholy a String –

Among the hundreds of visitors to Rydal Mount in the summer of 1832 was the
Royal Academician, Henry Pickersgill, who had been chosen to paint William's

portrait. The commission had caused great excitement and the result – at first – delighted all the Wordsworths, including William, who addressed a sonnet to his own picture.

378. Dorothy Wordsworth to William Rowan and Eliza Hamilton; Rydal Mount, 13 June 1831

This very moment a letter arrives – very complimentary – from the Master of St John's College, Cambridge (the place of my brother William's education), requesting him to sit for his portrait to some eminent artist, as he expresses it, "to be placed in the old House among their Worthies." He writes in his own name, and that of several of the Fellows. Of course my brother consents; but the difficulty is to fix on an artist. There never yet has been a good portrait of my brother. The sketch by Haydon, as you may remember, is a fine drawing – but what a likeness! all that there is of likeness makes it to me the more disagreeable.

379. Dora Wordsworth to Edward Quillinan; Rydal Mount, postmarked 8 October 1832

This [William's sonnet, *To the Author's Portrait*] I have transcribed thinking it the best proof I could give that your suspicions about the picture were quite wrong – It seems silly to say anything further on the subject but yet I feel as if enough could never be said – we do feel so deeply grateful to Pickersgill for giving us such a likeness of such a Father! My Mother is <u>perfectly</u> satisfied nay far far more – this I never expected could be the case – We all agree that Rotha's, darling Rotha's picture & this are the only <u>perfect</u> likenesses, that is <u>living</u> likenesses, we ever saw: in fact it is impossible to sit before either the one or the other five minutes without ones eyes filling with tears – . . .

Father's popularity is amazingly on the increase if we may judge from the odd & queer indeed impertinent I had almost said expedients that have been resorted to this summer by Strangers high & low to have a sight of him or his dwelling. One Man sent in a note well written with some needles to sell price 3d – "as a Lover of Poetry the Author of the Excursion would confer an additional great obligation by paying the bearer in person – " We have had two or three other notes quite as funny.

380. William Wordsworth to Eliza Hamilton; Rydal Mount, 10 January 1833

To come then to the point of your request – permission to transcribe
from my Letters – I cannot bring my mind to consent to this – it is
attaching far too much importance to words dropped in that way . . . I
have been so dejected in mind, by some private distresses, and still more
by the alarming State of public affairs in the two Islands, that I have not
been able to take the least pleasure in Poetry, or in my ordinary pursuits.
– In my Youth I witnessed in france the calamities brought upon all classes,
and especially the poor, by a Revolution, so that my heart aches at the
thought of what we are now threatened with – farewell

*381. William Wordsworth to his brother, Christopher; [Rydal Mount], 29
January [1833]*

You will grieve to hear that our dear Sister is very poorly and seems to
grow weaker every day. It was a month on Sunday since she left her room
– perhaps she caught some cold then – at all events she had an unusually
bad night and has never rallied since. Her legs began to swell – and the
swelling is accompanied with black spots, which alarm Mr Carr much;
and he has ordered her allowance of brandy and opium to be considerably
increased, apprehending mortification. She is not at all aware of this
<u>danger</u>, and I am happy to say that though unable now to rise from her
bed she is in a quiet state of mind. I will harrass you no more with
particulars, but will conclude with recommending her to your prayers. It
cannot be long before we must follow in course of Nature all those whom
we love, who are gone before us. When you write, do not let it appear
that I have sent you a desponding account.

382. Dora Wordsworth to Edward Quillinan; Rydal Mount, 22 February 1833

– A week ago – Monday night we little expected my dear Aunt would
look on this fair world again – Mr Carr too thought with us she had
scarcely an hour to live – Every day since that sad night she has rallied
wonderfully & is now freer from pain, & more comfortable in all respects, &
stronger than she was 7 weeks ago when she first was obliged to take to
her bed entirely – . . . I wash her face as she used to do mine some thirty
years ago she dear creature not having the power to do so much for herself
without great exhaustion – but she is happy & contented & only has

one regret – that she cannot read or even bear to be read to & as she cannot gain new ideas she knows she must lose some old ones – so she tells us –

383. William Wordsworth to Henry Crabb Robinson; [Rydal Mount], 5 February 1833

You mistake me in supposing me an Anti Reformer – <u>that</u> I never was – but an Anti-Bill man; heart and soul. – It is a fixed judgement of my mind, that an unbridled Democracy is the worst of all Tyrranies. Our Constitution had provided a check for the Democracy, in the regal prerogative influence & power, and in the house of Lords acting directly through its own Body and indirectly by the influence of individual Peers over a certain portion of the House of Commons – the old system provided in practise a check – both without and <u>within</u>. The extinction of the nomination-boroughs has nearly destroyed the internal check. The House of Lords, as a body, have been trampled upon, by the way in which the Bill has been carried, and they are brought to that point that the Peers will prove useless as an external check – while the regal power & influence has become, or soon will, mere shadows –

384. William Wordsworth to his family at Rydal; Moresby, Monday evening [1 April 1833]

. . . one day with another, I have scarcely walked less than 12 miles. The sea is a delightful companion & nothing can be more charming especially for a sequestered Mountaineer than to cast eyes over its boundless surface, and hear as I have done almost, from the brow of the steep in the Church field at Moresby, the waves chafing & murmuring in a variety of tones below, as a kind of base harmony to the shrill yet liquid music of the larks above. I took yesterday five minutes of this [?transport] before going into the Church and surely it was as good a prelude for devotion as any Psalm thou[gh] one of the Moresby female singers has a charming voice and manages it well. But concerning my employments I have a communication for Dora especially – shall I let it out, I have composed since I came here the promised Poem upon the birth of the Baby [John's first child, a daughter, Jane], and thrown off yesterday and to day in the course of a ride to Arlecdon (Mr Wilkinsons) a sober & sorrowful sequel to it which I fear none of you will like [*The Warning*]. They are neither yet fairly written out but I hope to send them for your impressions in this parcel . . . I have now scribbled so much that I must leave off or my eyes will scarcely serve for transcribing the Poems which are rather long for such occasion. Bear in mind with respect to 2nd especially that this will be its first appearance on paper and no doubt it will require altering.

385. William Wordsworth to Henry Crabb Robinson; [Rydal Mount], postmarked 6 May 1833

Public affairs are going on just as I apprehended. Nothing, I am persuaded but a course of affliction will bring back this Nation to its senses. And when it recovers then it will be a long time under the necessity of sacrificing liberty to order, probably under a military government at least under one unavoidably despotic. It would give me much pleasure to talk over these matters with you, and some, to write upon them, if my eyes were better, & my scrawl legible.

386. William Wordsworth to Mrs W. P. Rawson, of the Sheffield Female Anti-Slavery Society; [Rydal Mount, ?May 1833]

Your Letter which I lose no time in replying to, has placed me under some embarrassment, as I happen to possess some Mss verses of my own [*Humanity*]² upon the subject to which you solicit my attention. But I frankly own to you, that neither with respect to this subject nor to the kindred one, the Slavery of the Children in the Factories, which is adverted to in the same Poem, am I prepared to add to the excitement already existing in the public mind upon these, and so many other points of legislation and government. Poetry, if good for any thing, must appeal forcibly to the Imagination and the feelings; but what at this period we want above every thing, is patient examination and sober judgement. It can scarcely be necessary to add that my mind revolts as strongly as any one's can, from the law that permits one human being to sell another.

387. Dora Wordsworth to Edward Quillinan; Rydal Mount, 17 May 1833

Father has written several 100 lines this spring but only "tiresome small Poems" as Mother calls them who is vexed she cannot get him set down to his long work. I don't believe the "Recluse" will ever be finished He has written two or three sweet Poems – a few lines in one of them will please you especially, as shewing very happily the poetry of <u>Romanism</u> & making us wish that some of your Rites[3] had been retained by our Church – I wish we could persuade him to print but at present he is unpersuadable –

388. Ralph Waldo Emerson, American philosopher, essayist and poet, journal, 28 August 1833

He [Wordsworth] led me out into his garden, & showed me the walk in which thousands of his lines were composed. His eyes are inflamed. No loss, except for reading, because he never writes prose; and poetry, he carries even hundreds of lines in his memory, before writing it.!!

He said, he had just been to visit Staffa, &, within three days, had made three sonnets on Fingal's Cave, & was composing a fourth, when he was called in to see me! He said, "if you are interested in my verses, perhaps you will like to hear these lines." I assented gladly; & he recollected himself for a few moments, & then stood forth, & repeated in succession the three entire sonnets, with great spirit. I thought the second, & third, more *beautiful*, than any of his printed poems . . .

This reciting was so unexpected & extraordinary, – he, the old Wordsworth, standing forth & reciting to me in a garden walk, like a schoolboy "speaking his piece," – that I at first had nearly laughed; but, recollecting myself, that I had come thus far to see a poet, & he was chaunting poems to me, I saw, that he was right, & I was wrong, & gladly gave myself up to hear.

389. Eliza Fletcher, of Lancrigg, Easedale, holiday log book, 5 September 1833

The former [Mr Wordsworth] came he said to make Mrs Wordsworth's apology for not having sooner ask'd us to dine at Rydall Mount, and to announce "a family affliction." – the death of Mrs Wordsworth['s] eldest Brother – Notwithstanding the Poet was more facetious – talkative and good humour'd than it has been our chance to see him this summer.

Mr [Thomas] Hamilton explain'd this to Mary (aside) by saying that he had lately been deliver'd of <u>six Sonnets</u>. – This Litter as the unhallow'd Scoffers of Lake Poetry would call it. – was conceived on a late Highland or rather Hebridean Tour the Poet made with Mr Robinson an old friend of Mrs Barbauld's. It seems while the poetic <u>travail</u> is upon him, Our Bard is commonly sour, irritable and "easily provoked." – He was yesterday more in the mood of one who had to tell of some joyful occurrence than a messenger sent to announce "a family affliction" . . .

390. William Wordsworth to John Kenyon; Rydal Mount, 23 September [1833]

You speak of your own rambles, and allude to mine. It is true, as was affirmed in an offensive Paragraph in a Glasgow Paper, that I have been taking a peep at the Hebrides. My tour, which was only for a fortnight, included the Isle of Man (visited for the first time), Staffa, Iona, and a return thro' Burns' country, Renfrewshire and Airshire. The weather was mixed, but upon the whole I and my companions, Mr Robinson, an ex-Barrister, and my son John, were well repaid. About 10 days after my return I was summoned to Carlisle upon business, took Mrs W[ordsworth] along with me, and we came home up the banks of the Eden, by Corby and Nunnery, both charming places, to Lowther, and home by Ullswater. These two Excursions united, have since produced 22 sonnets, which I shall be happy to read to you; the more so because I cannot muster courage to publish them, or any thing else. I seem to want a definite motive – money would be one, if I could get it, but I cannot; I find by my Publisher's acc[oun]t, which I rec[eive]d the other day, that the last Ed[ition] of my Poems[4] owes us conjointly (my share being 2 thirds) nearly £200. The Ed[ition] was 2000, of which not quite 400 had been sold last June; a fact which, contrasted with the state of my poetical reputation, is wholly inexplicable, notwithstanding the depressed state of the book-market in England . . .

391. Dora Wordsworth to her cousin, Chris Wordsworth; Rydal Mount, 12 November [1833]

My Fathers eyes are better but too weak to allow of his writing or even looking at a book & as he may not yet employ his mind he finds as you may imagine these long fire & candle light evenings distressing & tiresome in the extreme – My Mother & I read to him a great great deal but as neither her chest nor my throat is of the very strongest we find it fatiguing & he cannot always keep awake & reading aloud is tiresome at best one gets on so slowly.

392. William Wordsworth to the poet, Mrs Felicia Hemans; [Rydal Mount, c.30 April 1834]

And now my d[ea]r Friend to a Subject which I feel to be of much delicacy – You have submitted what you had intended as a Dedication for your Poems to me. I need scarcely say that as a <u>private letter</u> such expressions from such a quarter, could not but have been rec[eive]d by me but [*sic*] with pleasure of <u>no ordinary kind</u>, unchecked by any consideration but the fear that my writings were overrated by you & my character thought better of than it deserved. But I must say that a <u>public</u> testimony in so high a strain of admiration is what I cannot but shrink from – be this modesty true or false, it is in me – you must bear with it & make allowance for it. And therefore as you have submitted the whole to my judgement, I am emboldened to express a wish that you would instead of this Dedication in which your warm & kind heart has overpowered you, simply inscribe them to me, with such expression of respect or gratitude, as would come within the limits of the rule which after what has been said above, will naturally suggest itself. Of course if the sheet has been struck off, I must hope that my shoulders may become a little more Atlantean than I now feel them to be.

393. Sara Hutchinson to Edward Quillinan; [Rydal Mount], 20 July [1834]

Perhaps Dora has not told Ro[tha] that her Father has consented to publish the Poems <u>on hand</u> – But not with Drawings, as was once talked, of but in a volume which will make a 5th to the last & uniform also with the preceding ones – a neat little Vol[ume] & not costly.

394. Dora Wordsworth to Henry Crabb Robinson; [Rydal Mount], postmarked 25 July 1834

You will be glad to hear that my Aunt Miss Wordsworth continues tolerably well – certainly stronger on the whole than when you were with us last year. My Father too has had no return of inflammation in his eyes – yet they are but of little service to him either for reading or writing which at this time he feels a more than usual inconvenience as he has at last yielded to our oft-repeated entreaties & is about to send his short M.S. Poems to press which when collected we expect will with a little <u>stuffing</u> make a Vol[ume] about the size of those of the last Edition which

Ed[ition] Longman tells us has sold better than any former one[5] – The Title of the new vol[ume] is to be 'Yarrow Revis[i]ted with other Poems' – so you will soon have all your favorite new Scotch sonnets without the trouble of transcribing.

On 25 July 1834 Samuel Taylor Coleridge died, aged sixty-one, in his lodgings at Highgate, London, where he had lived for eighteen years. His death was a tremendous shock to all the Wordsworths but for William, in particular, it marked the end of an era.

395. William Wordsworth to Samuel Taylor Coleridge's son-in-law, Henry Nelson Coleridge; [Rydal Mount], 29 July [1834]

I cannot give way to the expression of my feelings upon this mournful occasion; I have not strength of mind to do so – The last year has thinned off so many of my Friends, young and old, and brought with it so much anxiety private & public, that it would be no kindness to you were I to yield to the solemn & sad thoughts and remembrances which press upon me. It is nearly 40 years since I first became acquainted with him whom we have just lost; and though with the exception of six weeks when we were on the continent together, along with my Daughter, I have seen little of him for the last 20 years, his mind has been habitually present with me, with an accompanying feeling that he was still in the flesh. That frail tie is broken & I, & most of those who are nearest & dearest to me must prepare and endeavour to follow him.

396. Robert Perceval Graves to Mrs Hemans; 12 August 1834

One of the first things we heard from him was the death of one who had been, he said, his friend for more than thirty years. He then continued to speak of him, called him the most <u>wonderful</u> man that he had ever known, wonderful for the originality of his mind & the power he possessed of throwing out in profusion grand central truths from which might be evolved the most comprehensive systems. Wordsworth, as a Poet, regretted that German metaphysics had so much captivated the taste of Coleridge, – for he was frequently not intelligible on this subject – whereas if his energy & his originality had been more exerted in the channel of poetry, an instrument of which he had so perfect a mastery, Wordsworth thought he might have done more, permanently to enrich the literature & to influence the thought of the nation than any man of the age. As it was, however, he said he believed Coleridge's mind to have been a widely fertilizing one, & that the seed he had so lavishly sown in his conversational discourses & the Sibylline leaves (not the poem so called by him) which he had scattered abroad so extensively covered with his annotations, had done much to form the opinions of the highest-educated men of the day; although this might be an influence not likely to meet with adequate recognition.

397. William Wordsworth to his friend, the lawyer and dramatist, Thomas Noon Talfourd; Rydal Mount, 1 January 1835

Your letter brought a great shock to us all, I had not heard from yourself when you were here, that any thing was threatening [Charles] Lamb's health, & Miss Hutchinson who saw him late in the Spring reported that he was looking wonderfully well, & appeared in excellent Spirits. He has followed poor Coleridge within six months! It seems to us upon reflection, that his Sister will bear the loss of him better than he could have borne that of her: & we are bound to believe so, as it has pleased God to take him first . . .

My little Vol[ume] is printed off all but the last sheet – A Copy will be sent to you & the one designed for our dear departed friend may go to Moxon's to be delivered by Mrs M[oxon] to Miss Lamb whenever it shall be thought proper. Upon most carefully reviewing all that concerned the political Poem,[6] which you & I agreed had better be withheld – I determined to publish it – I felt it due to myself to give this warning to my Countrymen, at this awful Crisis – utterly useless it may prove, but I should have suspected myself of cowardice or selfish caution, if I had suppressed what I had thought & felt – upon that momentous change. The Reform bill I have ever deemed from the night on which L[or]d J[ohn] Russel brought forth his motion, an unwise measure, which could not be carried but by unworthy means. We are now about to gather the fruits of it in sorrow & vain repentance.

398. William Wordsworth to Henry Crabb Robinson; [Rydal Mount, c. 27 April 1835]

– At Breakfast this morning we received from some unknown Friend the Examiner, containing a friendly notice of my late Vol[ume] – Is it discreditable to say that these things interest me little, but as they may tend to promote the sale; which with the prospects of unavoidable expense before me, is a greater object to me much greater than it would other wise have been. – The private testimonies which I receive very frequently of the effect of my writings upon the hearts & minds of men, are indeed very gratifying – because I am sure they must be written under pure influences – but it is not necessarily or even probably so with strictures intended for the public. The one are effusions, the other compositions, and liable in various degrees to inter-mixtures that take from their value – It is amusing to me to have proofs how Critics & Authors differ in judgement, both as to fundamentals and Incidentals . . . If my writings are to last, it will I myself believe, be mainly owing to this characteristic. They will please for the single cause, 'that we have all of us one human heart!'[7]

farewell

399. *William Wordsworth to Robert Southey; [Rydal Mount], Sunday morning, 7 June [1835]*

We have been and are, in sad distress in this House. My Beloved Sisters days are drawing steadily to a close; She grows obviously weaker & weaker every day; And dear Miss Hutchinson [too] is still suffering under her severe attack; lumbago, at first, then rheumatic fever, with frequent delirium, which is not yet quite gone. We hope however & trust that she is recovering; Mr Carr, who has been very anxious about her, tells us that it is chiefly weakness that causes the symptoms, which continue to make us uneasy.

400. *Dora Wordsworth to Edward Quillinan; Rydal Mount, 1 June 1835*

Dear Father keeps up his spirits most patiently tho at times I see his heart is well nigh breaking; & when the blow does come I am sure he will meet it with resignation – how mercifully has this bitter blast been tempered to him!

Though the Wordsworths were prepared for Dorothy's death and waiting for it in hourly expectation, it was actually Sara Hutchinson who died, suddenly and unexpectedly, on 23 June 1835. The two aunts had been very close and Sara's death was the catalyst which finally plunged Dorothy into dementia. Lovingly cared for at Rydal Mount, she would survive another twenty years, outliving all her brothers, but she was merely the shell of her former self. The 'exquisite sister' who had been such an inspiration for William's poetry died with Sara.

401. *William Wordsworth to Edward Quillinan; [Rydal Mount, c.27 June 1835]*

I know not how she has escaped from us, but it was God's will that this excellent Creature should quit the earth. My poor dear Sister and Dora seem to bear up wonderfully – so does Mrs W[ordsworth] we have had Mrs [Mary] Hutchinson with us for a fortnight – a great blessing.

I know how you valued the dear departed, her loss [is] irreparable to us all. – It is astounding to me that she should have gone before my beloved Sister who is very feeble and suffers much at times – Her departed friend had little or no acute pain after the fever left – O – What a heavenly expression was on her face after the breath had left her body; it would have done your soul good to see it!

I write through tears, but scarcely tears of sorrow – so has it been often & often since she left us – farewell –

402. *William Wordsworth to Henry Crabb Robinson; [Rydal Mount], 6 July [1835]*

I fear you cannot read this Letter. I feel my hand-shaking, I have had so much agitation to-day, in attempting to quiet my poor Sister, and from being under the necessity of refusing her things that would be improper for her. She has a great craving for oatmeal porridge principal[ly] for the sake of the butter that she eats along with it and butter is sure to bring on a fit of bile sooner or later.

403. *William Wordsworth to Samuel Rogers; Lowther Castle, 28 September [1835]*

You will be desirous, I am sure to learn how our invalids are. My dear Sister in bodily health is decidedly better, though quite unable to stand; her mind however is I grieve to say, much shattered. The change showed itself upon the death of dear Miss Hutchinson, but probably was preparing before. Her case at present is very strange; her judgement, her memory, and all her faculties are perfect as ever, with [the] exception of what relates to her own illness, & passing occurrences. If I ask her opinion upon any point of Literature, she answers with all her former acuteness; if I read Milton, or any favourite author, and pause, she goes on with the passage from memory; but she forgets instantly the circumstances of the day. Considering that she is not 64 years of age, I cannot but hope that her mind may be restored, if her bodily health should go on improving.

My daughter is a good deal better, but very far from being strong & well. – [8]

404. Hartley Coleridge to his mother, Mrs Sarah Coleridge, Saturday [September 1835]

Perhaps I cannot tell you any thing more comfortable of our friends at Rydal than that Mrs. Wordsworth is gone to visit her son and daughter-in-law at Workington. Mr. Wordsworth is, all things considered, wonderfully well – I have often seen him lately, sometimes on his walks, sometimes at the Foxes, and sometimes at his own abode: (the day before yesterday, he call'd upon me – what think you for? to borrow a razor as he had not shaved that morning, and bethought him to call on the Parrys). Dora is not worse, I wish I could say she was much better. She has the same sweet smile as ever, and all the good spirits that can proceed from a kind and innocent heart in an afflicted body. (Miss Wordsworth is, I suppose, more comfortable as to her bodily feelings – suffers little or no pain, and is grown fat, but her memory is gone – so they say, at least, for I do not now see her. She never leaves her room.) I hope Mr. Wordsworth feels some consolation in the complete victory of his poetic fame. He may at least feel assured, that no Great Poet ever lived to see his name of so full an age as Wordsworth has done. His last volume is exquisite.

405. Mary Wordsworth to Dorothy's friend, Jane Marshall; [Rydal Mount, late December 1835]

Her [Dorothy's] memory is less confused & I think gradually strengthens – but the same childishness governs her – & lately her passions have been <u>more</u> ungovernable – But we must attribute this to the great change that has been made – only I am here checked by the recollection, that before we began to reduce the Opium, she was (except that her memory was then gone) much as she is at present . . . I wish you could but have seen the joy with which that countenance glistened at the sight of your never-to-be forgotten present. She was up & in her disturbed way, when I took them to her & held them before her, every sensation of irritation, or discomfort vanished, & she stroked & hugged the Turkey upon her knee like an overjoyed & happy child – exulting in, & blessing over & over again her dear, dearest friend – telling Jane [the servant], by whom I suppose she had fancied herself ill-used at the time "You see, I <u>have</u> good friends who care for me, tho' you do not" – Poor Jane gives hourly proof of her tender care & love of her, but this by the bye – The two beautiful lily white Chicken[s] were next the object of her admiration – & when Doro said it was a pity that such lovely creatures should have been killed, she scouted the regret, saying "what would they do for <u>her</u> alive, her friend knew best what she wanted – & she should eat them every bit herself."

406. Dora Wordsworth to her cousin, Chris Wordsworth; Rydal, 7 January [1836]

I wish it were allowed me to answer your quaeries [*sic*] respecting our dearest Aunt more favorably – the last few days she has been much quieter – but alas she is in a most melancholy state – it is some comfort to us that you are spared the pain of witnessing what daily nay indeed hourly we are called upon to witness & without being able in the slightest degree to minister to her comfort or happiness – nothing seems to give her pleasure not even the sight of her dear brother – & often & often he comes down from her room his eyes filled with tears – saying "Well all I can do for her now is to heat her night cap I have done it 20 times within the last ¼ of an hour & that seems to give her a momentary pleasure & that is some comfort." Her bodily health continues good as far as we can judge – but Mr Carr fears some mischief may be going on in the brain he has applied blisters behind the ears & by this means he hopes to keep down the inflammatory action otherwise he fears abcesses may form on the brain – if he be mistaken in this he at present sees nothing to cause alarm & thinks she may live for years – but dear Chris this is a melancholy prospect – for if her mind is to continue in its present state one & all of us would <u>joyfully</u> see her laid by that beloved Aunt who is gone before in our own quiet Churchyard in Grasmere – but I will not dwell longer on this sad subject it is hard for us both.

407. Mary Wordsworth to Mary Anne Marshall, daughter of Jane Marshall;
[Rydal Mount, 4 May 1836]

... her situation puzzles us sadly for, her good looks & the healthy &
flourishing appearance of her body <u>generally</u> & the functions not being
in the least deranged, lead one to think that no bodily disease exists. – Yet
she is almost constantly in a state of impatient discomfort – To <u>you</u> I may
venture to describe her state as I did this morn[in]g to her brother – that
she was exactly like a very <u>clever, tyrannical spoilt</u> Child (for she is acute &
discriminating to a marvellous degree) – Yet she has intervals of mildness &
is overcome by her old affections – & sometimes she is very languid &
weeps – which is very afflicting – She is interested with the letters of our
friends, & while she is reading them she seems as well as any one – but
this excitement being passed she relapses into restlessness & discomfort –
her brother who has been the last to observe that this was under such
influence – observed to her this morn[in]g – "I think Dorothy if we could
ply you up with letters to read, we should soon have you well." – This
observation excited anger. Poor thing! Still we hope that when she can
get into the Garden a change may take place.

Though the Wordsworths continued to hope against hope that Dorothy's condition would improve, it did not. She remained in this state for the rest of her life.

Chapter Eleven

1836–40

In the spring of 1836 William went to London for what turned out to be one of his busiest and most exhausting visits. He lobbied officials and government ministers in repeated attempts to get his post as Distributor of Stamps transferred to his younger son, who was unable to find other employment. He sought out medical advice for Dora, whose health had been in a state of steady decline for years, and attended the dentist on his own account. He harried his publishers, old and new, in an attempt to secure better terms for his next edition of poems. Then there was the usual social whirl, visiting old friends and being introduced to new: 'I see scores of people that are introduced to me but dont remember the names of one in ten', he told his family. There were trips to a prize-giving at Harrow, where his nephew, Chris, was now headmaster, and to Eton at the invitation of Edward Coleridge. He even found time to have 'an odd adventure', attending the notorious trial of Lord Melbourne, whom his friend Thomas Noon Talfourd was defending against what was generally considered a trumped-up charge of adultery with the society beauty and poetess, Mrs Caroline Norton. The visit had its desired effect in distracting William from his anxiety about his sister, but it was supposed to be a prelude to a long-anticipated two-month trip to Italy in the company of the affable Henry Crabb Robinson. As the date for his departure grew closer, William began to get cold feet.

408. William Wordsworth to his family; Mr Marshall's [London], 6 o'clock [June 1836]

Here follows Moxon's 2nd proposal received this morning –

Mr M[oxon] to print stereotype and pay all the expenses of an Edition of 3000 Copies of Mr W[ordsworth's] Poetry works in 6 vol[ume]s similar to the Edit[ion] in 5 vol[umes] 1827

Mr M[oxon] for the same to give Mr W[ordsworth] 1000£ the whole to be paid in cash immediately after the Publication of the 6th Vol[ume] (this I shall stipulate to be in 6 months)

Mr M[oxon] to give Mr W[ordsworth] for every future edit[ion] of

1000 Copies 400, to be paid in Cash within 6 months of the day of publication.

The Copyright & stereotype plates to be Mr Wordsworths –

So you see dearest Friends there is nothing like standing up for one's self, and one's own legitimate interest!

409. William Wordsworth to his family; [London], Saturday 2 o'clock [June 1836]

This London life wears me out – these long <u>tete</u> a tetes with strangers, and late dinners & luncheons and [calls] in the morning hours would soon make an end of me.

410. William Wordsworth to his family; [London, June 1836]

My dearest Friends,

My heart fails – I am so sad in a morning when I wake and think that more than 4 months will elapse before I see you again, if I go to Italy and after an absence of I believe 7 weeks. – I cannot bear to think of it having reached the age that we all have except you dearest Dora – I should have thought nothing of it 20 years ago – but now I sicken at the scheme as I draw near to the appointed time. Do let me put it off, and try the events of another year, that may [have] produced favorable changes among us; if not – it will be no disappointment to me.

I think I will return with Mr Graves, and do not <u>scold</u> me if I should. To say the truth in another point also – I have been much exhausted by these long London tete a tetes with people, foreigners among others, who wish to hear me talk & never [am] at rest.

411. William Wordsworth to his wife, Mary; [Hampstead], Thursday morning [30 June 1836]

– I cannot put off my journey home; for I am quite tired of this mode of life & worn out with it. It is easy for you to say go and spend a quiet day here or there, it is not in my power to spend a quiet day any where. People put so many questions to me, and think it so necessary to endeavour to put me upon talking, and to talk to me. You quite forget too my situation and my disposition when you talk to me of quiet and preservation from exhaustion – Should I go to Dr Davys he would invite his friends to meet me and so on –

Though Mary and Dora had been anxious that William should stay away from the distressing scenes at home for as long as possible, they could not resist his plea to be allowed to return. Back at Rydal Mount, William flung himself into the preparation of his new edition of collected poems which, for the first time, would be published by Moxon, rather than Longman.

412. *Mary Wordsworth to Henry Crabb Robinson; [Rydal Mount, 28 September 1836]*

Here we are in the Hall up to the ears in a muddle of counting lines to fill the 2nd vol[ume] – a body of finished sheets from the first, having arrived along with your letter – & their appearance after many changes gives great satisfaction to the Poet & his Clerk – His Journeyman in the Person of Mr Quillinan having left us last week, to my great regret, for he supplied my place, which he filled most admirably, and has quite thrown me into the shade. However the Poet is obliged to be thankful for his old helpmate & a busy house we have – working steadily till dinner time – & in a disorderly manner the rest of the day: tho' he finds time to walk with Mr Justice Coleridge, who with his family are residing in Foxhow . . . The juvenile pieces have caused great labor; but, as we proceed, we hope to go on with less difficulty – & that the Poet may leave home with a perfect holiday before him – &, but, I dare not say so – return to the Recluse; – and let me charge you, not to encourage the Muse to vagrant subjects – but gently recur, upon such indications should they arise, to Rogers' hint that "jingling rhyme does not become a certain age." entre nous –

413. *William Wordsworth to John Kenyon; [Rydal Mount, c.24 September 1836]*

I have had a great deal of dry & wearisome labour, of which I do not repent, however, in preparing my Poems for the new Edition, especially those which were among my first attempts.

I hear from many quarters of the impression which my writings are making, both at home & abroad, & to an old man it would be discreditable not to be gratified with such intelligence; because it is not the language of praise, for pleasure bestowed – but of gratitude for moral & intellectual improvement received.

414. *William Boxall, RA, portrait painter, to William Wordsworth; Hardwick House, near Bury St Edmunds, Suffolk, 29 August 1836*

. . . you have here a knot of true & sincere worshippers . . . I verily believe there is no book but the Bible that is to them so full of inspiration. You would be delighted to see the beautiful appreciation with which they read you & I believe nothing short of a pilgrimage to Rydal Mount will suffice them that they may themselves tell you how much gratitude they feel towards you – I envy you, my dear Sir; & yet with what pleasure I tell you that your words & thoughts live so cherished in their 'heart of hearts' – Can any poet wish for more than to feel that he has thus created happiness –

415. *William Wordsworth to his publisher, Edward Moxon; [Rydal Mount, late December 1836]*

Your account of the sale of the book [*Yarrow Revisited*] is as favourable as I ventured to expect: being myself quite at ease in regard to the reception which, writings that have cost me so much labour, will in the end meet with, I can truly say that I have not the least anxiety concerning the fate of this Edition, further than that you may speedily be repaid what you have generously advanced to me. The labour I have bestowed in correcting the style of these poems, now revised for the last time according to my best judgement, no one can ever thank me for, as no one can estimate it. The annoyance of this sort of work is, that progress bears no proportion to pains, & that hours of labour are often entirely thrown away – ending in the passage being left, as I found it.

416. *William Wordsworth to his friend, the civil servant and dramatist, Henry Taylor; Rydal, 4 November [1836]*

. . . I have seen the Print designed for the new Ed[ition] of my Poems: it is well engraved, but partly owing to a fault about the upper lip, & still more to its having preserved the inclination of the body (natural in a recumbent attitude) without an arm, to explain it, or account for it, the whole has an air of feebleness & decrepitude which I hope is not yet authorized by the subject.

417. *Mary Wordsworth to Jane Marshall; [Rydal Mount], Christmas Eve [1836]*

I take a greater liberty with you than common by forwarding <u>such</u> an untidy & I fear <u>illegible</u> letter, & must pray your forgiveness – writing with a Poet beside me ought not to be an excuse – tho' – as at this moment, he takes the pen – bad as it is, literally out of my hand – this reminds me of what <u>you</u> say of his <u>alterations</u>, or corrections. <u>I</u> must say that he never makes one that he does not <u>seem</u> to convince my understanding & judgment – but like you, not always my <u>feelings</u> – however we must give him credit for being right – & <u>we</u> can always cherish where we like, what we have loved & cling to – & hope that those to whom the Poems are new – may find a higher – I am sure not a <u>deeper</u>, pleasure from them than we have done.

At the age of sixty-six, William finally achieved his long-cherished ambition of taking a tour of Italy. His companion was Henry Crabb Robinson, though Edward Moxon accompanied them as far as Paris, where William called on Annette Vallon, their daughter, Caroline, and her family. Travelling in a carriage, William and Robinson drove through southern France to Italy, visiting Rome, Florence, Assisi and Venice (though not Naples, where cholera was raging), and returning through the Italian Lakes and Austria.

418. *William Wordsworth to his sister, Dorothy; [London], Friday afternoon [17 March 1837]*

My dear & very dear Sister,

Here I am waiting on the Dentist & have snatched a moment to tell you, that I am worn out with hurry. – You will be surprized but I hope not grieved to hear that I am starting for a trip upon the Continent with Mr Robinson. Our passports are procured, our carriage bought and we shall embark at the tower stairs on Sunday morning for Calais. How I wish you could have gone with us; but I shall think of you every where, and often shall we talk of you . . .

Farewell my dearest Sister and farewell my dear Joanna [Hutchinson], and kindest remembrances to all the household James Anne, Jane and Dorothy [the servants]; and mind that you all take care of yourselves and of each other.

Your most affectionate Brother
W Wordsworth

419. William Wordsworth to his friend, Isabella Fenwick; Paris, Friday 24 March [1837]

– What shall I say of Paris? – Many splendid edifices, and some fine streets have been added since I first saw it at the close of the year –91. But I have had little feeling to spare for novelties, my heart and mind having been awakened every where to sad & strange recollections of what was then passing, and of subsequent events, which have either occurred in this vast City, or which have flowed from it as their source.

420. Henry Crabb Robinson, diary, Nimes, 6 April 1837

At Nismes (*April 6th*) I took Wordsworth to see the exterior of both the Maison Carree and the Arena. He acknowledged their beauty, but expected no great pleasure from such things. He says, "I am unable, from ignorance, to enjoy these sights. I receive an impression, but that is all. I have no science, and can refer nothing to principle." He was, on the other hand, delighted by two beautiful little girls playing with flowers near the Arena; and I overheard him say to himself, "Oh, you darlings! I wish I could put you in my pocket, and carry you to Rydal Mount."

421. William Wordsworth to his wife, Mary, and daughter, Dora; [Rome], Saturday, postmarked 20 May 1837

But of churches and pictures and statues in them I am fairly tired – in fact I am too old in head limbs & eyesight for such hard work, such toiling and such straining, and so many disappointments either in finding the most celebrated picture covered up with curtains, the service going on so that one cannot ask to have a sight, or the church closed when one arrives at the door – All this will however be forgotten long before I get back to dear England and nothing but the pleasure, I hope, survive. The only very celebrated object which has fairly disappointed me on account of my ignorance I suppose, is the Pantheon. But after all it is not particular objects with the exception perhaps of the inside of St Peters, that make the glory of this City; but it is the boun[d]less variety of combinations of old & new, caught in ever varying connection with the surrounding country, when you look down from some one or other of the Seven hills, or from neighbouring eminences not including in [*sic*] the famous seven.

422. *William Wordsworth to his family; [Albano], Tuesday 19 May [1837]*

My dearest Friends,

It is just three weeks and two days since we reached Rome, and on Tuesday next we shall leave it to take the road for Florence. Since my last I have worked hard to see the most remarkable things in Rome & its immediate neighbourhood – Churches, Palaces, Villas, Ruins, Eminences, – not Cardinals, though I have seen numbers of these, but commanding points of view, and all these with very great pleasure, and only one drawback – the never wanting proof that I am rather too old for such <u>excessive</u> exertions, and that my bodily strength is much diminished within the latter part of these labours. But my health thank God continues very good, so I have every reason to be thankful.

. . . to tell you the truth I am not sorry to be so near the time of turning my face homewards; for the Tour of Italy is too much to be taken in less than 8 months unless a person be young and very strong. The country is inexhaustible for those who are well read in antient story and classical Poetry, and its natural beauty tempts you to exertion in every direction.

423. *Henry Crabb Robinson, diary, Riva [del Garda], 18 June 1837*

A day to saunter about in. We walked out before breakfast, taking the road to Arco above the lake. This lake is exposed to storms, of which Virgil has written alarmingly. Wordsworth soon left me, as he was annoyed by the stone walls on the road. I sauntered on, and found, on inquiry, that I was now in the Tyrol; but in this remote district no one asked for passport. On my return I breakfasted, and read Lady Wortley Montague, which formed my resource to-day; but I at length became anxious at Wordsworth's non-appearance. I remained in my room till half-past one, and still he had not returned, though he said he should be back to breakfast. I became very uncomfortable, for I feared some accident had occurred. I

could no longer rest, and went forth in search of him . . . Thinking he
would be attracted by a village and castles on the mountains, I took my
direction accordingly, and after proceeding some distance, the sound of a
waterfall caught my ear, and I felt sure that, if it had caught his, he would
have followed it. Acting upon this clue, I came to a mill, where I gained
tidings of him. He had breakfasted there, and gone higher up. I followed
on, and found a man who had seen him near Riva. This relieved me of
all apprehension. On my return to the inn, he had already arrived.

424. William Wordsworth to his family; [Salzburg], postmarked 13 July 1837

I have, however, to regret that this journey was not made some years ago,
to regret it I mean as a Poet; for though we have had a great disappointment
in not seeing Naples &c, and more of the country among the Apennines
not far from Rome, Horaces country for instance, and Ciceros Tusculum,
my mind has been enriched by innumerable images, which I could have
turned to account in verse, & vivified by feelings which earlier in my life
would have answered noble purposes, in a way they now are little likely
to do. But I do not repine, on the contrary I am very happy, wishing
only to see all your dear faces again, and to make amends for my frequent
bad behaviour to you all. Absence, absence in a foreign country and at a
great distance, is a condition, for many minds, at least for mine, often
pregnant with remorse. Dearest Mary, when I have felt how harshly I
often demeaned my self to you my inestimable fellow-labourer while
correcting the last Edition of my poems, I often pray to God that he
would grant us both life, that I may make some amends to you for that &
all my unworthiness. But you know into what an irritable state this
timed and overstrained labour often put my nerves. My impatience was
ungovernable as I thought then, but I now feel that it ought to have been
governed. You have forgiven me I know, as you did then, and perhaps
that somehow troubles me the more. I say nothing of this to you dear
Dora though you also have had some reason to complain.

425. Henry Crabb Robinson to his hostess in Rome, Frances Mackenzie; 2 Plowden Building, Temple, [London], 17 November 1837

You have from the poet himself a short Itinerary – I have little to add –
The spots he deeply enjoyed were the three Sanctuaries [the monasteries
of Laverna, Camaldi and Vallombrosa in the Apennines]. He began one

poem on hearing the *Cuckoo at L'Averna* which I trust he will finish I fear we are not entitled to expect much beyond – "I have" he said "A fund of thoughts & suggestions, if I had but youth & health to work them up" – You know how painfully he writes – But then when produced how glorious, how perfect the works are!

You must have observed how intensely as well as how delicately & disciminatingly W[ordsworth] enjoys the beauties of nature – He cares rather less than I wish for works of antiquity – he has a fine sense for the charms of colour, but is less susceptible to beauty of form either in Sculpture or Architecture – I overheard him exclaim with rapture at the sight of two children playing by the Amphitheatre at Nismes "Oh that I could steal those children & carry them off to Rydal Mount! ["] And on the top of the Colosseum he was admiring the rich verdure beyond as much as the sublime edifice below – He ought to have visited Italy many years before – Most likely I should he said but for the Edinburg[h] Reviewers – he sent a message to this effect to Jeffery [Francis Jeffrey of the *Edinburgh Review*] –

426. William Wordsworth to Edward Quillinan; Brinsop Court, Herefordshire, Wednesday, 20 September [1837]

I will conclude this matter of poetry my part of the letter with requesting that as an act of friendship at your convenience you would take the trouble a considerable one I own of comparing the corrections in my last Edition with the text in the preceding one. You know my principles of style better I think than any one else & I should be glad to learn if anything strikes you as being altered for the worse – You will find the principal changes are in The White Doe, in w[hic]h I had too little of the benefit of y[ou]r help & judgement there are several also in the Sonnets both miscellaneous & political – in the other poems they are nothing like so numerous but here also I should be glad if you w[oul]d take the like trouble.

427. William Wordsworth to his cousin, Elizabeth Fisher; Rydal Mount, 15 December [1837]

These observations lead me to speak with regret that Mrs Hemans' Poems have been put in her [Elizabeth Fisher's daughter's] way at so early an age; towards the close of my 6th Vol[ume] will be found a poem occasioned

by the death of the Ettrick Shepherd, which shews that I think highly of
that Lady's genius – but her friends, & I had the honor of being one
of them – must acknowledge with regret, that her circumstances, tho'
honorably to herself, put her upon writing too often & too much – she
is consequently diffuse; & felt herself under the necessity of <u>expanding</u>
the thoughts of others, & [hovering inside] their feelings which has
prevented her own genius doing justice to itself, & diminished the value
of her productions accordingly. This is not said with a view to the
withdrawing Mrs H[eman]'s works, but with a hope that it may be a
caution for you to place those of the elder Writers in your daughter's way,
in preference to modern ones, however great their merits. And in this
implied recommendation, I do not speak without allusion to my own.
Wherever I have written better than others, as far as style is concerned, it
has been mainly owing to my early familiarity with the Works of the truly
great Authors of past times – & where I have the least pleased myself in
style or versification I can trace it up to early communication with inferior
writers. One of my Schoolmasters, whom I most respected & loved, was,
unfortunately, for me, a passionate admirer of Dr Johnson's prose; &
having not been much exercised in prose myself, I have not till this day
got over the ill effects of that injudicious [? influence] upon my own way
of expressing myself.

*428. William Wordsworth to Sir William Rowan Hamilton, newly elected
President of the Royal Irish Academy; Rydal Mount, 21 December [1837]*

You pay me an undeserved compliment in requesting my opinion, how
you could best promote some of the benefits which the Society at whose
head you are placed – aims at; as to patronage you are right in supposing
that I hold it in little esteem for helping genius forward in the fine Arts;
especially those whose medium is words. Sculpture & painting <u>may</u> be
helped by it; but even in these departments there is much to be dreaded . . .

Genius in Poetry, or any department of what is called the Belles Lettres
is much more likely to be cramped than fostered by public Support –
better wait to reward those who have done their work, tho' even here
national rewards are not necessary, unless the Labourers be, if not in
poverty, at least in narrow circumstances – let the laws be but just to them
– & they will be sure of attaining competence, if they have not misjudged
their own talents, or misapplied them . . .

As to "better canons of criticism, & general improvement of Scholars,"

I really, speaking without affectation, am so little of a Critic or Scholar, that it would be presumptuous in me to <u>write</u> upon the Subject to you . . . It is somewhat mortifying to me to disappoint you – You must upon reflexion I trust perceive, that in attempting to comply with your wish, I should only lose myself in a wilderness. I have been applied to to give lectures upon Poetry in a public Institution in London, but I was conscious that I was neither compet[ent] to the Office, nor the Public prepared to receive what I should have felt it my duty to say, however in[adequately].

For thirty years William had been lobbying discreetly but persistently for a change in the copyright laws; as he approached his sixty-eighth birthday, this became a matter of greater urgency and personal importance to him. Most of his works had been in print for longer than the period protected by copyright and, on his death, could be reprinted at will by any publisher, without his or his family's permission, and without any payment to them. This was particularly galling for a poet who had only just begun to earn money for his work. He therefore lent enthusiastic support to attempts by his friend, Thomas Noon Talfourd, to secure a new Copyright Bill; in the short term Talfourd failed, but the campaign prepared the way for future efforts which were ultimately successful.

429. William Wordsworth to his friend, William Ewart Gladstone, MP; Rydal, 23 March 1838

Upon the general merits of this question, it would be presumptuous in me to enter in a Letter to you. But as to my own interest in it, it may not be superfluous to say that within the last three years or so my poetical writings have produced for me nearly 1.500 pounds, and that much the greatest part of them, either would be public property to-morrow, if I should die, or would become so in a very very few years. Is this just, or can a state of law which allows the possibility of such injustice be favorable to the production of solid literature, in any department of what is usually called Belles-Letters[?]

ever faithfully yours,
Wm Wordsworth

I need not say how much I should rejoice to see you at Rydal Mount.

430. William Wordsworth to Thomas Noon Talfourd; [Rydal Mount, 14 April 1838]

I have not been unmindful of your Copyright Bill, having written scarcely less than 50 notes or Letters, many of them to members of Parliament in support of it.

431. William Wordsworth to Sir Robert Peel, MP; Rydal Mount, 3 May 1838

Permit me to state a fact as throwing light upon the reasonableness of lengthening the term of copyright. My own poems, and I may add Mr Coleridge's, have been in demand since their first publication, but till lately only to that degree which confined both publisher and author, in common prudence, to small editions, the profits of which were accordingly small to the publisher, and the residue to the Author almost insignificant. I have gained much more from my long-published writings within the last five or six years than in the thirty preceding, and the Copy-right of much the greatest portion of them would die with me, or within the space of four years. And, if from small things we may ascend to great, how slowly did the Poetry of Milton make its way to public favor, nor till very lately, were the Works of Shakespear himself justly appreciated even within his own Country.

432. Mary Wordsworth to Isabella Fenwick; Rydal Mount, 3 May [1838]

Attending to little improvements in an adjoining field (Dora's property) has been a delightful occupation to her father – & a salutary recreation from indoor labours – otherwise, we should have passed our late weeks under depressed Spirits – but these duties have been beneficial – by driving the cause out of his habitual thoughts; & I now look forward with hope that our meeting may be a happy one . . . The presence of these dear Babes [John's children] have brought fresh life to this house – only our time is so much occupied, we cannot sufficiently profit by it – But the sound of their innocent voices, when we do not see them, is refreshing – & often I am sure gives spirit to the GrandFather's efforts – feeling that he is putting them forth with a view to their future benefit – at the same time, that he is labouring for the honor of literature – For ourselves personally, it is too late a day to expect benefit from the success of the measure, should it be successful, which we now scarcely expect.

433. George Ticknor, Professor of Belles Lettres, Harvard University, journal, 8 May [1838]

Mrs. Wordsworth asked me to talk to him about finishing the Excursion, or the Recluse; saying, that she could not bear to have him occupied constantly in writing sonnets and other trifles, while this great work lay by him untouched, but that she had ceased to urge him on the subject, because she had done it so much in vain. I asked him about it, therefore. He said that the Introduction, which is a sort of autobiography, is completed. This I knew, for he read me large portions of it twenty years ago. The rest is divided into three parts, the first of which is partly written in fragments, which Mr. Wordsworth says would be useless and unintelligible in other hands than his own; the second is the Excursion; and the third is untouched. On my asking him why he does not finish it, he turned to me very decidedly, and said, "Why did not Gray finish the long poem he began on a similar subject? Because he found he had undertaken something beyond his powers to accomplish. And that is my case."

434. William Wordsworth to Henry Crabb Robinson; [Rydal Mount, 18 June 1838]

Our way of life is wholly without interest or variety. We see few strangers, though they are beginning to make their appearance; and no new books not even periodicals, nothing in fact beyond what we value much, certain Vol[ume]s of Poems that have been sent us, by Mr Kenyon, Mr Milnes and Mr Trench. – I dont know when Mr Moxon will send forth my Sonnets; I have done with them; perhaps he may think that they would fall stillborn from the Press, if published till the ferment of the coronation [of Queen Victoria] is over, and then will come the dead time of the long vacation. But these considerations may be of no importance in a Book of which the materials are old. – You will find however 13 new sonnets, some of which I hope will please you.

On 28 July 1838 the University of Durham conferred an honorary degree on William. As it was technically a law degree, William derived much amusement from teasing his barrister friend, Henry Crabb Robinson, suggesting that he should 'not scruple when a difficult point of Law occurs, to consult me.' He was, however, embarrassed when he attended the ceremony because the oration was made in English, instead of Latin, which was the custom at older universities.

This honour was swiftly followed by another: he was invited by a student committee to stand for election as Rector of the University of Glasgow. Though he declined to do so, it was another indication of his growing reputation, especially among the young.

435. William Wordsworth to his nephew, Chris Wordsworth; [Rydal Mount, 16 August 1838]

One of the Durham papers had a transcript which might get into the London ones of the Speech of professor Jenkins, exactly as it was spoken. There is as you observe some thing very awkward in constraining a Man to hear his own praises, before many listeners, in his Mother tongue. – I object to the practice also as lowering the University; nor could I learn any satisfactory reason why the old usage had been abandoned –

436. William Wordsworth to James Hutcheson, secretary of the Wordsworth Committee, University of Glasgow; [Rydal Mount, October 1838]

As I cannot doubt that they will give me credit for having carefully weighed the reasons which have led me to decline the honor, I feel myself at liberty to declare at once the satisfaction which I have derived from this occurrence as an evidence of the sense entertained among the Students in your University of the importance of imaginative Literature. A right understanding upon the subject, & a just feeling is at all times momentous, but especially so in the present state of society, & the opinions now so prevalent respecting the relative value of intellectual pursuits.

437. Ellen Ricketts, a friend of Dora's, recollections of a three-day excursion to the Duddon Valley with Mr Wordsworth, 8–10 October 1838

I do not think I shall ever forget our dear old Poet's *Quixotic* appearance on this eventful little tour, or rather I should say he resembled more the representations of one [of] the Weird Sisters in Macbeth than any thing else I can think of. He had been lately recovered from a very severe attack of Sciatica, he had suffered so much, and 'felt for himself (as he said) so much', this being almost the only serious illness he had ever had, that he was determined to take every precaution against cold. He had a little cloth cap on his head with a piece of fur falling from the back of it, and serving occasionally as a Collar. He had one of those Sheppard Scotch Plaids, used in the Highlands, and the gift of one of his many fair admirers, this plaid being sewn up one side and end, he threw over his head; it formed a conical peak at the top of it and then hung down shapeless and lank straight down his back, and being too long for him the remainder generally trailed on the ground like a train. It is true he suddenly recollected (when he stumbled over it every now and then) to hold it up on one arm, but this never lasted *long* for in his eagerness in talking and walking, away went the poor train again, sweeping the ground. He had on a p[ai]r of dark glass spectacles, as he was suffering from inflammation in his Eyes, and as a further protection to them whenever there was the least wind, up went an old weather-beaten faded green Umbrella with some of the points coming out, but from the flexible state to which it was altogether reduced by constant usage, it accommodated itself most agreeably to its owner's wishes and suited itself to every point of the compass. This completed our Hero's *turn out*, and a fund of amusement did it occasion us, for we were saucy enough to laugh at him repeatedly, which seemed much to divert him.

438. William Wordsworth to Henry Crabb Robinson; [Rydal Mount, c.5 December 1838]

I undertook to write a few Sonnets, upon taking leave of Italy – these gave rise to some more; & the whole amount to 9 which I shall read to you when you come, as you kindly promised before you went away, that you would do, soon after your return. If however you prefer it, the 4 upon Italy shall be sent you, upon the one condition that you do not read them to verse-writers. We are all in spite of ourselves a parcel of thieves. I had a droll instance of it this morning – for while Mary was writing down for me one of these Sonnets, on coming to a certain line, she cried out somewhat uncourteously "that's a plagiarism" – from whom? "from yourself" was the answer. I believe she is right tho' she could not point out the passage, neither can I.

439. Henry Taylor, quoting a letter from Isabella Fenwick to himself; Ambleside, 28 March 1839

He worked, she says, 'seldom less than six or seven hours a day, or rather one ought to say the whole day, for it seemed always on his mind – quite a possession.' In the evening he used to come to her house to tell her of his work, 'of the difficulties he has had and how he had overcome them, of the *beautiful* additions he had made, and all the why and wherefore of each alteration.' Once he appeared 'quite radiant with joy', and presently the reason for his peculiar pleasure burst forth. '"I must tell you", he said, "what Mary said when I was dictating to her this morning. 'Well, William, I declare you are cleverer than ever'", and the tears started into his eyes and he added: "It is not often I have had such praise; she has always been sparing of it."'

While William and Mary were staying with Isabella Fenwick at Bath in the spring of 1839, a family crisis which had long been brewing came to a head. Two and a half years earlier, when Edward Quillinan had been at Rydal Mount, helping William to prepare a new edition of his collected poems, he and Dora had realized that, as Quillinan put it, they had each 'in my heart of hearts held you dearest of all for years too.' Dora held out for a platonic friendship but Quillinan wanted nothing less than marriage and eventually persuaded Dora to accept him. William and Mary were understandably horrified. Quillinan was forty-seven, Dora thirty-four; he was a Roman Catholic, she an Anglican; he was a widower with a reputation as a flirt and a roué, she was a naive virgin. Worst of all, he was penniless, without any real prospect of being able to support Dora, and, as it appeared to her parents, who knew nothing of the affair until their daughter told them of it herself, he had betrayed their trust by wooing and winning her covertly. Through the good offices of Isabella Fenwick an understanding had been reached: the engagement would be recognized but the marriage would be deferred until Quillinan could provide for a wife. This was now jeopardized by Quillinan's urging Dora, in her parents' absence, to risk marrying him without their consent. The intervention of Isabella Fenwick and Dora's brother, Willy (who had himself lost a fiancée whose parents disapproved of his penurious state and would not allow him to marry their daughter), prevented a complete breach, but it was only when William and Quillinan met face to face in London that a genuine reconciliation took place.

440. Mary Wordsworth to her daughter, Dora; [Bath], Friday 19th [and 23 April 1839]

. . . I must steer clear of thoughts nearest my heart. Only I must say that neither you nor Mr Q[uillinan] do your father's feelings justice, or shew him proper <u>respect even</u> – by such expressions retorted upon him as "£-s-d-" & "the business of the matter" – All the feelings for y[ou]r Sake, that he has extinguished – should not indeed my dearest have been met in this Spirit – by either of you – But I must not go on . . .

– My dearest Child – all I mean to say to you is, that since dearest W[illy] read his letter (which was written entirely at his own suggestion, we unknowing of his intention till he put it first into my hands, & then he read it to his Father) we have all been uninterruptedly calm, & think & talk of your situation, & hope of happiness as a matter decided upon – therefore my beloved Daughter, do not agitate the matter further, or call upon your <u>tender Father</u> (for he <u>does</u> deserve that epithet if ever Man did) for more than this passive countenance which he is I feel, ready to give – And may his, & your Mother's blessing be upon you both – When you write, write as I hope you now feel, with thankfulness – & hope – & in this spirit & if possible, regain your lost strength before we meet, as I trust we shall do with hearts overflowing with love to you – Dearest W[illy] who left us yesterday morning will if possible see Q – & I trust ere then his irritation may have subsided & that all will be well. I will say no more – but that what we owe to dear Miss Fenwick is beyond all possible conception –

441. William Wordsworth to his daughter, Dora; [Bath, c.24 April 1839]

My dear Daughter,

The Letter which you must have received from W[illia]m [i.e., Willy] has placed before you my judgement and feelings; how far you are reconciled to them I am unable to divine; I have only to add, that I believe Mr Q[uillinan] to be a most honorable and upright man; and further that he is most strongly and faithfully attached to you – this I must solemnly declare in justice to you both; and to this I add <u>my blessing upon you and him</u>; more I cannot do – and if this does not content you with what your B[rothe]r has said, we must all abide by God's decision upon our respective fates. Mr Q[uillinan] is, I trust, aware how slender my means are; the state of W[illy]'s health will undoubtedly entail upon us considerable expense, & how John is to get on without our aid I cannot foresee. No more at present, my time is out; I am going to join Miss Fenwick at Miss Pollard's.

                    ever your most tender hearted and affectionate Father
                                                        Wm Wordsworth

442. Thomas Carlyle, essayist and historian, to Ralph Waldo Emerson; Chelsea, 29 May 1839

Wordsworth is here at present; a garrulous, rather watery, not wearisome old man. There is a freshness as of brooks and mountain breezes in him; one says of him: Thou are not great, but thou are genuine; well speed *thou*.

443. Isabella Fenwick to her niece, Isabella Fenwick; Cambridge Terrace, London, 20 May 1839

I have not yet been able to contrive a meeting between the Poet & him [Isabella Fenwick senior's brother] – he has been engaged & preoccupied – ever since he has been in Town and it has only been a <u>chance</u> half hour that I have seen him myself except when I dined to meet him at Mr Marshalls – where he & Mrs Wordsworth have been staying the last fortnight – & where I believe there has been some great party to meet him every day – in the midst of all this gaiety however they have had much to grieve & agitate them – the death of [their nephew] Mr Charles Wordsworths [wife] in Child bed – William's [i.e., Willy's] continued bad health – and Dora's <u>Affair</u> – more than alloy enough in this London life however flattering & successful –

444. William Wordsworth to his wife, Mary; [London], Saturday morning, 8 June [1839]

Yesterday I had a long interview with Mr Quillinan; tell dearest Dora. – I fear it was not satisfactory to either party – he seems wretched at the thought of the marriage being put off; and, as I told him, I could not look at [it] with that chearfulness & complacency & hopefulness, which ought to accompany such a transaction. As the event is inevitable, I told him I felt it my duty to try to make the best of it; but how I should succeed I could not tell. But said I blame no one; I only do regret that the affair should have pressed on this way in my absence, this was [the] sum of all; only I must add that I felt easier for having seen him, & that our interview was perfectly friendly.

445. *William Wordsworth to his daughter, Dora; [London], [9 June 1839]*

                                        Sunday morning, nine o clock
My dearest Dora,
    I am looking for Mr Quillinan, every moment. I hope to revive
the Conversation of yesterday – The sum is: I make no opposition
to this marriage – I have no resentment connected with it towards
any one. You know how much friendship I have always felt towards
Mr Q[uillinan], and how much I respect him – I do not doubt the
strength of his love & affection towards you; this as far as I am
concerned is the fair side of the case – On the other hand, I cannot
think of parting with you, with that complacency, that satisfaction,
that hopefulness which I could wish to feel, there is too much of
necessity in the case for my wishes – but I must submit and do
submit; and God almighty bless you my dear Child and him who is
the object of your long & long tried preference & choice.
                                        Ever your affectionate father,
                                             Wm Wordsworth
I have said little above of your dear Mother, the best of women. O
how my heart is yearning towards her, and you, and my poor dear
Sister! –

446. *Edward Quillinan to Dora Wordsworth; [London], Monday 10 June*
1839

After that weary first interview of which I gave you so doleful & yet half
hopeful a report; I never was so thoroughly subdued by distress of mind
in my life. – That expression "too old to be transplanted" almost killed
me. – . . . on Sunday Morn[in]g I went again to Mr Marshal's by Mr
W[ordsworth]'s appointment. I was shewn in to all the family at breakfast
he among them; that being his breakfast-breakfast; the one to follow at
Kenyon's, was to be his talking breakfast. – Presently he went with me
into the Library & there read me that most kind letter which he had
written to you. – From that moment all was right: I dismounted from my
high horse, never more to get on its back, by my fault at least to him. –
Willy kindly gave up his seat in the Cabriolet & walked to Kenyon's, that
I might ride with his father to Harley Street – In the Cab, he spoke to me
with all the affection of a friend & a father – & if he holds to that, it must
be my delight as well as my duty to shew him that that is the right course.

19. William Wordsworth, 1821, a portrait in charcoal and chalk by Francis William Wilkin (1791–1842). Though admitted by all to be an excellent physical likeness, the Wordsworths thought it lacked the spiritual, poetic element. William himself observed drily that 'it is like [me] if you suppose all the finer faculties of the mind to be withdrawn' and called it 'Wordsworth the Chancellor of the Exchequer – Wordsworth the Speaker of the House of Commons'.

20. The artist, Benjamin Robert Haydon (1786–1846), friend and admirer of William, sketched in 1815 whilst sleeping by the Scottish painter, Sir David Wilkie.

21. A mid nineteenth-century engraving by 'W. P.' of Grosvenor Square, London. The Wordsworths often stayed in Grosvenor Square with the Beaumonts and the Marshalls when visiting London.

22. Sir Walter Scott (1771–1832), poet, novelist and friend of the Wordsworths; a copy, dated 1829, by John Graham Gilbert of his own earlier portrait.

23. Temple Church, engraved by Storer and Grieg, 1805. Henry Crabb Robinson, William's friend, was a barrister in the Temple and William often breakfasted with him there.

Windermere
REGATTA,

TO BE HELD

AT THE LOW WOOD INN,

On Thursday, the 23rd September, 1830.

The Stewards propose that the following arrangement of Sports be adopted:

A TRAIL HUNT will commence at 9 o'clock.—First Dog £1. second, 10s.

TEN O'CLOCK.

Rowing Match for Skiffs, single handed.

First Prize, £1.—Second (if more than two) 10s.

HALF-PAST TEN.

MATCH with FISHERMEN'S BOATS, double-handed, each to be rowed by the Men who have regularly fished in them, short Oars only.—First Prize, £1.—Second, 15s.—Third, 10s.—Fourth (if five Boats contend) 5s.

ELEVEN O'CLOCK.

ROWING MATCH

For Wherries, double-handed.

First Prize, £3.—Second Prize (if three Boats) £1.

HALF-PAST ELEVEN.

MATCH for PLEASURE BOATS single-handed.—First, £1—Second, 10s. Third (if more than three) 5s.

TWELVE O'CLOCK.

Match for Boys under 16 years of age,

In Skiffs, double-handed.—First prize 10s.—Second (if more than two) 5s.

Private Matches among Gentlemen Amateurs, and other amusements, will take place at this time.

ONE O'CLOCK.

It is requested that all SAILING BOATS rendezvous in the Bay at Low Wood, and form a Sailing Match for a NEW SUIT OF COLOURS.

TWO O'CLOCK.

A GRAND PROCESSION,

To be formed of all the Boats, to follow in succession—the Sail Boats to take the lead.

THREE O'CLOCK.

Grand Wrestling Matches.

All names to be entered at a quarter before three.—First prize, £6 and a handsome BELT.—Second Prize, £2.—Two falls out of three to decide the last contest.

A Cold Collation will be ready at this hour for Ladies and Gentlemen, at the Low Wood Inn.

A FOOT RACE

Will take place immediately before the wrestling.—First prize, 15s.—Second, 5s.

All disputes to be settled by the Stewards, or those appointed by them.

A SPLENDID EXHIBITION OF

VAUXHALL FIRE WORKS

Will take place (at dark) in the evening.

Stewards,

Professor WILSON,	I. L. BEETHOLME, Esq.
JAMES BRANKER, Esq.	ROBT. PARTRIDGE, Esq.

A Ball will take place on Friday evening, at the Low Wood Inn; dancing to commence at nine o'clock.

T. Richardson, Printer, Kendal.

24. Advertisement for the regatta on Lake Windermere, September 1830. The annual regattas were the social event of the Lakeland season and William attended the balls and picnics from being a schoolboy at Hawkshead until the last few years of his life.

25. A pen-and-ink sketch by John Harden of Brathay of skaters on a frozen lake in 1847. According to Dorothy Wordsworth, William was 'still the crack skater on Rydal Lake' at the age of sixty.

26. The annual rush-bearing festivities at Ambleside. The traditional ceremony, which marked the replacement of the rushes covering the church floor, survived in some northern towns and villages, including Ambleside and Grasmere. Hoops, decorated by local children with paper and flowers, were paraded through the streets before being displayed in the church.

27. Mary Wordsworth (1770–1859), aged sixty-nine, painted by Margaret Gillies in 1839.

28. Dorothy Wordsworth (1771–1855), aged sixty-one, painted by Samuel Crosthwaite in 1833, during a brief period of remission in her long illness before her final collapse into dementia in 1835.

29. Dora Wordsworth (1804–47), aged thirty-five, painted by Margaret Gillies in November 1839. The portrait was retouched after her death, at her widower's request, to make her appear more 'spiritualized'.

30. Edward Quillinan (1791–1851); the only known portrait of Dora's husband. The date and artist have not been identified.

William Wordsworth,
April 21st 1847

31. William Wordsworth, a portrait in chalk and pencil, dated 21 April 1847, by Leonard
Charles Wyon (1826–91). The sitting for this portrait was interrupted and never resumed
when William received the letter informing him that Dora had been diagnosed with
tuberculosis and had not long to live.

Having made his peace with Quillinan, William, accompanied by Willy, set off for Oxford, where he was to receive one of the greatest accolades of his career. Prompted by the leaders of the Oxford Movement – John Keble, the Fabers and John Henry Newman – the University had decided to confer an honorary degree upon him. This was a significant honour in itself, but it was the spontaneous reception given the 69-year-old poet by the masters and undergraduates which proved a more memorable tribute to his genius.

447. Mary Arnold, wife of Thomas Arnold, headmaster of Rugby, from the Arnold family notebook, [12 June 1839]

In June 1839 your father & Jane & I set out with the very dawn for Oxford, to be present at the Com[memoratio]n & see degrees conferred amongst others on Mr Bunsen & Mr Wordsworth . . . The whole scene at the theatre was very striking but the one Image w[hic]h dwells on my mind with the most powerful interest is that of Mr W[ordsworth] with his venerable dignifed & yet humble look as he advanced to receive the University distinction. His grey hair easily distinguished him nor was he less marked by the deafening shouts of applause & approbation w[hic]h were heard on all sides from the Grave looking body of Masters below, as well as from the more vehement Undergraduates above. – Every thoughtful person there must I think have contrasted in their minds this strong demonstration of approbation with the neglect & even contempt with w[hic]h his early works were received & yet here was the same man his system & principles unchanged, his own dignified simplicity the same both in himself & in his works & yet having conquered that public opinion w[hic]h he was content to wait for[,] sure that his principle was true & not over anxious about the early acknowledgment of it. In all this there is real greatness.

William was also capable of displaying real generosity. He had always freely allowed editors of poetry selections to use his poems if their purposes were charitable or educational. In 1837 a young American, Henry Reed, who was Professor of English Literature at the University of Pennsylvania, had produced an American edition of *The Poetical Works of William Wordsworth*. No copyright laws existed to protect English works from piracy so William had no control over the publication and received nothing for it. Despite this, Reed's obvious enthusiasm for, and understanding of, the poetry won William's approval. He wrote to thank Reed for 'the pains you have bestowed upon the work' and entered into a long correspondence with him, which often included his new poems and latest revisions, expressly for the purpose of enabling Reed to continue to produce the 'most correct' edition. Others less scrupulous than Reed were ready to take advantage of this attitude. William had long championed the early poets, who were not then well known, and when Thomas Powell proposed an edition of Chaucer in modernized English, William gave the project his enthusiastic backing. As Mary suspected right from the start, however, Powell wanted William's involvement so that he could use his name to sell the book.

448. *William Wordsworth to Henry Reed; Rydal Mount, 23 December 1839*

Your letters are naturally turned upon the impression which my Poems, have made, & the estimation they are held, or likely to be held in, thro' the Vast Country to which you belong; I wish I could feel as livelily as you do upon this subject – or even upon the general destiny of those works – pray do not be long surprized at this declaration. There is a difference of more than the length of your life, I believe, between our ages, I am standing on the brink of that vast ocean I must sail so soon – I must speedily lose sight of the shore & I could not once have conceived how little I now am troubled by the thought of how long or short a time they who remain upon that shore may have sight of me. The other day I chanced to be looking over a M.S. poem belonging to the year 1803 – tho' not actually composed till many years afterwards. It was suggested by visiting the neighbourhood of Dumfries, in which Burns had resided & where he died it concluded thus.

> Sweet mercy to the gates of heaven
> This Minstrel lead, his sins forgiven,
> The rueful conflict the heart riven
>   With vain endeavour,
> And memory of earth's bitter leaven
>   Effaced for ever.

Here the verses closed, but I instantly added the other day

> But why to Him confine the prayer,
> When kindred thoughts & yearnings bear
> On the frail heart the purest share
>   With all that live?

> The best of what we do & are,
> Just God, forgive!

The more I reflect upon this last exclamation, the more I feel & perhaps it may in some degree be the same with you, justified in attaching comparatively small importance to any literary monument that I may be enabled to leave behind. It is well however I am convinced that men think otherwise in the earlier part of their lives, & why it is so is a point I need not touch upon in writing to you.

449. William Wordsworth to Edward Moxon; [Rydal Mount, ?18 February 1840]

Mr Powell, my Friend, has some thought of preparing for Publication some portions of Chaucer modernized so far & no farther than is done in my treatment of the Prioress's Tale. That would in fact be his model. – He will have Coadjutors, among whom I believe will be Mr Leigh Hunt, a man as capable of doing the work well as any living Author. I have placed at my friend Mr Powell's disposal, in addition to the Prioress's Tale, three other pieces which I did long ago, but revised the other day. They are the Manciple's Tale, the Cuckoo and the Nightingale, and 24 Stanzas of Troilus and Cressida. This I have done mainly out of my love & reverence for Chaucer, in hopes that whatever may be the merit of Mr Powell's attempt, the attention of other Writers may be drawn to the subject; and a Work hereafter be produced by different pens which will place the treasures of one of the greatest of Poets within the reach of the Multitude which now they are not. I mention all of this to you, because, though I have not given Mr Powell the least encouragement to do so, he may sound you as to your disposition to undertake the Publication. – I have myself nothing further to do with it than I have stated. Had the thing been suggested to me by any number of competent Persons 20 years ago I would have undertaken the editorship, done much more myself, and endeavoured to improve the several Contributions where they seemed to require it. – But that is now out of the question – –

I am glad to hear so favorable an account of the Sale of the new Edition. The penny-postage[1] has let in an inundation of complimentary Letters upon me – Yesterday I had one that would amuse you by the language of awe, veneration gratitude &c in which it abounds, & two or three days ago I had one from a little Boy eight years old! – telling Me how he had been charmed with the Idiot Boy &c &c. – In several of these Letters there is one thing which gratifies, viz the frequent mention of the consolation which my Poems have afforded the Writer under affliction, & the calmness and elevation of mind which they have produced in him.

450. Mary Wordsworth to Isabella Fenwick; [Rydal Mount, c. March 1840]

It appears from a letter rec[eive]d yesterday that the projectors of the intended publication have changed their purpose of modernizing <u>all</u> Chaucer – but first of all, mean to give a Selection 'by way of feeling the pulse of the public' – & this sample is to consist of W[illia]m's Prioresses Tale already published – the Cuckoo & Nightingale (now in Mr P[owell]'s hands) & those before you. While the other coadjutors give one piece each – a much larger <u>quantity</u> perhaps – but will this be a fair Specimen of what they mean to send out afterwards without aught from the <u>Masters</u> hand! To me it seems plain what the motive is – they are in haste to appear in connection with a name of influence. – I hope you do not think there will be any thing dishonorable in Mr W——— changing his purpose at this late hour.

451. William Wordsworth to Thomas Powell; Rydal Mount, 16 October 1840

Yesterday I rec[eive]d a letter from a Lady from which I transcribe the following. "I have read in a Newspaper that you are about to publish Chaucer's Tales modernized" – & a friend also tells me that he has seen an advertizement of your Publication in which my name stands first in large letters – Now dear Sir, you will remember that the condition upon which I placed these things at your disposal was, that for many reasons I should not be brought prominently forward in the Matter – but that my communications, given <u>solely</u> out of regard for you & reverence for Chaucer, should appear as unostentatiously as possible. I am therefore much concerned for what has been done, as it cannot be undone.

Despite his displeasure, William did not allow this incident to sour his friendship with the man responsible. When another old friend wrote to solicit a work from his pen, however, William instantly dismissed the idea. The suggestion was, in any case, an odd one: that the poet should write a biography of his brother, Christopher, a churchman and scholarly author of esoteric ecclesiastical works, who was about to resign as Master of Trinity College, Cambridge.

452. *William Wordsworth to the Reverend Francis Merewether; Rydal Mount,*
29 April 1840

My undertaking, dear Sir, to write my Brothers Memoir, is a thing
impossible – such a work could not be in hands so likely to disappoint the
public as mine. It would be expected I should have much to say of him,
a knowledge of which could not have come to me, but as his Brother. Now
as I grievously lament we have had very, very little personal intercourse; I
am between 4 & 5 years his Senior which separated us, as it could not but
do, as Boys; we having lost our Parents when we were Children. I left
Col[lege] before he came thither, & I saw nothing of him during the
Vacations. Many years of my life were afterwards spent in rambling about
the Continent, & in residences in different parts of England; so that we
seldom met, & only for a very short time, during many years. When he
was at Bocking, as you know, I paid him a visit – & he has twice been in
this Country – except what might be gained from these & our own short
visits at Cambridge – (during which however he was always so much
occupied in his Study or other avocations, that I had little communication
with him there) – I am unacquainted with his pursuits & mode of life –
in short I have none of that knowledge which would be looked for in a
Brother writing his life – Besides it must be borne in mind that I have
entered my 71st year – & therefore in course of Nature he will outlive
me. As Mr Watson [Christopher's closest friend] who I know is acquainted
with, & has sympathized in all his views & undertakings, for substantial
reasons declines the office of his Biographer, it will naturally devolve upon
one of his [i.e., Christopher's] Sons – from whom I trust it may be
expected. Materials furnished me by Others, to which you advert, could
not supply these deficiencies, especially as they would relate to Professional
engagement, studies, & proceedings which lie in a walk so far apart from
my own. I could not enter into the Spirit of those materials, as one of his
cooperators & coadjutors. Enough has been said I trust to reconcile you,
to forgo the expectation that such a labor of love, could advantageously
come from me.

None of Christopher's three academic sons would produce a biography of their
father, whose life remains unwritten, but one of them, Chris, would become the
authorized biographer of his uncle. This was ironic, for Chris, headmaster of
Harrow, future bishop of Lincoln and author of scholarly church histories and
commentaries, would have made a far more appropriate biographer of his own

father. As one of William's friends commented, in words which echo the poet's own argument for declining to write his brother's biography, Chris 'did not know much of his Uncle, except by hearsay, and that was not the way to know Wordsworth.'

Chapter Twelve

1840–44

On 7 April 1840 William celebrated his seventieth birthday. Though he complained of minor ailments, particularly the recurrent problem with his eyes, his health and energy were undiminished. He was even still writing poetry, including a poem prompted by a cuckoo-clock, a birthday present from Isabella Fenwick.

453. Mary Wordsworth to Isabella Fenwick; [Rydal Mount], April [1840]

. . . I enclose you a trifling scrap from the <u>Septuagenarian's</u> own hand; & which ought to have been forwarded on that day, had I thought the offering sufficiently worthy. The improved copy of the Cuckoo Clock, is in your hands ere this, but I have to send a new reading of the last Stanza, which has not been yet forwarded to Dora – indeed it was only altered last night. I <u>do</u> trust that the last polish has now been given – it has however been a work of real pleasure – & well it may – for no children were ever more delighted with a new toy, than we are with the subject of it – Dear Miss Wordsworth was seated before it upon the top of the stairs the other day – & when the bird had performed its office, & the little door flapped to, I thought she would have dropped from her chair, she laughed so heartily at the sudden exit of the little Mimic.

454. William Wordsworth to his daughter, Dora, and Isabella Fenwick; [Rydal Mount], 7 April 1840

Sister is very comfortable – and we are going on nicely, though wishing much for your return. Yesterday I dined with Mrs Luff, after calling at the house high up Loughrigg side, where dwells the good woman who lost her two children in the flood last winter. The wind was high when I knocked at her door, and I heard a voice from within, that I knew not what to make of; though it sounded something like the lullaby of a Mother, to her Baby. after entering I found it came from a little sister of those drowned Children, that was singing to a bundle of clouts rudely put together to look like a Doll, which she held in her arms.

I tell you this little story in order that, if it be perfectly convenient, but on no account else, you may purchase a thing that may answer the purpose with some thing more of pride and pleasure to this youngling of a nurse. Such is your mother's wish, I should not have had the wit to think of it. No matter she says how common a sort of thing the Doll is, only let it be a good big one.

455. *Edward Quillinan to Dora; Canterbury, 11 April 1840*

. . . I was also greatly taken with that anecdote of Mr W[ordsworth] & the lone child & the doll: – <u>his</u> part in the affair is one of those small gems of trifles worth preserving in remembrance, one of the smaller lights to the best and deepest sanctuary of his nature.

456. *William Wordsworth to Thomas Powell; Rydal Mount, 1 May 1840*

Mrs W[ordsworth] & I have both been in good health during the spring which for beauty of weather has exceeded all that I remember. We have been eleven weeks almost without rain; and the east winds are so broken by our mountains and tempered, that being softened also by the warmth of the sun we have scarcely felt any annoyance from them. One beautiful feature of the Season has been most remarkable, – the profusion and size and splendor of the wild flowers; I do not remember having seen in England any thing like it. – I have almost lived in the open air, with nothing to complain of but that my eyes will not stand reading.

457. *William Wordsworth to Charles Henry Parry, who had just lost his eighteen-year-old daughter; Rydal Mount, 21 May 1840*

Pray impute to any thing but a want of due sympathy with you in your affliction my not having earlier given an answer to your Letter. In truth I was so much moved by it that I had not at first sufficient resolution to bring my thoughts so very close to your trouble as must have been done had I taken up the pen immediately. –

I have been myself distrest in the same way though my two children were taken from us at an earlier age, one in [her] fifth[1] and the other in his seventh years, and within half a year of each other. – I can therefore enter into your sorrow more feelingly than for others is possible who have not suffered like losses . . .

The consolation which Children and very Young Persons who have been religiously brought up, draw from the holy Scripture ought to be habitually on the minds of adults of all ages for the benefit of their own Souls, and requires to be treated in a loftier and more comprehensive train of thought and feeling than by writers has usually been bestowed upon it. It does not therefore surprize me that you hinted at my own pen being employed upon the subject as brought before the mind in your lamented Daughter's most touching case. I wish I were equal to any thing so holy, but I feel that I am not.

458. Mary Wordsworth to her nephew, Chris Wordsworth; Rydal Mount, 24 June [1840]

Your Uncle is remarkably well, and the wonder of all who hear that he has entered his 70th year – he has been hard at work for the last 3 or 4 months – and tho' he labours in constant fear of his eyes, and complains of discomfort from them – Yet in reality he has had very little suffering: and the work that has principally occupied him, you will imagine to have required deep thought and to be delicately treated, when I tell you that he has written 11 Sonnets 'On the punishment of Death!' More practical and [?airy] Subjects – even such as some 8 or 10 years hence – may interest your Daughter, have diversified his labours, all which I hope he may before long have the satisfaction of reading to you at Rydal.

Amongst the hundreds of visitors who called at Rydal Mount in the summer of 1840 was one of the most distinguished yet, the dowager Queen Adelaide, aunt of Queen Victoria. Much to the amusement of the Wordsworths' friends, she chose not to visit the haughty Lady le Fleming, who, highly offended, shut herself up at Rydal Hall, while her more famous tenant took his illustrious visitor on a tour of her ladyship's park.

459. William Wordsworth to Lady Frederick Bentinck; [Rydal Mount, 30 July 1840]

On Monday morning, a little before nine, a beautiful and bright day, the Queen Dowager and her sister appeared at Rydal. I met them at the lower waterfall, with which her Majesty seemed much pleased. Upon hearing that it was not more than half a mile to the higher fall, she said, briskly, she would go; though Lord Denbigh and Lord Howe felt that they were pressed for time, having to go upon Keswick Lake, and thence to Paterdale. I walked by the Queen's side up to the higher waterfall, and she seemed to be struck much with the beauty of the scenery . . .

Upon quitting the park of Rydal, nearly opposite our own gate, the Queen was saluted with a pretty rural spectacle; nearly fifty children, drawn up in [an] avenue, with bright garlands in their hands, three large flags flying, and a band of music. They had come from Ambleside, and the garlands were such as are annually prepared at this season for a ceremony called 'the Rush-bearing';[2] and the parish-clerk of Ambleside hit upon this way of showing at Rydal the same respect to the Queen which had been previously shown at Ambleside. I led the Queen to the principal points of view in our little domain, particularly to that, through the summer house, which shows the lake of Rydal to such advantage. The Queen talked more than once about having a cottage among the lakes, which of course was nothing more than a natural way of giving vent to the pleasure which she had in the country. You will think, I fear, that I have dwelt already too long upon the subject; and I shall therefore only add, that all went off satisfactorily, and that every one was delighted with her Majesty's demeanour.

460. Dora Wordsworth to her brother, Willy; [Rydal Mount], Monday night, 27 July 1840

Do you think Mammy will be able to sleep tonight after having been shaken by the hand at our own door by a Queen – having talked with the Queen in this very room – & her old husband the old Poet having walked side by side & talked with her Majesty a full hour I am sure – the World & his Wife were assembled on our front to see the cortege – & Tommy Troughton with his band, & all the flags, & all the rushbearings placed in two lines from the high waterfall gate to our gate made as pretty an avenue for the Queen to walk thro' roofed by the green trees & the bright blue sky as was ever seen – . . . If you had seen dear Mammy in Miss Fenwick's white satin bonnet this morning & black lace scarf, you w[oul]d have been proud of her & whether the servants & whole assembly of Natives were more proud of Mistress & the shaking of her hand by the Queen or of Master looking so handsome in his "fine new hat" & walking side by side ["]wit Queen" w[oul]d be hard to tell –

461. Edward Quillinan to his daughter, Rotha; Rydal Mount, 1 September 1840

. . . at breakfast I declared my intention to ride to Wyburn, 7 miles off, & go up the mountain. – "I will go with you:" said Dora. Every [body] cried out "Impossible. You cannot walk up Helvellyn, & it is known to be impossible to ride up all the way." However Dora was so anxious to try it, though Mrs W[ordsworth] would not hear of it for a long time, that I thought it might be worth while to let her make the attempt on a pony, & Mr Wordsworth not only assented to my proposal but offered to go with us! This was something worth accepting, So Father Daughter & I set out in the carriage, Ebba Hutchinson [Tom's daughter, William's niece] riding the little pony we had borrowed from Mr Roughsedge for the mountain. When we got to Wyburn, we were assured by the Guides, & the innkeeper that such a thing was never heard of as riding all the way up Helvellyn; that it [was] just impossible. Nothing moved, we determined to try it . . . & up we went, with no Guide but Mr Wordsworth – It was very steep, very hot work, very craggy at times, & in some places worse from being wet & spongy, but we effected the ascent in about two hours & ¼, Mr W[ordsworth] mostly poetising by himself the whole way, & Dora not once being suffered by me to get off her horse till we got to the very top! – No Lady that we hear of has ever done this . . . I wish you could have seen the Old Poet, seated from time to time, as we paused for breath, on a rock writing down his Waterloo Sonnet – for he composed one as we went up on the visit of Wellington to the Field of Waterloo 20 years after the Battle, as painted lately by Haydon the historical painter, to whom the Duke gave 5 sittings. Haydon sent Mr W[ordsworth] a fine print from his painting, urging a request that he would give him a Sonnet on the subject. – He complied & composed it on Helvellyn! – I have not time to tell you, with any particularity, of our whiskey & water bottle, our sandwiches, & gingerbread nuts, the pony, capital nice little fellow, trying to kick Dora off, our getting partially bogged once or twice, our strange & pleasant meeting with the Marshalls, three of the sisters (including that delightful poetess Mrs Elliott) and also two of their brothers, & Sir William Chatterton who (the men) were, or rather had been, grouse-shooting – our descent by another way, and in fine all our prosperous excursion. –

It is a curious fact, that even on that great steep mountain the Poet was followed by Strangers – rather a bore, yet an evidence of the reverence he is held in. – Nobody that is not here can have the least idea how he is hunted, flattered, puffed, carest &c &c. It is enough to <u>spoil</u> any human being.–

462. William Wordsworth to Edward Moxon; [Rydal Mount], 17 December 1840

You told me the Excursion was out of print. What do you say to reprinting it in double column stereotyped, all but the pages – so that the same plates might serve hereafter, the paging being altered, for the concluding part of the vol[ume] when the whole shall be published in one? I have two motives for this, the one a desire to make the book acceptable to Mechanics & others who have little money to spare, & next to shew from so many instances with which this would concur that books are as likely to be sold as cheap as they can be afforded, should the term of copy-right be extended, & that in fact, they could in that case be sold cheaper, as there being no dread of competition – Editions might be larger – & would of course be sold at less price. Let me hear from you on this point at your early convenience.

463. Henry Crabb Robinson to his brother; Rydal Mount, 12 January 1841

The poet is in full vigour of health & intellect Mrs W[ordsworth] as delightful as ever, being a model of goodness Poor Miss W[ordsworth] in an unexpectedly improved state – Her mind feeble but she talks nothing absolutely insane or irrational, but she has so little command of herself that she cannot restrain the most unseemly noises, blowing loudly & making a nondescript sound more shrill than the cry of a partridge & a turkey . . . From this she is to be drawn only by a request to repeat Verses which she does with affecting sweetness – She is fond of repeating her own pretty lines Which way does the wind blow? . . .

We have had less than the usual excitement of disputation – W[ords-worth]'s tone is far more liberal than it used to be. He does not abuse even the Non-Con[formist]s except in jest Nor the Whig-rad[ical]s at all – Party animosity seems to be dying away for want of nutriment.

Yet another attempt to reform the copyright laws was made by the pertinacious Thomas Noon Talfourd in the spring of 1841. This too failed, not because of opposition by the booksellers and publishers as on previous occasions, but because the author and Member of Parliament, Thomas Babington Macaulay, argued that copyright was a form of monopoly which was against the interest of the public and should not be extended under any circumstances. Macaulay could afford to be altruistic – he held a government post on the Supreme Council of India which paid him £10,000 a year – but William could not.

464. William Wordsworth to Thomas Noon Talfourd; Rydal Mount, 8 February 1841

My dear Sergeant Talfourd,

Tho' I have been silent you have been daily in my thoughts. Notwithstanding what I feel, I cannot bring myself to condole with you, upon the loss of the Copy-right bill, for this Session – Indignation stifles every other emotion but gratitude towards you, for the noble & persevering exertions which you have made so long. I have seen nothing of the debate but a me[a]gre report in the St. James' Chronicle that gives Macauleys speech at some length, but alots to your notice of it, only a few lines – Pray find a moment to tell me what had best be done in future – I would write & publish in my own name a letter addressed to you, in refutation of the trash advanced by Macauley if all that he has said had not been anticipated over & over by yourself & others. This same gentleman, if he has acted upon conscientious motives, without supposing him to be more stupid than I can think possible, ought to set about introducing a bill for the repeal of the law of Copyright as it now stands – in order to shorten its term, or rather abolish it altogether –

William was now hard at work on a new project, preparing his hitherto unpublished juvenile poems for publication: amongst these would be his Salisbury Plain poem, now called *Guilt and Sorrow*, and his tragedy, *The Borderers*.

465. William Wordsworth to Isabella Fenwick; [Rydal Mount], Friday evening [March 1841]

The weather here has been most glorious, as warm almost as June; yet two or three nights ago Windermere was skinned over with ice which could not have been but for the breathless calmness: Dearest Mary looks and is much better than when you left us; For myself I feel nervous and a good deal exhausted, because I cannot keep my poor brain quiet. I could sleep like a top all the afternoon, but in the night or rather morning after 4 o clock I make poor work of it. – Mary has transcribed all the Poems except the Sonnets and my work of correction is over. But I have not yet had courage to look at the tragedy – I composed a Sonnet on my walk home after I left you, and I have since written upwards of 100 Lines in blank Verse, the Scene Italy; about 50 more will I hope finish the Poem –

466. William Wordsworth to Edward Moxon; [Rydal Mount], 4 March [1841]

By way of <u>secret</u> I must let you know, that I have just been copying out about 2000 Lines of miscellaneous Poems, from Mss, some of which date so far back [as] 1793, and others from that time, at various periods, to the present day. – If I could muster a 1000 lines more, there would be enough for another Volume, to match pretty well in size with the rest; but this not being the case I am rather averse to publication – You will hear more of this hereafter. Mrs W[ordsworth] and I will not be in Town till the middle of May at the earliest. –

And now with many and sincere good wishes farewell.

ever faithfully yours

Wm Wordsworth

On 11 May 1841, after years of not-always-patient waiting, Edward Quillinan and Dora were married at St James' church, Bath. In an effort to sugar the pill for her father, the newly-weds and Isabella Fenwick accompanied her parents on a brief tour of the West Country, visiting the haunts of his youth, before William and Mary travelled on alone to London. The wedding, however, did not pass off without incident.

467. Edward Quillinan to his daughter, Rotha; Piper's Inn, Somerset, 12 May 1841

Dora & I were made one yesterday at Bath, her brother, John Wordsworth having kindly come from Cumberland on purpose to be the officiating clergyman. Mr & Mrs Wordsworth and William [i.e. Willy] and Miss Fenwick were also of the party: but Mr Wordsworth was so agitated at parting with his sole daughter that he said to me, almost at the last moment, "I have told Dora that I would accompany you to church if you wished it, but this interview with my child has already so upset me that I think I can hardly bear it." We all then begged him <u>not</u> to come, & it was agreed that his Son William should act for him; but he gave us his blessing very affectionately both before & after the wedding: nothing indeed could be kinder than he & all have been. – Ebba Hutchinson & Miss Tudor were the Bridesmaid. – There was as usual, a breakfast afterwards, confined to the family circle & two or three friends . . . Mr & Mrs Wordsworth & Miss Fenwick will join us here tomorrow at breakfast & take us on with them to Bridgwater, Nether-Stowey the birthplace of Coleridge, & Alfoxden where Mr Wordsworth once lived & where he first knew Coleridge . . .³

468. Isabella Fenwick to Henry Taylor; 20 May 1841

We had two perfect days for our visit to Wells, Alfoxden, &c. They were worthy of a page or two in the poet's life. Forty-two years, perhaps, never passed over any human head with more gain and less loss than over his. There he was again, after that long period, in the full vigour of his intellect, and with all the fervent feelings which have accompanied him through life; his bodily strength little impaired, but grey-headed, with an old wife and not a young daughter. The thought of what his sister, who had been his companion here, was then and now is, seemed the only painful feeling that moved in his mind. He was delighted to see again those scenes (and they were beautiful in their kind) where he had been so happy – where he had felt and thought so much. He pointed out the spots where he had written many of his early poems, and told us how they had been suggested . . . Dear Dora and Mr Quillinan parted with us at Bridgewater; they proceeded to Rydal Mount and we to Bagborough [where Isabella Fenwick's sister lived], where we have been spending some very pleasant days. Mr Wordsworth and the Squire do very well together. The latter thinks the former a very sensible man, and the former thinks the latter a very pleasant one. The people in Somersetshire know nothing of the poet. They call him Wentworth and Wedgewood and all sorts of names. But they are kind and hospitable, and he likes to be met on the ground of his common humanity.

469. William Wordsworth to Isabella Fenwick; from the Bishop of London's, Fulham Palace, London, 29 June 1841

This is a wretchedly dull Letter; but I really know not what to touch upon, among the multiplicity of topics; and what would it avail to tell you that at a large dinner table, or in such and such a throng I have seen or had a few minutes converse with such a Person or Personage. But O, my dear Friend, the hollowness of London society – but what an abuse of the term, and not only the hollowness but the tediousness especially among Dabblers in Literature – to me their talk, and their flattery above all, is insupportable.

470. William Wordsworth to Isabella Fenwick; Harrow, 10 July 1841

I steal a moment, my beloved Friend, to write you a few words; and tell you in part how I have been employed. On Wednesday last we came here from Hampstead. Sir Robert Peel attended the speeches that day, and saw two prizes for Latin prose and Verse adjudged to his Son. I took that opportunity to request an interview with him upon the Copyright Bill, and accordingly it took place yesterday at his own House, Whitehall. – I could not induce him to look favorably upon the Bill; in fact he was obviously afraid of being charged with favouring <u>monopoly</u>, if he gave it his support. He assigned some reasons for thinking that undeserving authors would profit by the privilege to the injury of the community. He acknowledged however the [*sic*] both the justice and expediency of giving the privilege to particular Persons, and expressed a hope that Parliament would aid in such a measure. – I urged many and I think cogent objections to this scheme; combated his notion that any injury to the public would accrue from the quarters to which he had adverted; and gave many reasons for the belief that the literature of the Country would derive great benefit from the extension of the term, and that, though the number of Authors who might profit from it by means of works now existing was deplorably small, still we had just reasons for believing that the number would be encreased to the benefit and honor of the nation, and in the service of mankind at large. I made, however, little or no impression, none indeed to encourage hope that he would support that or a similar measure. – My day's labour was not however thrown away, for I called on Mr Lockhart, reported to him what had passed and succeeded in persuading Him to write an Article for the Quarterly, in support of the cause.

471. William Wordsworth to Isabella Fenwick; [Rydal Mount, 5 August 1841]

It was neither rheumatism nor s[c]iatica with which I was troubled, but only the effect of a straining of the muscles from too much exercise, and imprudently climbing styles & gates, without due consideration of my age, and only looking at my natural lightness of body and activity. The pain which when I stooped or rose inconsiderately from my chair &c – was very acute, gradually went away and has for some days wholly disappeared. But it has taught me that I must yield to the invisible changes which Time makes in One's constitution. –

As the quieter winter months approached, William returned to the preparation of his new volume, *Poems, Chiefly of Early and Late Years*, which Moxon would publish in 1842. He was more than usually nervous about this work, partly because the book trade was in a parlous state, and partly because he feared that the juvenile pieces it contained might rouse the old antagonism of the critics.

472. William Wordsworth to Henry Crabb Robinson; [Rydal Mount, late November 1841]

(Private)

My dear Friend

We shall soon be looking out for your visit; and you must excuse me if I put you to a little trouble before you Leave London. I was thinking of publishing a Vol[ume] of poems this winter and have given some little of our late leisure to prepare it for the Press; but I am checked by the fear which has been expressed to me 'that Moxon may Crash'; could you in a quiet way collect for me any information upon this point. I know that the publishing trade is in general in a most agitated state And I know no reason for thinking that his concerns are an exception but send for a contrary opinion. I should be glad if I could get some light from you –

473. Henry Crabb Robinson to William Wordsworth; [London], 15 December 1841

I called also on our friend Moxon to day – I enquired about you, announcing my intended visit – He informed me of your having a few weeks back written about the publication of a new volume – he supposes you have been deterred by the sad report of the late Sale of the edition on hand – This he says is certainly very bad, but not <u>peculiarly</u> so – He says that the whole book selling returns in London at this season do not amount to more than a sixth of what they were a year ago!!!!!! He seemed still to think that this is hardly a good reason for not publishing the new volume – which might serve as a spur to the back volumes – besides being in itself profitable –

474. William Wordsworth to his daughter, Dora; Lowther Castle, 7 December [1841]

The Autumn has been delightfully mild; in fact most charming weather. To day it is most beautiful; and through a veil of tall leafless trees, I have a prospect of silver & sunny clouds as pleasing as one could wish to look at. I am anxious to be at home for many reasons, one that I wish for quiet and repose as I have exhausted myself a good deal of late, in disentangling a composition or two in which I have been engaged from awkwardnesses that annoyed me much.

475. William Wordsworth to his friend, Sir William Gomm; Rydal Mount, 10 March 1842

We have both weathered the winter stoutly, though latterly a good deal over exerted in preparing and carrying through the Press a new Vol[ume] of Miscellaneous Poems of which some were written as far back as 1793, and several others within these last 4 or 5 years, up almost to yesterday. –

476. William Wordsworth to Edward Moxon; Rydal Mount, [27 March 1842]

You will perhaps have thought that I was splenetic in insisting upon this volume not being sent to the Reviews – it is a thing which I exceedingly dislike, as done, seemingly, to propitiate. If any work comes from an Author of distinction, they will be sure to get hold of it; if they think it would serve their publication so to do; & if they be inclined to speak well of it, either from its own merits or their good opinion of the Author in general, sending the book is superfluous; & if they are hostile it would only gratify the Editor's or Reviewer's vanity, & set an edge upon his malice – These are secrets of human nature which my turn for dramatic writing (early put aside) taught me – or rather that turn took its rise from the knowledge of this kind with which observation had furnished me.

Mrs W[ordsworth] protests against all this, & says if I am to write in such a strain I had better take the pen in to my own hand.

477. Mary Wordsworth to Edward Moxon; [Rydal Mount, 1 April 1842]

Mr W[ordsworth] bids me add that he regrets you have nothing more favorable to hold out than that the book is likely to have a "very <u>fair</u> sale" – cold comfort he says for him who has wasted so much health & strength in minute correction which nobody will either thank him for, nor care any thing about & which wasted health & strength (I now write from his dictation <u>observe</u>) might in part have been recovered if the profits of this volume would have left him free in conscience to take a recreative trip to Paris or elsewhere! – such stuff my good husband compels me to write –

On the eve of William's seventy-second birthday a watered-down version of the Copyright Bill which he had fought so long to secure was passed. It transformed the position of authors, extending the period of protection of copyright from twenty-eight to forty-two years from the date of first publication, or seven years after the author's death, whichever was longer.

478. William Wordsworth to Viscount Mahon; Rydal Mount, 11 April 1842

Dear Lord Mahon,

Let me begin with thanking you cordially for your Letter, but above all for your zealous exertions on behalf of the Literature of the Country. The result is lamentably short of what it must have been, if the House (I mean the majority of it) could have seen the matter in its true light, either as a question of justice, of feeling, or of policy. One point however is gained and that a very important one. The <u>principle</u> of postobit remuneration will be established if Sir Robert Peel's amendment become[s] Law. Seven years are indeed only a beggarly allowance; why did not Sir R[obert] propose at least <u>nine</u>? and then there would have been a year for each of the Nine Muses, Urania included!!!

In May William, Mary and Willy went to London. The object of their visit was two-fold: to visit Dora, who was living there, and to lobby once again for a government office for Willy. Lord Lowther, who was now Postmaster-General, revived the old idea of transferring William's office of Distributer of Stamps to his son, who had been acting as his sub-distributer in Carlisle for some years, so was not unqualified for the post. He could, however, only hold out a hope that Sir Robert Peel, as Prime Minister, would grant William a government pension to make up for the £400 a year loss in income he would sustain. Pension or not, William and Mary were simply happy to see their youngest son settled: they looked forward to the probability of having to make strict economies with perfect equanimity.

479. *William Wordsworth to Isabella Fenwick; [7 Upper Spring Street, Baker Street, London, 24 May 1842]*

Every thing here is lost in hurry and distraction. Yesterday I dined at the Whig Lord Stanleys; and there I met Mr [Thomas] Carlysle, who inquired kindly after you. To day I dine at the B[isho]p of Londons; and thence go to the grand affair at the Dutchess of Sutherlands where of the Post of this Morning tells us 800 of the haute Ton, including several branches of the royal family will be assembled. – To morrow I dine at the Marquis of Lansdown's. Thursday at Home, and go to the House of Lords, it is the Copy right day – But I find Mary has told you all this: Let me say a word about dear Dora, I wish it could be a more hopeful one. I cannot but think that she looks worse and worse. What she wants is absolute <u>tranquillity</u> and rest of body and mind. Both her temperament and her situation are against her having either one or the other; nor do I see how they are to be attained, so that I cannot but despond as to the issue. Fresh air she has none, exercise she has only had since we came, yesterday, when Miss Rogers took her out kindly for an airing. But [when] we have the happiness of seeing you again, you shall have all particulars –

The transfer of the office I shall know more about in a day or two, whether it will be effected and if so, upon what terms. Nothing can exceed Lord Lonsdales kindness, or that of all the members of his family. No doubt if the Transfer does take place, it will be under circumstances that will cause a great reduction of the income, W[illia]m & I have together drawn from it, so that unless a pension follows in a reasonable time, we shall be much straitened, and stand in need of the most rigid economy; and <u>that</u> will not be hard for us to practice –

480. *Mary Wordsworth to Isabella Fenwick; [Rydal Mount], Sunday morning [August 1842]*

Poor dear Willy parted with his home & his new acquisitions in very depressed spirits – he foolishly dwells on the 'sacrifice' which he considers his Father to have made for him, & which in fact is none at all, but the reverse – & I may truly say, were it not for his sake, & that of good Mr. Carter [the Stamp Office clerk], to both of whom, his Father having a Pension, would be a satisfaction, I would rather not have one . . . The removal of the Stamps, seemed a sort of breaking up, for seeing the last of what has been a nearly 30 years interest could not but be seriously felt by us, at our age – & it was felt, but with thankfulness that what had been so great a benefit to us (in educating our Children, & enabling us to live for so many years in the sort of hospitality we liked best) had passed into the hands of our beloved Son – & grateful are we to those who have aided us in this object. But as Cook says, it was like a funeral going out of the house, when after so much bustle, & pulling down in the Office they had all passed away. I however next day set about building up again & we are now comfortably reconciled to our loneliness; in the delightful hope that you will, in a few months dearest Friend come back to us . . .

481. *Mary Wordsworth to Isabella Fenwick; [Rydal Mount], 4 October 1842*

My dearest Friend

I know not where I may find you but I cannot let this our fortieth wedding-day pass (& such a day of bright gorgeous autumn is not very often seen) without dividing my heart-felt thankfulness with you – who, I know, wherever you may be, your thoughts & blessings will be with us, especially if it occurs to you, that from this day we look back upon 40 years of wedded life with grateful thanks to our heavenly Father for leading us thro' such a long course of uninterrupted harmony. – We like all mortals have had our sorrows, but these have been endeared to us by perfect sympathy, & only drawn us more closely to each other. – Then this beautiful region in which we have been permitted to live – & in such home-society! Our two beloved Sisters, the one gone before, & the other changed – yet how graciously have these deprivations been made up to us by the blessing of you, dearest Friend, being sent to comfort us for the loss of our Companion Child. Would that we could look forward for but a portion of our happiness consequent upon her union.

482. William Wordsworth to William Ewart Gladstone MP; Rydal Mount,
17 October 1842

Rydal Mount, Oct[ober] 17th 42.

My dear Mr Gladstone,

I do not lose a moment in letting you know that Sir Robert Peel
has made me an offer of a Pension of £300 per ann[um] for my life,
and in terms which have above measure enhanced the satisfaction I
feel upon the occasion.

I will not run the risk of offending you by a renewal of thanks for
your good offices in bringing this about, but will content myself
with breathing sincere and fervent good wishes for your welfare.
Believe me, my dear Mr Gladstone,

faithfully yours
Wm Wordsworth

483. Lady Frederick Bentinck, daughter of Lord Lonsdale, to William
Wordsworth; 18 October 1842

It has come later in y[ou]r Life than y[ou]r Friends think right but still,
after what pass'd here in the Summer, it has come sooner, than we were
prepared to expect.

484. William Wordsworth to his young friend and admirer, the poet Aubrey de
Vere; Rydal Mount, 16 November 1842

For many reasons connected with advanced life, I read but little of new
works either in prose or verse. [Samuel] Rogers says of me, partly in joke
and partly in earnest, as he says of himself and others as frankly, and has
avowed in one of his letters written when he was an old man, "I read no
poetry now but my own." In respect to myself, my good old friend ought
to have added that if I do read my own, it is mainly, if not entirely, to
make it better. But certain it is that old men's literary pleasures lie chiefly
among the books they were familiar with in their youth; and this is still
more pointedly true of men who have practised composition themselves.
They have fixed notions of style and of versification, and their thoughts
have moved on in a settled train so long that novelty in each or all of these,
so far from being a recommendation, is distasteful to them, even though,
if hard put to it, they might be brought to confess that the novelty was all

improvement. You must be perfectly aware of all that I have said, as characteristic of human nature to a degree which scarcely allows of exceptions, though rigidity or obtuseness will prevail in some minds more than in others. For myself, however, I have many times, when called upon to give an opinion on works sent, felt obliged to recommend younger critics as more to be relied upon, and that for the reason I have mentioned. It is in vain to regret these changes which Time brings with it; one might as well sigh over one's grey hairs . . .

You enquire after my MS. poem on my own life. It is lying, and in all probability will lie, where my "Tragedy," and other "Poems" lay ambushed for more than a generation of years. Publication was ever to me most irksome; so that if I had been rich, I question whether I should ever have published at all, though I believe I should have written.

485. William Wordsworth to Professor Henry Reed; Rydal Mount, 27 March 1843

. . . it may afford you some satisfaction to be told that in the Mss Poem upon my own Poetic education there is a whole Book of about 600 Lines upon my obligations to writers of imagination, and chiefly the Poets, though I have not expressly named those to whom you allude – and for whom & many others of their age I have a high respect. The character of the School Master about whom you inquire, had like the Wanderer in the Excursion a solid foundation in fact & reality, but like him it was also in some degree a Composition; I will not & need not call it an invention – it was no such thing: – But were I to enter into details I fear it would impair the effect of the whole upon your mind, nor could I do it at all to my own satisfaction.

On 21 March 1843 Robert Southey died and the post of Poet Laureate fell vacant. For forty years Southey had shared in the weals and woes of the Wordsworth family, as they had in his, but his last years had been marred by mental illness and a second marriage which caused irreparable rifts in his own family. His widow pointedly did not invite William to the funeral but he went anyway, with his son John and his grandson William, who was Southey's godson. On 30 March the Lord Chamberlain wrote to William and offered him the Laureateship.

486. William Wordsworth to Lady Frederick Bentinck; [Rydal Mount, 1 April 1843]

Had I been several years younger I should have accepted the office with pride and pleasure; but on Friday I shall enter into, God willing, my 74th year, and on account of so advanced an age I begged permission to decline it, not venturing to undertake its duties. For though, as you are aware, the formal task-work of New Year and Birthday Odes was abolished when the appointment was given to Mr. Southey, he still considered himself obliged in conscience to produce, and did produce, verses, some of very great merit, upon important public occasions. He failed to do so upon the Queen's Coronation, and I know that this omission caused him no little uneasiness. The same might happen to myself upon some important occasion, and I should be uneasy under the possibility; I hope, therefore, that neither you nor Lord Lonsdale, nor any of my friends, will blame me for what I have done.

It was the Prime Minister's prerogative to make the appointment and Sir Robert Peel was determined that William would be the next Poet Laureate. He wrote a personal letter, undertaking 'that you shall have nothing required from you' and assuring him that the offer had been made solely 'in order to pay you that tribute of Respect which is justly due to the first of living Poets.' William was forced to concede defeat and on 4 April, three days before his seventy-third birthday, he accepted the appointment, on condition that 'it is to be considered merely honorary.' Miss Fenwick decided to ensure that the new Laureate's birthday would be celebrated in style.

487. Edward Quillinan to Henry Crabb Robinson; Ambleside, 19 April 1843

We have a tea-drink tomorrow in Mr North's field to 120 or 130 school-children (all girls, for the boys are too boisterous). When I say we, Dora & I (assisted by the Robinson's & Brigges) are only the managers; & the nominal entertainers of all that young rabble. Miss Fenwick pays the piper – or rather the Fidler, for we mean to make them dance. – She gives the fete to Dora to celebrate her Father's Birthday which has been put off in royal fashion from the 7th to the 20th of April.

Mr W[ordsworth] will probably not be in town this year unless a foreign Tour sh[oul]d be resolved on. But that is not unlikely, for he seems bent Italy-ward, or at all events, abroad-ward.

488. Edward Quillinan to Henry Crabb Robinson; Belle Isle, Windermere, 23 July 1843

Mr. Wordsworth ought to have been at Buckingham Palace, at the Queen's Ball, for which he received a formal invitation: – "The Lord Chamberlain presents his compliments. He is commanded by Her Majesty to invite Mr. William Wordsworth to a ball at Buckingham Palace, on Monday, the 24th July – ten o'clock. Full dress." To which he pleaded, as an apology for non-attendance, the non-arrival of the invitation (query command?) in time. He dated his answer from this place, "The Island, Windermere," and that would explain the impossibility; for the notice was the shortest possible, even if it had been received by first post. But a man in his seventy-fourth year would, I suppose, be excused by Royalty for not travelling 300 miles to attend a dance, even if a longer notice had been given – though probably Mr. Wordsworth would have gone had he had a fortnight to think of it, because the Laureate *must* pay his personal respects to the Queen sooner or later; and the sooner the better, he thinks.

489. William Wordsworth to Henry Reed; Rydal Mount, 2 August 1843

This Spring I have not left home for London or any where else and during the progress of it and the Summer I have had much pleasure in noting the flowers & blossoms as they appeared & disappeared successively, an occupation from which, at least with regard to my own grounds, a Residence in Town for the three foregoing Spring season[s] cut me off. Though my health continues, thank God to be very good, and I am active as most men of my age, my strength for very long walks among the mountains is of course diminishing, but weak or strong in body, I shall ever remain in heart and mind faithfully your much obliged Friend

Wm Wordsworth

The autumn of 1843 brought a series of misfortunes which hit the Wordsworths hard: their daughter-in-law, Isabella, was in such poor health that the doctors insisted she went to Madeira for the winter; their nephew, Richard Wordsworth's son, was diagnosed with pulmonary consumption, which could only be fatal; Mary's sister, Joanna, died of a paralytic stroke and Jane Winder, their much-loved servant for more than fifteen years, also died suddenly. On 19 March 1844 William's friend and patron, Lord Lonsdale, died, aged eighty-six, followed shortly afterwards by the wife of an old friend, the 82-year-old poet, William Lisle Bowles.

490. William Wordsworth to an unidentified correspondent; Rydal Mount, 4 October [actually November] 1843

First let me express my sympathy with your sorrows, and a hope that time and reflections acting in concert with God's grace will restore tranquillity to your mind and consolation to your heart. The elegiac poem upon the decease of your Son, you submit to me not merely as a Man who may have suffered as I have in fact done from like bereavements, but also as a Poet and a Critic. – This I somewhat regret for your grief is yet too keen to allow of your treating the Subject in that mitigated tone that <u>Poetry</u> requires. And therefore though there are in your verses, many touching passages and profound thoughts, yet as a whole the anguish which is given vent to at such length stands in the way of the general effect. Emotion remembered in a state of mind approaching to tranquillity as I have elsewhere said is more favorable to the production of verses filled to give frequent and general pleasure. Pray do not be hurt at what I have written, which I have had but little scruple in writing as the Lines which you have sent me both upon this sad subject, and upon others afford abundant proof of the poetical mind, while the execution is oftentimes exceedingly happy.

491. Edward Quillinan to Henry Crabb Robinson; Ambleside, 9 December 1843

I have been dining at Rydal – after walking about a considerable part of the morning through the waters & the mists with the Bard who seems to defy all weathers; & who called this a beautiful, soft solemn day; & so it was; though somewhat insidiously soft, for a mackintosh was hardly proof against its insinuation. He is in great force, & in great vigour of mind. He has just completed an epitaph on Southey, written at the request of a Committee at Keswick for Crosthwaite Church. I think it will please you.–

492. William Wordsworth to Edward Moxon; Rydal Mount, 11 March 1844

There are several strong reasons why I should go to London this spring, and I hope to do so, yet I become every year less inclined to face the way of life into which I am cast when I am there as a New-comer . . .

It pleases me to learn that my Poems are going off so well. Within this last week I have had three Letters, one from an eminent High-churchman and most popular Poet, the other from a Quaker, and the third from a Scottish Free-Church-man, that prove together how widely the Poems interest different classes of men.

493. William Wordsworth to an unidentified correspondent; Rydal Mount, 26 March 1844

Two letters from you have at different, and I regret to say, distant times reached me, the latter accompanied by an Mss of verses of your own Composition.

You must have thought me ungracious and unkind in not noticing long ago these communications. But you must allow me to state frankly the reasons. So exceedingly numerous are the Letters & Mss transmitted to me, that I have sometime since been obliged to leave them unacknow-ledged, and without any exception, unless they happen to come, which is rare, from persons with whom I am acquainted – You will therefore see that in omitting to notice your's there was no disrespect on my part to yourself. The fact is, my age and domestic position and an infirmity of eyesight, which disables me from reading at all by candlelight, are insurmountable objections to my meeting the wishes of those who may actually be anxious to have my opinion of their Productions. There is no young Person under my roof whom I could employ either as my Reader or Amanuensis; and my Wife's eyes (she is the same age as myself) are nearly worn out with long & unremitting service in various ways.

You will perhaps be surprized when I say that nearly every day, the year through, or rather at the rate of every day in the year, I have either Books sent me, or Mss, or applications for Autographs. I am therefore brought to the necessity above stated, and after what has been said, I cannot doubt from the openness & friendly candour of your last Letter, That you will excuse my Silence hitherto in regard to yourself.

494. William Wordsworth to Lady Frederick Bentinck; [Rydal Mount], 31 March 1844

But, how much is there to be thankful for in every part of Lord Lonsdale's life to its close! How gently was he dealt with in his last moments! and with what fortitude and Christian resignation did he bear such pains as attended his decline, and prepared the way for his quiet dissolution! Of my own feelings upon this loss I shall content myself with saying, that as long as I retain consciousness I shall cherish the memory of your father, for his inestimable worth, as one who honoured me with his friendship, and who was to myself and my children the best benefactor.

495. William Wordsworth to the Reverend William Lisle Bowles; Rydal Mount, 17 May 1844

It is indeed a sad thing to be left alone, as it were, after having been so long blessed as you have been with a faithful companion; no one can judge of this but they who have been so happily placed, and either have been doomed to a like loss, or, if the tie still be unbroken, are compelled daily to think how soon it certainly must, by one or other being called away. Under this consciousness, I venture to break in upon you, and to offer my heartfelt sympathy. The separation cannot be long between you, nor would I advert to so obvious a reflection were it not that from the advanced age which my wife and I have, through God's blessing, attained together, I feel the power of it to soothe and mitigate and sustain, far beyond what is possible for your young friends to do. –

It is more than half a century since, through your poetry, I became acquainted with your mind and feelings, and felt myself greatly your debtor for the truth and beauty with which you expressed the emotions of a mourner – My Remembrance is thrown back upon those days with a Sadness which is deep, yet far from painful – A beloved Brother with whom I first read your Sonnets (it was in a recess upon London Bridge[)], perished by Shipwreck long ago, and my most valued friends are gone to their graves. 'But not without hope we sorrow and we mourn' So I wrote when I lost that dear brother. So have I felt ever since, and so I am sure, my dear Friend, you do now – God bless you through time and through eternity.

496. William Wordsworth to Professor Henry Reed; Rydal Mount, 5 July 1844

In your last Letter you speak so feelingly of the manner in which my birthday has been noticed, both privately in your Country, and somewhat publicly in my own neighbourhood that I cannot forbear saying a word or two upon the subject. It would have delighted you to see the assemblage in front of our House, some dancing upon the gravel platform, old and young, as described in Goldsmiths travels, and others, children I mean, chacing each other upon the little plot of Lawn to which you descend by steps from the platform. We had music of our own preparing, and two sets of casual Itinerants, Italians, & Germans, came in successively, and enlivened the festivity. There were present upward of 300 children, and about 150 adults of both sexes and all ages – the children in their best attire, and of that happy and I may say beautiful race which is spread over this highly favoured portion of England. The Tables were tastefully arranged in the open air, oranges and Gingerbread in piles decorated with evergreens & spring flowers and all partook of tea, the young in the open air and the old within doors – I must own I wish that little commemorations of this kind were more common among us; It is melancholy to think how little that portion of the community which is quite at ease in their circumstances have to do in a <u>social</u> way with the humbler classes. They purchase commodities of them, or they employ them as labourers, or they visit them in charity for the sake of supplying the most urgent wants by alms-giving. But this alas is far from enough – One would wish to see the rich mingle with the poor as much as may be upon a footing of fraternal equality. The old feudal dependencies and relations are almost gone from England, and nothing has yet come adequately to supply their place. There are tendencies of the right kind here and there, but they are rather accidental, than aught that is established in general manners.

Though William had long been reconciled to his daughter's marriage, his son-in-law's failure to provide for Dora financially remained a source of irritation. When William offered to build a house at Rydal for Isabella Fenwick – but not for his equally homeless daughter – it almost caused a complete breach between the friends. Miss Fenwick insisted that William's first duty was to his daughter; William refused to take on himself what he considered should be Quillinan's responsibility.

497. William Wordsworth to Isabella Fenwick; Rydal Mount, Wednesday morning [17 July 1844]

. . . my most dear Friend, I do feel from the bottom of my heart, that I am unworthy of being constantly in your sight. Your standard is too high for my hourly life; – when I add to what you blame, the knowledge which I bear about all day long of my own internal unworthiness I am oppressed by the consciousness of being an object unfit to be from morning to night in your presence. Among ten thousand causes which I have to thank God for his goodness towards me, is that for more than forty years I have had a Companion who can bear with my offences, who forgets them, and enters upon a new course of love with me when I have done wrong, leaving me to the remorse of my own Conscience. Of this chastisement I have had my portion, and the feeling seems to be gathering strength daily & hourly; only let me believe that I do not love others less, because I seem to hate myself more.

498. William Wordsworth to Isabella Fenwick; [Rydal Mount, 22 July 1844]

Thanks for your long and affectionate Letter. You scarcely touch upon the point that was nearest to my heart; and I do not see how you well could; so we will let the matter rest till we have the happiness of meeting again & in the meanwhile you must try to think as well of me as you can. To one thing only will I now advert, viz, that I will not bind myself, circumstanced as Dora is, to make her any fixed allowance. I am convinced it would be wrong to do so, as it would only produce in certain quarters[4] an effect which I should exceedingly deprecate. Be assured I will take care while I live, that she should <u>not suffer</u> in mind for scantiness of income. That she may be somewhat straitened, acting as She has chosen to do with my strongest disapprobation I deem fit and right. – But no more of the subject; nor will I return to it again.

499. William Wordsworth to Isabella Fenwick; Rydal, Thursday [19 September 1844]

I know not whether you have been told how much Miss Fletcher enjoyed her Tour to, and upon the banks of the Duddon. Mr Quillinan was Charioteer, and nobody could be kinder or more ready to serve, or more generally amiable than he was. Neither this nor any thing else however reconciles me to his course of life. You say he could not procure employment – I say, that he does not <u>try</u>. He has now taken again to hard labour on his translation of Camoens, a work which can not possibly turn to profit of any kind either pecuniary or intellectual.[5] All that ought to be looked at from it is his own amusement at <u>leisure</u> hours. The fact is he cannot bring himself to stoop in the direction he ought to stoop in. His pride looks and works the wrong way – and I am hopeless of a cure – but I am resolved not to minister to it, because it ought not to exist, circumstanced as he is. His inaction mortifies me the more because his talents are greatly superior to those of most men who earn a handsome livelihood by Literature. –

William's harsh words, however, were belied by his actions. Though he had no wish to finance Quillinan's idle way of life, he could not let his daughter suffer. He did not build her a house or pay her a fixed allowance, as Miss Fenwick wished, but he did subsidize the Quillinans to the extent that he paid out more than £80 a year in rent and servants' wages to secure them a comfortable home in Rydal and took pleasure in surprising Dora with generous gifts of cash whenever the need arose.

Chapter Thirteen

1844–8

500. Caroline Fox, journal, 6 October 1844

He [Wordsworth] took us to his Terrace, whence the view is delicious: he said, 'Without those autumn tints it would be beautiful, but with them it is exquisite.' It had been a wet morning, but the landscape was then coming out with perfect clearness. 'It is,' he said, 'like the human heart emerging from sorrow, shone on by the grace of God.' We wondered whether the scenery had any effect on the minds of the poorer people. He thinks it has, though they don't learn to express it in neat phrases, but it dwells silently within them. 'How constantly mountains are mentioned in Scripture as the scene of extraordinary events; the Law was given on a mountain, Christ was transfigured on a mountain, and on a mountain the great Act of our Redemption was accomplished, and I cannot believe but that when the poor read of these things in their Bibles, and the frequent mention of mountains in the Psalms, their minds glow at the thought of their own mountains, and they realise it all more clearly than others.'

Thus ended our morning with Wordsworth.

The delicious views from Rydal Mount were now under a threat more serious than anything they had ever faced before. The railway boom was at its height and a company was formed to build a railway between Kendal and Lowwood, close to Ambleside, thus opening up the Lakes to tourists from the industrial towns of Yorkshire and Lancashire. Though it was claimed that this was as far as it would go, the obvious next step would be to link it to Keswick, a route that would inevitably bring the railway through the Vale of Rydal. In private letters to those he knew and in poetry and prose, published in the national press and in pamphlet form, William rose to the defence of the Lakes. It was a deeply unfashionable and controversial thing to do, provoking charges of elitism and selfishness, but his words planted the seed for what would become the idea of establishing the Lake District as a National Park; and, though he failed to prevent the railway between Kendal and Windermere being built, he succeeded in ensuring its termination at Bowness, several miles from Ambleside, thus preventing any further development into the heart of the Lakes.

501. William Wordsworth to his friend, General Charles William Pasley, Inspector General of Railways; Rydal Mount, 15 October [1844]

. . . all the old resident Gentlemen and Proprietors of this neighbourhood are greatly annoyed, with scarcely an exception, by the project of a Railway from Kendal to the head of Windermere. The shares are already subscribed for and at a premium, which will not surprize you who are better, probably, than any one else, acquainted with the excesses to which the Railway Mania drives people on the present superabundances of Capital. Excuse my writing to you upon this occasion which I do to beg that when it comes before you, as probably it will, you would give it more attention than its apparent importance may call for. The traffic will be found quite contemptible, the staple of this country is its beauty and that will be destroyed by such a nuisance being carried through these narrow vales. at present nothing is publicly said of its being carried farther than within a mile of Ambleside, but that is all nonsense. attempts will assuredly be made and at no distant Period, to carry it on to Keswick, to Maryport [on the Cumberland coast], notwithstanding the high ground that parts Westmorland from Cumberland.

502. William Wordsworth to the editor of the Morning Post; *Rydal Mount, 17 December 1844*

The time of life at which I have arrived may, I trust, if nothing else will, guard me from the imputation of having written from any selfish interests, or from fear of disturbance which a railway might cause to myself. If gratitude for what repose and quiet in a district hitherto, for the most part, not disfigured but beautified by human hands, have done for me through the course of a long life, and hope that others might hereafter be benefited in the same manner and in the same country, *be* selfishness, then, indeed, but not otherwise, I plead guilty to the charge. Nor have I opposed this undertaking on account of the inhabitants of the district *merely*, but, as hath been intimated, for the sake of every one, however humble his condition, who coming hither shall bring with him an eye to perceive, and a heart to feel and worthily enjoy.

503. William Wordsworth to Isabella Fenwick; [Rydal Mount, early January 1845]

. . . the <u>beauty</u> of the Season with us, has exceeded any thing – such glorious effects of sunshine & shadow, and skies that are quite heavenly, in the evenings especially; with moon & mountain-clouds setting each other off in a way that really has transported us to look upon . . . I am glad you approve of my Railway Letter, but it has drawn upon me as I knew it would, from the low-minded & ill-bred a torrent of abuse, through the Press – both in London Glasgow & elsewhere, but as it has afforded me an opportunity of directing attention to some important truths I care little for such rancorous scurrility, the natural outbreak of self conceit and stupid ignorance.

In the spring of 1845 Quillinan succeeded in persuading William and Mary that he should be allowed to take Dora to Portugal, where, he hoped, the climate would restore her health. They were naturally reluctant to part with her, fearing that, as they were both in their mid seventies, they might not live to see her again. A renewed invitation to the Queen's Ball gave William the excuse to accompany his daughter as far as London to delay his parting from her.

504. Edward Quillinan to Henry Crabb Robinson; Ambleside, 18 April 1845

But I have kept my best news back, & almost grudge them to you: one William Wordsworth "a wicked imp they call a poet" is to be our companion to London, but will go straight from Euston Square to Moxon's, where he will remain till his <u>business</u> in town is over: his business being to attend the Queen's Ball on Friday night, by H.M.'s gracious command. Think of the Laureate 75 invited again to go 300 miles to a Ball! But he cannot "decline the honour" & it is but right & decent that he should make his appearance at the Queen's Levee, & this will be his opportunity; the same day too. – I don't know whether he will have anything to say to his old London friends after he has made his debut in the palace of a young Queen, but you will have him among you & can try –

505. William Wordsworth to Edward Moxon; [Rydal Mount], 18 April 1845

An invitation from the Lord Chamberlain to attend the Queen's Ball on Friday the 25th has left me without a choice as to visiting London; – And in consequence I purpose to start on Wednesday next with Mr & Mrs Quillinan who are going to Oporto he to attend his Brother's marriage, and she accompanying him in the hope of benefiting her health which as you know has been declining for several years . . . If it be in your power to accommodate me pray let me know by return of Post. – I have another favor to ask, which is that you would mention my errand to Mr Rogers, and perhaps he could put me in the way of being properly introduced and instructed how to behave in a situation, I am not sorry to say, altogether new to me. My stay in London for several cogent reasons will be very short.

506. Aubrey de Vere to Isabella Fenwick; [London, April 1845]

I never saw him in greater force or energy, either of body or mind. He gave us a lively account of his visit to Mr. Rogers, and his trying on Mr. Rogers's court dress which fortunately fits him so well that, with the help of Sir Humphry Davy's sword "science and art being thus fraternally united" he will have no trouble about his apparel.

507. Mrs Brookfield, London society hostess: diary, 6 May 1845

May 6th, 1845: I dined at Moxon's, where were Wordsworth, A[lfred] Tennyson, H. Lushington, Harness, Dyce, and self. A. Tennyson and Lushington came home with me for an hour. Wordsworth described his presentation to the Queen at the Ball last Friday but one . . . and speaking of the graciousness of it added, "I daresay it was *my years*, most likely she had not read many of my works." He added that he had stipulated with the Lord Chamberlain that he should not just pass through the crowd but should be noticed. I remarked that the Queen had done herself good by her reception of him, and that he could not have bestowed his patronage on a more depressed cause than that of Queendom – unless the Clergy . . . which raised a great laugh. I, however, begged to amend my speech and to express my gratitude for his patronage of the Clergy. He said he was quite content with my first compliment.

508. Elizabeth Barrett Browning, poet, to Hugh Stuart Boyd; [London], 30 April 1845

You will be delighted to hear that Wordsworth is in London, – having been "commanded" up to attend the queen's ball. The majesty of England, when she saw him, was quite "*fluttered*", Mrs. Jameson heard from one of the maids of honour – and I am well contented that it should be so.

509. Aubrey de Vere, memories of Alfred Tennyson, written in 1897

There was another occasion on which the Poet whose great work was all but finished, and the youthful compeer whose chief labours were yet to come, met in my presence. It was at a dinner given by Mr Moxon. The ladies had withdrawn, and Wordsworth soon followed them. Several times Tennyson said to me in a low voice, "I must go: I cannot wait any longer." At last the cause of his disquiet revealed itself. It was painful to him to leave the house without expressing to the old Bard his sense of the obligation which all Englishmen owed to him, and yet he was averse to speak his thanks before a large company. Our host brought Wordsworth back to the dining-room; and Tennyson moved up to him. He spoke in a low voice, and with a perceptible emotion. I must not cite his words lest I should mar them; but they were few, simple and touching. The old man looked very much pleased, more so indeed than I ever saw him look on any other occasion; shook hands with him heartily, and thanked him affectionately. Wordsworth thus records the incident in a letter to his accomplished American friend, Professor Reed: "I saw Tennyson when I was in London several times. He is decidedly the first of our living poets, and I hope will live to give the world still better things. You will be pleased to hear that he expressed in the strongest terms his gratitude to my writings. To this I was far from indifferent."

510. William Wordsworth to George Huntly Gordon; Rydal Mount, 24 June 1845

When I had but a glimpse of you at Mr Moxon's I was troubled with an inflammation in one of my eyes from which I am only just recovered and you must kindly accept this as excuse for not replying sooner to your friendly Letter. The Extract which [you] have sent me is very pleasing, but I do not feel I could make any thing of it in a poem, as you recommend.

Besides, there is some thing wayward In matters of this kind. When a subject was proposed to Gainsborough for a picture, if he liked it he used to say, "What a pity I did not think of it myself" –

My own practice is odd even in respect to subjects of my own chusing. It was only a few days ago that I was able to put into Verse the Matter of a Short Poem ['Forth from a jutting ridge'] which had been in my mind with a determination and a strong desire to write upon it for more than thirty years; nor is this the first time when the like has occurred –

On his return from London William tried to forget his anxiety about Dora by immersing himself in his garden and in preparing a new edition of his collected poems for Moxon. In a break from past practice, this was to be a single volume, with engravings by the celebrated William Finden of a picture of Rydal Mount on its title page and of Sir Francis Chantrey's bust of the poet himself as a frontispiece. 'A handsome Vol[ume] which makes a beautiful present', as Henry Crabb Robinson commented, it would be published just in time for the Christmas market. An expensively bound copy, inscribed with a set of specially composed presentation verses, was sent to the Queen with her Poet Laureate's compliments.

511. William Wordsworth to Henry Crabb Robinson; Rydal Mount, 7 August [1845]

I have not been well lately from two causes; I overlaboured and overheated myself with my axe and saw, and caught cold in the evening. and when I was recovering from this I had [a] very ugly fall from the top of the Mount, which shook me sadly, and of which I shall feel the effects for some time . . . The reprinting of my Poems is going on regularly, the Book will be stereotyped and from what I hear through the Bookseller, there will be no small demand for it; partly for its own sake, & partly to class with Byron and Southey etc who are already in the same forms. The alterations of which you heard, are almost exclusively confined to a few of the Juvenile Poems –

512. Mary Wordsworth to Catherine Clarkson; Rydal Mount, 7 September [1845]

After a season more than usually broken in upon by visitors we are ourselves intending, in the course of the next fortnight, going for the <u>last time to Brinsop</u> to see our dear friends there. My poor disabled Brother

[Tom, who as a result of a fall from his horse in 1837, was paralyzed from the waist down] has at length made up his mind, & has given up his farm, & they are to leave that Spot to which each & all of the family, are so much attached, in the Spring. This will be a great trial to them all, but as they are going to reside with their elder Son, (who has a small living in pretty county Leominster) I hope after a little time they will be reconciled to the change – & feel themselves relieved from much anxiety.

513. William Wordsworth to Edward Moxon; [Rydal Mount, 4 November 1845]

My late wanderings have unavoidably caused some delay, but the next sheet will conclude the Poetry and bring us to the Notes, which will be followed by the Prefaces and then we shall be done with this tedious work. Looking over the Proofs has been trying to my eyes, but I feel much indebted to Mr Carter [his old Stamp Office clerk], as I am sure you will also for the care which he has taken in correcting the proofs; I feel obliged to you also for your own attentions to this important part of the concern. – I have not yet seen (Mr Carter being now at Carlisle) a specimen of the sheets as struck off; my only fear is that the margin will not be broad enough for binding as one could wish – Will it not be cramped? We are about to publish this expensive Vol[ume] at a most unfavorable time. Nothing is now thought of but railway shares. The Savings-banks are almost emptied of their old deposits, and scarcely any thing new comes into them. All gone to Railway Speculation – a deplorable state of things – –

Are the engraving of the Bust and the view of the House finished?

Mr Carter is making an Index of first lines; which I hope will be of some use, for it is impossible to give titles to a third part of this multifarious collection of Poems. –

514. Harriet Martineau, novelist and essayist, Autobiography, *[winter 1845]*

It was one of the pleasures of my walks, for the first few years of my residence here [in Ambleside], to meet with Wordsworth when he happened to be walking, and taking his time on the road. In winter, he was to be seen in his cloak, his Scotch bonnet, and green goggles, attended perhaps by half-a-score of cottagers' children, – the youngest pulling at his cloak, or holding by his trowsers, while he cut ash switches out of the hedge for them.

On Christmas Eve 1845 the Wordsworths were devastated to learn that their youngest grandson, Edward, had died of fever in Rome. His parents' marriage was effectively at an end, his mother having remained on the Continent with the children while his father returned to England. John now insisted that his family should return home and (with £75 given for the purpose by William) went in person to Italy to retrieve his four surviving children, leaving his wife to follow at a more leisurely pace with her mother. John's family life was in ruins – as, also, was his home, for his newly-built vicarage at Brigham was about to be demolished to make way for a railway between Cockermouth and Workington. To add to these griefs, William's nephew, Richard's son, John, still lingered on in the final stages of consumption and, on 2 February 1846, William's younger brother, Christopher, died after a short illness. It was hardly surprising that William's usually cheerful spirits gave way to depression.

515. William Wordsworth to the Reverend William Jackson; [Rydal Mount, March 1846]

My first words must be to beg pardon for not haveing [*sic*] written to you, both to inform you of what had been done, and to acknowledge your great kindness. But the fact is we have been subject for some time to anxieties and sorrows in no common degree; and we wanted courage to communicate with our friends, in consequence; and in addition to this I have for more than a month been obliged to abstain both from writing and reading & what is still worse almost from thinking, by my old complaint inflammation in one of my eyes.

516. William and Mary Wordsworth to Isabella Fenwick; [Rydal Mount, 13 May 1846]

[William writes] – My dear Wife keeps herself quite well by marvellous activity of mind and body. I wish I could do the same – but many things do not touch her which depress me, public affairs in particular – my contempt for the management of these both in England and Ireland is quite painful – I have almost confined myself in this Sheet to personal news, and I must beg you my dear Friend excuse the dullness of what I write. My pleasures are among Birds and Flowers, and of these enjoyments, thank God, I retain enough; but my interests in Literature and books in general seem to be dying away unreasonably fast – nor [do] I look or much care for a revival in them. This I do not suppose to be a universal attendant upon the age which I have reached, but I fear it is very common. Mason the Poet used to say latterly that he read no poetry but his own – I could not speak in this strain, for I read my own less than any other – and often think that my life has been in a great measure wasted. I will now lay down my pen as we are going to see my poor nephew, who continues to languish and waste as he may for months to come – . . .

[Mary writes] W[illia]m sometimes talks of our going to London for a fortnight – I wish to defer this if we move at all till there is a chance of meeting the Q[uillinan]s – but do not like to discourage it altogether – for he does seem to require some change – a change in spirits & habits I am sorry to say has taken place since the times I mentioned to you before – he sits more over the fire in silence &c &c & is sooner tired on his walks – which he is ever unwilling to commence unaccompanied by me – but dearest friend I must be done.

517. *William Wordsworth to Henry Crabb Robinson; Rydal Mount, Wednesday, [20] May 1846*

The other day James drove Mrs W[ordsworth] Miss Quillinan and myself down Windermere side, and home by Hawkshead, and the beautiful Vale, my old School-day haunts which I make a point of seeing every year – but how changed! In my time we had more than a 100 Boys playing and roaming about the Vale; now not one was to be seen, the School being utterly deserted. –

At the end of June the Quillinans returned from Portugal to live for the first time in a home of their own: John Carter had built a cottage under Loughrigg and, as he spent most of the year working for Willy in Carlisle, he offered them the tenancy. The Wordsworths' joy at Dora's return was marred only by the death of her cousin, John Wordsworth, aged thirty-one, on 18 August; he was buried next to Thomas and Catharine in what had now become the family plot in the corner of Grasmere churchyard.

518. *William Wordsworth to John Gardner, the surgeon to whom John Wordsworth had been apprenticed; Rydal Mount, 20 August 1846*

> Rydal Mount
> Ambleside
> Aug[u]st 20–1846

My dear Sir

The illness under which your Pupil and Friend John Wordsworth has been declining so long, terminated on Tuesday last. He died at his Residence in Ambleside being gradually worn out. His Mother was with him, and also his Cousin William, my Son. On Saturday he will be laid in Grasmere Churchyard. I ought to mention that his mind was clear and bright to the very last; I need not add that he will long be greatly lamented by all who enjoyed an intimacy with him.

> Believe me
> my dear Sir
> Sincerely and faithfully yours
> Wm Wordsworth

519. *William Wordsworth to an unidentified correspondent; Rydal Mount, 30 October 1846*

The Edition of my Poems in one Vol[ume] double column published last year, is nearly out of print; and Mr Moxon is going to press with another – the last was two thousand copies. – The annual sale[1] for the last nine years annually has been about a thousand, which is remarkable as it is upwards of half a century since I began to publish.

520. *William Wordsworth to Isabella Fenwick; Rydal Mount, [early November 1846]*

The papers will have told you that I was proposed as a Candidate for the Lord Rectorship [of the] University of Glasgow,[2] and had a majority of votes, 21 I believe out of 200; but owing to the <u>form</u> of Election the decision fell to the Lord Rector, whose deputy voted for the opposing Candidate Lord John Russell. Be assured I am truly glad of this, as if Lord J[ohn] accepts the Office, I shall be spared the disagreeableness of a refusal, or what would be still worse at this season, a journey to Glasgow, and a public exhibition there to which I should be exceedingly averse –

Dora with the assistance of her Husband has just concluded the Revision of her Journal [of her residence in Portugal]. I am anxious to read it, or rather that Mary should read [it] a loud to me during our lonely Evenings. It never before happened to us to pass so much time together without other companionship; and what cause have we to be thankful that neither by bodily infirmity, or any other evil we are prevented from mutual enjoyment; though we cannot help earnestly wishing that You, our beloved Friend, were with us to make a Third in our society.

521. Henry Crabb Robinson to his brother; Liverpool, 4–5 February 1847

The fact is that during my late visit I had much less than I used to have of conversation with him [Wordsworth] – He spoke very little to any one And said on one occasion when it was remarked that he was silent – "Yes, the Silence of old age". It was not that his judgement or sense was in any respect impaired, but his activity – He was quite happy quite cordial quite amiable; but not so animated or energetic as he used to be.

He allowed me uncontradicted to state heresies which would not have been tolerated a few years ago – This is the full extent of what I consider as the inroad of age – . . .

On 20 January 1847, the Wordsworths's youngest son, Willy, married Fanny Elizabeth Graham, the daughter of a retired Cumberland stockbroker who lived in Brighton. None of his family was fit enough to make the long journey south in the depths of winter to attend the wedding but Dora took great delight in preparing the little cottage Willy had rented at Brisco, just outside Carlisle, for the newly-weds' return. Ironically, though Quillinan prohibited Dora from going to Brighton, it was at Brisco that she caught the cold which would terminate so fatally.

522. Dora Wordsworth to Isabella Fenwick; Rydal Mount, 14 December 1846

I was delighted with the Cottage so lowly looking & yet the rooms so good – such convenient closets & cupboards & every thing in such perfect order –

Mr Quillinan has put his veto on my accompanying William to Brighton he fears my taking cold, wandering about from house to house in this severe weather, with us it is clear & bright & beautiful but nipping cold –

Father & Mother are looking forward to their visit to Bath with real pleasure – one word of their arrangements – Father declares against taking man or maid with them, now it is not <u>fit</u> that they should go alone & my Mother feels that neither of them are now equal to take care of themselves & look after the luggage at the Rail way Stations – my Mother would like to take James [Dixon], or if more convenient to you a maid servant – but I fancy perhaps James might be most useful to <u>you</u> in Bath & equally so to them – now my reason for writing all this is to ask you to mention in some of your letters to Father that <u>you</u> hope he will bring a servant with him & you say w[ha]t you w[oul]d prefer & then it will be a <u>real</u> pleasure to him to come into this arrangement so necessary for their comfort in travelling & for our peace of mind in thinking of them –

In February 1847 William and Mary (with James in attendance) set off from Rydal Mount on a round of visits which would take them not only to Miss Fenwick at Bath but also to their Hutchinson relations in Herefordshire and to London, where they would stay with Mrs Hoare in Hampstead and their nephew, Chris Wordsworth, at Westminster. While at Bath, William received a letter containing the request that he should write an ode for the installation of Prince Albert as Chancellor of the University of Cambridge; the ode was to be set to music by Thomas Attwood Walmisley, Professor of Music at the University, and performed at the ceremony on 6 July 1847. Though not expressly a royal command to the hitherto silent Poet Laureate, nor even a request to him made in the right of his office, the letter was couched in such a way that William could not refuse.

523. William Wordsworth to Charles Beaumont Phipps, private secretary to the Prince Consort; Bath, 15 March 1847

Bath
15 March 1847

Sir
The request with which through your hands his Royal Highness the Prince Albert has honored me could not but be highly gratifying; and I hope that I may be able upon this interesting occasion to retouch a harp which, I will not say with Tasso oppressed by misfortunes and years has been hung up upon a cypress, but which has however for some time been laid aside.

I have the honor to be
with sincere respect,
faithfully your

> most obedient Serv[a]nt
> William Wordsworth

The Hon[ora]ble C. B. Phipps &c &c &c

---

524. William Wordsworth to Thomas Attwood Walmisley, Bath; 26 March 1847

I cannot but wish you had a Fellow-labourer more worthy of his office than myself – for it is some time since I ceased to write verse, and gave up the intention of ever resuming the employment – All I can say at present is, that though I have not yet composed a Line, I will endeavour to meet your wish speedily; only be so kind as to let me know, whether you would prefer an irregular style of versification Like Gray's Ode on the Installation of the Duke of Grafton, or a regular form of stanza to be repeated to the Conclusion – As soon as I am apprized of this, I shall set about the Work in order to to comply with your request without delay.

---

525. Sara Coleridge to Isabella Fenwick; Chester Place, [London], 26 April 1846

Last Saturday I saw dear Mr and Mrs Wordsworth, probably for the last time during this visit of theirs to the south. He has looked remarkably well since he came to town; when I have seen him there has been a rosy hue over his face, and he struck my nephew, JDC., who saw him on his arrival at Paddington, as wondrously full of vigour, quite a grand old man, and as one might expect the poet Wordsworth to be . . . I was not able to obtain a dinner or breakfast-visit from the great man, though several times promised it. But I believe he dined out nowhere, and even declined breakfasting at Mr Robinson's. You have heard, no doubt, that he has written part of the Installation Ode; Miss F says that there is a great deal of thought in it; but he says himself that it is but superficial thought, and that it is not worth much. However, I am glad that his mind is still lithe enough to perform such tasks, even in an ordinary manner, if ordinary it be. There will probably be a manner in it that reports of himself, even if the substance be not very new or powerful.

William had always found writing to order an almost impossible task. In trying to write the Installation Ode he found himself under uniquely difficult circumstances. Whilst in London he had received increasingly worrying reports from home about the state of Dora's health. Unable to concentrate on the task in hand, he fell back on a strategem he had used on at least two previous occasions: he asked his son-in-law for help. He had once said of Quillinan that 'you know my principles of style better I think than any one else'.[3] Quillinan's gift for imitation now proved invaluable and it is surely ironic that Walmisley preferred the first version of the Ode, which was closer to Quillinan's original text, than the later one, which William had reworked more extensively. Before he could send this latter version, however, William received the news that he had been dreading. Dora, who had taken her turn with the rest of the family in devotedly nursing her dying cousin, John, had contracted his pulmonary consumption. It was, as they all knew, a death sentence, and, on learning of the diagnosis, William and Mary immediately left London for Rydal Mount. It was against this background that the ill-fated Installation Ode had to be completed.

526. William Wordsworth to his daughter-in-law, Fanny Elizabeth Wordsworth; Hampstead Heath, 20 April 1847

I ordered Doras Book [*Journal of a Few Months' Residence in Portugal and Glimpses of the South of Spain*, which Moxon had just published] to be sent you, I have only had time to look into it, but like what I have seen. O that we were less anxious about her – we remain here and in London solely because we think she will do better without than with us – Again most affectionately farewell.

527. Mary Wordsworth, note in a copy of The Installation Ode *presented by the ornamental binder, Frederick Westley, to Mary Wordsworth, [April–May 1847]*

The Plan, & Composition of this Ode was chiefly prepared by Mr. Quillinan, but carefully Revised in M.S. by Mr. Wordsworth, who being in a state of deep domestic affliction, could not otherwise have been able to fulfil the engagement with Prince Albert, previously made, in time for the Installation. M. W.

528. Edward Quillinan, diary, April 1847

23 April: Mr Fell for the first time expressed fears for Dora
27 April: Mr & Mrs W[ordsworth] arrived from London –
28 April: Mr Gough of Kendal examined D[ora] – & gave us no <u>hope</u> –
   "a question only of time": –

*529. William Wordsworth to Thomas Attwood Walmisley; Rydal Mount, 29
April 1847*

Here is the promised Ode corrected as well as under distressing domestic
circumstances I was able to do it –

My Nephew Dr [Chris] Wordsworth gave me hope that it would
answer our mutual purpose, that is, that the words would suit your music.

*530. Thomas Attwood Walmisley to William Wordsworth; Trinity College,
Cambridge, 3 May 1847*

. . . I wish to ask your indulgence if I make one or two remarks upon the
difference between the first & second versions; . . . I so much prefer
the former version . . . Could you add another Stanza which would
cause the Ode to end more joyously than the previous termination, which
seems rather sombre – . . . Should you prefer the second version in all
these instances, perhaps you would allow me to retain the former version
in my musical exposition of your poem, and a different Edition might be
printed . . . with the following note: – "In this Copy of the Ode, a few
alterations have been been made to suit the musical arrangement."

*531. William Wordsworth to Thomas Attwood Walmisley; Rydal Mount, 5
May 1847*

The alterations were made in the notion, mistaken as it seems, that they
might better suit your music. Be pleased to understand that you may adopt
or reject any alterations as they suit you or not, and whether the note you
suggest for the printed Ode may be requisite we will leave to after-
consideration. . . .

The heavy domestic affliction that presses on me, the very dangerous
illness of my only daughter, makes it impossible for me to exert myself
satisfactorily in this task.

532. *Hartley Coleridge to Thomas Blackburne; [May 1847]*

You never knew her [Dora] – perhaps never saw her. I have known her from her infancy. But if you had seen her as I have seen her and seen how a beautiful Soul can make a face not beautiful most beautiful, if you had seen how by the mere strength of affection she entered into the recesses of her Father's Mind and drew him out to gambol with her in the childishness that always hung upon her womanhood, you would feel, as we do, what earth is about to lose and Heaven to gain. May God support her Father and Mother under the loss and to that end join your prayers to mine.

533. *Hartley Coleridge to his sister, Sara; Nab [Cottage, Rydal], 18 May 1847*

I have nothing more hopeful to relate of Dora. She is sometimes easy, and sometimes in considerable pain – suffers most at night. She has been at her own request, fully informed of her state, and is not only resign'd but happy. Her parents bear up like Christians, but are quite absorb'd by their sorrow. I have not seen them – (excepting Mr. Wordsworth on the road, as I told you before). I would gladly go, if I could be of any use or comfort, but the Doctor advises me not. They wish to see no one. If they should wish to speak to me, they will probably send for me. Poor William was over from Carlisle a day or two ago, to take leave. John was at Rydal lately and administered the sacrament to his sister, a trying duty which he well supported. From what I gather, I anticipate it will not be long be very long. [*sic*] God's will be done –

534. *Mrs Thomas Arnold to Henry Crabb Robinson; Fox How, 1 June 1847*

. . . our dear friends are anxious to keep all around them as quiet, and as free from excitement as possible – and I therefore feel it the truest kindness and compliance with their wishes, neither to go or send, but to satisfy myself with such opportunities as I can find of enquiring, as to the daily progress of the fatal malady. Dear Mr Wordsworth comes forth occasionally to see his old friends. & yesterday morning when I saw him slowly & sadly approaching by our Birch tree, I hastened to meet him, & found that he would prefer, walking with me around our own garden boundary to entering the House, & encountering a larger party – So we wandered about here – & then I accompanied him to Rydal – & he walked back again with me through the great field as you can so well picture to yourself. This quiet intercourse gave me an opportunity of seeing how entirely our dear friends are prepared to bow with submission to God's will. No one can tell better than yourself how much they will feel it, for you have had full opportunities of seeing how completely Dora was the joy and sunshine of their lives, but she is herself by her own composure and cheerful submission & willingness to relinquish all earthly hopes & possessions – teaching them to bear the greatest sorrow which could have befallen them. Her father described her as gradually sinking, & said that they felt she might at any time or at any hour be taken from them – but I shall always feel with you that these lingering weeks have been most mercifully ordered for them, & are full of present comfort & of consoling memories for the future.

535. Mary Wordsworth to Lady Monteagle [née Mary Anne Marshall]; [Rydal Mount], 1 June [1847]

We are thank God wonderfully supported – The afflicted Father, not having the consolatory <u>duty</u> of nursing to turn his thoughts from our deep sorrow – in this season of suspense, suffers most. But I trust he, as well as the rest of us will be upheld to the close, by the sustaining will of our blessed Redeemer.

536. Mary Wordsworth to her cousin and sister-in-law, Mary Hutchinson; [Rydal Mount], Thursday, [7] July 1847

By no means think of coming to me, I shall find my support – in the quiet example she has set me – No change will she admit that she knows of, in the house on her acc[oun]t – We are to sit as usual in the room below – the breakfast & dinner bell is to be rung as usual – 'No fuss' – is her watchword –

Dora died on 9 July 1847, a few weeks before her forty-fourth birthday, and was buried in Grasmere churchyard close to her aunt, Sara Hutchinson. The plot was carefully chosen to allow room for the later interment of her father and husband on either side. Dora's death almost destroyed William: as his old friend, Henry Crabb Robinson, described it, he seemed lost in 'fixed and irremovable grief', so much so that his family and friends began to fear that he was sinking into the same state as his sister.

537. William Wordsworth to Edward Moxon; Rydal Mount, 9 August 1847

We bear up under our affliction as well as God enables us to do – but O my dear Friend our loss is immeasurable –

538. Edward Quillinan to Isabella Fenwick; Loughrigg Holme, 13 October 1847

Mrs W[ordsworth] with as much feeling, & with a _mother's_ feeling to boot, has a happier method of dealing with her sorrows. – Her remaining children, her grand children & her husband occupy her mind & heart usefully. – But as to the outward world it _must_ be now a blank to both; & as to the reputation of literature it is the veriest bubble; there is no heart in it, nor the least atom of consolation for a man like Wordsworth. That he has been a good moral preacher, or teacher, however, must be some consolation to him in his old age.

539. William and Mary Wordsworth to Isabella Fenwick; [Rydal Mount], 6 December [1847]

[William writes] I ought to have written to you, my very very _dear_ Friend upon our return hither [from a visit to his sons at Brigham and Carlisle], and _perhaps_ I _did_, for I really have no distinct remembrance of any thing that passes. – The best thing I have to say is that the Mother of our departed Child preserves her health, and stirs about the House upon every occasion, as heretofore. You kindly express a hope that Mr Quillinan and I walk together – this has not been so, I cannot bear to cross the Bridge and Field that lead to his Abode; and he does not come hither, so that, except once on the Highway, and once or twice at Church, and one evening when he dined[4] here with Mr Scott his Friend, I have not seen him at all . . .

The weather here as is usual at this season is much broken, and as I have had a troublesome cold I have seldom ventured lately further than the Walks of the Terraces and the Garden. Hannah Cookson [a family friend] has been staying with us a few days. No one can be kinder and she is very useful to me in many ways. I suffer most in heart and mind before I leave my bed in a morning – Daily used She to come to my bedside and greet me and her Mother, and _now_ the blank is terrible. But I must stop. She is ever with me and will be so to the last moment of my life. – . . .

[Mary writes] Beloved friend I am thankful that this one solitary effort has been made – tho' it too painfully speaks of my poor Husband's state, & this will be a pain to you –

540. Mary Wordsworth to Isabella Fenwick; [Rydal Mount], 27 December 1847

We had much pleasure & comfort from the visit of Dr C[hris] Wordsworth & his excellent wife – You will be glad to hear what I think I have not mentioned to you before, that Chris undertook to prepare, after his Uncle's day, some biographical notices, which, being understood that such is intended to appear from that quarter, may prevent indifferent persons to take upon them to Publish – as poor Cottle & others have done for Coleridge. Susan took from her Uncle some notes, & they were referred to You dear friend, for what you could help them to, if in God's goodness it should please him that you survive us – & for those notes regarding the time, & circumstances connected with the publication of his several poems – by the bye how far did you get in this work which you so patiently & kindly undertook? If I remember rightly – Mr Q[uillinan] – transcribed your copy – He must be applied to at some proper time to aid Christopher, perhaps he may be hurt that he was not asked to be principal in the work (Christopher who had been talking with Willy on the subject offered his service) for you know he is easily offended.

541. Henry Crabb Robinson to Isabella Fenwick, written after his annual Christmas visit to Rydal Mount; Manchester, 10 January 1848

I have no doubt you will be anxious to hear my report of the condition of our excellent friends. It is but a sad one And yet not worse than you will be prepared to hear – Of Mrs W[ordsworth] it is decidedly better than I expected to be able to make. She is able to talk with composure of her loss: And tho' her countenance bears marks of suffering & age combined; yet she seems to discharge the business of the day with her ordinary activity – Not so with Mr W[ordsworth]: I was able latterly to make him walk out every day when the weather was favorable, and even make calls: but Mrs W[ordsworth] tells me that after such walks, he would retire to his room sit alone & cry incessantly – I witnessed several such bursts of grief occasioned by the merest accidents, such as my proposing to call with him on Mrs Arnold – He was unable to take leave of me for sobbing when I came away – During my three weeks stay, it was very seldom that I could engage him in any conversation.

542. *Mary Wordsworth to Isabella Fenwick; [Rydal Mount], 2 February [1848]*

... I do feel sorrow to tell you that I have no help from my beloved Mourner – he is bowed to the dust – & our dear comers & goers seem rather to have increased, than dissipated his dejection – His mind & spirits (except for a brief while when with almost <u>indifferent</u> Persons, he can rally a little & appear quite himself) is in the lowest state of <u>humiliation</u> & deep sorrow. But I doubt not you will agree with me in the hope that this must work for good & that time will bring comfort. – May the Almighty in his mercy see fit to send support ere long –

543. *Edward Quillinan to Henry Crabb Robinson; Loughrigg Holme, 23 July 1848*

At this time of the year, leisure hours, & indeed all hours of the day, are <u>there</u> [i.e. at Rydal Mount] necessarily divided among strangers who coming from a distance with introductions must be received, or strangers who happen to be visitors of "friends who live within an easy walk" – and I think such perpetual interruptions, which would drive some men mad, are rarely disagreeable to Mr Wordsworth; and in my opinion all these callers do him good, by taking him out of himself – though they leave his Wife but little time for the indulgence of a more quiet intercourse with such friends as you some 300 miles off. – You are not to infer from what I have said that there is any unusual bustle of pilgrims to the Poet's house this year, as compared with former years, except the last; but as hardly any one was admitted, and few sought to be admitted, last year, and as a good many of the strangers now in the lake-country do find their way up to him, he and Mrs W[ordsworth] have perhaps in reality just now more demands upon their energies than they ever had formerly when they were some years younger & the world was brighter, and they had a daughter.[5] – This evening however they have none with them but persons who are in some sort of their own family. I just now left them at tea with "quite a family party" – Mr [John] Monkhouse, my two girls Jemima & Rotha, two of John Wordsworth's boys, Johnny & Charley, Mr

Herbert Hill [husband of Bertha Southey] & one of his little boys, and Mr <u>Hartley Coleridge</u>. – . . .

It is Johnny Wordsworth's birthday today, & to morrow is Charley's, & the Poet's two grand-children have invited all the children in the country & some adults to celebrate the two birthdays to-morrow evening. James Dixon has prepared a balloon which is to be sent up; & I know not what besides is to astonish the Country. Poor Rydal! & happy children.

544. Mary Wordsworth to Isabella Fenwick; [Rydal Mount], 2 August [1848]

After a long season of comers & goers we find our household reduced to our own scanty number, & my husband & I are alone, at least at <u>breakfast</u> – Soon afterwards we may look for Tourists, who by hook or by crook make their way to us. It seems to me as if America had broken loose so many, especially from New York, of that Country make their way to the Poet – for my part I see few of them – but my dear Husband receives all Strangers cordially – and it does him good to talk to them . . .

At this moment a groupe of Young Tourists are standing before the window (I am writing in the Hall) & W[illia]m reading a newspaper – & on lifting up his head a profound bow greeted him from each – they look as if come up from the Steamer for the day. I wish you could have seen them.

545. Edward Quillinan to Henry Crabb Robinson; Loughrigg Holme, 12 August [1848]

Yesterday as I happened to be on the Terrace at Rydal Mount, no less than 50, or 60 (I counted 48 & then left off) Cheap-trainers invaded the poet's premises at once. They walked about all over the terraces & garden, without leave asked, but did no harm; & I was rather pleased at so many humble men & women & lasses having minds high enough to feel interest in Wordsworth. I retreated into the house; but one young lady rang the bell, asked for me, & begged me to give her an autograph of Mr W[ordsworth]. – I had none. "Where could she get one?" I did not know. – Her pretty face looked as sad as if she had lost a lover.

546. George John Douglas Campbell, 8th Duke of Argyll, describing a visit to Rydal Mount to the Reverend J. G. Howson; 8 September 1848

When tea was over, we renewed our request that he sh[oul]d read to us. He said "Oh dear, that is terrible" but consented, asking what we chose. He jumped at "<u>Tintern Abbey</u>" in preference to any part of the <u>Excursion</u>.

He told us that he had written Tintern Abbey in 1798 – taking four days to compose it – the last 20 lines or so being composed as he walked down the hill from Clifton to Bristol. It was curious to feel that we were to hear a Poet read his own verses composed 50 years before –

He read the introductory lines descriptive of the Scenery in a low clear voice But when he came to the thoughtful and reflective lines His tones deepened, and he poured them forth with a fervour and almost passion of delivery which was very striking and beautiful. I observed that Mrs Wordsworth was strongly affected, during the reading. The strong emphasis that he put on the words addressed personally to the person to whom the poem is addressed struck me as almost unnatural at the time – "My <u>dear, dear</u> friend" and in the words "In thy wild eyes" It was not till after the reading was over that we found out that the old Paralytic, and <u>doited</u> woman we had seen in the morning was the <u>sister</u> to whom Tintern Abbey was addressed, and her condition now accounted for the fervour with which the old Poet read lines which reminded Him of their better days. But it was melancholy to think that the vacant silly stare we had seen in the morning was from the "Wild eyes" of 1798!

Wordsworth apologised to the D[uche]ss for having read so loud – and excused Himself by referring to the now condition of his sister. But we c[oul]d not have had so good an opportunity of bringing out in his reading, the source of the inspiration of his poetry – which it was impossible not to feel was the poetry of the heart.

Mrs Wordsworth told me it was the first time he had read since his daughter's death – and that she was thankful to us for having made him do it – as he was apt to fall into a listless languid state.

Chapter Fourteen

1848–50

547. *Mary Wordsworth to her niece by marriage, Mrs Chris Wordsworth; Rydal Mount, 28 December [1848]*

. . . I think I may say, with much thankfulness, that y[ou]r dear Uncle's spirits <u>begin</u> to revive, <u>even</u> when he is <u>not</u> in company. His memory, as regards <u>present things merely</u> is sadly failed – or perhaps it is rather, that his thoughts being elsewhere, it <u>is absence</u> & not a lack of memory – but so it is, hourly occurrences make no impression on his mind. Do not notice this dear Susan –

On 6 January 1849 Hartley Coleridge died, aged fifty-two. The Wordsworths had loved and cared for him since childhood, providing him with a second home and protecting him, as best they could, from his own failings, especially after all his own family had left the Lakes. As Hartley's brother and sister gratefully acknowledged, they had been indefatigable in their care of him until the very last.

548. *Sara Coleridge to her cousin, the Reverend Edward Coleridge; 10 Chester Place, Regent's Park, [London], January 1849*

Our old friends, Mr and Mrs Wordsworth, are more endeared to me and Derwent [her brother] than ever, by the love and tender interest they have shown; not more, indeed, than I should have looked for from them, but all I could have thought of or hoped. "You should have heard the old man say, 'Well! God bless him!' and then turn away in tears. 'It is a sad thing for me, who have known him so long! He will be a sad loss to us; and let him lie as near to us as possible, leaving room for Mrs Wordsworth and myself. It would have been his wish.'"

In another letter, when all was over, D[erwent] says – "Mr and Mrs W[ordsworth] had been at the cottage during my absence. Mrs

W[ordsworth] kissed the cold face thrice, said it was beautiful, and decked the body with flowers. This has also been done by others. Mr W[ordsworth] was dreadfully affected, and could not go in . . ."

549. Henry Crabb Robinson to Isabella Fenwick; 30 Russell Square, [London], 15 January 1849

The account I have to give of our friends is so much better than that of last year that I should certainly have sent it, tho' I had not received a friendly intimation of your wish to hear from me.

I found Mr Wordsworth more calm & composed than I expected – Whatever his feelings may be, the outward expression of them he can repress – I heard no sighs, no moaning – And he never refused to join in any conversation on the topics of the day.[1] I feared that the visit to the Churchyard last Tuesday with Mr [Derwent] Coleridge to fix on the spot where Hartley might be interred would overset him, but, on the contrary, I returned with him alone – and he talked on a literary subject[2] on our return with perfect self-possession and full of the subject. But his mind is not as active as it was – and Mrs W[ordsworth] s[ays] he has not composed a line during the year and scarcely <u>written</u> one. I can therefore account for the report concerning the supposed loss of his faculties [which] was a gross exaggera[tion] if not a malicious misrepresentation of his actual condition

It was only in the Evening that there was any sensible difference between what he now is, and what he was when we together played a rubber with them – Cards have never been introduced yet. But if I live to make another Christmas visit, I trust I shall not again forget to make my annual contribution for the amusement of the coming year.

The most agreeable circumstance is that he goes occasionally to Mr Quillinan's And that they stand in a friendly relation towards each other – Every unpleasant impression on the mind of Mr Qu[illinan] is quite removed –

Dear Mrs Wordsworth is what she always was – I see no change in her, but that the wrinkles of her careworn countenance are somewhat deeper

Poor Miss W[ordsworth] I thought sunk still deeper in insensibility – By the bye, Mrs Wordsworth says that almost the only enjoyment Mr Wordsworth seems to feel is in his attendance on her – and that her death would be to him a sad calamity!!!

*550. Edward Quillinan to Henry Crabb Robinson; Loughrigg Holme,
12 January 1849*

Mr Wordsworth today came to me through snow and sleet, and sate for
an hour in his most cheerful mood. Some talk about his grand-children
led him back to his own boyhood, and he related several particulars which
it would have done you good to listen to, for some of them were new to
me & probably would have been so to you. He talked too a great deal
about the Coleridges, especially the STC. – If I had been inclined to
Boswellise, this would have been one of my days for it. He was particularly
interesting.

*551. William Wordsworth, on his seventy-ninth birthday, to Isabella Fenwick;
[Rydal Mount], 7 April 1849*

I was sitting down to write to You, my beloved Friend, a few lines upon
my entering, this day, my eightieth year, when your affectionate Letter
was brought to me. Pray accept my heart-felt thanks for the good wishes
which it breathes. I wish I could add that I was more at ease in the recesses
of my own nature, but God's will be done.

*552. Edward Quillinan to Henry Crabb Robinson; Loughrigg Holme, 14
October 1849*

You will find your old and faithful friend the poet pretty much as he was
on y[ou]r last visit. The same social cheerfulness – company cheerfulness
– the same fixed despondency (uncorrected)[3] I esteem him for both: I
love him best for the latter. – I have put up a beautiful headstone to Dora's
Grave. I wonder if you will like it. – God bless you, friend Crabb.

To his lasting regret, Henry Crabb Robinson did not pay his usual Christmas
visit to Rydal Mount in 1849. He therefore missed his last opportunity to see the
poet. The winter of 1849–50 was long and hard: heavy snowfalls were followed
by rain and then severe frosts. For days on end Quillinan and his daughters were
snowed up in their cottage under Loughrigg. William, too, was imprisoned by
his fireside, though chafing for his daily walk. On 10 March 1850, he braved the
weather to walk with Quillinan and, as a result, caught a bad cold which developed
into a serious chest infection.

553. Edward Quillinan, diary, 10 March 1850

10 Mar[ch]: very keen cold weather – Mr W[ordsworth] in the even[in]g proposed to join me on my walk towards Grasmere ... I remonstrated with him on being so thinly clad. "I care nothing about it" was his answer as if poor man he was invulnerable.

554. Edward Quillinan to Isabella Fenwick; Loughrigg Holme, 22 March 1850

I was very uneasy at Mrs W[ordsworth]'s indefatigable nursing – I believe she had not slept, at least not had a good sleep, for several nights & days; and she is very unwilling to accept help, thinking, no doubt quite justly, that her services are more acceptable to her husband than those of anyone else, though she very highly praises the patient assiduity of the Housemaid, Hannah Holmes ... Miss W[ordsworth] is as usual, & has behaved very well; making little or no noise, which must have been a great effort at self-management on her part.

555. Mary Wordsworth to her cousin and sister-in-law, Mary Hutchinson; [Rydal Mount, March 1850]

You will be glad to hear that dear William is better – yet I dare say it will be some time before he thinks himself as well as he was previous to this ugly attack – which to any one who did not know him as I do, would have thought it [*sic*] a frightful one – to me it has brought back his old habit of exaggerating his bodily ailments, which for nearly 3 years he has never seemed conscious of having one to complain of, so completely has his mind been engrossed by our sorrows.

This beautiful season, lovely as it is, is too cold for him to venture out to refresh his mind or I should hope soon to see him well, but creeping over a hot fire as he does, I fear you will not find him even so well, as he was when we were at Mathon [near Malvern, where the Wordsworths had visited the Hutchinsons in 1849] in this respect, for I cannot conceal from myself, that a sensible change, during the last year has clouded his memory. – But I am not without hope that the presence of these dear Girls [Mary's daughters, Ebba and Sarah Hutchinson], & the expectation of seeing you may rouse him so that you may not discover in him the change which I have been afraid you would find. But enough of my forebodings.

556. Mary Wordsworth to Isabella Fenwick; [Rydal Mount], Monday afternoon,
[8–9 April 1850]

Since Tea he has awaked &, so sweetly! asking me "if I thought he would
ever get well"? & upon my expressing my thoughts & explaining why he
was so weak & what was to be done to regain lost strength He jocosely
observed – 'You preach very nicely' – 'Now read to me' this office I
turned over to Eliz. [Ebba], to whom he said 'You must excuse me if I fall
asleep' – And truly it is even so – Yet at this instant Sister is come to see
him, rather inopportunely – as he is too sleepy to be kept awake, & this
is not desireable just now. –

7 oc[lock] Tuesday m[ornin]g
The hopes beloved F[rien]d which lingered about my heart when last
Ev[enin]g I wrote so far; <u>have</u> after a quiet night, passed away, & I feel I
must – I feel I must no longer[4] rest them <u>here</u> I have your prayers & your
invaluable love

God bless you
M.W.
P.S.

I do not look for a speedy termination to our anxieties – rather the
contrary – But God knoweth best & we must stand & wait his blessed
Will.

557. Edward Quillinan to Mrs Chris Wordsworth; Loughrigg Holme, 9 April
1850

[Dr Davy] thought him, as he told me, in a precarious state but <u>not</u> a
<u>hopeless</u> one . . . His being so long in bed must be against him, as so
contrary to his life-long habits of being much out of doors. But his
constitution was so vigorous, & so <u>unabused</u>, that he may yet retain power
which w[oul]d fail most men at his age after such an illness.

558. John Wordsworth to his cousin, Chris Wordsworth; Rydal Mount, Thursday
morning [11 April 1850]

I did not expect him to survive many days last week; Sunday night however
he somewhat improved, & in some respects has continued to do so up to
this hour. What we have now, I think, most cause to apprehend, is his
falling into a condition in some respects similar to our dear Aunt's – (She

however is much better since this illness of her B[rothe]rs which causes her to think less about her own uncomfortable sensations.) Habitual somnolence, apathy, or paralytic affection is I think to be apprehended. We get him on to an easy chair for about an hour daily – This is a most painful operation, to all the parties concerned, though on his part it arises in a great measure from extreme sensitiveness & nervous apprehension. From the lusty manner in which he screams out when touched he cannot be as weak as he appears to be . . . I think the present state of things is likely to continue for some time, with very little perceptible change. It is a most painful subject to write upon. I suppose Chr[is]'s engagements are such as to prevent his coming down here for a few days. I think <u>his moral</u> influence would be beneficial. I hold up to my dear F[athe]r the example of Sir W[alter] Scott, who manfully said, "If I am to die, I would rather die of the remedies than of the disease." <u>He</u> on the contrary gives way to the disease in every way – but this <u>in fact</u> mainly is <u>the disease</u> – there is no organic mischeif [*sic*] going on. My Mother is wonderfully supported.

559. Edward Quillinan to Henry Crabb Robinson; Loughrigg Holme, 23 April 1850

John & William are here: (that is, at Ryd[a]l M[oun]t) also the Miss Hutchinsons who chanced to be on a visit when the illness began; & whose Mother is daily expected; Mrs Hutchinson will probably be of much help & solace to Mrs W[ordsworth] who bears all this wonderfully, so far. Miss W[ordsworth] too is as much herself as she ever was in her life, & has an almost absolute <u>command</u> of her own will! does not make noises; is not all self; thinks of the feelings of others (Mrs W[ordsworth]'s for example), is tenderly anxious about her brother; &, in short, but for age & bodily infirmity, is almost <u>the</u> Miss Wordsworth we knew in past days. Whether this will last, or be the sign that she will not long survive her brother, is beyond us. – Mr W[ordsworth]'s mind is, when it is brought out, <u>perfectly clear</u>, & has been so throughout; but tranquil & reserved; he has for the most part been so quiet as almost to seem asleep when he was not so; except when aroused by those about him, or by his <u>doctors</u>. All of the latter he has dreaded; he felt that they disturbed him, or caused him to be disturbed, by ordering him 'to be <u>got up</u>' (of all things what he most shrinks from) or by suggesting other expedients that did him no good; & perhaps he thought, perhaps knew, that they <u>could</u> do no good.

It seems doubtful whether he may not yet survive many days, & have much suffering to go through; or whether he may pass away very soon & almost insensibly.–

560. *Willy Wordsworth to his wife, Fanny; Rydal Mount, 11 a.m., 23 April 1850*

. . . and now for our dear Father, who became so much worse early last evening that we scarcely thought he could get over the night. I sat up with him till past five o'clock – a sad sad night I had of it; but when I called Hannah & James to take my place his breathing was a trifle better, & now at Eleven O'clock, his life is hanging, as Dr Davy has just said, "by so slight a thread that he questions much whether it will hold together many hours longer". I will keep this open till the very last moment so that you shall have the latest possible intelligence – We have given up all intention of ever <u>attempting</u> to move or even disturb him again. He lies on a small bed at the foot of his own & dear Mother's – Poor dear Mother was sadly overcome last night – ! She went to bed at eleven, & she only got out of her bed once during my stretch to have a look at poor dear Father, & try to wrap up his poor cold feet in a warm flannel shawl, to w[hic]h he was as averse as ever the moment he felt the clothes being moved – Dear Mother did however gain snatches of sleep & pleased I was whenever I heard her poor sobs subdued by them – John got here a little before 8 pm. He has got a substitute I'm glad to say for next Sunday if not longer. Dear Aunt Hutchinson much to dearest Mother's comfort arrived by mail this morning. . . . I wish you were both here this lovely day & could hear that glorious thrush that has been singing on the mount ever since day break – I must now go upstairs. . . .

I had not finished writing my initials before I was summoned to our dearest Father's bedside & within ten minutes of my being in the room his Spirit passed away & all <u>was over</u> at a quarter before twelve o'clock in the presence of our dearest Mother, John, Aunt Hutchinson, Hannah, James, Elizabeth & little Hannah – Dearest Aunty being in her chair on the front & is not yet aware of her & our loss –

Oh how thankful we all feel that he is now in peace Had he been spared a little longer how indescribable must his sufferings have been – The Lord's Will has truly been mercifully done –

561. *Edward Quillinan to Sara Coleridge; Loughrigg Holme, 23 April 1850*

We had known for two or three days, at least, that there was no hope; but we were led to believe that the end was not as yet. At twelve o'clock this day, however, he passed away, very very quietly. Mrs Wordsworth is quite resigned; . . .

It is said that Shakspeare died, on his birthday, April 23, if that be the real date. This great man, Wordsworth, was no Shakspeare, and the dramatic power perhaps was not in him. But he had a grand and tender genius of his own that will live in the heart of his country; and these mountains will be his noblest monument. His life was a long & prosperous life, and he was rewarded in the latter part of it at least, for the virtuous use he had made of the great power entrusted to him, with "honour, love, obedience, troops of friends, & all that should accompany old age."[5] He has, no doubt, now a higher reward: he is gone to Dora.

562. *Edward Quillinan to Sara Coleridge; Loughrigg Holme, 28 April 1850*

Yesterday was a day which will long be remembered in these vales, for almost all their population was in the Church & Church-Yard of Grasmere. Very few, none indeed but those of the family who happened to be here, were invited to the Funeral; but many came. It was a fine morning, and its brightness seemed to deepen the solemnity of the gathering. Mrs Wordsworth saw her husband lowered into his Grave, and bore up better that I feared she could, from the moment she left the house till she returned to it. She is to-day very composed. – Conformably to what she knew to be <u>his</u> wish, & what she felt strongly to be her own, he was buried <u>close</u> to Dora, and the Grave was dug deep enough to admit her coffin too hereafter. The narrowness of the space, between Dora & Sara Hutchinson, did not allow room for two separate Graves; so dear Mrs Wordsworth herself ordered this arrangement; and John & William took care that it should be exactly complied with. This morning she expressed to me her heartfelt satisfaction that she now felt sure that She, as well as the Father, would lie beside their beloved daughter.[6]

Abbreviations Used in Notes and Sources

The following abbreviations have been used to indicate those locations most frequently cited:

Amherst: Archives & Special Collections, Amherst College, Amherst, Massachusetts.

Berg: The Henry W. & Albert A. Berg Collection of English and American Literature, The New York Public Library, New York.

BL: Manuscript Collections, British Library, London.

Cornell: Department of Manuscripts and Archives, Cornell University, New York.

Cottle: J. Cottle, *Reminiscences of Samuel Taylor Coleridge and Robert Southey* (Lime Tree Bower Press, 1970).

CRO: Cumbria Record Office, The Castle, Carlisle.

DC: Wordsworth Trust, Dove Cottage, Grasmere.

DW: Dr Williams's Library, London.

Estimate: *An Estimate of William Wordsworth by his Contemporaries*, edited by E. Smith (Blackwell, Oxford 1932).

Fenwick Notes: *The Fenwick Notes of William Wordsworth*, edited by J. Curtis (Bristol Classical Press, 1993).

Hamilton: *Life of Sir William Rowan Hamilton* by R. P. Graves (Longman, Green & Co., London, 1882), 3 vols.

Harvard: The Houghton Library, Harvard University, Cambridge, Massachusetts.

HCRD: *Diary, Reminiscences, and Correspondence of Henry Crabb Robinson*, edited by T. Sadler (Macmillan & Co., London, 1872), 3 vols.

HCRWC: *The Correspondence of Henry Crabb Robinson with the Wordsworth Circle (1808–1866)*, edited by E. J. Morley (Clarendon Press, Oxford, 1927), 2 vols.

Hunt: Department of Manuscripts, The Huntington Library, San Marino, California.

LDW: *Letters of Dora Wordsworth*, edited by H. P. Vincent (Packard & Co., Chicago, 1944).

LHC: *The Letters of Hartley Coleridge*, edited by G. E. & E. L. Griggs (Oxford, 1941).

LWDW: *The Letters of William and Dorothy Wordsworth*, edited by E. de Selincourt, C. L. Shaver, M. Moorman & A. G. Hill (Clarendon Press, Oxford, 1967–93), 8 vols.

Memoirs: Christopher Wordsworth, *Memoirs of William Wordsworth* (London, 1851).

MLSC: *Memoir and Letters of Sara Coleridge*, edited by E. Coleridge (London, 1873), 2 vols.

NLS: Manuscripts Division, National Library of Scotland, Edinburgh.

PM: Department of Literary & Historical Manuscripts, The Pierpont Morgan Library, New York.

Princeton: Robert H. Taylor Collection, Rare Books & Special Collections, Princeton University Library, Princeton, New Jersey.

Prose: *The Prose Works of William Wordsworth*, edited by W. J. B. Owen & J. W. Smyser (Clarendon Press, Oxford, 1974), 3 vols.

Romantic Bards: *Romantic Bards and British Reviewers*, edited by J. O. Hayden (Routledge & Kegan Paul, London, 1971).

Sandford: Elizabeth Sandford, *Thomas Poole and his Friends* (Friarn Press, 1996), reprint of the original 2 vols., bound as one.

STCL: *Collected Letters of Samuel Taylor Coleridge*, edited by E. L. Griggs (Clarendon Press, Oxford, 1956–71), 6 vols.

Ticknor: G. Ticknor, *Life, Letters and Journals*, edited by G. S. Hillard (Sampson Low et al., 1876), 2 vols.

UCL: Manuscript Room, Sharpe Papers, University College, London.

UV: McGregor Room, Autograph Collection, Special Collections Department, The Library, University of Virginia, Charlottesville, Virginia.

V&A: Forster Collection, National Art Library, Victoria and Albert Museum, London.

Notes

Introduction

1. William Wordsworth to Basil Montagu, [?Sept 1844]: MS in Paul C. Richards Collection, Boston University; *The Journal of Thomas Moore*, edited by W. S. Dowden (London & Toronto, 1988), v, 1, 988.

2. William Wordsworth to David Laing, 11 Dec 1835: MS in Special Collections, Edinburgh University Library.

3. William Wordsworth to Edward Moxon, [4 Jan 1836]: MS Hunt: HM 22095.

4. William Wordsworth to Sir Henry Bunbury, 30 July [1838]: MS Hunt: HM 12304.

5. William Wordsworth to Samuel Carter Hall, 15 Jan 1837: MS Harvard.

6. William Wordsworth to Basil Montagu, [?Sept 1844]: MS in Paul C. Richards Collection, Boston University.

7. William Wordsworth to Edward Moxon, 10 Dec 1835: MS Berg.

8. See above, note 1.

Chapter One

1. Spedding slightly misquotes the opening lines of William's prize-winning poem, *Lines Written as a School Exercise at Hawkshead, Anno Aetatis 14*.

2. Charlotte Smith (1749–1806), poet, novelist, and a distant relation by marriage of the Wordsworths. William was an admirer of her poetry.

3. Helen Maria Williams (1761–1827), poet and pro-Revolutionary, to whom William had addressed his first ever published poem, *Sonnet on Seeing Miss Helen Maria Williams Weep*, which appeared in the *European Magazine* (March 1787).

Chapter Two

1. The poet, Thomas Gray (1716–61), in his *Journal in the Lakes* (1775).
2. The 'Salisbury Plain' poem would eventually be published as *Guilt and Sorrow* in 1842; thirty stanzas of it were published in *Lyrical Ballads* (1798) as *The Female Vagrant*.
3. This word is obscure in the manuscript: though it appears to be 'resolute', *LWDW, Early Years*, 125 transcribes it as 'severe'.
4. John Praetor Pinney, however, was under the mistaken impression that his son's new tenants would be paying rent.
5. Nicholas Leader (1773–1836), one of Godwin's radical circle in London.
6. Seven ships and hundreds of men from the Royal Navy fleet were lost off the notoriously treacherous Dorset coast during a storm on 17 November 1795.
7. A quote from Shakespeare's *A Midsummer Night's Dream*, Act V, Scene i.
8. 'The Recluse' was long-projected but never completed: the only substantial portion of it to be published was *The Excursion* (1814). *The Prelude*, William's autobiographical poem, was intended to be an introduction to 'The Recluse'.

Chapter Three

1. '2d edition': John means the first volume of *Lyrical Ballads* (1800), which was a reissue, and therefore a second edition, of *Lyrical Ballads* (1798).
2. 'cut at it': before writing 'cut at it', Dorothy originally wrote 'employed himself' but deleted only the second word so that the manuscript actually reads 'employed cut at it . . .'
3. 'The Pedlar': a section of 'The Recluse', which would eventually be published as part of *The Excursion* (1814).

Chapter Four

1. ' – I gave him the wedding ring . . . blessed me fervently': these two sentences have been deleted in the manuscript by a different hand.
2. 'Tuesday': or possibly Thursday, the manuscript is unclear.
3. 'between': written 'bewween' in the manuscript.
4. Sally Green, a former nursemaid to the Wordsworth children, who had just lost her parents; they had died in a snowstorm while crossing the fells between Easedale and Langdale on 19 March 1808, leaving twelve orphans. The Wordsworths set up a subscription to raise funds for the care and education of the five youngest and, although they had intended to replace Sally, they kept

her on as a member of their household, sending her to school and teaching her needlework to enable her to secure employment in future.

5. This experience resulted in a poem, 'Pressed with conflicting thoughts of love and fear', which was not published in William's lifetime.

Chapter Five

1. Sara Hutchinson, who was now a permanent member of the Wordsworth household, had recently ruptured a blood vessel and been seriously ill.

2. Sir George Beaumont (1753–1827) was a talented amateur artist as well as a generous patron of the arts; he provided a drawing to be engraved as the frontispiece of *The White Doe of Rylstone* (1815).

3. The phrase in square brackets has been deleted in the manuscript, possibly by Dorothy herself.

4. Most of the last two sentences are written in the shorthand code Robinson used when discussing sensitive matters.

5. Mary had already learnt of Catharine's death before William could get to Hindwell: she had been in the room when Sara's letter was handed to their brother Tom, and, realizing immediately that something was wrong, had insisted on knowing the truth.

6. 'Wife . . . Wilson': all inhabitants of Greta Hall, Keswick, which was home to the Southey family: Southey's wife, Edith Fricker, was the sister of Sarah Coleridge and Mary Lovell; Mary Barker lived in the other half of the Hall and Mrs Wilson was the housekeeper.

7. Dorothy originally wrote 'must be indulged at times' but then deleted the last two words.

Chapter Six

1. Once the expensive first edition had sold out, William intended to reprint *The Excursion* in a cheaper format to make it more widely accessible. This was his usual practice, enabling him to maximize his earnings for new work whilst also reaching the widest possible readership.

2. John Scott (1783–1821), a Wordsworth enthusiast, was editor of *The Champion* in which he published his own, very favourable, review of *The White Doe*.

3. William habitually stated that Catharine was four when she died, though, in fact, she was three months short of her fourth birthday: see also letter 457.

4. The Habeas Corpus Act (limiting the right to imprison without charge to 48 hours) was suspended in the spring of 1817 in response to serious disturbances

in agricultural and manufacturing districts throughout the country, some of which were forcibly suppressed by the military. The distresses of the labouring poor had been aggravated by the cessation of war, the high price of provisions, the introduction of machinery and the consequent rise in unemployment.

5. Schedoni was the monk with the blood-chilling gaze in Ann Radcliff's romance about the Inquisition, *The Italian* (1797).

6. Phrenology was the popular pseudo-science of divining character by locating and identifying the bumps on the skull, each of which was believed to be an organ representing a trait such as poetry or philosophy.

7. Haydon is quoting William's own lines from 'I wandered lonely as a cloud', ll.21-2.

8. Though he was now standing against the Lowther interest, Henry Brougham (1778–1868) had approached Lord Lonsdale in 1806 in the hope of securing a parliamentary seat through his influence: William repeatedly urged that this hypocrisy should be publicly exposed but Lonsdale refused to do so.

9. William Westall's recently published *Views of the Caves near Ingleton, Gordale Scar, and Malham Cove in Yorkshire.*

Chapter Seven

1. 'a spurious Peter': John Hamilton Reynolds's *Peter Bell: A Lyrical Ballad*, a witty parody of William's poetic style, anticipated William's own publication, which had been widely advertised.

2. The last two sentences are written in the shorthand code Robinson used when discussing sensitive matters.

3. *LWDW, Later Years*, i, 3 dates this letter 10 January 1821, but the manuscript clearly reads '6th Jan[ua]ry 1821'.

4. William is here arguing that he is still a democrat even though he no longer believes in the principle of one man one vote. His modified position is that he wants to see the franchise widened to increase the number of those eligible to vote, but only so long as it remains in the hands of those with some property.

5. Frederick William Goddard, a young American on a Swiss tour of his own, met the Wordsworths at Lucerne and accompanied them on their ascent of the Righi mountain; he was drowned a few days later in a freak storm on Lake Zurich. William wrote *Elegiac Stanzas* in his memory and later transmitted a copy to Goddard's mother.

Chapter Eight

1. The phrase in square brackets is deleted in the manuscript, probably by Quillinan himself.
2. 'seekers-out': the word is obscure in the manuscript: it may read 'cutters-out'.
3. 'to mend himself': i.e., to improve his position by getting better terms for his work.
4. John Murray (1788–1843), founder of the *Quarterly Review* and publisher of Lord Byron, for which reasons he was particularly disliked by the Wordsworth women.
5. Dorothy was staying with the Hutchinsons, who had moved from Hindwell in Radnorshire to Brinsop Court near Hereford.
6. Southey's youngest daughter, fourteen-year-old Isabel, had died in July 1826.
7. Hamilton had sent William a long poem, 'It haunts me yet, that dream of earthly love', which he had written at Ambleside on 13 September.

Chapter Nine

1. Reynolds had, in fact, printed only two of the five sonnets submitted, as William discovered two months later.
2. The manuscript date actually reads 22 January 1828 but this is clearly the writer's mistake, as the letter is legibly postmarked 24 January 1829: *LWDW, Later Years*, II, 4 further misdates the letter to 12 January.
3. 'to look after the Constellation Farm': i.e., to inspect the freehold property in Langdale which William had purchased as part of a consortium of family and friends in 1818–9; the joint ownership entitled each member of the consortium to vote in Westmorland elections.
4. Felicia Dorothea Hemans (1793–1835), a popular poetess of the day, best known now for her *Songs of the Affections* and 'The boy stood on the burning deck'.
5. Isabella Curwen (1808–49), whom John Wordsworth married on 11 October 1830. Hartley Coleridge was right in suspecting that the Curwen fortune was not secure: when the family coal mines at Workington were swamped by the sea in 1837 Isabella lost her allowance and her inheritance. The pressures of living with five children solely on John's clerical income contributed to the eventual breakdown of their marriage.
6. This letter exists only in a handwritten transcript by William's niece by marriage, Susan Wordsworth, for her husband's biography, *Memoirs of William*

Wordsworth (1850): the words 'and economically' have been deleted, presumably by the editor and because they were deemed inappropriate.

7. Sir George Beaumont had died on 7 February 1827 and William had been under pressure since then to produce verses in his memory.

Chapter Ten

1. Tithonus: a son of the King of Troy, he was so beautiful that Aurora, goddess of the dawn, fell in love with him and granted his request for immortality. As he failed to ask for perpetual youth, however, his body continued to age.

2. *Humanity* was written in the autumn of 1829 but remained unpublished until 1835.

3. 'your Rites': Quillinan was a Roman Catholic by birth although he had baptized both his daughters into the Anglican church and attended the Church of England himself.

4. *The Poetical Works of William Wordsworth* (Longman & Co., 1832), 4 vols.

5. Although the last edition of William's collected poems, published in 1832, had sold better than any previous edition, it had still performed badly: see letter 390. *Yarrow Revisited, and Other Poems* (1835) was William's first critical and commercial success and it transformed his reputation.

6. *The Warning*, composed at Moresby in 1833 as a sequel to the poem suggested by the birth of his first legitimate grandchild: see above no. 384. William had originally decided to omit it from *Yarrow Revisited* because it was so different in tone to the rest of the poems.

7. Quoted from William's own poem, *The Old Cumberland Beggar*, l.153.

8. The deaths of Catharine and Thomas had made the Wordsworths understandably over-anxious about the health of their remaining children, but Dora's tendency to 'unwellness', as she called it, had been exacerbated in recent years by what would now be recognized as anorexia: see Juliet Barker, *Wordsworth: A Life* (Viking, 2000), for a detailed discussion of her condition.

Chapter Eleven

1. Sir Rowland Hill (1795–1879) had secured the introduction of the penny postage in the budget of 1839: it revolutionized the postal system by changing the onus for paying for letters from the recipient to the writer.

Chapter Twelve

1. Catharine was actually in her fourth year: see Chapter 6, note 3.
2. 'rush-bearing': a medieval festival, still celebrated in some churches in the north of England, marking the day each year when the old rushes covering the church floor were removed and replaced with new ones. The children decorated hoops with paper which were then hung in the church.
3. Quillinan is mistaken: Coleridge was born at Ottery St Mary, Devon, though he later lived at Nether Stowey: he had already met William in Bristol in 1795 and stayed with the Wordsworths at Racedown Lodge before they moved to Alfoxton.
4. 'certain quarters': William originally wrote 'a certain quarter' but seems to have decided this was too pointed a reference to Quillinan, and altered it to 'certain quarters'.
5. Quillinan was still working on his unfinished translation of *The Lusiads*, Luis de Camoens' sixteenth-century Portuguese epic poem, when he died in 1851.

Chapter Thirteen

1. 'sale': The manuscript actually reads 'sold' though William clearly meant 'sale'; the word 'about' which follows in the same sentence may actually be 'above', but the reading is unclear.
2. This was William's second nomination to the post: see letter 436.
3. See letter 426.
4. It is an indication of William's unusual confusion of mind that he first wrote 'he drank tea here', then deleted 'drank' and wrote over it 'dined', but forgot to delete the word 'tea'; though the sense is obvious, the manuscript therefore reads 'he dined tea here'.
5. 'and they had a daughter': these words have been scribbled over in the manuscript.

Chapter Fourteen

1. 'The outward expression . . . of the day': this sentence is deleted in the manuscript.
2. 'on a literary subject': deleted in the manuscript.
3. 'Despondency' and 'Despondency Corrected' are the titles of the third and fourth books of *The Excursion*.

4. This confused sentence is an indication of Mary's distress: she also deleted a second 'no longer' which she wrote after the first.

5. The quotation is a paraphrase of Shakespeare's *Macbeth*, V. iii. 24–5.

6. When Mary died, in January 1859, she was buried as she wished in the same grave as her husband and therefore next to that of their daughter.

Sources

1. *Memoirs*, i, 7–9.
2. DC: WLL/DW/1/1.
3. *Memoirs*, i, 10–13.
4. DC: WLMS A/Spedding/66a.
5. T. W. Thompson, *Wordsworth's Hawkshead* (OUP, London, 1970), 344.
6. *Memoirs*, i, 13–14.
7. *LWDW, Early Years*, 18, n.4 (MS not located).
8. DC: WLMS SH 2/11/11.
9. DC: WLMS SH 2/11/13.
10. DC: WLL/DW/1/9.
11. *Memoirs*, i, 14–15.
12. DC: WLL/WW/1/10.
13. *Memoirs*, i, 15.
14. Cornell.
15. DC: WLL/DW/1/14.
16. BL: Add. MS 46136 fos.3–4.
17. DC: WLMS 2/45.
18. BL: Add. MS 46136 fos.7–8.
19. DC: WLL/DW/1/16.
20. DC: WLL/WW/1/17.
21. DC: WLL/DW/1/19.
22. BL: Add. MS 46136 fos.9–10.
23. *Memoirs*, i, 77.
24. G. M. Harper, *Wordsworth's French Daughter* (Princeton, 1916).
25. DC: WLL/DW/1/23.
26. DC: WLL/DW/1/25.
27. DC: WLL/DW/1/27.
28. DC: WLL/DW/1/28.
29. BL: Add. MS 46136 fos.11–12.
30. *Memoirs*, i, 82.
31. DC: WLL/DW/1/31.
32. DC: WLMS 2/47.
33. BL: Add. MS 46136 fos. 13–14.
34. Ibid. fos.15–17.
35. Ibid. fos.18–19.
36. Ibid. fos.20–21.
37. DC: WLL/DW/1/38.
38. Berg.
39. Hunt: HM 22055.
40. DC: WLL/DW/1/40.
41. Pinney Papers, Letter Book 13 no.9, University of Bristol.
42. BL: Add. MS 46136 fos.22–3.
43. *Memoirs*, i, 96.
44. Hunt: HM 22057.
45. DC: WLL/DW/1/43.
46. *Memoirs*, i, 98–9.
47. *STCL*, i, 325.
48. *Memoirs*, i, 102–4.
49. Sandford, 130.
50. Nicolas Roe, *Wordsworth and Coleridge: The Radical Years* (Oxford, 1988), 248.
51. Ibid., 261.
52. Sandford, 134.
53. *Memoirs*, i, 106, 113.

54. *LWDW, Early Years*, 195 (ms in private hands).

55. Ibid. 197 n.1 (MS not located).

56. Princeton.

57. Cottle, 175.

58. DC: WLL/DW/1/51.

59. BL: Collection of Autographs Mus. Brit. Jure Emptionis 18204 fos. 486–7.

60. *LWDW, Early Years*, 221, 224 (MS not located: not New York Genealogical & Biographical Society, as in *LWDW*).

61. *Fenwick Notes*, 15.

62. *Prose*, i, 116.

63. *Romantic Bards*, 5.

64. MS in private hands, on loan to DC, Dec 2001.

65. *STCL*, i, 445.

66. DC: WLL/WW/1/55.

67. DC: WLL/DW/1/56.

68. DC: WLL/WW/1/58.

69. *STCL*, i, 490–91.

70. DC: WLMS H1/1/2.

71. V&A: MS 48G 3/1–3/2.

72. BL: Add. MS 35344 fos.138–40.

73. *STCL*, i, 543.

74. DC: WLL/WW/1/65.

75. DC: WLL/DW/2/154.

76. DC: WLL/WW/2/120.

77. DC: WLL/WW/2/126.

78. DC: WLMS H 1/8/4.

79. *Letters of Charles and Mary Lamb*, edited by E. W. Marrs (Cornell University Press, 1975), i, 221.

80. V&A: MS 48G 5/1–5/2.

81. *LWDW, Early Years*, 267 (MS not located).

82. Cottle, 259–60.

83. DC: WLL/WW/1/70.

84. DC: MS DC 20 fo.33.

85. Berg.

86. Harvard.

87. *Prose*, i, 122–3, 125–6, 149–50.

88. Berg.

89. Hunt: HM 12303.

90. DW: HCR corresp.1800–1803 no.23.

91. DC: WLL/JW/15.

92. DC: WLL/WW/1/75.

93. DC: MS DC 25.

94. Ibid.

95. Ibid.

96. *LWDW, Early Years*, 366–7 (MS not located).

97. DC: WLMS SH 33/2.

98. DC: WLMS SH 16/3.

99. DC: MS DC 31.

100. DC: WLL/DW/1/84.

101. DC: MS DC 31.

102. DC: MS DC 167.

103. DC: WLL/DW/1/93.

104. BL: Add. MS 36997 fos.1–2.

105. *STCL*, ii, 975.

106. Ibid., 978.

107. BL: Add. MS 36997 fos.3–4.

108. Ibid. fos.5–6.

109. BL: Add. MS 41186 fos.3–4.

110. Hunt: HM 22059.

111. BL: Add. MS 36997 fos.9–10.

112. DC: WLL/WW/1/99.

113. *LWDW, Early Years*, 454 (MS not located).

114. BL: Add. MS 36997 fos.11–12.

115. PM: MA 1581 (Wordsworth) 1.

116. DC: WLL/DW/1/111.

117. DC: WLMS 2/53.

118. DC: WLL/WW/1/118.

119. Wordsworth MSS, Manuscripts Dept., Lilly Library, Indiana University, Bloomington, Indiana.
120. DC: WLL/WW/1/127.
121. DC: WLL/WW/2/137.
122. DC: WLL/WW/2/139.
123. DC: WLL/DW/2/140.
124. DC: WLL/DW/2/151.
125. DC: WLL/DW/2/156.
126. PM: MA 1581 (Wordsworth) 9.
127. NLS: MS 3875 fo.240.
128. PM: MA 1581 (Wordsworth) 16.
129. NLS: MS 3876 fos.12–13, 165–6.
130. BL: Add. MS 36997 fos.54–5.
131. *Romantic Bards*, 10.
132. Ibid., 17, 19, 20, 23.
133. *Estimate*, 74.
134. PM: MA 1581 (Wordsworth) 24.
135. NLS: MS 3876 fos.165–6.
136. BL: Add. MS 36997 fos.66–7.
137. DC: WLL/WW/2/185a.
138. Ibid.
139. DC: MS G1/1/1.
140. *STCL*, iii, 113–14 (MS not located).
141. PM: MA 1581 (Wordsworth) 27.
142. BL: Add. MS 36997 fos.70–71.
143. DC: WLL/SH/5.
144. DC: WLL/DW/3/197.
145. BL: Add. MS 34046 fo.207.
146. Ibid. fos.208–9.
147. Hunt: HM 22066.
148. DC: Copy (MS in private hands).
149. DC: WLL/WW/3/202.
150. BL: Add. MS 35344 fos.151–2.
151. BL: Add. MS 34046 fos.220–21.
152. BL: Add. MS 36997 fos.82–3.
153. DC: WLL/1/12/14 (copy).
154. PM: MA 1581 (Wordsworth) 30.
155. BL: Add. MS 36997 fos.84–5.
156. DC: WLL/DW/3/213.
157. DC: MS G1/2/2.
158. DC: MS G1/2/5.
159. BL: Add. MS 36997 fos.100–101.
160. *LWDW, Middle Years*, i, 471 (MS not located).
161. BL: Add. MS 36997 fos.104–5.
162. DC: WLL/SH/13.
163. DC: WLL/DW/4/235.
164. DC: MS G1/4/3.
165. *STCL*, iii, 403.
166. DW: MS HCR Diary, 1812.
167. Ibid.
168. *STCL*, iii, 410–11.
169. DW: MS HCR Diary, 1812.
170. DC: MS G1/4/4.
171. DC: MS G1/5/1.
172. DC: MS G1/1/8.
173. Cornell.
174. DC: MS G1/1/11.
175. DC: WLL/1/12/15 (copy).
176. CRO: MS.D.Lons. L1/2/55/5.
177. CRO: MS.D.Lons. L1/2/55/6.
178. CRO: MS.D.Lons. L1/2/55/7.
179. DC: WLL/DW/4/259.
180. DC: WLL/SH/17.
181. DC: WLL/SH/18.
182. DC: WLL/SH/16.
183. DC: WLL/SH/19.
184. BL: Add. MS 36997 fos.122–3.
185. DC: WLL/WW/4/267.
186. BL: Add. MS 36997 fos.124–5.
187. BL: Add. MS 35344 fos.156–8.
188. BL: Add. MS 36997 fos.126–7.

189. DC: WLL/SH/21.

190. DC: MS G1/1/14.

191. *Romantic Bards*, 39–40.

192. PM: MA 4500 R–V.

193. DC: WLL/MW/10.

194. BL: Add. MS 36997 fo.132.

195. DC: WLL/DW/4/283.

196. *The Diary of Benjamin Robert Haydon*, edited by W. B. Pope (Harvard University Press, 1960), i, 450.

197. *Estimate*, 226–7.

198. Ibid., 217.

199. BL: Add. MS 36997 fos.140–41.

200. DC: (copy).

201. *LWDW, Middle Years*, ii, 299 (MS not located: not Hunt, as in *LWDW*).

202. BL: Add. MS 36997 fos.148–9.

203. Ibid., 321, 322–3 (MS not located).

204. DW: HCR corresp.1809–17 no.127.

205. DC: WLL/SH/27A.

206. DC: WLL/SH/32.

207. Princeton.

208. BL: Add. MS 34046 fos.228–9.

209. BL: Add. MS 36997 fos.154–5.

210. *New Letters of Robert Southey*, edited by K. Curry (Columbia University Press, 1965), ii, 160–61.

211. DC: WLL/SH/34.

212. BL: Add. MS 41186 fos.29–30.

213. B. R. Haydon, *Autobiography* (Oxford University Press, 1927), 359–62.

214. DC: WLL/SH/36.

215. CRO: MS D.Lons. L1/2/55/25.

216. CRO: MS D.Lons. L1/2/55/34.

217. CRO: MS D.Lons. L1/2/55/38.

218. DC: WLL/SH/44.

219. DC: WLL/MW/19.

220. DC: WLL/CW/63.

221. DC: WLL/WW/4/328.

222. DC: WLL/MW/22.

223. CRO: MS D.Lons. L1/2/55/53.

224. Hunt: HM 22073.

225. DC: WLL/CW/66.

226. Ticknor, i, 237–8.

227. DC: WLL/WW/4/331.

228. DC: WLL/SH/53.

229. CRO: MS D.Lons. L1/2/55/45.

230. *Estimate*, 302–3.

231. Ibid., 302.

232. Ibid., 310–11.

233. *Romantic Bards*, 109.

234. CRO: MS D.Lons. L1/2/55/59.

235. DC: WLL/SH/54.

236. DC: WLL/MW/24.

237. DC: WLL/SH/58.

238. DC: WLL/SH/62.

239. *LWDW, Middle Years*, ii, 593–4 (MS not located).

240. *HCRD*, i, 350.

241. *Estimate*, 325.

242. Ibid., 336.

243. DC: WLL/DW/4/339.

244. DC: WLL/DW/4/340.

245. DC: WLL/MW/29.

246. CRO: MS D.Lons. L1/2/55/75.

247. DC: MS DC 90.

248. *HCRD*, i, 358–9.

249. CRO: MS D.Lons. L1/2/55/76.

250. DW: MS HCR Journal 1820.

251. *HCRD*, i, 365.

252. PM: MA 1581 (Wordsworth) 36.

253. DC: 2002.57.4.

254. DW: HCR corresp. 1818–26 no. 55.

255. BL: Add. MS 36997 fos.183–4.

256. DC: WLL/MW/39.

257. BL: Add. MS 36997 fos.185–6.

258. Ibid. fos.187–9.

259. Ibid. fos.190–91.

260. DC: WLL/SH/75.

261. DC: WLL/SH/76.

262. DC: WLL/WW/5/351.

263. BL: Add. MS 36997 fos.192–3.

264. DC: WLL/SH/79.

265. DW: HCR corresp. 1818–26 no.76.

266. Special Collections, University of California at Davis, California.

267. *Estimate*, 353.

268. Ibid., 344.

269. V&A: MS 48 e.2 no.51.

270. DC: WLMS 13/1/5a.

271. DC: WLL/DW/5/356.

272. DC: WLL/MW/44.

273. DC: WLL/MW/48.

274. DC: WLL/DW/5/357.

275. DC: WLL/MW/51.

276. DW: HCR corresp.1818–26 no.86/87.

277. DC: WLL/WW/5/358a.

278. DC: 2002.57.8.

279. DC: MS DC 102.

280. DC: WLL/DW/5/363.

281. *LWDW, Later Years*, i, 224 (MS not located).

282. V&A: MS 48 e.2 no.52.

283. CRO: MS D.Lons. L1/2/55/88.

284. Beinecke Rare Book and Manuscript Library, Yale University, New Haven, Connecticut.

285. DC: WLMS H 1/15/7.

286. DC: WLL/WW/5/376.

287. DC: WLL/MW/61.

288. DC: WLL/MW/62.

289. DC: WLL/SH/103.

290. DW: HCR corresp. 1818–26 no.137.

291. UCL: Folder 18 fos.43–4.

292. DC: WLL/DW/5/379.

293. *LWDW, Later Years*, i, 343–4 (MS not located).

294. DC: WLMS A/Beaumont, Sir George/82.

295. PM: MA 1581 (Wordsworth) 41.

296. DW: HCR corresp. 1818–26 no.127.

297. UCL: Folder 18 fos.43–4.

298. *LWDW, Later Years*, i, 380–81 (MS not located).

299. DC: WLMS A/Jones, Robert/6 (transcript only).

300. UV: MS 10547–S, box 8, folder William Wordsworth 1823–41.

301. DC: WLL/SH/114.

302. Ibid.

303. MS in private hands, copy at DC.

304. DC: WLL/SH/116.

305. Part DC: WLL/WW/5/388; part Princeton.

306. MS Misc.177, Carl H. Pforzheimer Collection of Shelley and his Circle, New York Public Library, New York.

307. DC: WLL/SH/116.

308. BL: Add. MS 27925 fos.109–10.

309. DC: 2002.57.7.

310. DW: HCR corresp. 1818–26 no.171.

311. DW: HCR corresp. 1827–9 no.1.

312. Amherst: William Wordsworth MS A6.

313. NLS: MS 3436 fos.155–6.

314. Cornell.

315. Hamilton, i, 262.

316. Cornell.

317. BL duplicates, Gratz Case 11, Box 14 (Copy), Historical Society of Pennsylvania, Philadelphia, PA.

318. Cornell.

319. BL: Ashley MS 4641 fo.1.

320. J. H. Overton & E. Wordsworth, *Christopher Wordsworth, Bishop of Lincoln 1807–1885* (London, 1888), 64–5.

321. DC: WLL/MW/69.

322. W. Knight, *The Life of William Wordsworth* (Edinburgh, 1889), iii, 132.

323. Bodley: MS Autogr.C.24/3 fos.370r–371r.

324. Cornell.

325. *LDW*, 45.

326. BL: Add. MS 46136 fos.34–5.

327. Cornell.

328. DC: WLL/WW/5/402.

329. Harvard.

330. DC: WLL/Dora/17.

331. Harvard.

332. Cornell.

333. Cornell.

334. *Memoirs*, ii, 184–92.

335. DW: HCR corresp. 1827–9 no.121c.

336. DW: HCR corresp. 1827–9 no.118.

337. Cornell.

338. DC: WLL/DW/5/427.

339. DC: WLL/Dora/23.

340. DC: WLL/Dora/25.

341. Hunt: HM 22076.

342. Cornell.

343. DC: WLL/DW/6/431.

344. DC: WLL/DW/6/434.

345. Cornell.

346. *LWDW, Later Years*, ii, 264–5 (MS not located).

347. Cornell.

348. DC: WLL/SH/137.

349. UCL: Folder 18 fos.73–4.

350. *LHC*, 111–12.

351. Cornell.

352. DC: WLL/WW/6/441.

353. DC: WLL/WW/6/444.

354. DC: WLL/1/12/27 (transcript).

355. Hamilton, i, 424–5 (MS not located).

356. DC: WLL/WW/6/449.

357. *The Greville Memoirs 1814–1860*, edited by L. Strachey & R. Fulford (London, 1938), ii, 122–3.

358. DC: WLL/EQ/28.

359. Berg.

360. *LWDW, Later Years*, ii, 395–6 (MS not located).

361. Hamilton, i, 428–9 (MS not located).

362. DC: WLL/DW/6/452.

363. *LWDW, Later Years*, ii, 407–8 (MS not located).

364. DC: 2002.57.

365. NLS: MS 3919 fos.147–8.

366. *Fenwick Notes*, 50–51.

367. Cornell.

368. Berg.

369. *Memoirs*, ii, 242–3.

370. *LDW*, 91.

371. Cornell.

372. *LDW*, 94.

373. BL: Add. MS 46137 fos.230–31.

374. *Memoirs*, ii, 252–4.

375. BL: MS 46137 fos.61–2.

376. Cornell.

377. Harvard.

378. Hamilton, i, 430 (MS not located).

379. DC: WLL/Dora/44.

380. Cornell.

381. BL: Add. MS 46136 fos.75–6.

382. DC: WLL/EQ/42.

383. DW: HCR corresp.1832–3 no.91.

384. DC: WLL/WW/6/466.

385. DW: HCR corresp.1832–3 no.117.

386. Ryl.Eng. MS.415/165, John Rylands Library, University of Manchester.

387. DC: WLL/Dora/48.

388. R. W. Emerson, *Journals and Miscellaneous Notebooks*, edited by M. M. Sealts (Harvard University Press, 1973), x, 555–6.

389. DC: WLMS A/Fletcher, E/2.

390. *LWDW, Later Years*, ii, 641–2 (MS not located).

391. DC: WLL/Dora/56.

392. Harvard.

393. DC: WLL/SH/160.

394. DW: HCR corresp.1834–5 no.46b.

395. BL: Add. MS34225 fos.192–3.

396. DC: WLMS A/Graves/4.

397. Berg.

398. DW: HCR corresp.1834–5 no.95.

399. Hunt: HM 12312.

400. DC: WLL/Dora/64.

401. DC: WLL/WW/6/485.

402. DW: HCR corresp.1834–5 no.113.

403. UCL: folder 18 fos.96–7.

404. *LHC*, 176.

405. DC: WLL/MW/85.

406. DC: WLL/Dora/65a.

407. DC: WLL/MW/91.

408. DC: MS G1/7/8.

409. DC: MS G1/8/2.

410. DC: MS G1/8/5.

411. DC: MS G1/8/9.

412. DW: HCR Papers, Misc. Bundle 2 iv g.

413. DC: 2002.57.16.

414. DC: WLMS A/Boxall/1.

415. Hunt: HM 22097.

416. Bodley: MS Eng.lett.C.1 fos.343r–v.

417. DC: WLL/DW/6/505.

418. DC: WLL/WW/6/512.

419. DC: WLL/WW/6/513.

420. *HCRD*, ii, 188.

421. DC: WLL/WW/7/518.

422. DC: WLL/WW/7/519.

423. *HCRD*, ii, 196–7.

424. DC: WLL/WW/7/523.

425. Cornell.

426. DC: WLL/WW/7/537.

427. Cornell.

428. Cornell.

429. BL: Add. MS 44356 fos.24–5.

430. Cornell.

431. Cornell.

Sources

331

432. DC: WLL/MW/120.
433. Ticknor, ii, 167.
434. DW: HCR corresp.1838–40
no.36.
435. DC: WLL/WW/7/543.
436. DC: WLMS A/Hutcheson/2.
437. *LWDW, Later Years*, iii, 761–2.
438. DW: HCR corresp.1838–40
no.67.
439. *The Correspondence of Henry
Taylor*, edited by E. Dowden
(London, 1888), 117–18.
440. DC: WLL/MW/127.
441. BL: Ashley MS A 4649 fos.40–41.
442. *The Collected Letters of Thomas and
Jane Welch Carlyle*, edited by
C. R. Sanders et al. (Duke
University Press, 1985), xi, 121.
443. DC: MS E462.2.1.
444. DC: WLL/WW/7/550.
445. DC: WLL/WW/7/551.
446. DC: WLL/EQ/88.
447. DC: WLMS A/Arnold/45/7.
448. Cornell.
449. Hunt: HM 22119.
450. DC: WLL/WW/7/553.
451. UV: MS 10547–S, box 8, folder
William Wordsworth 1823–41.
452. Cornell.
453. DC: WLL/MW/136.
454. BL: Ashley MS 4641 fos.11–12.
455. DC: WLL/EQ/97.
456. UV: MS 10547–S, box 8, folder
William Wordsworth 1823–41.
457. Hunt: HM 12314.
458. *The Letters of Mary Wordsworth
1800–1855*, edited by
M. E. Burton (Clarendon Press,
1958), 244 (MS not located).
459. *Memoirs*, ii, 367–8.
460. DC: WLL/Dora/72.
461. DC: WLL/EQ/101.
462. Hunt: HM 22123.
463. DW: HCR corresp.1841–2
no.4.
464. Berg.
465. DC: WLL/WW/7/567.
466. Hunt: HM: 22126.
467. DC: WLL/EQ/114.
468. Henry Taylor, *Autobiography
1800–1875* (London, 1885), i,
388–9.
469. DC: WLL/WW/7/570.
470. DC: WLL/WW/7/572.
471. DC: WLL/WW/7/574.
472. DW: HCR corresp.1841–2
no.107.
473. Ibid., no.109.
474. DC: WLL/WW/7/581.
475. Hunt: HM 6877 (wrongly
catalogued in Hunt: as written
to Sir William Gordon).
476. Hunt: HM 22133.
477. Hunt: HM 22134.
478. *LWDW, Later Years*, iv, 322–2
(MS not located; not Chevening
as in *LWDW*, nor Centre for
Kentish Studies where Stanhope
MSS now located).
479. DC: WLL/WW/8/584.
480. DC: WLL/MW/147.
481. MS in private hands, typescript
at DC.
482. BL: Add. MS 44359 fos.202–3.
483. DC: G 1/14/5.
484. Aubrey de Vere, *Recollections*
(London, 1897), 127–8.
485. Cornell.

486. *Memoirs*, ii, 398–9.

487. DW: HCR corresp.1843 no.34.

488. *HCRD*, ii, 242.

489. Cornell.

490. *LWDW, Later Years*, iv, 492–3
(MS not located: not Yale as in
LWDW).

491. DW: HCR corresp.1843
no.125.

492. Hunt: HM 22150.

493. Cornell.

494. *Memoirs*, ii, 407.

495. DC: WLL/WW/8/601.

496. Cornell.

497. DC: WLL/WW/8/602.

498. DC: WLL/WW/8/603.

499. DC: WLL/WW/8/605.

500. *The Journals of Caroline Fox
1835–1871*, edited by W. Monk
(Elek Books Ltd, London 1972),
157–8.

501. BL: Add. MS 41964 fos.261–2.

502. *Prose*, iii, 355.

503. DC: WLL/WW/8/611.

504. DW: HCR corresp.1845 no.30b.

505. Hunt: HM 22165.

506. *LWDW, Later Years*, iv, 669 n.3.

507. *Mrs Brookfield and her Circle* by
C. & F. Brookfield (London,
1905), i, 150–51.

508. *Elizabeth Barrett to Mr Boyd*,
edited by B. P. McCarthy
(London, John Murrray, 1955),
276.

509. H. Tennyson, *Alfred, Lord
Tennyson: A Memoir* (London,
1897), i, 210.

510. Cornell.

511. DW: HCR corresp.1845 no.80b.

512. DC: WLL/MW/151.

513. Hunt: HM 22171.

514. Harriet Martineau, *Autobiography*
(Virago, 1983), ii, 236.

515. Berg.

516. DC: WLL/WW/8/621.

517. DW: HCR corresp.1846 no.25.

518. Miriam Lutcher Stark
Collection, Harry Ransom
Humanities Research Center,
University of Texas at Austin.

519. MS L W926 1846, Special
Collections, University of Iowa.

520. DC: WLL/WW/8/626.

521. DW: HCR corresp.1847 no.8a.

522. MS in private hands.

523. Royal Archives, Windsor Castle:
MS RA VIC/F36/73.

524. DC: MS DC 170.

525. *MLSC*, ii, 111–12.

526. DC: WLL/WW/8/632.

527. DC: Frederick Westley
presentation copy of *The
Installation Ode* to Mary
Wordsworth.

528. DC: WLMS 13/5/5.

529. Amherst: William Wordsworth
MS 8.

530. DC: WLMS A/Walmisley/2.

531. *LWDW, Later Years*, iv, 846 (MS
not located).

532. *LHC*, 293.

533. Ibid., 294.

534. DW: HCR corresp.1847 no.28a.

535. DC: WLL/MW/164.

536. DC: WLL/MW/169.

537. Hunt: HM 22194.

538. DC: WLL/EQ/132.

539. DC: WLL/WW/8/636.

540. DC: WLL/MW/173.

541. DW: HCR corresp.1848 no.3b.

542. DC: WLL/MW/175.

543. DW: HCR corresp.1848 no.38a.

544. DC: WLL/MW/181.

545. DW: HCR corresp.1848 no.43b.

546. DC: WLMS A/Argyll/1.

547. DC: WLL/MW/187.

548. *MLSC*, ii, 211–12.

549. DW: HCR Papers Misc. Bundle 2 vii a–b.

550. DW: HCR corresp.1849 no.4.

551. DC: WLL/WW/8/639.

552. DW: HCR corresp.1849 no.43a.

553. DC: WLMS 13/5/8.

554. DC: WLL/EQ/136.

555. DC: WLL/MW/200.

556. DC: WLL/MW/202.

557. DC: WLL/EQ/139.

558. DC: WLMS 1/4/1.

559. DW: HCR corresp.1850 no.27a.

560. DC: WLL/WW/2/51.

561. DC: WLL/EQ/141a.

562. DC: WLL/EQ/141b.

General Index

The abbreviation WW refers to William Wordsworth; page numbers in italics indicate that the subject is the addressee of the letter.